Intelligent Evolutionary Optimization

Intelligent Evolutionary Optimization

HUA XU

Tsinghua University, Beijing, P.R. China

YUAN YUAN

Beihang University, Beijing, P.R. China

Elsevier
Radarweg 29, PO Box 211, 1000 AE Amsterdam, Netherlands
125 London Wall, London EC2Y 5AS, United Kingdom
50 Hampshire Street, 5th Floor, Cambridge, MA 02139, United States

Notices
Knowledge and best practice in this field are constantly changing. As new research and experience broaden our understanding, changes in research methods, professional practices, or medical treatment may become necessary.

Practitioners and researchers must always rely on their own experience and knowledge in evaluating and using any information, methods, compounds, or experiments described herein. In using such information or methods they should be mindful of their own safety and the safety of others, including parties for whom they have a professional responsibility.

To the fullest extent of the law, neither the Publisher nor the authors, contributors, or editors, assume any liability for any injury and/or damage to persons or property as a matter of products liability, negligence or otherwise, or from any use or operation of any methods, products, instructions, or ideas contained in the material herein.

ISBN: 978-0-443-27400-8

For Information on all Elsevier publications
visit our website at https://www.elsevier.com/books-and-journals

Publisher: Mara Conner
Editorial Project Manager: Naomi Robertson
Production Project Manager: Fahmida Sultana
Cover Designer: Mark Rogers

Typeset by MPS Limited, Chennai, India

Contents

Part I Evolutionary algorithm for many-objective optimization

List of figures

List of tables

List of algorithms

About the authors

Hua Xu is a leading expert on intelligent natural interaction and service robots. He is currently a Tenured Associate Professor at Tsinghua University, Editor-in-Chief of Intelligent Systems with Applications, and Associate Editor of Expert Systems with Applications. He has authored the books, "Data Mining: Methodology and Applications" (2014), "Data Mining: Methods and Applications — Application Cases" (2017), "Evolutionary Machine Learning" (2021), "Data Mining: Methodology and Applications (2nd edition)" (2022), "Natural Interaction for Tri-Co Robots (1) Human—Machine Dialogue Intention Understanding" (2022), and "Natural Interaction for Tri-Co Robots (2) Sentiment Analysis of Multimodal Interaction Information" (2023), and published more than 140 papers in top-tier international journals and conferences. He is the Core Expert of the No. 03 National Science and Technology Major Project of the Ministry of Industry and Information Technology of China, a senior member of the CCF, a member of CAAI and ACM, the Vice Chairman of Tsinghua Collaborative Innovation Alliance of Robotics and Industry, and a recipient of numerous awards, including the Second Prize of National Award for Progress in Science and Technology, First Prize for Technological Invention of CFLP, and First Prize for Science and Technology Progress of CFLP.

Yuan Yuan is a Professor in the School of Computer Science at Beihang University. He received his PhD in computer science from Tsinghua University in 2015. His research interests include computational intelligence, machine learning, intelligent software engineering, and multiobjective optimization. To date, he has published dozens of papers as a first author in top international academic journals and conferences such as IEEE TSE, IEEE TEVC, IEEE TASE, ACM TOSEM, and ACM GECCO, with over 3000 citations on Google Scholar. As a core member of several projects, he has participated in the Major Science and Technology Program of the 02 Project and the National Natural Science Foundation of China, among others, and has received the first prize of the China Federation of Logistics and Purchasing for Science and Invention. He has also been actively involved in academic service and leadership roles. He has served as a guest editor for several authoritative international journals, including IEEE TITS, IEEE TETCI, and Memetic Computing. He has been a program committee member and chair of several well-known international conferences in the field of artificial intelligence, such as ACM GECCO, IEEE CEC, ICSE, and IJCAI. In addition, he has served as a reviewer for several top international journals in the field of artificial intelligence for many years.

Preface

Evolutionary algorithms (EAs) are a class of population-based global optimization algorithms that simulate the biological evolution process in nature. EAs have been successfully applied in the field of multiobjective optimization, opening up a new path for solving multiobjective optimization problems (MOPs). Owing to the unique advantages of EAs in multiobjective optimization, which can effectively overcome the limitations of traditional methods, the study of multiobjective evolutionary algorithms (MOEAs) has become a hot direction in the field of evolutionary computation (EC) and has been developed into an important and active research branch: evolutionary multiobjective optimization (EMO).

This book focuses on decomposition-based MOEAs as the research object and conducts research work at both the method and application levels, aiming to further improve the performance of such algorithms in high-dimensional multiobjective optimization and extend their new application areas, providing efficient solution methods for complex MOPs in the field of production scheduling. At the theoretical method level, this book systematically studies the methods of balancing convergence and diversity in aggregation-based MOEAs, the new dominance relation-based MOEAs, the comparative study of variation operators in decomposition-based MOEAs, target dimensionality reduction in multiobjective optimization, and high-cost multiobjective evolutionary optimization methods assisted by dominance prediction. At the level of engineering optimization applications, for the process scheduling optimization problem in the actual integrated circuit manufacturing field, the complex production environment with multiple chambers, multiple robots, multiple processing paths, multiple optimization objectives, and so on, is abstracted as a multiobjective flexible job shop scheduling problem (FJSP), and the book systematically studies the hybrid harmony search (HHS) method for single-objective optimization problems, the integrated search method of hybrid harmony search and large neighborhood search (HHS/LNS) for single-objective optimization in high-dimensional space, and the memetic evolutionary method based on target importance decomposition for multiobjective optimization.

As evolutionary multiobjective optimization is a rapidly developing research field, limited by the author's knowledge and cognitive scope, mistakes and shortcomings in the book are inevitable. We sincerely hope that you can give us valuable comments and suggestions for our book. Please contact xuhua@tsinghua.edu.cn or a third party in the open-source system platform https://thuiar.github.io/ to give us a message. All the related source codes and datasets for this book have also been shared on https://github.com/thuiar/Books.

The research and writing of this book have been supported by the National Natural Science Foundation of China (Project No. 61673235, 61175110, 60875073, and 60575057). We deeply appreciate the following students from the State Key Laboratory of Intelligent Technology and Systems, Department of Computer Science, Tsinghua University, for their hard work: Xiaofei Chen and Xiaohan Zhang. We also deeply appreciate Jiadong Yang, Bo Wang, and other students for the related research directions of cooperative innovation work. Without the efforts of the members of our team, the book could not be presented in a structured form in front of every reader.

Hua Xu
Yuan Yuan

PART I

Evolutionary algorithm for many-objective optimization

Part I introduces the key challenges in the field of multiobjective optimization and proposes innovative algorithms to address these challenges. We discuss the balance between convergence and diversity in multiobjective optimization, objective reduction techniques, and surrogate-assisted evolutionary algorithms. Through experiments and comparisons, we demonstrate the superiority of these algorithms on multiple benchmark problems and their competitiveness against existing algorithms. This part provides valuable insights and methods for readers interested in multiobjective optimization.

1

PART I

Evolutionary algorithm for many-objective optimization

CHAPTER 1

Preliminary

Contents

In various domains of social production, people constantly pursue maximum benefits with minimum costs. Minimizing costs and maximizing benefits form a contradictory pair, and when both aspects are considered, it becomes a typical multiobjective optimization problem (MOP). Many specific problems in scientific research and engineering practice require the simultaneous consideration of multiple optimization objectives. For example, when a military enterprise designs a missile, it generally aims to maximize its range, accuracy, and fuel efficiency while minimizing its weight. However, improving these design objectives may conflict with each other. For instance, increasing the missile's range may result in increased fuel consumption, leading to the need for a compromise between different design objectives. As MOPs are widely present in the real world, researching multiobjective optimization algorithms to help people better solve such problems holds great theoretical significance and practical value.

Solving MOPs is generally more challenging than solving single-objective optimization problems (SOPs). In SOPs, as the solutions have a total order relationship, there is usually only one unique optimal solution. However, in MOPs, due to the existence of conflicts between objectives, the solutions only have a partial order relationship. Therefore, instead of obtaining a single optimal solution, a set of compromised solutions, known as the Pareto optimal solution set or nondominated solution set, is typically obtained. In addition, when solving practical MOPs, decision-makers often select one or more solutions from the Pareto optimal solution set based on personal preferences or decision methods as the final optimal solution to the problem. Obtaining the

Intelligent Evolutionary Optimization
DOI: https://doi.org/10.1016/B978-0-443-27400-8.00001-0

Pareto optimal solution set is the primary and essential step in solving MOPs, which is also the core content of this book. Traditional algorithms for solving MOPs include linear weighting method [1], ϵ-constraint method [1], max–min method [2], goal programming method [3], and satisfactory method [4]. While these methods inherit the mechanisms of classic algorithms for solving SOPs, they share a common flaw. To obtain the Pareto optimal solution set of the original problem, the algorithms must run multiple times. As the solution processes of each run are independent and difficult to share information between them, the results obtained from each run may be incomparable, making it challenging for decision-makers to make effective decisions. Furthermore, running the algorithm multiple times also incurs significant computational overhead, reducing the efficiency of problem-solving. It is worth noting that these traditional methods often have certain requirements for the differentiability of objective functions and the convexity of the Pareto front. For example, linear weighting methods cannot effectively handle the concave parts of the Pareto front, and they are generally difficult to use for large-scale problems, limiting their practical applications. Evolutionary algorithms (EAs) are a type of population-based global optimization algorithm that simulates the natural evolution process in biology. EAs have been successfully applied in the field of multiobjective optimization, opening up a new path for solving MOPs. EAs are particularly suitable for solving MOPs for the following reasons: First, they can simultaneously handle a set of solutions, known as a population, and obtain multiple Pareto optimal solutions in a single run to approximate the Pareto optimal solution set. Second, EAs are insensitive to the shape and continuity of the Pareto front. For example, they can easily handle discontinuous or concave Pareto fronts. In addition, EAs can effectively handle large-scale search spaces, making them ideal for solving NP-hard problems. Due to the unique advantages of EAs in multiobjective optimization, which can effectively overcome the limitations of traditional methods, research on multiobjective evolutionary algorithms (MOEAs) has become a hot topic in the field of evolutionary computation (EC) and has developed into an important and active branch of research known as evolutionary multiobjective optimization (EMO). Currently, EMO has achieved fruitful results in both method and application levels, with novel algorithms and successful applications continuously emerging. In the top-tier journal of the EC field, IEEE Transactions on Evolutionary Computation, two out of the five most cited articles among those published from 1997 to 2023 are related to EMO research achievements [5,6]. The two leading international conferences in the EC field, the Genetic and Evolutionary Computation Conference (GECCO) hosted by ACM and the IEEE Congress on Evolutionary Computation (CEC) hosted by IEEE, also have the most subconferences related to EMO each year. CEC 2009 even held an algorithm competition specifically for MOEAs. Many well-known scholars in the EC field, such as Kalyanmoy Deb and Carlos A. Coello Coello, have also published relevant monographs on EMO.

In recent years, research in the EMO field has gradually shifted toward many objective optimization problems (MaOPs), which are MOPs with more than three objectives [7]. The rise of such research is mainly due to two reasons. On the one hand, optimization problems involving many objectives are widespread in various practical applications, such as control system design [8,9], industrial scheduling [10], software engineering [11,12], etc. Therefore practitioners urgently need effective optimization methods to solve these problems. On the other hand, popular Pareto-dominance-based MOEAs, such as nondominated sorting genetic algorithm II (NSGA-II) [5], strength Pareto evolutionary algorithm 2 [13], Pareto envelope-based selection algorithm II [14], etc., have limitations when dealing with high-dimensional MaOPs. Therefore research on MaOPs has become increasingly important in the EMO field. Although they have shown excellent performance in MOPs with two or three optimization objectives, MOEAs encounter significant difficulties in high-dimensional many-objective optimization. The main reason is that as the number of objectives increases, the proportion of nondominated solutions in the population increases sharply, and it is even possible that all solutions are nondominated. In this case, Pareto-dominance-based selection mechanisms cannot provide enough selection pressure on the population as they do in low-dimensional objectives. As a result, the evolution of the population will slow down, or even stagnate. Several early studies on high-dimensional many-objective optimization [15−17] have already verified this through analysis or experimentation.

Recently, thanks to the continuous efforts of researchers, some initial progress has been made in the study of high-dimensional many-objective optimization. Among them, decomposition-based MOEAs may be the most promising class of techniques for solving MaOPs. This type of technique uses the idea of decomposition to either decompose the original problem into multiple single-objective subproblems or to directly decompose the objective space of the original problem into multiple objective subspaces, effectively reducing the difficulty of solving the original problem. However, there are still many deficiencies and drawbacks in both the method and application aspects of these techniques:

1. At the methodological level, some algorithms face difficulties in maintaining population diversity, while others have insufficient convergence. Therefore how to balance convergence and diversity more effectively in these algorithms is an urgent issue to be addressed. Additionally, these algorithms rarely explore how to balance the relationship between exploration and exploitation more effectively in the decision space. There is significant research space in this area as well.

2. At the application level, current algorithms of this type often fail to integrate multi-objective search with problem-specific knowledge when solving practical problems. As a result, they may have insufficient optimization capabilities.

1.1 Fundamental concepts and basic framework

Intelligent evolutionary solutions to MOPs are the focus of this book. In the following section, we will first explain the fundamental concepts of MOPs and the basic framework of MOEAs.

1.1.1 Multiobjective optimization problems

Without loss of generality, this book considers MOPs with the following mathematical form:

$$\min f(x) = (f_1(x), f_2(x), \ldots, f_m(x))^{\mathrm{T}}$$

$$\text{subject to } x \in \Omega \subseteq \mathbb{R}^n \tag{1.1}$$

Here, $x = (x_1, x_2, \ldots, x_n)^{\mathrm{T}}$ is an n-dimensional decision vector in the decision space Ω. The function $f: \Omega \to \Theta \subseteq \mathbb{R}^m$ is an m-dimensional objective vector that maps the n-dimensional decision space Ω to the m-dimensional objective space Θ. Fig. 1.1 provides a schematic representation of this mapping. Several important definitions of MOPs are presented below.

1. **Definition 1**: Given two decision vectors $x, y \in \Omega$, x Pareto-dominates y, denoted as $x \prec y$, if and only if for every index $i \in \{1, 2, ..., m\}$, $f_i(x) \leq f_i(y)$ and there exists at least one index $j \in \{1, 2, ..., m\}$ such that $f_j(x) \leq f_j(y)$.
2. **Definition 2**: A decision vector $x^* \in \Omega$ is a Pareto optimal solution if and only if there does not exist a decision vector $x \in \Omega$ such that $x \prec x^*$.
3. **Definition 3**: The Pareto optimal solution set $x \prec x^*$, denoted as

$$PS = \{x \in \Omega | x \text{ is a Pareto optimal solution}\} \tag{1.2}$$

4. **Definition 4**: The Pareto front PF, denoted as

$$PF = \{f(x) \in \mathbb{R}^m | x \in PS\} \tag{1.3}$$

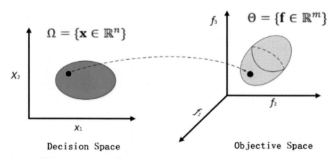

Figure 1.1 Illustration of the mapping from the decision space to the objective space in multiobjective optimization.

5. **Definition 5**: The ideal point $z^* = \left(z_1^*, z_2^*, \ldots, z_m^*\right)^{\mathrm{T}}$, where for each index $i \in \{1, 2, \ldots, m\}$, z_i^* is the infimum of f_i.

6. **Definition 6**: The nadir point $z^{\mathrm{nad}} = \left(z_1^{\mathrm{nad}}, z_2^{\mathrm{nad}}, \ldots, z_m^{\mathrm{nad}}\right)^{\mathrm{T}}$, where for each index $i \in \{1, 2, \ldots, m\}$, z_i^{nad} is the supremum of f_i over the Pareto front PS.

For MOPs, the objective of MOEAs is to find a set of nondominated objective vectors that are as close as possible to the Pareto front in the objective space, that is, convergence, and to distribute them as uniformly as possible along the Pareto front, that is, diversity.

1.1.2 Introduction to multiobjective evolutionary algorithms

MOEAs are the inheritance and development of EAs in the field of multiobjective optimization. Like EAs, MOEAs also exhibit the following three notable characteristics [18]:

1.1.2.1 Population-based
MOEAs maintain a set of feasible solutions, called the population, and optimize the problem solution space in a parallel manner. The evolutionary process is based on the population.

1.1.2.2 Fitness-oriented
Each feasible solution in the population, called an individual or chromosome, has its genetic representation, called the encoding. The quality of each individual's performance is characterized by its fitness value. Based on the natural law of survival of the fittest, individuals with higher fitness values have a higher probability of being retained, while those with lower fitness values are more likely to be eliminated. This selection mechanism is the basis for the algorithm to converge to the optimal solution.

1.1.2.3 Variation-driven
During the problem-solving process, MOEAs change the genetic representation of individuals through variation operators, mimicking the process of genetic change in biological evolution. This is the fundamental basis for the algorithm to effectively search the solution space.

MOEAs first generate an initial population using random or heuristic methods, with the number of chromosomes or individuals in the initial population being the population size. Then, MOEAs enter the iterative process, as shown in Fig. 1.2. In each generation, first, mating selection is performed to select which individuals in the current population will generate offspring individuals. Then, variation operators are applied to the selected individuals to generate several offspring individuals. Common variation operators include crossover and mutation in genetic algorithms. Next, the offspring individuals are evaluated by computing all the objective values corresponding to the solutions. Finally, environmental selection is performed to select which individuals in the population will be the next generation. If only one offspring individual is

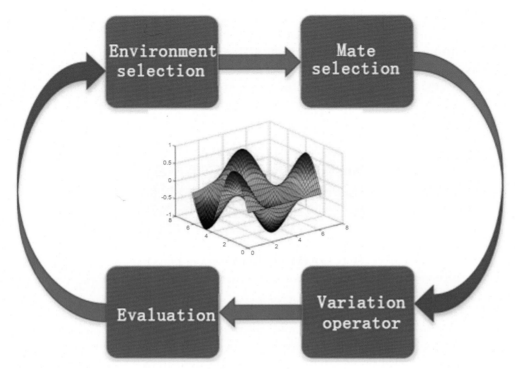

Figure 1.2 Illustration of the evolutionary iteration process of MOEAs.

generated in each generation, the algorithm is said to use the steady-state mode. If the number of offspring individuals generated in each generation is equal to the population size, the algorithm is said to use the generational mode.

In EAs for solving SOPs, variation operators are the focus of research, mainly considering how to design more efficient variation operators to balance exploration and exploitation in the decision space, that is, the balance between wide search and concentrated search. Researchers have developed various effective variation operators for SOPs, such as the estimation of distribution algorithm [19], which establishes a probability model based on the distribution of the optimal individuals and generates offspring individuals through random sampling based on the model, and differential evolution (DE) [20], which generates offspring individuals based on the differences between parent individuals. Environmental selection is relatively simple in single-objective EAs because the objective function directly reflects the quality of the individuals. However, it is the focus of research for MOEAs. For example, for MOEAs that use the generational mode, the key problem is how to carry out reasonable fitness assignment, selecting half of the individuals from a population of twice the population size as the next generation of individuals, while balancing convergence and diversity in the objective space.

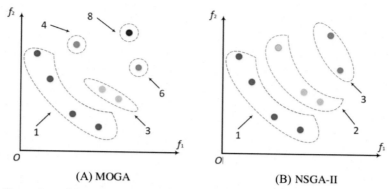

Figure 1.3 Illustration of the fitness assignment methods used in MOGA (A) and NSGA-II (B).

Fig. 1.3 illustrates the fitness assignment methods used in the well-known multiob-jective genetic algorithm (MOGA) [21] and NSGA-II. In MOGA, the fitness of all nondominated individuals is set to 1, and the fitness of other individuals is set to the number of individuals that dominate it plus 1. Under this method, individuals with the same fitness will be further selected using the fitness-sharing mechanism. In NSGA-II, the fitness of all nondominated individuals in the population is initially set to 1, and then these nondominated individuals are temporarily ignored. New nondo-minated individuals are determined in the remaining population, and their fitness is set to 2. This process continues until all individuals in the population are assigned fitness values. Individuals with the same fitness values form the nondominated layers in NSGA-II, and their differences are further distinguished using the crowding distance.

While research on variation operators in MOEAs is relatively limited, they still play a crucial role. Some studies have shown that the requirements of MOEAs for convergence and diversity in the objective space (which are to some extent in opposi-tion) increase the difficulty of balancing exploration and exploitation in the decision space, which in turn places higher demands on variation operators [22]. Therefore the design of MOEAs should take into account two balances: the balance between con-vergence and diversity in the objective space and the balance between exploration and exploitation in the decision space. The second balance provides greater potential for the first balance, while the first balance establishes a better foundation for the second balance. Therefore these two balances are interdependent and mutually reinforcing.

1.2 Provides an overview of related research

High-dimensional MOPs are currently at the forefront of research in the field of EMO. This section will provide an overview of the current status of related research in this area.

1.2.1 Evolutionary high-dimensional multiobjective optimization

The MaOPs pose serious challenges to existing MOEAs [15−17,23−25], especially to the widely used Pareto-dominance-based MOEAs. In existing research, there are generally two types of techniques that can overcome the shortcomings of Pareto-dominance-based MOEAs in solving MaOPs.

The main idea of the first type of technique is to use new preference relations (such as relaxed Pareto dominance or other sorting methods) to introduce finer-grained ordering relationships in the objective space. There has been extensive research in this area. ϵ-Dominance is one of the most representative works, which divides the objective space into many grids and only allows one solution in each grid. Deb et al. [26] combined this concept with a multiobjective search to develop a steady-state MOEA that quickly achieves a good distribution of solutions. In addition to ϵ-dominance, many other optional preference relations have prospects in high-dimensional multiobjective optimization, such as average ranking (AR) and maximum ranking (Mr) [27], supporting relations [28], fuzzy Pareto dominance [29,30], expansion relations [31], preference order sorting [32], L-dominance, and others [33−37]. Several similar studies [38−41] have explored the advantages and disadvantages of different preference relations to some extent.

Another type of technique aims to improve the mechanism for maintaining diversity. This type of technique is based on the following consideration, since Pareto dominance cannot generate sufficient selection pressure towards the Pareto front in high-dimensional multiobjective space, selection almost completely depends on diversity maintenance operators, which are generally considered as the second-level selection operators in MOEAs. However, most existing diversity maintenance metrics, such as crowding distance [5] or k-nearest distance [13], prefer solutions that are dominance-resistant [15,24], that is, those solutions that have high performance in at least one objective but poor performance in other objectives. This can lead to a bias towards solutions that are far from the global Pareto front, even though these solutions may have good diversity distribution in the objective space. Therefore diversity maintenance strategies in high-dimensional multiobjective optimization need to be carefully considered to avoid or alleviate this phenomenon. Compared to the first type of technique, research related to this type of technique is much less abundant. Adra and Fleming [42] proposed two mechanisms for managing diversity and studied their impact on the overall convergence of algorithms in high-dimensional multiobjective optimization. Deb and Jain [43] proposed an improved NSGA-II algorithm, called NSGA-III, which replaces the crowding distance operator in NSGA-II with a clustering operator that is performed with the help of a set of uniformly distributed reference points. Li et al. [44] developed a general strategy for modifying diversity metrics for Pareto-dominance-based MOEAs, called the transfer-based density estimation strategy, which combines the distribution and convergence information of solutions.

In contrast to Pareto dominance-based MOEAs, the other two types of MOEAs, namely indicator-based and decomposition-based MOEAs, are generally considered more suitable for solving MaOPs because they either use other preference relations to promote convergence or employ efficient diversity maintenance mechanisms. However, they also face their challenges when dealing with MaOPs.

Indicator-based MOEAs directly consider the desired performance of the algorithm and aim to optimize a performance indicator that can provide an ideal ordering relationship among the sets of solutions that approximate the Pareto front. Due to its good theoretical properties, the hypervolume (HV) [6] is the most commonly used performance indicator. The main advantage of HV is that maximizing HV is equivalent to finding the Pareto front for a given MOP problem [45]. In existing literature, some mature algorithms use HV, such as the indicator-based evolutionary algorithm, the S metric selection evolutionary algorithm [46], and the multiobjective covariance matrix adaptation evolution strategy [47]. However, the computational cost of HV grows exponentially with the number of objectives and it is generally difficult to apply in high-dimensional multiobjective situations with more than five objectives. To address this issue, a possible strategy is to only know the ordering relationship of solutions obtained based on HV, without the need for precise HV calculation. The HypE algorithm [48] uses this strategy, where the value of HV is approximated by Monte Carlo simulation. Another strategy is to use other performance indicators to replace HV, which have much lower computational costs and also have good theoretical properties, such as $R2$ [49] and Δ_p [50]. This strategy has been implemented in some recent indicator-based MOEAs [51−54].

Decomposition-based MOEAs can be further divided into two types: aggregation-based MOEAs and reference-point-based MOEAs, depending on the form of decomposition. Aggregation-based MOEAs use a weight vector to combine all optimization objectives of an MOP into an aggregation function. A set of weight vectors (or directions) will produce multiple aggregation functions, and each aggregation function defines an SOP. Maintaining population diversity is implicitly achieved by specifying a set of uniformly distributed weight vectors in the objective space. The problem decomposition-based multiobjective evolutionary algorithm (MOEA/D) [55,56] and multiple single-objective Pareto sampling (MSOPS) [57] are two of the most representative aggregation-based MOEAs. Recently, a new search framework based on NSGA-II called ensemble fitness ranking (EFR) [58] was proposed for high-dimensional multiobjective optimization, which is more general than MSOPS. Formally, EFR can be seen as an extension of AR and Mr [27]. The significant difference is that EFR uses a more general fitness function (aggregation function) instead of the objective function used by AR and Mr. In recent years, aggregation-based MOEAs have become very popular in high-dimensional multiobjective optimization, as they have shown quite good performance on MaOPs [23,59−62]. However, they still have limitations in high-dimensional multiobjective search. For example, MOEA/D can generally bring the population close to the Pareto front even in high-dimensional multiobjective spaces, but it often faces difficulties in maintaining diversity, which can result in poor coverage of the Pareto front. This finding has been confirmed by several recent studies [35,43,63], which is largely attributed to the contour properties of the aggregation function, which will be further elaborated in Chapter 3 of this book. Other aggregation-based MOEAs, such as MOSOP and EFR, also suffer from similar problems, as they are driven by the aggregation function. Additionally, it is worth mentioning that MOEA/D, as one of the mainstream frameworks for designing MOEAs, has been extensively studied, such as in combination with swarm intelligence algorithms [64,65], embedding adaptive mechanisms [66—68], mixing with local search [69,70], and introducing stable matching in selection [71]. However, most of these new algorithms have not been validated on MaOPs. To the best of our knowledge, except for a few recent papers [72,73], research on MOEA/D in high-dimensional multiobjective optimization still focuses on exploring its search behavior in experiments [60,61,74—76].

Reference-point-based MOEAs are a promising technique for solving MaOPs and can effectively alleviate several difficulties associated with dealing with high-dimensional objectives [43]. Unlike aggregation-based MOEAs, reference-point-based MOEAs do not rely on aggregation functions and do not have multiple explicit single-objective subproblems. Instead, they directly decompose the objective space into multiple objective subspaces using multiple reference points (or reference directions) and search them in parallel during the evolution process. TC-SEA [77], MOEA/D-M2M [78], NSGA-III [43], and I-DBEA [73] are representative reference-point-based MOEAs. TC-SEA generates a set of uniformly distributed attraction points (reference points) using Manhattan distance in every iteration. Each solution is attached to the nearest attraction point, and the solutions attached to the same attraction point compete locally based on the Manhattan distance indicator to produce the next generation of solutions. MOEA/D-M2M decomposes an MOP into multiple MOPs defined on the objective subspaces using a set of uniformly distributed reference lines and assigns a subpopulation with a certain number of individuals to solve each corresponding MOP. The individual competition in each subpopulation is achieved using Pareto nondominated sorting. NSGA-III attaches each individual in the considered population to the corresponding reference line of the corresponding reference point using a set of uniformly distributed reference points and emphasizes selecting nondominated individuals that are closer to the attached reference line during environmental selection. I-DBEA uses similar criteria to NSGA-III in environmental selection, but uses a steady-state mode during the evolution process, while NSGA-III uses a generational mode. Since reference-point-based MOEAs explicitly divide the objective space into multiple subspaces, they have certain advantages in maintaining solution diversity. However, these methods mainly bring the population close to the Pareto front through Pareto dominance relationships, such as MOEA/D-M2M, NSGA-III, and I-DBEA, which can lead to insufficient convergence when solving MaOPs.

Finally, it should be noted that the use of decomposition-based approaches for solving MOPs has been present in some earlier studies on MOEAs, such as MOGLS [79,80].

This book will also cover change operators in MOEAs. Although change operators have a significant impact on algorithm performance, research in this area is still relatively scarce.

1.2.2 Evolutionary operators for variation in multiobjective optimization algorithms

In the field of EMO, most studies, such as those in references [5,13], focus on the environmental selection process.

To enhance the search capability of MOEAs in the decision space, some studies [81,82] have proposed new variation operators for MOPs. Additionally, another research direction in this regard is to integrate the effects of multiple existing variation operators. This is based on the fact that different variation operators are often suited for different fitness landscapes and may even be suitable for different stages of the optimization process. Thus the organic combination of different variation operators can be expected to achieve complementary advantages in search capability. This general idea has been utilized by many researchers in multiobjective optimization over the past few decades. Vrugt and Robinson [83] proposed using different variation operators simultaneously in NSGA-II to generate offspring individuals and an adaptive strategy was also employed that tends to select the variation operator with the highest regeneration success rate. Tan et al. [22] proposed an adaptive variation operator that utilizes the binary representation structure of genes and integrates the functions of crossover and mutation. Elhossini et al. [84] proposed a hybrid algorithm for solving MOPs that combines particle swarm optimization (PSO) with genetic operators, with the genetic operators being improved to preserve the information used by PSO. Some recent similar works can be found in Refs. [68,85–87]. Moreover, it should be mentioned that this type of approach usually adopts adaptive control mechanisms to coordinate the selection of different variation operators.

Studies on the impact of variation operators on algorithm performance in high-dimensional multiobjective optimization are relatively scarce. However, recent research has shown that this is a particularly important issue when dealing with high-dimensional multiobjective problems. Sato et al. [88] found that as the number of objectives increases, the gene expression of the true Pareto optimal solutions becomes significantly diversified, and they suggest that traditional variation operators may become too disruptive and lose effectiveness in this scenario. Based on this analysis, they further proposed controlling the maximum number of crossed genes in the crossover operator, which can significantly improve the performance of several MOEAs on MaOPs. Ishibuchi et al. [89] observed that when solving high-dimensional multiobjective knapsack problems, algorithm performance can be significantly improved when the distance between parent individuals and offspring individuals in the algorithm is small. To further verify this observation, they implemented a distance-based crossover operator, which provides a custom parameter to control the distance between parent and offspring individuals.

1.2.3 Applications of the proposed algorithms

Our proposed algorithms, such as θ-DEA, have been successfully applied to many practical problems by other researchers. Li et al. [90] combined our θ-DEA with integrated decision making for the problem of combined heat and power economic emission dispatch.

Liao and Zhang [91] applied θ-DEA to the optimization of several high-performance analog and RF integrated circuits in different CMOS technologies. Nayeem et al. [92] modeled the transit network design problem as a many-objective problem and solved it efficiently using θ-DEA. Echevarría et al. [93] used our θ-DEA to learn human-understandable models for the health assessment of Li-ion batteries. Chabbouh et al. [94] searched for oblique decision trees for imbalanced binary classification using our θ-DEA. Garcia and Trinh [95] used our θ-DEA and EFR-RR to solve the modular cell design problem for novel biocatalysis. Gupta and Nanda [96] proposed an improved θ-DEA to handle cloud detection problem in satellite imagery. Ebadifard and Babamir [97] proposed to schedule scientific workflows on virtual machines based on θ-DEA. Zhang et al. [98] used EFR-RR to obtain the optimal feature subset for anomaly detection in a cloud environment. Kaur et al. [99] proposed a secure and energy-efficient Internet of things (IoT) model for e-health based on θ-DEA. Biswas et al. [100] adapted θ-DEA to solve the multiobjective influence maximization problem with three conflicting objectives and real-world constraints. Rahimi et al. [101] investigated the performance of θ-DEA and EFR-RR on the next software release problem.

1.3 Conclusion

This chapter provides an introduction to MOPs and their importance, as well as a discussion of the application of decomposition-based MOEAs to high-dimensional MOPs. Additionally, the chapter highlights the challenges in environmental selection for MOEAs, particularly in balancing diversity and convergence in fitness assignments. Several fitness assignment methods, such as those used in MOGA and NSGA-II, are introduced as potential approaches to address this issue. This chapter provides a foundation and guidance for the discussions in the subsequent chapters.

References

[1] Cohon JL. Multiobjective programming and planning. Chelsea: Courier Corporation; 2004.

[2] Osyczka A. An approach to multicriterion optimization problems for engineering design. Computer Methods in Applied Mechanics and Engineering 1978;15(3):309−33.

[3] Laundy RS. Multiple criteria optimisation: theory, computation and application. Journal of the Operational Research Society 1988;39(3):879−86.

[4] Koski J. Multicriterion optimization in structural design. Tampere University of Technology; 1981.

[5] Deb K, Pratap A, Agarwal S, et al. A fast and elitist multiobjective genetic algorithm: NSGA-II. IEEE Transactions on Evolutionary Computation 2002;6(2):182−97.

[6] Zitzler E, Thiele L. Multiobjective evolutionary algorithms: a comparative case study and the strength Pareto approach. IEEE Transactions on Evolutionary Computation 1999;3(4):257−71.

[7] Ishibuchi H, Tsukamoto N, Nojima Y. Evolutionary many-objective optimization: a short review. In: Proceedings of the 10th IEEE congress on evolutionary computation. IEEE; 2008. p. 2419−26.

[8] Fleming PJ, Purshouse RC, Lygoe RJ. Many-objective optimization: an engineering design perspective. In: Proceedings of the 2nd evolutionary multi-criterion optimization, 2005;5. p. 14−32.

[9] Herrero JG, Berlanga A, López JMM. Effective evolutionary algorithms for many-specifications attainment: application to air traffic control tracking filters. IEEE Transactions on Evolutionary Computation 2008;13(1):151−68.

[10] Sülflow A, Drechsler N, Drechsler R. Robust multi-objective optimization in high dimensional spaces. In: Proceedings of the 4th evolutionary multi-criterion optimization; 2007. p. 715−26.

[11] Harman M, Yao X. Software module clustering as a multi-objective search problem. IEEE Transactions on Software Engineering 2010;37(2):264−82.

[12] Sayyad AS, Menzies T, Ammar H. On the value of user preferences in search-based software engineering: a case study in software product lines. In: Proceedings of the 35th international conference on software engineering. IEEE; 2013. p. 492−501.

[13] Zitzler E, Laumanns M, Thiele L. SPEA2: improving the strength Pareto evolutionary algorithm. TIK-report 2001;103.

[14] Corne DW, Jerram NR, Knowles JD, et al. PESA-II: region-based selection in evolutionary multi-objective optimization. In: Proceedings of the 3rd annual conference on genetic and evolutionary computation; 2001. p. 283−90.

[15] Ikeda K, Kita H, Kobayashi S. Failure of Pareto-based MOEAs: does non-dominated really mean near to optimal? In: Proceedings of the 14th congress on evolutionary computation, vol. 2. IEEE; 2001. p. 957−62.

[16] Khare V, Yao X, Deb K. Performance scaling of multi-objective evolutionary algorithms. In: Proceedings of the 2nd evolutionary multi-criterion optimization; 2003. p. 376−90.

[17] Purshouse RC, Fleming PJ. Evolutionary many-objective optimisation: an exploratory analysis. In: Proceedings of the 15th congress on evolutionary computation, vol. 3; 2003. p. 2066−73.

[18] Yu X, Gen M. Introduction to evolutionary algorithms. Springer Science & Business Media; 2010.

[19] Larrañaga P, Lozano JA. Estimation of distribution algorithms: a new tool for evolutionary computation. Springer Science & Business Media; 2001.

[20] Storn R, Price K. Differential evolution—a simple and efficient heuristic for global optimization over continuous spaces. Journal of Global Optimization 1997;11(4):341.

[21] Fonseca C. Genetic algorithms for multiobjective optimization: formulation discussion and generalization. In: Proceedings of the 5th international conference on genetic algorithms; 1993. p. 416−23.

[22] Tan KC, Chiam SC, Mamun AA, et al. Balancing exploration and exploitation with adaptive variation for evolutionary multi-objective optimization. European Journal of Operational Research 2009;197(2):701−13.

[23] Hughes EJ. Evolutionary many-objective optimisation: many once or one many? In: Proceedings of the 17th IEEE congress on evolutionary computation, vol. 1. IEEE; 2005. p. 222−7.

[24] Purshouse RC, Fleming PJ. On the evolutionary optimization of many conflicting objectives. IEEE Transactions on Evolutionary Computation 2007;11(6):770−84.

[25] Knowles J, Corne D. Quantifying the effects of objective space dimension in evolutionary multiobjective optimization. In: Proceedings of the 4th evolutionary multi-criterion optimization; 2007. p. 757−71.

[26] Deb K, Mohan M, Mishra S. Towards a quick computation of well-spread pareto-optimal solutions. In: Proceedings of the 2nd evolutionary multi-criterion optimization; 2003. p. 222−36.

[27] Bentley PJ, Wakefield JP. Finding acceptable solutions in the pareto-optimal range using multiobjective genetic algorithms. In: Proceedings of the soft computing in engineering design and manufacturing; 1998. p. 231−40.

[28] Drechsler N, Drechsler R, Becker B. Multi-objective optimisation based on relation favour. In: Proceedings of the 1st evolutionary multi-criterion optimization; 2001. p. 154−66.

[29] Köppen M, Vicente-Garcia R, Nickolay B. Fuzzy-pareto-dominance and its application in evolutionary multi-objective optimization. In: Proceedings of the 3rd evolutionary multi-criterion optimization; 2005. p. 399−412.

[30] He Z, Yen GG, Zhang J. Fuzzy-based Pareto optimality for many-objective evolutionary algorithms. IEEE Transactions on Evolutionary Computation 2013;18(2):269−85.

[31] Sato H, Aguirre HE, Tanaka K. Controlling dominance area of solutions and its impact on the performance of MOEAs. Lecture Notes in Computer Science 2007;4403:5.

[32] Di Pierro F, Khu ST, Savic DA. An investigation on preference order ranking scheme for multiobjective evolutionary optimization. IEEE Transactions on Evolutionary Computation 2007;11 (1):17−45.

[33] Kukkonen S, Lampinen J. Ranking-dominance and many-objective optimization. In: Proceedings of the 15th IEEE congress on evolutionary computation. IEEE; 2007. p. 3983−90.

[34] Le K, Landa-Silva D. Obtaining better non-dominated sets using volume dominance. In: Proceedings of the 15th 2007 IEEE congress on evolutionary computation. IEEE; 2007. p. 3119−26.

[35] Yang S, Li M, Liu X, et al. A grid-based evolutionary algorithm for many-objective optimization. IEEE Transactions on Evolutionary Computation 2013;17(5):721−36.

[36] Coello CAC, Oyama A, Fujii K. An alternative preference relation to deal with many-objective optimization problems. In: Proceedings of the 7th evolutionary multi-criterion optimization; 2013. p. 291−306.

[37] Yuan Y, Xu H, Wang B. An improved NSGA-III procedure for evolutionary many-objective optimization. In: Proceedings of the 16th annual conference on genetic and evolutionary computation; 2014. p. 661−8.

[38] Garza-Fabre M, Pulido GT, Coello CAC. Ranking methods for many-objective optimization. In: Proceedings of the 8th Mexican international conference on artificial intelligence; 2009. p. 633−45.

[39] Jaimes AL, Santana-Quintero LV, Coello CAC. Ranking methods in many-objective evolutionary algorithms. Nature-Inspired Algorithms for Optimisation 2009;193:413−34.

[40] Jaimes AL, Coello CAC. Study of preference relations in many-objective optimization. In: Proceedings of the 11th annual conference on genetic and evolutionary computation; 2009. p. 611−8.

[41] Fabre MG, Pulido GT, Coello CAC. Alternative fitness assignment methods for many-objective optimization problems. In: Proceedings of the 9th artifical evolution international conference, evolution artificielle; 2010. p. 146−157.

[42] Adra SF, Fleming PJ. Diversity management in evolutionary many-objective optimization. IEEE Transactions on Evolutionary Computation 2010;15(2):183−95.

[43] Deb K, Jain H. An evolutionary many-objective optimization algorithm using reference-point-based nondominated sorting approach, part I: solving problems with box constraints. IEEE Transactions on Evolutionary Computation 2013;18(4):577−601.

[44] Li M, Yang S, Liu X. Shift-based density estimation for Pareto-based algorithms in many-objective optimization. IEEE Transactions on Evolutionary Computation 2013;18(3):348−65.

[45] Fleischer M. The measure of Pareto optima applications to multi-objective metaheuristics. In: Proceedings of the 2nd evolutionary multi-criterion optimization; 2003. p. 519−33.

[46] Beume N, Naujoks B, Emmerich M. SMS-EMOA: multiobjective selection based on dominated hypervolume. European Journal of Operational Research 2007;181(3):1653−69.

[47] Igel C, Hansen N, Roth S. Covariance matrix adaptation for multi-objective optimization. Evolutionary Computation 2007;15(1):1−28.

[48] Bader J, Zitzler E. HypE: an algorithm for fast hypervolume-based many-objective optimization. Evolutionary Computation 2011;19(1):45−76.

[49] Brockhoff D, Wagner T, Trautmann H. On the properties of the R2 indicator. In: Proceedings of the 14th annual conference on genetic and evolutionary computation; 2012. p. 465−72.

[50] Schutze O, Esquivel X, Lara A, et al. Using the averaged Hausdorff distance as a performance measure in evolutionary multiobjective optimization. IEEE Transactions on Evolutionary Computation 2012;16(4):504−22.

[51] Phan DH, Suzuki J. R2-IBEA: R2 indicator based evolutionary algorithm for multiobjective optimization. In: Proceedings of the 17th IEEE congress on evolutionary computation; 2013. p. 1836−45.

[52] Trautmann H, Wagner T, Brockhoff D. R2-EMOA: focused multiobjective search using R2-indicator-based selection. In: Proceedings of the 7th learning and intelligent optimization; 2013. p. 70−4.

[53] Gómez RH, Coello CAC. MOMBI: a new metaheuristic for many-objective optimization based on the R2 indicator. In: Proceedings of the 15th IEEE congress on evolutionary computation. IEEE; 2013. p. 2488−95.

[54] Villalobos CAR, Coello CAC. A new multi-objective evolutionary algorithm based on a performance assessment indicator. In: Proceedings of the 14th annual conference on genetic and evolutionary computation; 2012. p. 505−12.

[55] Zhang Q, Li H. MOEA/D: a multiobjective evolutionary algorithm based on decomposition. IEEE Transactions on Evolutionary Computation 2007;11(6):712−31.

[56] Li H, Zhang Q. Multiobjective optimization problems with complicated Pareto sets, MOEA/D and NSGA-II. IEEE Transactions on Evolutionary Computation 2008;13(2):284−302.

[57] Hughes EJ. Multiple single objective Pareto sampling. In: Proceedings of the 5th congress on evolutionary computation, vol 4. IEEE; 2003. p. 2678−84.

[58] Yuan Y, Xu H, Wang B. Evolutionary many-objective optimization using ensemble fitness ranking. In: Proceedings of the 16th annual conference on genetic and evolutionary computation; 2014. p. 669−76.

[59] Wagner T, Beume N, Naujoks B. Pareto-, aggregation-, and indicator-based methods in many-objective optimization. In: Proceedings of the 4th evolutionary multi-criterion optimization; 2007. p. 742−56.

[60] Ishibuchi H, Sakane Y, Tsukamoto N, et al. Evolutionary many-objective optimization by NSGA-II and MOEA/D with large populations. In: Proceedings of the 14th IEEE international conference on systems; 2009. p. 1758−63.

[61] Hadka D, Reed P. Diagnostic assessment of search controls and failure modes in many-objective evolutionary optimization. Evolutionary Computation 2012;20(3):423−52.

[62] Li M, Yang S, Liu X, et al. A comparative study on evolutionary algorithms for many-objective optimization. In: Proceedings of the 7th evolutionary multi-criterion optimization; 2013. p. 261−75.

[63] Wang R, Purshouse RC, Fleming PJ. Preference-inspired coevolutionary algorithms for many-objective optimization. IEEE Transactions on Evolutionary Computation 2012;17(4):474−94.

[64] Martínez SZ, Coello CAC. A multi-objective particle swarm optimizer based on decomposition. In: Proceedings of the 13th annual conference on genetic and evolutionary computation; 2011. p. 69−76.

[65] Ke L, Zhang Q, Battiti R. MOEA/D-ACO: a multiobjective evolutionary algorithm using decomposition and antcolony. IEEE Transactions on Cybernetics 2013;43(6):1845−59.

[66] Ishibuchi H, Sakane Y, Tsukamoto N, et al. Adaptation of scalarizing functions in MOEA/D: an adaptive scalarizing function-based multiobjective evolutionary algorithm. In: Proceedings of the 5th evolutionary multi-criterion optimization; 2009. p. 438−52.

[67] Zhao SZ, Suganthan PN, Zhang Q. Decomposition-based multiobjective evolutionary algorithm with an ensemble of neighborhood sizes. IEEE Transactions on Evolutionary Computation 2012;16(3):442−6.

[68] Li K, Fialho A, Kwong S, et al. Adaptive operator selection with bandits for a multiobjective evolutionary algorithm based on decomposition. IEEE Transactions on Evolutionary Computation 2013;18(1):114—30.

[69] Sindhya K, Miettinen K, Deb K. A hybrid framework for evolutionary multi-objective optimization. IEEE Transactions on Evolutionary Computation 2012;17(4):495—511.

[70] Martínez SZ, Coello CAC. A direct local search mechanism for decomposition-based multi-objective evolutionary algorithms. In: Proceedings of the 17th IEEE congress on evolutionary computation. IEEE; 2012. p. 1—8.

[71] Li K, Zhang Q, Kwong S, et al. Stable matching-based selection in evolutionary multiobjective optimization. IEEE Transactions on Evolutionary Computation 2013;18(6):909—23.

[72] Asafuddoula M, Ray T, Sarker R. A decomposition based evolutionary algorithm for many objective optimization with systematic sampling and adaptive epsilon control. In: Proceedings of the 7th evolutionary multi-criterion optimization; 2013. p. 413—27.

[73] Asafuddoula M, Ray T, Sarker R. A decomposition-based evolutionary algorithm for many objective optimization. IEEE Transactions on Evolutionary Computation 2014;19(3):445—60.

[74] Ishibuchi H, Hitotsuyanagi Y, Tsukamoto N, et al. Many-objective test problems to visually examine the behavior of multiobjective evolution in a decision space. In: Proceedings of 9th international conference on parallel problem solving from nature; 2010. p. 91—100.

[75] Ishibuchi H, Akedo N, Nojima Y. Relation between neighborhood size and MOEA/D performance on many-objective problems. In: Proceedings of the 7th evolutionary multi-criterion optimization; 2013. p. 459—74.

[76] Ishibuchi H, Akedo N, Nojima Y. Behavior of multiobjective evolutionary algorithms on many-objective knapsack problems. IEEE Transactions on Evolutionary Computation 2014;19(2):264—83.

[77] Moen HJF, Hansen NB, Hovland H, et al. Many-objective optimization using taxi-cab surface evolutionary algorithm. In: Proceedings of the 7th evolutionary multi-criterion optimization; 2013. p. 128—42.

[78] Liu HL, Gu F, Zhang Q. Decomposition of a multiobjective optimization problem into a number of simple multiobjective subproblems. IEEE Transactions on Evolutionary Computation 2013;18 (3):450—5.

[79] Ishibuchi H, Murata T. A multi-objective genetic local search algorithm and its application to flow-shop scheduling. IEEE Transactions on Systems, Man, and Cybernetics, Part C (Applications and Reviews) 1998;28(3):392—403.

[80] Ishibuchi H, Yoshida T, Murata T. Balance between genetic search and local search in memetic algorithms for multiobjective permutation flowshop scheduling. IEEE Transactions on Evolutionary Computation 2003;7(2):204—23.

[81] Chan TM, Man KF, Kwong S, et al. A jumping gene paradigm for evolutionary multiobjective optimization. IEEE Transactions on Evolutionary Computation 2008;12(2):143—59.

[82] Li M, Yang S, Li K, et al. Evolutionary algorithms with segment-based search for multiobjective optimization problems. IEEE Transactions on Cybernetics 2013;44(8):1295—313.

[83] Vrugt JA, Robinson BA. Improved evolutionary optimization from genetically adaptive multimethod search. Proceedings of the National Academy of Sciences 2007;104(3):708—11.

[84] Elhossini A, Areibi S, Dony R. Strength Pareto particle swarm optimization and hybrid EA-PSO for multi-objective optimization. Evolutionary Computation 2010;18(1):127—56.

[85] Hadka D, Reed P. Borg: an auto-adaptive many-objective evolutionary computing framework. Evolutionary Computation 2013;21(2):231—59.

[86] Nebro AJ, Durillo JJ, Machín M, et al. A study of the combination of variation operators in the NSGA-II algorithm. In: Proceedings of the 15th advances in artificial intelligence: 15th conference of the Spanish Association for Artificial Intelligence, CAEPIA 2013, Madrid, Spain, September 17—20, 2013. Proceedings 15. Berlin Heidelberg: Springer; 2013. p. 269—78.

[87] Shim VA, Tan KC, Tang H. Adaptive memetic computing for evolutionary multiobjective optimization. IEEE Transactions on Cybernetics 2014;45(4):610—21.

[88] Sato H, Aguirre HE, Tanaka K. Genetic diversity and effective crossover in evolutionary many-objective optimization. In: Proceedings of the 5th learning and intelligent optimization: 5th international conference; 2011. p. 91−105.

[89] Ishibuchi H, Tanigaki Y, Masuda H, et al. Distance-based analysis of crossover operators for many-objective knapsack problems. In: Proceedings of the 13th international conference; 2014. p. 600−10.

[90] Li Y, Wang J, Zhao D, et al. A two-stage approach for combined heat and power economic emission dispatch: combining multi-objective optimization with integrated decision making. Energy 2018;162:237−54.

[91] Liao T, Zhang L. Efficient parasitic-aware hybrid sizing methodology for analog and RF integrated circuits. Integration 2018;62:301−13.

[92] Nayeem MA, Islam MM, Yao X. Solving transit network design problem using many-objective evolutionary approach. IEEE Transactions on Intelligent Transportation Systems 2018;20 (10):3952−63.

[93] Echevarría Y, Blanco C, Sánchez L. Learning human-understandable models for the health assessment of li-ion batteries via multi-objective genetic programming. Engineering Applications of Artificial Intelligence 2019;86:1−10.

[94] Chabbouh M, Bechikh S, Hung CC, et al. Multi-objective evolution of oblique decision trees for imbalanced data binary classification. Swarm and Evolutionary Computation 2019;49:1−22.

[95] Garcia S, Trinh CT. Comparison of multi-objective evolutionary algorithms to solve the modular cell design problem for novel biocatalysis. Processes 2019;7(6):361.

[96] Gupta R, Nanda SJ. Improved framework of many-objective evolutionary algorithm to handle cloud detection problem in satellite imagery. IET Image Processing 2020;14(17):4795−807.

[97] Ebadifard F, Babamir SM. Scheduling scientific workflows on virtual machines using a Pareto and hypervolume based black hole optimization algorithm. The Journal of Supercomputing 2020;76 (10):7635−88.

[98] Zhang Z, Wen J, Zhang J, et al. A many objective-based feature selection model for anomaly detection in cloud environment. IEEE Access 2020;8:60218−31.

[99] Kaur M, Singh D, Kumar V, et al. Secure and energy efficient-based E-health care framework for green internet of things. IEEE Transactions on Green Communications and Networking 2021;5 (3):1223−31.

[100] Biswas TK, Abbasi A, Chakrabortty RK. An improved clustering based multi-objective evolutionary algorithm for influence maximization under variable-length solutions. Knowledge-Based Systems 2022;256:109856.

[101] Rahimi I, Gandomi AH, Nikoo MR, et al. A comparative study on evolutionary multi-objective algorithms for next release problem. Applied Soft Computing 2023;110472.

CHAPTER 2

New dominance relation-based evolutionary algorithm for many-objective optimization

Contents

2.1 Introduction

Many–objective optimization has become a topic of increasing interest in the evolutionary multiobjective optimization (EMO) community [1,2]. This type of optimization involves problems with four or more objectives, and it poses a significant challenge to classical Pareto dominance-based multiobjective evolutionary algorithms (MOEAs).

Intelligent Evolutionary Optimization
DOI: https://doi.org/10.1016/B978-0-443-27400-8.00002-2

The rise of evolutionary many-objective optimization research can be attributed to two main factors. Firstly, real-world applications often involve optimization problems with a large number of objectives, and practitioners require effective optimizers to solve these problems. Secondly, popular MOEAs based on Pareto dominance have struggled in many-objective optimization, despite performing well on problems with two or three objectives. This is mainly because as the number of objectives increases, almost all solutions in the population become nondominated, which leads to a loss of selection pressure toward the Pareto front (PF).

The main contribution of this chapter is to propose a new evolutionary algorithm called θ-dominance-based evolutionary algorithm (θ-DEA) for many-objective optimization. This algorithm combines the strengths of two existing many-objective optimizers, nondominated sorting genetic algorithm III (NSGA-III) and MOEA/D, to overcome their weaknesses.

NSGA-III is effective in emphasizing population members that are Pareto nondominated and close to the reference line of each reference point. However, in high-dimensional objective space, the Pareto dominance relied on by NSGA-III may not provide enough selection pressure to pull the population toward the PF, resulting in a focus on diversity rather than convergence.

MOEA/D, on the other hand, maintains diversity via diverse weight vectors and can generally approach the PF well using an aggregation function-based selection operator. However, in many-objective optimization, replacement decisions that are based solely on aggregation function values may lead to a loss of diversity in MOEA/D. This is because a solution may achieve a good aggregation function value but be far away from the corresponding weight vector in high-dimensional objective space, causing MOEA/D to miss some search regions.

2.2 Preliminaries

This section provides an overview of multiobjective optimization and introduces the original MOEA/D and NSGA-III algorithms, which serve as the foundation for the proposed algorithm.

2.2.1 Basic definitions

The mathematical definition of a multiobjective optimization problem (MOP) is presented:

$$\min \mathbf{f}(\mathbf{x}) = (f_1(\mathbf{x}), f_2(\mathbf{x}), \ldots, f_m(\mathbf{x}))^{\mathrm{T}}$$
$$\text{subject to } \mathbf{x} \in \Omega \subseteq \mathbb{R}^n. \tag{2.1}$$

The decision variables of MOP are represented by an n-dimensional vector, $\mathbf{x} = (x_1, x_2, \ldots, x_n)^{\mathrm{T}}$, which belongs to the decision space Ω. The objective functions of MOP are represented by a set of m functions, $\mathbf{f} = (f_1(\mathbf{x}), f_2(\mathbf{x}), \ldots, f_m(\mathbf{x}))$, which map the decision space Ω to the objective space Θ. The objective space Θ is a subset of m-dimensional Euclidean space, $\mathbb{R}^m$.

Given two decision vectors $\mathbf{x}$ and $\mathbf{y}$ belonging to the decision space Ω, $\mathbf{x}$ is said to Pareto dominate $\mathbf{y}$, represented as $\mathbf{x} \prec \mathbf{y}$, if and only if for every objective function i in the set $\{1, 2, \ldots, m\}$, $f_i(\mathbf{x})$ is less than or equal to $f_i(\mathbf{y})$, and for at least one objective function j in the set $\{1, 2, \ldots, m\}$, $f_j(\mathbf{x})$ is strictly less than $f_j(\mathbf{y})$.

A decision vector $\mathbf{x}^* \in \Omega$ is Pareto optimal if it is not possible to improve any of the decision criteria without making at least one of them worse, considering all the feasible decision vectors $\mathbf{x} \in \Omega$.

The Pareto set (PS) is defined as

$$PS = \{\mathbf{x} \in \Omega \,|\, \mathbf{x} \text{ is Pareto optimal}\}. \tag{2.2}$$

The PF is defined as

$$PF = \{\mathbf{f}(\mathbf{x}) \in \mathbb{R}^m \,|\, \mathbf{x} \in PS\}. \tag{2.3}$$

The ideal point $\mathbf{z}^*$ is a vector $\mathbf{z}^* = (z_1^*, z_2^*, \ldots, z_m^*)^{\mathrm{T}}$, where z_i^* is the infimum of f_i for each $i \in \{1, 2, \ldots, m\}$.

The nadir point $\mathbf{z}^{\mathrm{nad}}$ is a vector $\mathbf{z}^{\mathrm{nad}} = (z_1^{\mathrm{nad}}, z_2^{\mathrm{nad}}, \ldots, z_m^{\mathrm{nad}})^{\mathrm{T}}$, where z_i^{nad} is the supremum of f_i over the PS for each $i \in \{1, 2, \ldots, m\}$.

The goal of MOEAs is to simultaneously achieve two main objectives: convergence and diversity. Convergence refers to the ability to move the nondominated objective vectors toward the PF, which represents the set of all Pareto optimal solutions. On the other hand, diversity refers to the ability to generate a well-distributed set of nondominated objective vectors over the PF, covering different regions of the solution space.

2.2.2 MOEA/D

The MOEA/D is a multiobjective optimization algorithm that decomposes a complex MOP into a set of single-objective optimization subproblems. The key idea is to use aggregation functions to combine the multiple objectives into a single-objective function, which can be optimized more efficiently. By solving these subproblems in parallel, the MOEA/D can identify a set of Pareto optimal solutions that approximate the true PF. The optimal solution to each subproblem is a Pareto optimal solution of the original MOP, and the set of optimal solutions represents a diverse approximation of the true PF. The MOEA/D uses different aggregation functions to balance the trade-offs among the objectives. Considering Chebyshev as an example, let $\lambda_1, \lambda_2, \ldots, \lambda_N$

be a set of evenly spread weight vectors to transform the multiple objectives into a single-objective function, which can be solved using standard single-objective optimization techniques.

$$g_j^{\text{te}}\left(\mathbf{x}|\boldsymbol{\lambda}_j, \mathbf{z}^*\right) = \max_{k=1}^{m}\left\{\lambda_{j,k}\left|f_k(\mathbf{x}) - z_k^*\right|\right\} \tag{2.4}$$

where $j = 1, 2, \ldots, N$ and $\boldsymbol{\lambda}_j = \left(\lambda_{j,1}, \lambda_{j,2}, \ldots, \lambda_{j,m}\right)^{\text{T}}$.

MOEA/D is an optimization algorithm that initializes a set of weight vectors $\boldsymbol{\lambda}_j$ and computes a neighborhood set $B(j)$ for each vector. The neighborhood set consists of T weight vectors that are closest to $\boldsymbol{\lambda}_j$ based on Euclidean distance. The jth subproblem's neighborhood includes all subproblems whose weight vectors are in $B(j)$. The algorithm maintains a population of N solutions $\mathbf{x}_1, \mathbf{x}_2, \ldots, \mathbf{x}_N$, where each $\mathbf{x}_j$ is the solution to the jth subproblem. MOEA/D has two unique characteristics: mating restriction and local replacement. During reproduction, the jth offspring is produced by randomly selecting two indexes k and l from $B(j)$ and using genetic operators to generate a new solution $\mathbf{y}$ from $\mathbf{x}_k$ and $\mathbf{x}_l$. Local replacement is used to compare $\mathbf{y}$ with each neighboring solution $\mathbf{x}_u$, where u is in $B(j)$. If $g^{\text{te}}(\mathbf{y}|\boldsymbol{\lambda}_u, \mathbf{z}^*) < g^{\text{te}}(\mathbf{x}_u|\boldsymbol{\lambda}_u, \mathbf{z}^*)$, then $\mathbf{x}_u$ is replaced by $\mathbf{y}$. Once all N offsprings are produced, a new population is created and the process is repeated until the stopping criterion is met. For more information on MOEA/D, refer to [3,4].

2.2.3 NSGA-III

The basic framework of NSGA-III is an extension of the well-established NSGA-II algorithm [5], but it introduces significant changes in its selection mechanism to improve its performance and scalability. The main procedure of NSGA-III can be summarized as follows.

NSGA-III is a multiobjective optimization algorithm that begins by defining a set of reference points to guide the search toward the nondominated regions of the objective space. The algorithm then generates an initial population consisting of N solutions, where N is the population size. The next steps are iterated until the termination criterion is satisfied. During each iteration, NSGA-III uses the current parent population P_t to produce an offspring population Q_t at generation t.

The offspring population Q_t is generated by applying a combination of operators, including random selection, simulated binary crossover (SBX) operator, and polynomial mutation [6]. NSGA-III combines populations of parent solutions P_t and offspring solutions Q_t to form a new population R_t of size $2N$. The goal is to select the best N members from R_t to form the next parent population P_{t+1}. To achieve this, NSGA-III uses nondominated sorting based on Pareto dominance to classify solutions in R_t into different nondomination levels (F_1, F_2, etc.). The algorithm then constructs a new population S_t by selecting members of different nondomination levels one at a time, starting from F_1. The selection process continues until the size of S_t is equal to N or for the first time becomes greater than N. The solutions beyond the lth level are rejected, and members in $S_t \backslash F_l$ are already chosen for P_{t+1}. To maintain diversity in the population, NSGA-III uses a new selection mechanism that conducts a systematic analysis of members in S_t with respect to the supplied reference points. The algorithm selects the solutions that are closest to the reference points while ensuring that the selected solutions are well-spread across the objective space. This selection procedure helps NSGA-III to identify a diverse set of high-quality solutions that approximate the true PF of the multiobjective problem [7]. In contrast to the original NSGA-II, which used the crowding distance measure to select solutions, NSGA-III's selection mechanism is more effective on many-objective problems.

To achieve this, NSGA-III uses a reference point-based selection mechanism that selects solutions based on their proximity to the reference points.

First, NSGA-III normalizes the objective values and the supplied reference points to have an identical range. The ideal point of the set S_t is then set to the zero vector, and the perpendicular distance between each member in S_t and each reference line is computed. Each member in S_t is then associated with a reference point having the minimum perpendicular distance. Next, NSGA-III computes the niche count ρ_j for each reference point, which is the number of members in $S_t \backslash F_l$ that are associated with the jth reference point. The algorithm then executes a niche-preservation operation to select members from F_l that are associated with each reference point. To perform the niche-preservation operation, NSGA-III first identifies the reference point set J_{min} with the minimum ρ_j value. If J_{min} has more than one reference point, a reference point $\bar{j}$ is randomly chosen. If no member in level F_l is associated with the $\bar{j}$th reference point, the reference point is excluded from further consideration. Otherwise, the value of $\rho_{\bar{j}}$ is considered. If $\rho_{\bar{j}}$ equals 0, NSGA-III chooses the member from F_l that has the shortest perpendicular distance to the $\bar{j}$th reference line and adds it to P_{t+1}. The count of $\rho_{\bar{j}}$ is then increased by one. If $\rho_{\bar{j}}$ is greater than or equal to 1, a randomly chosen member from level F_l that is associated with the $\bar{j}$th reference point is added to P_{t+1}, and the count of $\rho_{\bar{j}}$ is increased by one. This niche operation is repeated until the remaining population slots of P_{t+1} are filled. By using the reference points and the niche-preservation operation, NSGA-III aims to identify a diverse set of high-quality solutions that approximate the true PF of the multiobjective problem. For more details, please refer to the original paper [8].

2.3 Proposed algorithm: θ-DEA

2.3.1 Overview

The proposed θ-DEA algorithm is a framework for solving MOPs. The algorithm is described in Algorithm 2.1, which consists of several steps. First, the algorithm generates a set of N reference points, which are denoted as $\lambda_j(j \in \{1, 2, ..., N\})$. For a problem with m objectives, each reference point $\lambda_j(j \in \{1, 2, ..., N\})$ is an m-dimensional vector represented by $\lambda_j = (\lambda_{j,1}, \lambda_{j,2}, \ldots, \lambda_{j,m})^T$. The components of λ_j satisfy the conditions $\lambda_{j,k} \geq$ or $k = 1, 2, ..., m$, and $\sum_{k=1}^{m} \lambda_{j,k} = 1$. Next, the algorithm produces an initial population P_0 with N members. The members of the population are randomly generated.

In Step 3, the algorithm initializes the ideal point z^*. While it can be time-consuming to compute the exact values of z_i^*, the algorithm estimates the minimum value found so far for each objective f_i. The ideal point is updated during the search to reflect the current best-performing solutions.

In Step 4, the algorithm initializes the nadir point z^{nad}, which is used in the normalization procedure. The algorithm assigns the largest value of f_i found in the initial population P_0 to z_i^{nad}. The nadir point is also updated during the search to ensure that the normalization procedure is effective.

Steps 6–23 are iterated until a satisfactory set of solutions is identified. In Step 7, the algorithm produces an offspring population Q_t by using the recombination operator. The offspring population is then combined with the current population P_t to form a new population R_t. S_t is the union of all the Pareto nondomination levels, F_i, in R_t up to the τth level. The value of τ is determined by the condition that the sum of the sizes of the preceding levels, $\sum_{i=1}^{\tau-1} |F_i|$, is less than N, while the sum of the sizes of the preceding levels up to the τth level is greater than or equal to N. For problems with numerous objectives, S_t is typically dominated by the first Pareto nondomination level, F_1, as a significant portion of the population consists of Pareto nondominated solutions.

Step 11 involves normalizing S_t using the assistance of z^* and z^{nad}. Once the normalization is complete, the clustering operator is employed to divide the elements of S_t into N distinct clusters, denoted as $\mathcal{C} = \{C_1, C_2, ..., C_N\}$. Each cluster, C_j, is identified by a reference point, λ_j.

Next, S_t is sorted into distinct θ-nondomination levels (F_1', F_2', etc.) using a nondominated sorting method that is based on θ dominance instead of Pareto dominance. The concept of θ dominance is fundamental to θ-DEA and will be further explained later. After the sorting process based on θ-nondomination is complete, the remaining steps involve filling the population slots in P_{t+1} one level at a time, beginning with F_1'.

In contrast to the selection methods utilized in NSGA-II and NSGA-III, in θ-DEA, solutions are chosen randomly from the final accepted level, F_l. This is because θ dominance places emphasis on both convergence and diversity. However, it is still possible to utilize various strategies to improve diversity in Step 20. The succeeding sections will provide a comprehensive explanation of the crucial procedures involved in θ-DEA.

Algorithm 2.1: Framework of the proposed θ-DEA.

1: $\Lambda \leftarrow$ Generate Reference Points ()
2: $P_0 \leftarrow$ Initialize Population ()
3: $\mathbf{z}^* \leftarrow$ Initialize Ideal Point ()
4: $\mathbf{z}^{nad} \leftarrow$ Initialize Nadir Point ()
5: $t \leftarrow 0$
6: while the termination criterion is not met do
7:           $Q_t \leftarrow$ Create Of spring Population (P_t)
8:           $R_t \leftarrow P_t \cup Q_t$
9:           $S_t \leftarrow$ Get Pareto Nondominated Fronts (R_t)
10: Update Ideal Point (S_t)
11:           Normalize $(S_t, \mathbf{z}^*, \mathbf{z}^{nad})$
12: $C \leftarrow$ Clustering (S_t, Λ)
13: $\{F'_1, F'_2, \ldots\} \leftarrow \theta$–Nondominated-sort (S_t, C)
14: $P_{t+1} \leftarrow \varnothing$
15: $i \leftarrow 1$
16: while $|P_{t+1}| + |F'_i| < N$ do
17:           $P_{t+1} \leftarrow P_{t+1} \cup F'_i$
18:           $i \leftarrow i + 1$
19:     end while
20:     Random Sort (F'_j)
21:     $P_{t+1} \leftarrow P_{t+1} \cup F'_i [1:(N - |P_{t+1}|)]$
22:     $t \leftarrow t + 1$
23: end while

2.3.2 Reference points generation

In θ–DEA, the generation of structured reference points follows the systematic approach introduced by Das and Dennis [9]. This approach is utilized in various earlier algorithms [10], including MOEA/D and NSGA-III, to enhance the diversity of the resulting solutions. The number of reference points generated depends on the dimensionality of the objective space, m, and another positive integer, H. Let us take a closer look at this process:

$$\sum_{i=1}^{m} x_i = H, x_i \in \mathbb{N}, i = 1, 2, \ldots, m. \tag{2.5}$$

We can determine the number of solutions to Eq. (2.5) by performing a calculation:

$$N = \binom{H + m - 1}{m - 1}. \tag{2.6}$$

Assuming that $(x_{j,1}, x_{j,2}, ..., x_{j,m})^{\mathrm{T}}$ represents the jth solution, we can derive the corresponding reference point, λ_j, by using Eq. (2.7):

$$\lambda_{j,k} = \frac{x_{j,k}}{H}, \ k = 1, 2, ..., m. \tag{2.7}$$

From a geometric perspective, each reference point, $\lambda_1, \lambda_2, ..., \lambda_N$, is situated on the hyperplane defined by the equation $\sum_{i=1}^{m} f_i = 1$. The value of H determines the number of divisions considered along each objective axis.

It should be noted that if H is less than m, no intermediate reference points will be generated using this method. On the other hand, when m is relatively large (e.g., $m = 8$), having $H \geq m$ would result in an enormous number of reference points, leading to an excessively large population size. To address this problem, the proposed θ-DEA utilizes two-layered reference points with smaller values of H, as suggested in [8]. Suppose the number of divisions for the boundary layer and the inner layer is H_1 and H_2, respectively. In this case, the population size can be expressed as follows:

$$N = \binom{H_1 + m - 1}{m - 1} + \binom{H_2 + m - 1}{m - 1}. \tag{2.8}$$

The distribution of two-layered reference points for a three-objective problem with H_1 set to 2 and H_2 set to 1 is depicted in Fig. 2.1.

2.3.3 Recombination operator

In many-objective optimization, the recombination operator may not be as effective. This is primarily because in high-dimensional objective space, there is a higher likelihood of selecting widely separated solutions for recombination, resulting in the production of inferior offspring solutions, also referred to as lethals [11,12]. There are typically two approaches to address this problem. One method involves utilizing a mating restriction scheme [13], in which the recombination operator only operates on neighboring solutions, as seen in MOEA/D. The other approach involves employing a specialized recombination scheme, such as the SBX operator with a large distribution index [8], where emphasis is placed on using near-parent solutions, as seen in NSGA-III.

Similar to NSGA-III, θ-DEA adopts the latter approach to address the recombination issue. During the recombination process, two parent solutions are randomly chosen from the current population, P_t. The child solution is then generated by applying the SBX operator, which utilizes a large distribution index, and polynomial mutation.

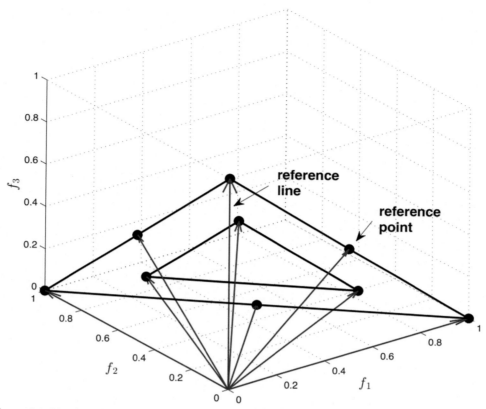

Figure 2.1 Distribution of two-layered reference points in the 3D objective space. Six points on the boundary layer ($H_1 = 2$) and three points on the inner layer ($H_2 = 1$).

2.3.4 Adaptive normalization

To tackle the problems in which the PF has objective values that are disparately scaled, θ-DEA integrates a normalization procedure. This procedure involves the replacement of objective $f_i(\mathbf{x})$, where i ranges from 1 to m, with the following expression:

$$\tilde{f}_i(\mathbf{x}) = \frac{f_i(\mathbf{x}) - z_i^*}{z_i^{\text{nad}} - z_i^*}. \tag{2.9}$$

As previously mentioned, z_i^* can be estimated using the best value discovered thus far for objective f_i. However, estimating z_i^{nad} is a more challenging endeavor, as it necessitates knowledge of the entire PF [14,15]. The process of estimating z_i^{nad} in θ-DEA is similar to that of NSGA-III, but differs in the identification of extreme points.

To begin the process of normalizing the population, S_t, the extreme point $\mathbf{e}_j$ is identified in the objective axis f_j. This is achieved by selecting the solution, $\mathbf{x} \in S_t$, that minimizes the following achievement scalarizing function:

$$ASF(\mathbf{x}, \mathbf{w}_j) = \max_{i=1}^{m} \left\{ \frac{1}{w_{j,i}} \left| \frac{f_i(\mathbf{x}) - z_i^*}{z_i^{\text{nad}} - z_i^*} \right| \right\}. \tag{2.10}$$

Eq. (2.10) defines the achievement scalarizing function, where $\mathbf{w}_j = (w_{j,1}, w_{j,2}, ..., w_{j,m})^T$ denotes the axis direction of the objective axis f_j. The values of $w_{j,i}$ are such that if $i \neq j$, then $w_{j,i} = 0$; otherwise, $w_{j,i} = 1$. In cases where $w_{j,i} = 0$, it is replaced with a small number, 10^{-6}. Furthermore, z_i^{nad} represents the ith dimension of the nadir point estimated in the previous generation. Finally, the objective vector of the discovered solution $\mathbf{x}$, that is, $\mathbf{f}(\mathbf{x})$, is assigned to the extreme point $\mathbf{e}_j$.

Once all m objective axes have been taken into account, we can obtain m extreme points, denoted as $\mathbf{e}_1, \mathbf{e}_2, ..., \mathbf{e}_m$.

These m extreme points are subsequently employed in constructing a m-dimensional linear hyperplane. The intercepts of the hyperplane with the directions $(1, z_2^*, ..., z_m^*)^T, (z_1^*, 1, ..., z_m^*)^T, ..., (z_1^*, ..., z_{m-1}^*, 1)^T$ are represented by $a_1, a_2, ..., a_m$, respectively. Given the matrix $\mathbf{E} = (\mathbf{e}_1 - \mathbf{z}^*, \mathbf{e}_2 - \mathbf{z}^*, ..., \mathbf{e}_m - \mathbf{z}^*)^T$ and $\mathbf{u} = (1, 1, ..., 1)^T$, we can compute the intercepts as follows:

$$\begin{pmatrix} \left(a_1 - z_1^*\right)^{-1} \\ \left(a_1 - z_2^*\right)^{-1} \\ ... \\ \left(a_1 - z_m^*\right)^{-1} \end{pmatrix} = \mathbf{E}^{-1} \mathbf{u}. \tag{2.11}$$

Subsequent to this, the values of z_i^{nad} are adjusted to a_i, with i ranging from 1 to m. Further, by employing Eq. (2.9), the population S_t can be normalized. An illustration of the construction of the hyperplane and the formation of intercepts in a 3D objective space can be seen in Fig. 2.2.

It is important to take note that if the rank of matrix E is less than m, the m extreme points will not be able to form a m-dimensional hyperplane. Even if the hyperplane can be constructed, there is still a possibility that no intercepts can be obtained in certain directions, or some intercepts a_i may not meet the constraint of $a_i > z_i^*$. In any of the aforementioned situations, for each $i \in \{1, 2, ..., m\}$, z_i^{nad} is assigned to the largest value of f_i among the nondominated solutions in S_t.

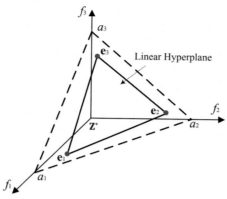

Figure 2.2 Illustration of constructing linear hyperplane by extreme points and computing intercepts in 3D objective space.

2.3.5 Clustering operator

At every generation in θ–DEA, the clustering operator is employed on population S_t. The clustering is implemented in the normalized objective space, where the origin represents the ideal point. Assume that $\tilde{\mathbf{f}}(\mathbf{x}) = (\tilde{f}_1(\mathbf{x}), \tilde{f}_2(\mathbf{x}), ..., \tilde{f}_m(\mathbf{x}))^T$ denotes the normalized objective vector for solution x. Let L be a line that passes through the origin with the direction $\boldsymbol{\lambda}_j$, and u represents the projection of $\tilde{\mathbf{f}}(\mathbf{x})$ on L. The distance between the origin and u is given by $d_{j,1}(\mathbf{x})$, while the perpendicular distance between $\tilde{\mathbf{f}}(\mathbf{x})$ and L is represented by $d_{j,2}(\mathbf{x})$. These quantities can be calculated, respectively, as follows:

$$d_{j,1}(\mathbf{x}) = \frac{||\tilde{\mathbf{f}}(\mathbf{x})^T \boldsymbol{\lambda}_j||}{||\boldsymbol{\lambda}_j||}, \tag{2.12}$$

$$d_{j,2}(\mathbf{x}) = \left|\left| \tilde{\mathbf{f}}(\mathbf{x}) - d_{j,1}(\mathbf{x}) \left(\frac{\boldsymbol{\lambda}_j}{||\boldsymbol{\lambda}_j||} \right) \right|\right|. \tag{2.13}$$

Fig. 2.3 visually depicts the distances, $d_{j,1}(\mathbf{x})$ and $d_{j,2}(\mathbf{x})$, in a 2D objective space.

In the clustering operator, only $d_{j,2}$ is taken into account, while $d_{j,1}$ will be used later in the definition of θ dominance. A solution $\mathbf{x}$ is assigned to the cluster C_j that has the smallest value of $d_{j,2}(\mathbf{x})$. The procedure for the clustering process is presented in Algorithm 2.2, which provides a more comprehensive explanation of the clustering process.

Algorithm 2.2: Clustering (S_t, Λ, C).

1: $\{C_1, C_2, \ldots, C_N\} \leftarrow \{\varnothing, \varnothing, \ldots, \varnothing\}$
2: **for** each solution $\mathbf{x}$ in S_t **do**
3: n $\leftarrow$ 1
4: min $\leftarrow d_{1,2}(\mathbf{x})$
5: **for** j $\leftarrow$ 2 to N **do**
6:    **if** $d_{1,2}(\mathbf{x}) <$ min **then**
7:      min $\leftarrow d_{1,2}(\mathbf{x})$
8:      n $\leftarrow$ j
9:    **end if**
10: **end for**
11: $C_n \leftarrow C_n \cup \{\mathbf{x}\}$
12: **end for**

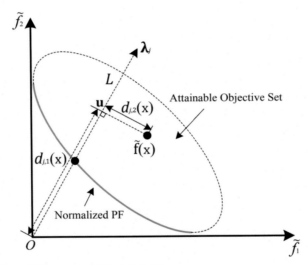

Figure 2.3 Illustration of distances $d_{j,1}(x)$ and $d_{j,2}(x)$.

2.3.6 θ-Dominance

The proposed θ-dominance operates on population S_t, utilizing a set of reference points Λ. Each solution in S_t is assigned to a cluster from a set of clusters C, determined by the clustering operator. The function $\mathcal{F}_j(\mathbf{x}) = d_{j,1}(\mathbf{x}) + \theta d_{j,2}(\mathbf{x})$, where $j \in \{1, 2, ..., N\}$ and θ is a predefined penalty parameter, is employed. The form of $\mathcal{F}_j(\mathbf{x})$ is identical to that of the penalty boundary intersection (PBI) function [3]. However, in this case, both distances, $d_{j,1}$ and $d_{j,2}$, are calculated in the normalized objective space. In general, $d_{j,2}(\mathbf{x}) = 0$ guarantees that $\mathbf{f}(\mathbf{x})$ is always on L, resulting in optimal diversity, while a smaller value of $d_{j,1}(\mathbf{x})$ under the condition $d_{j,2}(\mathbf{x}) = 0$ indicates better convergence. By defining $\mathcal{F}_j$ and C, several key concepts related to θ dominance can be defined as follows.

If there are two solutions, $\mathbf{x}$ and $\mathbf{y}$, within population S_t, then $\mathbf{x}$ is considered to θ-dominate $\mathbf{y}$, denoted as $\mathbf{x} \prec_\theta \mathbf{y}$, if $\mathbf{x} \in C_j, \mathbf{y} \in C_j$, and $\mathcal{F}_j(\mathbf{x}) < \mathcal{F}_j(\mathbf{y})$, where $j \in \{1, 2, ..., N\}$.

Definition 2.1:

A solution $\mathbf{x}^* \in S_t$ is considered to be θ-optimal if there does not exist any other solution $\mathbf{x} \in S_t$ such that $\mathbf{x} \prec_\theta \mathbf{x}^*$.

Definition 2.2:

The collection of all solutions that are θ-optimal within S_t constitutes the θ-optimal set (θ-OS), while the associated mappings of θ-OS in the objective space comprise the θ-optimal front.

Using the definition of θ dominance, we can observe the following three properties that demonstrate the irreflexivity, asymmetry, and transitivity of the relation $\prec_\theta$.

Property 2.1:

If a solution $\mathbf{x} \in S_t$, then $\mathbf{x} \not\prec_\theta \mathbf{x}$.

Proof: Let $\mathbf{x} \not\prec_\theta \mathbf{x}$, then there exists $j \in \{1, 2, ..., N\}$ such that $\mathbf{x} \in C_j$ and $\mathcal{F}_j(\mathbf{x}) < \mathcal{F}_j(\mathbf{x})$. Nonetheless, $\mathcal{F}_j(\mathbf{x})$ is equal to $\mathcal{F}_j(\mathbf{x})$. Therefore $\mathbf{x}$ cannot be θ-dominated by itself, and the relation $\prec_\theta$ is irreflexive.

Property 2.2:

If two solutions $\mathbf{x}, \mathbf{y} \in S_t$ satisfy $\mathbf{x} \not\prec_\theta \mathbf{y}$, then $\mathbf{y} \not\prec_\theta \mathbf{x}$.

Proof: Assume that $\mathbf{y} \not\prec_\theta \mathbf{x}$, then there exists $j \in \{1, 2, ..., N\}$ such that $\mathbf{y} \in C_j$, $\mathbf{x} \in C_j$, and $\mathcal{F}_j(\mathbf{y}) < \mathcal{F}_j(\mathbf{x})$. However, based on the fact that $\mathbf{x} \prec_\theta \mathbf{y}$, it follows that $\mathcal{F}_j(\mathbf{x}) < \mathcal{F}_j(\mathbf{y})$. As a result, the supposition is false, and the proposition is correct. This demonstrates that the relation $\prec_\theta$ is asymmetric.

Property 2.3:

Suppose there are three solutions, $\mathbf{x}$, $\mathbf{y}$, and $\mathbf{z}$, within S_t such that $\mathbf{x} \prec_\theta \mathbf{y}$ and $\mathbf{y} \prec_\theta \mathbf{z}$.

Prove as follows, given that $\mathbf{x} \prec_\theta \mathbf{y}$, we can conclude that there exists $j \in \{1, 2, ..., N\}$ such that $\mathbf{x} \in C_j$, $\mathbf{y} \in C_j$, and $\mathcal{F}_j(\mathbf{x}) < \mathcal{F}_j(\mathbf{y})$. Additionally, based on $\mathbf{y} \prec_\theta \mathbf{z}$, we know that $\mathbf{z} \in C_j$ and $\mathcal{F}_j(\mathbf{y}) < \mathcal{F}_j(\mathbf{z})$. As a result, we can deduce that $\mathbf{x} \in C_j$, $\mathbf{z} \in C_j$, and $\mathcal{F}_j(\mathbf{x}) < \mathcal{F}_j(\mathbf{z})$. Therefore $\mathbf{x} \prec_\theta \mathbf{z}$ is true, and the relation $\prec_\theta$ is transitive.

Since the θ dominance satisfies the aforementioned three properties, it defines a strict partial order on S_t. Therefore the fast nondominated sorting approach [5] can be directly applied in the context of θ dominance, resulting in S_t being divided into distinct θ-nondomination levels.

It should be noted that in the context of θ dominance, there is no competition between clusters, allowing for the use of different θ values in each cluster. To further explore this aspect, we have developed the proposed θ-DEA. In the normalized objective space, if λ_j represents the axis direction, we assign a high θ value ($\theta = 10^6$) to cluster C_j, while a normal θ value is used for other clusters. The high θ values in clusters corresponding to axis directions can help θ-DEA better capture the nadir point in higher-dimensional objective spaces, leading to more stable normalization processes.

2.3.7 Computational complexity of θ-DEA

The primary factor dictating the computational complexity of θ-DEA within a single generation is the clustering operator, which is outlined in Algorithm 2.2 under general conditions. For each solution $\mathbf{x}$ in S_t, Algorithm 2.2 requires the calculation of N distances, denoted $d_{1,2}(\mathbf{x}), d_{2,2}(\mathbf{x}), ..., d_{N,2}(\mathbf{x})$, with each distance calculated via $O(m)$ computations.

The total number of computations required for Algorithm 2.2 is $O(mN|S_t|)$. Given that $|S_t|$ is at most $2N$, the worst-case computational complexity for one generation of θ-DEA is approximately $O(mN^2)$.

2.4 Experimental design

The focus of this section is to outline the experimental design used to evaluate the performance of the proposed θ-DEA. We begin by presenting the test problems and quality indicators utilized in our experiments. Next, we provide a brief introduction to eight state-of-the-art algorithms used for comparison purposes. Lastly, we detail the experimental settings used in this study.

2.4.1 Test problems

This section outlines the test problems utilized in our experiments for comparing the performance of various algorithms. Specifically, we utilize two popular test suites for many-objective optimization, namely Deb−Thiele−Laumanns−Zitzler (DTLZ) [16] and Walking Fish Group (WFG) [17]. To ensure reliable computation of the quality indicators, we only consider DTLZ1−4 and DTLZ7 problems from the DTLZ test suite, as the nature of DTLZ5 and DTLZ6 PFs is unclear beyond three objectives [17]. Additionally, we incorporate two scaled test problems, namely scaled DTLZ1 and DTLZ2 problems [8], which are modifications of DTLZ1 and DTLZ2 problems, respectively. For instance, if the scaling factor is 10^i, then the objectives f_1, f_2, and f_3 for the three-objective scaled DTLZ1 problem are multiplied by 10^0, 10^1, and 10^2, respectively. Throughout our experiments, we refer to scaled DTLZ1 and DTLZ2 problems as SDTLZ1 and SDTLZ2, respectively.

The test problems used in our experiments can be scaled to accommodate any number of objectives and decision variables. We consider the number of objectives, m, to be within the range $\{3, 5, 8, 10, 15\}$.

The total number of decision variables for DTLZ1−4, DTLZ7, SDTLZ1, and SDTLZ2 problems is expressed as $n = m + k - 1$, unless otherwise specified. Specifically, k is set to 5 for DTLZ1 and SDTLZ1, 10 for DTLZ2−4 and SDTLZ2, and 20 for DLTZ7, as recommended in [8,16].

In the case of all WFG problems, unless explicitly mentioned otherwise, the number of decision variables is fixed at 24. Additionally, the position-related parameter is defined as $m - 1$ in accordance with [17,18]. For SDTLZ1 and SDTZL2 problems with different numbers of objectives, Table 2.1 displays the scaling factors employed.

The test problems utilized in our experiments possess diverse characteristics that challenge different aspects of an algorithm's performance. These characteristics include linear, mixed (convex/concave), multimodal, disconnected, degenerate, and disparately scaled PFs. Table 2.2 provides a summary of the primary features of all the test problems employed in our study.

Table 2.1 Scaling factors for SDTLZ1 and SDTLZ2 problems.

No. of objectives (m)	Scaling factor	
	SDTLZ1	SDTLZ2
3	10^i	10^i
5	10^i	10^i
8	3^i	3^i
10	2^i	3^i
15	1.2^i	2^i

Table 2.2 Features of the test problems.

Problem	Features
DTLZ1	Linear, multimodal
DTLZ2	Concave
DTLZ3	Concave, multimodal
DTLZ4	Concave, biased
SDTLZ1	Linear, multimodal, scaled
SDTLZ2	Concave, scaled
DTLZ7	Mixed, disconnected, multimodal, scaled
WFG1	Mixed, biased, scaled
WFG2	Concave, disconnected, multimodal, nonseparable, scaled
WFG3	Linear, degenerate, nonseparable, scaled
WFG4	Concave, multimodal, scaled
WFG5	Concave, deceptive, scaled
WFG6	Concave, nonseparable, scaled
WFG7	Concave, biased, scaled
WFG8	Concave, biased, nonseparable, scaled
WFG9	Concave, biased, multimodal, deceptive, nonseparable, scaled

2.4.2 Quality indicators

To evaluate the performance of various algorithms, quality indicators are utilized. In the EMO literature, one of the most commonly employed indicators is the inverted generational distance (IGD) [19], which provides a comprehensive evaluation of the convergence and diversity of a solution set. To calculate IGD, a set of uniformly distributed points along the known PF is required. While the true PFs for most benchmark problems are known, it is relatively straightforward to sample the points on the 2D or 3D front. However, for high-dimensional PFs, ensuring that sampled points are uniformly distributed and determining how many points are necessary to represent the true front are challenging issues. In fact, several studies [20−22] focused on many-objective optimization, where IGD serves as the quality indicator, failed to clarify how they sampled points along the PF.

In a recent study, Deb and Jain [8] proposed a novel approach for computing IGD in MOEAs that rely on supplied reference points or reference directions, such as MOEA/D and NSGA-III. This approach works as follows: for each reference direction $\boldsymbol{\lambda}_j, j = 1, 2, ..., N$, its targeted point $\mathbf{v}_j$ on the known PF in the normalized objective space can be accurately located. The set of all N targeted points constitutes $\mathbf{V} = \{\mathbf{v}_1, \mathbf{v}_2, ..., \mathbf{v}_N\}$. Let A be the set of final nondominated points obtained in the objective space for any algorithm. Then, IGD is calculated as follows:

$$\text{IGD}(\mathbf{A}, \mathbf{V}) = \frac{1}{|\mathbf{V}|} \sum_{i=1}^{|\mathbf{V}|} \min_{\mathbf{f} \in \mathbf{A}} d(\mathbf{v}_i, \mathbf{f}). \tag{2.14}$$

The formula for computing IGD involves calculating the Euclidean distance $d(\mathbf{v}_i, \mathbf{f})$ between the points $\mathbf{v}_i$ and $\mathbf{f}$, where f is a point in the set A. It is important to note that, for scaled problems, the objective values in set A need to be normalized using the ideal and nadir points of the exact PF before computing IGD. The set A with smaller IGD values is considered to be better.

The above method for computing IGD is particularly relevant to reference point/direction-based MOEAs, as these algorithms aim to find Pareto-optimal points close to the supplied reference points to some extent. Therefore it is sensible to use the aforementioned approach to calculate IGD. Since the proposed θ-DEA is also based on reference points, we will utilize IGD as defined by Eq. (2.14) to evaluate and compare its performance in the experiments.

The aforementioned IGD approach is not applicable to MOEAs that do not use reference points/directions, such as HypE [23] and shift-based density estimation (SDE) [22]. For these algorithms, the primary objective is to find a sparsely distributed set of Pareto-optimal points across the entire PF [24]. In such cases, the hypervolume (HV) [25] is frequently utilized as a performance indicator. The HV is a strict Pareto-compliant [19] indicator that possesses excellent theoretical qualities, rendering it a fair and reliable measure of performance. Assume that we have an algorithm that yields a set of final nondominated points in the objective space, which we denote by A. Additionally, suppose that $\mathbf{r} = (r_1, r_2, ..., r_m)^T$ is a reference point in the objective space that is dominated by any point in set A. The HV indicator value of A with respect to $\mathbf{r}$ is calculated as the volume of the region that is both dominated by A and bounded by $\mathbf{r}$. This value can be expressed as:

$$\text{HV}(\mathbf{A}, \mathbf{r}) = \text{volume}\left(\bigcup_{\mathbf{f} \in \mathbf{A}} \left[f_1, r_1\right] \times \ldots \left[f_m, r_m\right] \right). \qquad (2.15)$$

The HV is capable of evaluating both the convergence and diversity of a solution set. A higher HV value, given a reference point $\mathbf{r}$, indicates better quality. The selection of the appropriate reference point is a crucial factor in HV computation. Research has shown that values of r_i that are slightly greater than z_i^{nad} are preferable as they maintain a balance between solution set convergence and diversity [26,27]. In our experiments, we set $\mathbf{r}$ to 1.1 times $\mathbf{z}^{\text{nad}}$, where $\mathbf{z}^{\text{nad}}$ can be determined analytically for all of the test problems we employed.

Following the approach suggested in [2,28], we exclude any points that do not dominate the reference point when computing the HV. In instances where the PFs have objective values that are scaled differently, we normalize the objective values of both the points in A and the reference point r using $\mathbf{z}^{\text{nad}}$ and $\mathbf{z}^*$ (which is 0 for all test problems used) before computing HV via Eq. (2.15).

As a result, the HV value for an instance with m objectives in our experiments ranges from 0 to 1.1 m − Vm, where Vm represents the HV of the region that is bounded by the coordinate axes and the exact normalized PF. Furthermore, for problems that feature no more than 10 objectives, we determine HV with exact precision by utilizing the recently developed WFG algorithm [29]. In the case of problems that involve 15 objectives, we estimate the HV using a Monte Carlo simulation method detailed in [23]. To ensure accuracy, we employ 10,000,000 sampling points in our approximation.

2.4.3 Other algorithms in comparison

To validate the efficacy of the proposed θ-DEA, we compare its performance against eight state-of-the-art algorithms that function as benchmark algorithms.

1. Grid-based evolutionary algorithm (GrEA) [20]: GrEA leverages the grid's capabilities to augment the selection pressure on the PF and simultaneously maintain a broad and evenly distributed assortment of solutions. To achieve this, GrEA incorporates several components, including grid dominance, grid difference, three grid-based criteria (grid ranking, grid crowding distance, and grid coordinate point distance), as well as a fitness adjustment strategy.

2. Preference ordering genetic algorithm (POGA) [30]: The ranking phase of MOEAs in preference order-based approaches is based on an optimality criterion. By utilizing the definition of efficiency of order in subsets of objectives, the NSGA-II framework implements a ranking procedure that applies greater selection pressure to objective spaces of varying dimensionality than the conventional Pareto dominance-based ranking scheme.

3. NSGA-III [8]: NSGA-III is a many-objective optimization algorithm that is based on a reference point system. Its framework bears similarities to the original NSGA-II, but it differs in that diversity maintenance among population members which is facilitated by supplying and dynamically updating a series of well-dispersed reference points. In essence, NSGA-III prioritizes population members that are nondominated yet situated close to a given set of reference points.

4. SDE [22]: This technique is a broad adaptation of density estimation strategies that enables Pareto dominance-based MOEAs to be more effective in addressing many-objective optimization problems. The fundamental concept behind this approach is to leverage the preference of density estimators for solutions located in sparse regions. In order to assign poor converging solutions higher density values, they are relocated into crowded regions via SDE. This enables them to be eliminated more efficiently during the evolutionary process. SDE is straightforward to implement and can be utilized with any specific density estimator, requiring minimal computational resources and no extra parameters. In this chapter, SPEA2 + SDE is employed, as it displays the most superior performance among the three versions (NSGA-II + SDE, SPEA2 + SDE, and PESA-II + SDE) that were considered in [22].

5. MOEA/D [3]: This algorithm is an exemplar of the decomposition-based approach. To address problems that feature complex PSs, a new variant of MOEA/D (MOEA/D-DE) that employs differential evolution (DE) [31] was proposed in [4]. However, in this study, the original MOEA/D with the PBI function is chosen due to the findings reported in [8], which indicate that MOEA/D-DE performs poorly on many-objective problems. PBI is deemed more appropriate for tackling problems with a high-dimensional objective space.

6. Decomposition-based multiobjective particle swarm optimizer (dMOPSO) [32]: dMOPSO is an MOEA that expands upon the particle swarm optimization [33] approach and incorporates a decomposition-based framework. It updates the position of each particle by employing a group of solutions that are deemed globally best based on the decomposition-based approach. A significant aspect of this algorithm is its implementation of a memory reinitialization process that seeks to enhance the swarm's diversity. Like MOEA/D, the PBI function is also selected for use in dMOPSO.

7. HypE [23]: This algorithm is a HV-based evolutionary approach that is designed for many-objective optimization. It utilizes Monte Carlo simulation to estimate the precise HV values. The primary concept behind HypE is that only the solution rankings generated by the HV indicator are significant, while the actual values of the indicator are not crucial. HypE achieves a balance between the precision of the estimates and the computational resources at hand, thereby facilitating the application of HV-based search to many-objective problems.

8. Many-objective metaheuristic based on the R2 indicator (MOMBI) [18]: This metaheuristic is designed for many-objective optimization and is rooted in the R2 indicator. In order to incorporate R2 into the selection mechanism, this algorithm employs a nondominated scheme that is based on the adopted utility functions. The fundamental concept of this algorithm is to assign the first rank to solutions that demonstrate the best performance on any of the selected utility functions. Once these solutions are identified, they are removed, and a new second rank is established using the same approach. This iterative process of assigning ranks based on the utility functions persists until all of the solutions have been categorized.

The majority of categories of techniques for many-objective optimization are encompassed by the eight selected algorithms. Table 2.3 presents a summary of the chosen algorithms for comparison. The Metal framework [34] is utilized to implement all of the algorithms, including the proposed θ-DEA. The execution is performed on an Intel 2.83 GHz Xeon processor with 15.9 Gb of RAM. The final population is utilized for computing quality indicators for all algorithms except SDE, which uses the final archive.

Table 2.3 includes the following categories: C1 refers to Adoption of new preference relations; C2 refers to Adoption of new diversity promotion mechanisms; C3 refers to Decomposition-based approach; C4 refers to Indicator-based approach; and C5 refers to Reference-point based approach.

Table 2.3 Summary of the algorithms employed in comparison.

Algorithm name	Algorithm category
GrEA	C1 [20]
POGA	C1 [30]
NSGA-III	C2, C5 [8]
SDE	C2 [22]
MOEA/D	C3 [3]
dMOPSO	C3 [32]
HypE	C4 [23]
MOMBI	C4 [18]

2.4.4 Experimental settings

The experimental setup comprises general and parameter settings. The following are the general settings.

1. Number of Runs: For each test instance, each algorithm is executed independently 20 times.
2. Termination Criterion: To specify the termination criterion of each algorithm for each run, we utilize the maximum number of generations (MaxGen) in our experiment. Due to the varying computational complexity of the test problems, we have employed different MaxGen values for different problems.
3. Significance Test: In some cases, we have utilized the Wilcoxon signed-rank test [35] to test for statistical significance between two competing algorithms based on their assessment results. The significance level for this test was set at 5%.

Regarding the parameter settings, we initially provide several common settings for the algorithms, listed as follows.

1. Population Size: The population size N for NSGA-III, MOEA/D, and θ-DEA cannot be arbitrarily chosen, as it is governed by the parameter H. For problems with 8, 10, and 15 objectives, we have created intermediate reference points using two-layered reference points. Table 2.4 provides the population sizes utilized in this study for problems with varying numbers of objectives. We have slightly adjusted their population size to a multiple of four, as done in the original NSGA-III study [8].
2. Penalty Parameter θ: As the PBI function is utilized by MOEA/D, dMOPSO, and θ-DEA, it is necessary to set the penalty parameter θ for these algorithms. In the present chapter, we have set θ to 5 for both MOEA/D and dMOPSO, following the recommendation in [3]. However, other studies, such as [24,36], have suggested that the optimal specification of θ for MOEA/D may vary depending on the specific problem being solved and the number of objectives involved. In regards to the proposed θ-DEA, we have set θ to 5.
3. Parameters for Crossover and Mutation: All of the considered algorithms, with the exception of dMOPSO, employ the SBX and polynomial mutation [6]. The parameter values for crossover and mutation for GrEA, POGA, SDE, MOEA/D,

Table 2.4 Setting of the population size.

No. of objectives (m)	Divisions (H)	Population size (N)
3	12	91
5	6	210
8	3, 2	156
10	3, 2	275
15	2, 1	135

HypE, and MOMBI can be found in Table 2.5. The settings for NSGA–III and θ-DEA are slightly different, in accordance with [8], where η_c has a value of 30.

In addition to the aforementioned parameters, GrEA, SDE, MOEA/D, dMOPSO, and HypE each possess their own unique set of parameters. These parameters are established primarily based on the recommendations provided by their creators.

1. Parameter Setting in GrEA: The grid division (*div*) is a crucial parameter that must be specified. Given that the population size and termination criterion differ significantly from those of the initial GrEA study [20], we have modified div based on the recommendations provided in [20] for each problem instance, as illustrated in Table 2.6. Our objective is to achieve an optimal balance between convergence and diversity.

2. Parameter Setting in SDE: We have set the archive size equal to the population size.

Table 2.5 Parameter settings for crossover and mutation.

Parameter	Value
Crossover probability (p_c)	1.0
Mutation probability (p_m)	$1/n$
Distribution index for crossover (η_c)	20
Distribution index for mutation (η_m)	20

Table 2.6 Setting of grid division in GrEA.

Problem	No. of objectives (*m*)	Grid division (*div*)
DTLZ1	3, 5, 8, 10, 15	14, 17, 12, 17, 28
DTLZ2	3, 5, 8, 10, 15	15, 12, 12, 12, 12
DTLZ3	3, 5, 8, 10, 15	17, 19, 19, 19, 33
DTLZ4	3, 5, 8, 10, 15	16, 11, 12, 17, 18
DTLZ7	3, 5, 8, 10, 15	16, 12, 9, 11, 10
SDTLZ1	3, 5, 8, 10, 15	16, 16, 11, 17, 29
SDTLZ2	3, 5, 8, 10, 15	16, 10, 12, 15, 12
WFG1	3, 5, 8, 10, 15	6, 14, 13, 13, 13
WFG2	3, 5, 8, 10, 15	18, 16, 15, 19, 17
WFG3	3, 5, 8, 10, 15	16, 14, 12, 14, 16
WFG4	3, 5, 8, 10, 15	10, 13, 10, 11, 11
WFG5	3, 5, 8, 10, 15	10, 11, 12, 14, 14
WFG6	3, 5, 8, 10, 15	10, 12, 12, 14, 15
WFG7	3, 5, 8, 10, 15	10, 11, 12, 14, 14
WFG8	3, 5, 8, 10, 15	10, 12, 10, 14, 11
WFG9	3, 5, 8, 10, 15	9, 12, 12, 15, 13

3. Parameter Setting in MOEA/D: We have established a neighborhood size of 20, denoted as T.
4. Parameter Setting in dMOPSO: We have defined an age threshold, denoted as T_a, and set its value to 2.
5. Parameter Setting in HypE: We have set the reference point bound to 200, while the number of sampling points M has been established at 10,000.

2.5 Experimental results

In this section, we aim to authenticate the efficacy of θ-DEA. Our experiments have been segregated into three distinct parts. The primary segment involves a comparative analysis of θ-DEA with the other two MOEAs that employ reference points/directions, specifically, NSGA-III and MOEA/D. Our objective is to showcase the superior performance of θ-DEA, which is a reference point-based algorithm, in terms of achieving the desired balance between convergence and diversity. The second segment of our experiments involves a comparison of θ-DEA with several other many-objective optimization techniques. Our goal is to demonstrate the exceptional capability of θ-DEA as a general many-objective optimizer in effectively exploring sparsely distributed nondominated points across the entire PF. The third component of our experiments involves an analysis of the impact of the parameter θ on the performance of the proposed algorithm.

2.5.1 Comparison with NSGA-III and MOEA/D

In this section, we utilize IGD as an evaluation metric for the algorithms. Given that all of the experimental configurations, including the method for computing IGD, are aligned with those applied in the initial NSGA-III study [8], we compare the IGD outcomes of θ-DEA with those of NSGA-III and MOEA/D-PBI, as presented in [8].

To commence our comparison, we initially employ the normalized test problems, namely DTLZ1−4. These problems have an equivalent range of values for each objective over the PF. DTLZ1 has a straightforward, linear PF $\sum_{i=1}^{m} f_i = 0.5$, but presents a challenge due to the presence of $11^5 - 1$ local optima in the search space. The primary difficulty in this problem is to converge to the hyperplane. On the other hand, DTLZ2−4 have PFs with the same geometrical shape $\sum_{i=1}^{m} f_i^2 = 1$, but they are tailored to challenge different capacities of an algorithm.

In Table 2.7, the outcomes of θ-DEA and NSGA-III on the four problems are presented, indicating the best, median, and worst IGD values. Based on the results in Table 2.7, θ-DEA consistently exhibits superior performance compared to NSGA-III

Table 2.7 Best, median, and worst IGD values for θ-DEA and NSGA-III on m-objective DTLZ1−4 problems.

Problem	m	MaxGen	θ-DEA	NSGA-III
DTLZ1	3	400	5.655E − 04	**4.880E − 04**
			1.307E − 03	1.308E − 03
			9.449E − 03	**4.880E − 03**
	5	600	**4.432E − 04**	5.116E − 04
			7.328E − 04	9.799E − 04
			2.138E − 03	**1.979E − 03**
	8	750	**1.982E − 03**	2.044E − 03
			2.704E − 03	3.979E − 03
			4.620E − 03	8.721E − 03
	10	1000	**2.099E − 03**	2.215E − 03
			2.448E − 03	3.462E − 03
			3.935E − 03	6.869E − 03
	15	1500	**2.442E − 03**	2.649E − 03
			8.152E − 03	**5.063E − 03**
			2.236E − 01	**1.123E − 02**
DTLZ2	3	250	**1.042E − 03**	1.262E − 03
			1.569E − 03	**1.357E − 03**
			5.497E − 03	**2.114E − 03**
	5	350	**2.720E − 03**	4.254E − 03
			3.252E − 03	4.982E − 03
			5.333E − 03	5.862E − 03
	8	500	**7.786E − 03**	1.371E − 02
			8.990E − 03	1.571E − 02
			1.140E − 02	1.811E − 02
	10	750	**7.558E − 03**	1.350E − 02
			8.809E − 03	1.528E − 02
			1.020E − 02	1.697E − 02
	15	1000	**8.819E − 03**	1.360E − 02
			1.133E − 02	1.726E − 02
			1.484E − 02	2.114E − 02
DTLZ3	3	1000	1.343E − 03	**9.751E − 04**
			3.541E − 03	4.007E − 03
			5.528E − 03	6.665E − 03
	5	1000	**1.982E − 03**	3.086E − 03
			4.272E − 03	5.960E − 03
			1.911E − 02	**1.196E − 02**
	8	1000	**8.769E − 03**	1.244E − 02
			1.535E − 02	2.375E − 02
			3.826E − 02	9.649E − 02
	10	1500	**5.970E − 03**	8.849E − 03
			7.244E − 03	1.188E − 02
			2.323E − 02	**2.083E − 02**
	15	2000	**9.834E − 03**	1.401E − 02
			1.917E − 02	2.145E − 02
			6.210E − 01	**4.195E − 02**

(Continued)

Table 2.7 (Continued)

Problem	m	MaxGen	θ-DEA	NSGA-III
DTLZ4	3	600	**1.866E − 04**	2.915E − 04
			2.506E − 04	5.970E − 04
			5.320E − 01	**4.286E − 01**
	5	1000	**2.616E − 04**	9.849E − 04
			3.790E − 04	1.255E − 03
			4.114E − 04	1.721E − 03
	8	1250	**2.780E − 03**	5.079E − 03
			3.098E − 03	7.054E − 03
			3.569E − 03	6.051E − 01
	10	2000	**2.746E − 03**	5.694E − 03
			3.341E − 03	6.337E − 03
			3.914E − 03	1.076E − 01
	15	3000	**4.143E − 03**	7.110E − 03
			5.904E − 03	3.431E − 01
			7.680E − 03	1.073E + 00

Best performance is shown in bold.

on all instances, with the exception of three cases, namely the 15-objective DTLZ1 and 3-objective DTLZ2 problems. In certain iterations, θ-DEA fails to approximate the PF for the 15-objective DTLZ1 and DTLZ3 problems, as indicated by the significant worst IGD value. Our analysis suggests that the potential reason for the suboptimal performance of θ-DEA on the 15-objective DTLZ1 and DTLZ3 problems is its failure to capture the nadir point in high-dimensional objective space and incorrect normalization. On the other hand, for the 15-objective DTLZ4 problem, θ-DEA consistently exhibits excellent performance in all iterations, while NSGA-III often faces challenges in achieving optimal convergence and diversity on DTLZ4 problems with more than five objectives. A noteworthy observation is that neither θ-DEA nor NSGA-III could consistently achieve optimal performance on the three-objective DTLZ4 problem.

MOEA/D-PBI does not integrate the normalization technique. Therefore, to conduct a more equitable comparison against MOEA/D-PBI, we eliminate the normalization procedure from θ-DEA and label this variant as θ-DEA*. Table 2.8 presents the comparative outcomes between θ-DEA and MOEA/D-PBI. The results indicate that θ-DEA*, which omits the normalization procedure, surpasses MOEA/D-PBI on the DTLZ1, DTLZ3, and DTLZ4 problems. However, MOEA/D-PBI outperforms θ-DEA* on the DTLZ2 problem. The superior performance of θ-DEA* is especially noticeable on the DTLZ4 problem. We have observed that the outcomes of θ-DEA* are generally superior to those of θ-DEA, as presented in Table 2.7. This finding suggests that normalization may not be essential for the normalized problems. Furthermore, in contrast to θ-DEA, θ-DEA* exhibits optimal performance in all iterations for the

Table 2.8 Best, median, and worst IGD values for θ-DEA* and MOEA/D-PBI on m-objective DTLZ1−4 problems.

Problem	m	MaxGen	θ-DEA*	MOEA/D-PBI
DTLZ1	3	400	**3.006E − 04**	4.095E − 04
			9.511E − 04	1.495E − 03
			2.718E − 03	4.743E − 03
	5	600	3.612E − 04	**3.179E − 04**
			4.259E − 04	6.372E − 04
			5.797E − 04	1.635E − 03
	8	750	**1.869E − 03**	3.914E − 03
			2.061E − 03	6.106E − 03
			2.337E − 03	8.537E − 03
	10	1000	**1.999E − 03**	3.872E − 03
			2.268E − 03	5.073E − 03
			2.425E − 03	6.130E − 03
	15	1500	**2.884E − 03**	1.236E − 02
			3.504E − 03	1.431E − 02
			3.992E − 03	1.692E − 02
DTLZ2	3	250	7.567E − 04	**5.432E − 04**
			9.736E − 04	**6.406E − 04**
			1.130E − 03	**8.006E − 04**
	5	350	1.863E − 03	**1.219E − 03**
			2.146E − 03	**1.437E − 03**
			2.288E − 03	**1.727E − 03**
	8	500	6.120E − 03	**3.097E − 03**
			6.750E − 03	**3.763E − 03**
			7.781E − 03	**5.198E − 03**
	10	750	6.111E − 03	**2.474E − 03**
			6.546E − 03	**2.778E − 03**
			7.069E − 03	**3.235E − 03**
	15	1000	7.269E − 03	**5.254E − 03**
			8.264E − 03	**6.005E − 03**
			9.137E − 03	9.409E − 03
DTLZ3	3	1000	**8.575E − 04**	9.773E − 04
			3.077E − 03	3.426E − 03
			5.603E − 03	9.113E − 03
	5	1000	**8.738E − 04**	1.129E − 03
			1.971E − 03	2.213E − 03
			4.340E − 03	6.147E − 03
	8	1000	6.493E − 03	**6.459E − 03**
			1.036E − 02	1.948E − 02
			1.549E − 02	1.123E + 00
	10	1500	5.074E − 03	**2.791E − 03**
			6.121E − 03	**4.319E − 03**
			7.243E − 03	1.010E + 00
	15	2000	7.892E − 03	**4.360E − 03**
			9.924E − 03	1.664E − 02
			1.434E − 02	1.260E + 00

(*Continued*)

Table 2.8 (Continued)

Problem	m	MaxGen	θ-DEA*	MOEA/D-PBI
DTLZ4	3	600	**1.408E − 04**	2.929E − 01
			1.918E − 04	4.280E − 01
			5.321E − 01	**5.234E − 01**
	5	1000	**2.780E − 04**	1.080E − 01
			3.142E − 04	5.787E − 01
			3.586E − 04	7.348E − 01
	8	1250	**2.323E − 03**	5.298E − 01
			3.172E − 03	8.816E − 01
			3.635E − 03	9.723E − 01
	10	2000	**2.715E − 03**	3.966E − 01
			3.216E − 03	9.203E − 01
			3.711E − 03	1.077E + 00
	15	3000	**4.182E − 03**	5.890E − 01
			5.633E − 03	1.133E + 00
			6.562E − 03	1.249E + 00

Best performance is shown in bold.

15-objective DTLZ1 and DTLZ3 problems. This observation suggests that normalization may limit the performance of θ-DEA to some degree on these two instances.

Subsequently, θ-DEA, NSGA-III, and MOEA/D-PBI were subjected to a performance assessment using two WFG problems, WFG6 and WFG7. These problems share a common PF shape, which is a segment of a hyperbola with radii $r_i = 2i, i = 1, 2, ..., m$. WFG6 is a problem that cannot be separated, whereas WFG7 is a problem with a bias.

The comparison results are presented in Table 2.9. It is noteworthy that NSGA-III outperforms the other algorithms on WFG6 problems and three-objective WFG7, whereas the proposed θ-DEA exhibits superior performance on WFG7 with more than three objectives. MOEA/D-PBI, on the other hand, was found to be inferior to θ-DEA on both WFG6 and WFG7 problems.

To delve deeper into the performance of θ-DEA on problems with objectives having different scales, we analyzed the SDTLZ1 and SDTLZ2 problems. The results of the comparison are tabulated in Table 2.10. In the case of SDTLZ1, the situation is analogous to that of DTLZ1, where NSGA-III performs better on 3- and 15-objective instances, while θ-DEA outperforms NSGA-III on the remaining instances. On the other hand, θ-DEA clearly outperforms NSGA-III for the SDTLZ2 problem.

In light of the aforementioned comparisons, it is safe to infer that the proposed θ-DEA algorithm can effectively balance convergence and diversity by leveraging structured reference points. In fact, by testing on problems that exhibit diverse characteristics, θ-DEA surpasses NSGA-III and MOEA/D-PBI on most of them in terms of IGD values, thereby demonstrating its superiority.

Table 2.9 Best, median, and worst IGD values for θ-DEA, NSGA-III, and MOEA/D-PBI on m-objective WFG6 and WFG7 problems.

Problem	m	MaxGen	θ-DEA	MOEA/D-PBI
WFG6	3	400	2.187E − 02	1.015E − 02
			2.906E − 02	3.522E − 02
			3.355E − 02	1.066E − 01
	5	750	2.430E − 02	8.335E − 03
			3.270E − 02	4.230E − 02
			3.661E − 02	1.058E − 01
	8	1500	2.528E − 02	1.757E − 02
			3.140E − 02	5.551E − 02
			3.727E − 02	1.156E − 01
	10	2000	2.098E − 02	**9.924E − 03**
			3.442E − 02	4.179E − 02
			4.183E − 02	1.195E − 01
	15	3000	3.759E − 02	1.513E − 02
			4.892E − 02	6.782E − 02
			6.380E − 02	1.637E − 01
WFG7	3	400	5.524E − 03	1.033E − 02
			6.951E − 03	1.358E − 02
			8.923E − 03	1.926E − 02
	5	750	**5.770E − 03**	8.780E − 03
			6.854E − 03	1.101E − 02
			8.100E − 03	1.313E − 02
	8	1500	**4.405E − 03**	1.355E − 02
			5.603E − 03	1.573E − 02
			8.527E − 03	2.626E − 02
	10	2000	**7.069E − 03**	1.041E − 02
			8.322E − 03	1.218E − 02
			9.664E − 03	1.490E − 02
	15	3000	8.915E − 03	**7.552E − 03**
			1.059E − 02	1.063E − 02
			1.236E − 02	2.065E − 02

Best performance is shown in bold.

2.5.2 Comparison with state-of-the-art algorithms

The comparison will also include the unnormalized version of θ-DEA, that is, θ-DEA*. The performance of the algorithms will be evaluated using the HV indicator.

Table 2.11 presents the mean HV values obtained from evaluating DTLZ1−4, DTLZ7, SDTLZ1, and SDTLZ2 problems, while Table 2.12 depicts the results from evaluating WFG problems. Additionally, Table 2.13 provides a summary of the significance tests conducted on the HV results, comparing the proposed θ-DEA (θ-DEA*)

Table 2.10 Best, median, and worst IGD values for θ-DEA and NSGA-III on scaled m-objective DTLZ1 and DTLZ2 problems.

Problem	m	MaxGen	θ-DEA	NSGA-III
SDTLZ1	3	400	8.153E − 04	**3.853E − 04**
			3.039E − 03	**1.214E − 03**
			1.413E − 02	**1.103E − 02**
	5	600	**8.507E − 04**	1.099E − 03
			1.225E − 03	2.500E − 03
			6.320E − 03	3.921E − 02
	8	750	**4.043E − 03**	4.659E − 03
			4.938E − 03	1.051E − 02
			8.734E − 03	1.167E − 01
	10	1000	4.100E − 03	**3.403E − 03**
			4.821E − 03	5.577E − 03
			6.676E − 03	3.617E − 02
	15	1500	5.037E − 03	**3.450E − 03**
			1.078E − 02	**6.183E − 03**
			4.774E − 01	**1.367E − 02**
SDTLZ2	3	250	**9.709E − 04**	1.347E − 03
			1.926E − 03	2.069E − 03
			7.585E − 03	**5.284E − 03**
	5	350	**2.755E − 03**	1.005E − 02
			3.521E − 03	2.564E − 02
			6.258E − 03	8.430E − 02
	8	500	**7.790E − 03**	1.582E − 02
			9.015E − 03	1.788E − 02
			1.091E − 02	2.089E − 02
	10	750	**7.576E − 03**	2.113E − 02
			8.680E − 03	3.334E − 02
			1.068E − 02	2.095E − 01
	15	1000	**9.373E − 03**	2.165E − 02
			1.133E − 02	2.531E − 02
			1.401E − 02	4.450E − 02

Best performance is shown in bold.

with the other algorithms. In this table, "B" ("W") next to Alg_1 versus Alg_2 indicates that the results of Alg_1 are significantly better (worse) than those of Alg_2 on the listed number of instances. Moreover, "E" signifies that no statistical significance exists between the results of Alg_1 and Alg_2 on the given number of instances.

In order to illustrate the distribution of the acquired solutions in a high-dimensional objective space, we have employed a 15-objective WFG7 instance as a case study. Fig. 2.4 portrays a parallel coordinates plot of the final solutions obtained by four competitive algorithms, namely θ-DEA, GrEA, NSGA-III, and SDE, in a

Table 2.11 Performance comparison of θ-DEA to different algorithms with respect to the average HV values on DTLZ1–4, DTLZ7, SDTLZ1, and SDTLZ2 problems.

Problem	m	MaxGen	θ-DEA	θ-DEA*	GrEA	POGA	NSGA-III	SDE	MOEA/D	dMOPSO	HypE	MOMBI
DTLZ1	3	400	1.116137	**1.118329**	1.072987[a]	1.083131[a]	1.117600	1.097010[a]	1.116679[b]	1.074976[a]	1.117483[b]	1.072413[a]
	5	600	1.576983	**1.577892**	1.509905[a]	0.000000[a]	1.577027[a]	1.545051[a]	1.577632[b]	1.482412[a]	1.466936[a]	1.509007[a]
	8	750	2.137924	**2.137998**	2.105894[a]	0.000000[a]	2.137837[b]	2.089314[a]	2.136337[a]	1.824428[a]	1.999087[a]	2.018629[a]
	10	1000	2.592719	2.592696	2.566547[a]	0.000000[a]	**2.592792**	2.562563[a]	2.592233[a]	2.317805[a]	2.520526[a]	2.470400[a]
	15	1500	4.131873	4.175713	3.914267[a]	0.169237[a]	**4.176773**	4.083228[a]	4.169859[b]	3.394256[a]	3.702937[a]	3.623057[a]
DTLZ2	3	250	0.743778	0.744320	0.740172[a]	0.698084[a]	0.743523[a]	0.742896[a]	0.744137[b]	0.712523[a]	**0.753191**	0.703623[a]
	5	350	1.306928	**1.307368**	1.304274[a]	0.853065[a]	1.303638[a]	1.299877[a]	1.307343	1.239853[a]	0.756079[a]	1.142958[a]
	8	500	1.977904	1.978469	**1.989406**	0.181198[a]	1.969096[a]	1.980826	1.978216[b]	1.816420[a]	0.892917[a]	1.373654[a]
	10	750	2.514259	2.514485	**2.515566**	0.368282[a]	2.508717[a]	2.505222[a]	2.515040	2.428399[a]	1.174930[a]	1.623827[a]
	15	1000	4.137225	4.137766	4.070080[a]	0.600316[a]	4.133743[a]	4.105103[a]	4.137792	3.931332[a]	**1.407601**	1.891898[a]
DTLZ3	3	1000	0.736938	0.738977	0.678608[a]	0.699556[a]	0.737407[b]	0.739591	0.736044	0.665529	**0.750325**	0.702072[a]
	5	1000	1.303987	**1.305846**	1.135837[a]	0.000000[a]	1.301481[a]	1.300661	1.303168	1.252229[a]	0.740621[a]	1.138243[a]
	8	1000	1.968943	**1.970805**	1.622438[a]	0.000000[a]	1.954336[a]	1.968342	1.251873[a]	1.428208[a]	0.881516[a]	1.325053[a]
	10	1500	2.512662	**2.514027**	2.306975[a]	0.000000[a]	2.508879[a]	2.507127[a]	2.406221	2.107556[a]	1.175350[a]	1.643232[a]
	15	2000	3.788788	**4.136332**	3.215646[a]	0.311735[a]	4.123622[b]	4.072396[b]	2.722371[b]	2.269634[a]	1.553939[a]	1.901460[a]
DTLZ4a	3	600	0.729265	0.602951	0.573359[c]	0.702980[c]	**0.744634**	0.630875[c]	0.406020[a]	0.677459[c]	0.549999[c]	0.691034[c]
	5	1000	**1.308945**	1.308934	1.307539[a]	0.996996[a]	1.308698[a]	1.289331[a]	1.205512[a]	1.203429[a]	1.014145[a]	1.128597
	8	1250	1.980779	1.977231	**1.981321**	0.058851[a]	1.980236[a]	1.966667[a]	1.826489[a]	1.829561[a]	0.925370[a]	1.326579
	10	2000	2.515436	**2.515468**	2.514960[a]	0.080187[a]	2.515172[a]	2.500043[a]	2.423727[a]	2.438748[a]	1.235517[a]	1.453693[a]
	15	3000	4.138203	**4.138225**	4.132426[a]	1.482621[a]	4.138154	4.109571[a]	3.978200[a]	3.936754[a]	2.056801[a]	1.263883[a]
DTLZ7	3	1000	0.415753	0.406455	0.417124	0.416076	0.415824	**0.427114**	0.404236[c]	0.411552[c]	0.397286[a]	0.409400[c]
	5	1000	0.448398	0.371751	0.521976	0.413607[c]	0.493987	**0.528809**	0.366661[a]	0.365309[a]	0.411226[c]	0.491190
	8	1000	0.506288	0.152916	**0.581912**	0.445509[c]	0.528482	0.345470[c]	0.012948[a]	0.121468[c]	0.262019[c]	0.452561[c]
	10	1500	0.594612	0.122341	**0.651955**	0.445526[c]	0.615565	0.173690[c]	0.001891[a]	0.036388[a]	0.272124[c]	0.508263[c]
	15	2000	0.747688	0.059097	**0.764778**	0.502990[c]	0.751188	0.042080[c]	0.000425[a]	0.000220[a]	0.069042[a]	0.581946[c]

(Continued)

Table 2.11 (Continued)

Problem	m	MaxGen	θ-DEA	θ-DEA*	GrEA	POGA	NSGA-III	SDE	MOEA/D	dMOPSO	HypE	MOMBI
SDTLZ1	3	400	**1.117365**	0.724709	1.096990[c]	1.084446[c]	1.116023	1.086490[c]	0.332926[a]	0.470223[a]	1.100216[c]	1.075055[c]
	5	600	**1.577751**	0.722800	1.501184[c]	0.000000[a]	1.575525[c]	1.491374[c]	0.556767[a]	0.233560[a]	0.753613[c]	1.508512[c]
	8	750	**2.137936**	1.413738	2.112299[c]	0.000000[a]	2.126815[c]	1.712786[c]	1.319874[a]	0.810944[a]	1.072366[a]	2.021830[c]
	10	1000	**2.592726**	2.158027	2.568992[c]	0.000000[a]	2.587997[c]	2.285257[c]	2.068300[a]	1.378952[a]	1.490181[a]	2.465309[c]
	15	1500	4.164391	4.056134	3.960558[a]	0.033188[a]	**4.176670**	4.084369[c]	3.972655[a]	3.218729[a]	2.988263[a]	3.590185[a]
SDTLZ2	3	250	0.743746	0.378277	0.740767[c]	0.697453[c]	0.743277[c]	0.706272[c]	0.210273[a]	0.205731[a]	**0.753099**	0.703222[c]
	5	350	**1.306804**	0.405596	1.303628[c]	0.856364[c]	1.290520[c]	0.667578[c]	0.251787[a]	0.246862[a]	0.386773[a]	1.142126[c]
	8	500	1.977826	0.729306	**1.990325**	0.231584[a]	1.963251[c]	0.888944[c]	0.414793[a]	0.479764[a]	0.441930[a]	1.365266[c]
	10	750	**2.514252**	0.866187	1.851829[c]	0.265022[a]	2.504209[c]	1.004728[c]	0.486005[a]	0.584936[a]	0.544107[a]	1.630979[c]
	15	1000	**4.137314**	1.529079	4.079169[c]	0.858370[a]	4.129375[c]	1.861987[c]	0.715960[a]	0.466954[a]	1.323373[a]	1.898389[c]

The best average HV value among the 10 algorithms for each instance is highlighted in bold.
[a]The result is significantly outperformed by both θ-DEA and θ-DEA*.
[b]The result is significantly outperformed by θ-DEA*.
[c]The result is significantly outperformed by θ-DEA.

Table 2.12 Performance comparison of θ-DEA to different algorithms with respect to the average HV values on WFG problems.

Problem	m	MaxGen	θ-DEA	θ-DEA*	GrEA	POGA	NSGA-III	SDE	MOEA/D	dMOPSO	HypE	MOMBI
WFG1	3	400	0.704526	0.697356	0.846287	0.766621	0.669729[a]	0.803966	0.657143[a]	0.403170[a]	**0.976181**	0.885760
	5	750	1.138794	1.23603	1.268898	1.109501[a]	0.859552[a]	1.354217	1.349888	0.461233[a]	0.911020[a]	**1.528811**
	8	1500	1.875997	1.905395	1.769013[a]	1.745597[a]	1.424963[a]	1.883743	1.755326[a]	0.484046[a]	1.536599[a]	**2.042375**
	10	2000	2.364268	2.386742	2.365107	2.355532	2.249535[a]	2.375338	1.799394[a]	0.536340[a]	2.268813[a]	**2.465608**
	15	3000	4.003682	3.867407	3.811128[a]	3.528350[a]	4.085931	3.903864[b]	1.772444[a]	0.750153[a]	4.028462	**4.122918**
WFG2	3	400	1.227226	1.221941	1.226099	1.208077[a]	1.226956	1.224626[b]	1.111085[a]	1.125810[a]	**1.244737**	1.192808[a]
	5	750	1.597188	1.564818	1.570086[b]	1.591412[b]	**1.598410**	1.579667[b]	1.520168[a]	1.478517[a]	1.535704[a]	1.596152[b]
	8	1500	2.12411	2.055014	2.102930[b]	2.136409	2.136525	2.107484[b]	2.016854[a]	1.971067[a]	2.084336[b]	**2.136910**
	10	2000	2.578311	2.491268	2.570389[b]	**2.591798**	2.58104	2.573254[b]	2.459026[a]	2.406484[a]	2.556327[b]	2.589607
	15	3000	3.467983	3.961793	4.094032	4.163488	**4.173427**	4.143102	3.921513[c]	3.822155[c]	4.126212	4.157740
WFG3	3	400	0.814962	0.798550	0.834432	0.829395	0.819758	0.834035	0.757034[a]	0.774135[a]	**0.847567**	0.835361
	5	750	1.028412	0.999933	1.013341[b]	**1.064772**	1.013941[b]	0.956846[a]	0.906075[a]	0.957250[a]	0.977617[a]	0.959638[a]
	8	1500	1.147203	1.17453	1.263233	**1.427165**	1.221543	1.127832	0.770754[a]	1.093482[a]	1.351959	1.352012
	10	2000	1.573090	1.359598	1.577058	**1.770022**	1.567908	1.370175[b]	0.524917[a]	1.004506[a]	1.720463	1.699805
	15	3000	2.510031	0.904082	2.711461	2.534502	2.510223	2.458935	0.579003[a]	0.535783[a]	**2.793994**	2.702406
WFG4	3	400	0.729664	0.720486	0.717433[a]	0.679313[a]	0.728892[b]	0.720904[b]	0.685079[a]	0.643591[a]	**0.750714**	0.687819[a]
	5	750	**1.286861**	1.259362	1.271279[b]	1.096965[a]	1.285072[b]	1.220702[a]	1.161435[a]	1.074986[a]	0.855942[a]	1.146019[a]
	8	1500	**1.964648**	1.858132	1.933492[b]	1.448769[a]	1.962156	1.784107[a]	1.188847[a]	1.078243[a]	1.137827[a]	1.373071[a]
	10	2000	**2.504065**	2.232877	2.481299[b]	1.696742[a]	2.502319[b]	2.292594[a]	1.432285[a]	1.330296[a]	1.557451[a]	1.683372[a]
	15	3000	**4.136892**	2.990774	3.893931[b]	2.748079[a]	4.136393	3.683401[b]	1.694794[a]	0.991603[a]	2.551034[a]	1.872957[a]
WFG5	3	400	0.687005	0.676813	0.669193[a]	0.655342[a]	0.687220	0.683408[b]	0.656189[a]	0.633971[a]	**0.698642**	0.646584[a]
	5	750	**1.222746**	1.190345	1.219312[b]	1.080845[a]	1.222480[b]	1.173486[a]	1.120619[a]	1.049378[a]	0.893813[a]	1.061277[a]
	8	1500	1.850361	1.727167	**1.862278**	0.936887[a]	1.850281	1.711954[a]	1.279934[a]	0.671722[a]	1.183477[a]	1.286271[a]
	10	2000	2.346521	2.092514	2.335886[b]	1.138726[a]	**2.346581**	2.204977[b]	1.541144[a]	0.303028[a]	1.659310[a]	1.428448[a]
	15	3000	3.833116	2.719208	3.400492[b]	3.455143[b]	**3.833242**	3.184516[b]	1.864379[a]	0.089205[a]	2.764870[b]	1.455641[a]
WFG6	3	400	0.690060	0.679787	0.677130[b]	0.640068[a]	0.685939	0.685988[b]	0.654956[a]	0.657493[a]	**0.708633**	0.646929[a]
	5	750	1.223099	1.189960	**1.224094**	1.026995[a]	1.219001	1.176927[a]	1.041593[a]	1.116645[a]	0.441287[a]	1.071505[a]
	8	1500	1.841974	1.727171	**1.858232**	1.266641[a]	1.843340	1.695095[a]	0.698152[a]	1.087488[a]	0.475371[a]	1.285725[a]
	10	2000	**2.333417**	2.011900	2.331650	1.610767[b]	2.326666	2.175824[b]	0.811370[a]	1.189267[a]	0.627106[a]	1.482006[a]
	15	3000	**3.723823**	2.338636	3.571653[b]	2.063536[b]	3.717982	3.164650[b]	0.594620[a]	1.134651[a]	1.123090[a]	1.550496[a]

(Continued)

Table 2.12 (Continued)

Problem	m	MaxGen	θ-DEA	θ-DEA*	GrEA	POGA	NSGA-III	SDE	MOEA/D	dMOPSO	HypE	MOMBI
WFG7	3	400	0.731157	0.722678	0.721095[a]	0.68454[a]	0.729030[b]	0.732513	0.619351[a]	0.589746[a]	**0.752768**	0.693879[a]
	5	750	1.295864	1.263840	**1.298471**	0.997043[a]	1.291999[b]	1.249762[a]	1.073783[a]	0.992021[a]	0.525322[a]	1.143173[a]
	8	1500	1.973601	1.843617	**1.992683**	1.233529[a]	1.971529[b]	1.786518[a]	0.813288[a]	0.986483[a]	0.521515[a]	1.391605[a]
	10	2000	**2.508710**	2.280858	2.503361	1.663976[a]	2.507511[b]	2.337352[b]	0.950840[a]	1.154313[a]	1.234357[a]	1.666138[a]
	15	3000	**4.136189**	3.174241	3.829786[b]	2.538966[a]	4.134418[b]	3.898443[b]	0.772304[a]	1.134836[a]	2.267561[a]	1.847512[a]
WFG8	3	400	0.666959	0.655503	0.656139[b]	0.613089[a]	0.665932	0.662973[b]	0.633207[a]	0.491854[a]	**0.686264**	0.631815[a]
	5	750	**1.183904**	1.147459	1.173895[b]	0.973151[a]	1.182260[b]	1.136938[a]	0.968246[a]	0.836739[a]	0.340591[a]	0.623923[a]
	8	1500	**1.768213**	1.714995	1.733031[b]	1.295632[a]	1.759882[b]	1.666713[a]	0.326124[a]	0.195763[a]	0.693903[a]	1.313675[a]
	10	2000	**2.297054**	2.198196	2.252147[b]	1.684519[a]	2.280276[b]	2.168904[b]	0.255629[a]	0.237683[a]	1.014398[a]	1.636747[a]
	15	3000	**3.854067**	2.756205	3.667292[b]	2.734447[b]	3.815520	3.717599[b]	0.706627[a]	0.265396[a]	1.596445[a]	1.961387[a]
WFG9	3	400	0.680306	0.671742	0.688081	0.626639[a]	0.670081	0.695933	0.564686[a]	0.652229[a]	**0.733841**	0.663962[a]
	5	750	1.224104	1.159929	**1.238784**	0.318624[a]	1.212266[b]	1.186947[b]	1.028928[a]	1.031762[a]	1.053354[a]	0.949513[a]
	8	1500	1.842840	1.627886	**1.860060**	0.842951[a]	1.803989[b]	1.694549[b]	0.882226[a]	1.017887[a]	1.526635[a]	1.343829[a]
	10	2000	**2.364149**	1.956897	2.343906[b]	1.641153[a]	2.326700[b]	2.204423[b]	1.095281[a]	1.125591[a]	2.044502[b]	1.688538[a]
	15	3000	**3.862664**	2.472073	3.687303[b]	0.976440[a]	3.801860	3.466938[b]	1.002115[a]	0.804192[a]	2.591612[b]	2.188369[a]

The best average HV value among the 10 algorithms for each instance is highlighted in bold.
The result is significantly outperformed by both θ-DEA and θ-DEA*.
[a]The result is significantly outperformed by θ-DEA.
[b]The result is significantly outperformed by θ-DEA*.

Table 2.13 Summary of the significance test between θ-DEA (θ-DEA*) and the other algorithm.

		θ-DEA	θ-DEA*	GrEA	POGA	NSGA-III	SDE	MOEA/D	dMOPSO	HypE	MOMBI
θ-DEA vs	B	–	55	52	69	39	64	66	78	62	67
	W	–	17	22	9	14	10	8	2	17	13
	E	–	8	6	2	27	6	6	0	1	0
θ-DEA* vs	B	17	–	22	57	20	27	72	76	51	52
	W	55	–	53	19	58	41	3	1	26	27
	E	8	–	5	4	2	12	5	3	3	1

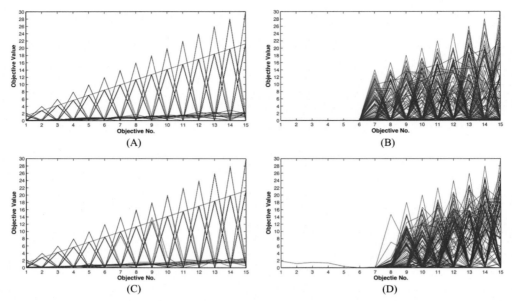

Figure 2.4 Final solution set of the (A) θ-DEA, (B) GrEA, (C) NSGA-III, and (D) SDE on the 15-objective WFG7 instance, shown by parallel coordinates.

single run. The plot enables a visual comparison of the performance of the algorithms. The aforementioned run has been selected based on its proximity to the average HV value. Fig. 2.4 clearly indicates that θ-DEA and NSGA-III are capable of achieving a good approximation and coverage of the PF. In contrast, GrEA and SDE are only able to converge to a portion of the PF.

In order to establish a comprehensive ranking of the algorithms, we have introduced a performance score [23]. The score is computed by considering all the algorithms Alg_1, Alg_2, ..., Alg_l involved in the comparison for a given problem instance. Let $\delta_{i,j}$ denote 1 if Alg_j significantly outperforms Alg_i in terms of HV, and 0 otherwise. Then, the performance score $P(\text{Alg}_i)$ for each algorithm Algi is determined as follows:

$$P\left(\text{Alg}_i\right) = \sum_{\substack{j=1 \\ j \neq i}}^{l} \delta_{i,j} \tag{2.16}$$

The value indicates the number of algorithms that significantly outperform the corresponding algorithm on the test instance being considered. A smaller value is indicative of superior algorithm performance. Fig. 2.5 presents a summary of the average performance score for various test problems and number of objectives. Fig. 2.6

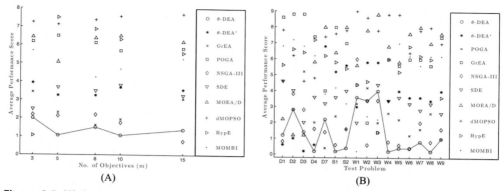

Figure 2.5 (A) Average performance score over all test problems for different number of objectives. (B) Average performance score over all objective dimensions for different test problems, namely DTLZ (Dx), SDTLZ (Sx), and WFG (Wx). The smaller the score, the better the PF approximation in terms of HV. The values of θ-DEA are connected by a solid line to easier assess the score.

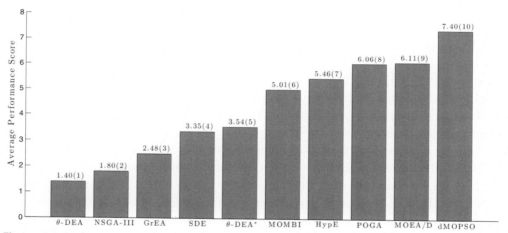

Figure 2.6 Ranking in the average performance score over all test problem instances for the selected 10 algorithms. The smaller the score, the better the overall performance in terms of HV.

illustrates the average performance score across all 80 problem instances for the 10 selected algorithms. The corresponding rank of each algorithm based on the score is also provided in brackets.

The aforementioned results have enabled us to draw some noteworthy observations for each algorithm. The proposed θ-DEA algorithm performs exceptionally well on almost all of the considered instances, exhibiting the best overall performance on DTLZ4, SDTLZ1, SDTLZ2, and WFG4−9 problems. However, θ-DEA's performance is relatively less outstanding on WFG1−3 problems. In the case of the WFG2 problem, θ-DEA displays a notable search behavior, maintaining competitiveness on 3-, 5-, 8-, and 10-objective instances, but exhibiting the worst performance on the 15-objective instance. On the other hand, θ-DEA* demonstrates an advantage on the normalized test problems, specifically the DTLZ1–4 problems. However, when it comes to addressing scaled problems, θ-DEA* cannot be compared to the superior performance of θ-DEA. In fact, out of the 60 scaled problem instances, θ-DEA outperforms θ-DEA* on 53 of them, thus confirming the effectiveness of the normalization procedure in θ-DEA.

In general, GrEA is highly proficient in tackling scaled problems, as evident from its competitive results on DTLZ7, SDTLZ1, SDTLZ2, and most WFG problem instances. The reason behind GrEA's effectiveness in handling scaled problems is its approach of dividing each dimension of the objective space into an equal number of divisions. This approach results in implicit objective normalization during the evolutionary process. It is noteworthy that the performance of GrEA is highly dependent on the parameter div.

While POGA demonstrates highly competitive performance on the WFG2 and WFG3 problems, achieving the best performance on the 10-objective WFG2 instance and the 5-, 8-, and 10-objective WFG3 instances, it generally fails to obtain satisfactory results on the other problems. It is noteworthy that POGA obtains zero HV values on 5-, 8-, and 10-objective instances for the DTLZ1, DTLZ3, and SDTLZ1 problems, but nonzero values for the 15-objective instance. The PFs of these three problems have numerous local PFs, so it is not surprising that POGA fails to converge to the PFs and obtains zero HV values. However, the reason for the nonzero HV values (especially poor) on the 15-objective instances is yet to be explored.

NSGA-III delivers performance that is the closest to the proposed θ-DEA, and it can perform exceptionally well across a broad spectrum of test problems. The results of NSGA-III and θ-DEA are not significantly different in 27 out of 80 instances. It is intriguing to note that NSGA-III performs poorly on 3-, 5-, 8-, and 10-objective instances for the WFG1 problem, but secures second place on the 15-objective instance.

SDE is a fairly decent performer when it comes to solving various problems, as compared to other algorithms. While it does not always come out on top, it still manages to secure the fourth position in terms of average performance across all instances, as illustrated in Fig. 2.6. However, it is interesting to observe that SDE outperforms other algorithms when it comes to solving the DTLZ7 problem, particularly on instances involving three or five objectives. Unfortunately, SDE's performance tends to deteriorate as the number of objectives increases beyond that range.

When it comes to solving normalized test problems, MOEA/D manages to perform quite well, except for DTLZ4, where it does not fare too well. However, when it comes to scaled test problems, MOEA/D does not produce satisfactory results, leading to its poor ranking in Fig. 2.6. It is worth noting that this does not necessarily mean that MOEA/D is a subpar optimizer for many-objective problems, since a simple normalization procedure could potentially improve its ability to solve scaled problems, as suggested by previous research [3]. On the other hand, dMOPSO is an algorithm that does not perform very well even on normalized problems, earning it a relatively low ranking.

HypE stands out as a highly competitive algorithm when it comes to solving three-objective instances, as evident from Fig. 2.5A. In fact, it performs better than other algorithms on 12 out of the 16 three-objective instances. However, its performance does not show any significant advantage over other algorithms when it comes to solving problems with more than three objectives, except for WFG3, where it performs exceptionally well on 8-, 10-, and 15-objective instances. It is worth noting that HypE calculates HV-based fitness values exactly when the number of objectives is less than or equal to three. However, when it comes to problems with a higher number of objectives, it relies on fitness value estimation using Monte Carlo simulation. This may account for its relatively poor performance on such problems due to inaccurate fitness estimation. While increasing the number of sampling points may improve accuracy, it may also lead to an unacceptable increase in computational effort. Despite being a popular many-objective optimizer, our experimental results suggest that HypE does not fare as well as some of the newly proposed many-objective algorithms. This observation has also been reported in several recent studies [20−22].

MOMBI exhibits strong performance on a majority of problem instances in the WFG1−3 set, with particularly impressive results on WFG1. Indeed, MOMBI outperforms other algorithms on 5-, 8-, 10-, and 15-objective instances of WFG1. However, its performance on other problems is not as remarkable.

As we have invested more computational resources toward solving problems with higher numbers of objectives, it becomes challenging to analyze the scalability of performance across all instances. Based on our experimental results, it is not entirely clear whether the performance of each algorithm deteriorates as the number of objectives increases. However, for the proposed θ-DEA algorithm, it manages to maintain strong performance even on instances with up to 15 objectives. This is evident from the results obtained on problems with regular geometric shapes, such as DTLZ1−4, SDTLZ1, SDTLZ2, and WFG4−9 problems. The average HV values obtained by θ-DEA on these instances are close to $1.1^{15} \approx 4.177$, suggesting that it can provide a good approximation of the PF even in high-dimensional objective spaces.

Although not the primary focus of this chapter, we aim to briefly explore the impact of increasing the number of decision variables (n) on test problems. To provide an example, we have chosen a normalized problem DTLZ2 and a scaled problem WFG7 to investigate the impact of increasing the number of decision variables. For DTLZ2, we set k to 98, resulting in $n = m + 97$. For WFG7, we set n to 100, while keeping the position-related parameter at m 2212 1. We execute three competitive algorithms, namely θ-DEA, NSGA-III, and SDE on the two problems, keeping the algorithm parameters and termination criterion unchanged. The average HV results are presented in Table 2.14, revealing that all three algorithms produce smaller HV values compared to the original problem instances, suggesting that larger n presents a greater challenge to all of them. However, the comparison between the algorithms changes to some extent. In the case of the DTLZ2 problem, θ-DEA outperforms SDE significantly on the initial 3-, 5-, and 10-objective instances. However, when the number of decision variables is increased, SDE significantly outperforms θ-DEA on the same instances. It appears that SDE is less susceptible to the impact of increasing the number of decision variables than θ-DEA when it comes to the DTLZ2 problem. It is worth noting that a cooperative coevolution technique [37] has been developed specifically to tackle MOPs with a large number of decision variables.

Ultimately, our goal is to extract valuable insights from the extensive experimental results presented in this section. One crucial observation is that an algorithm's performance is not solely determined by its ability to tackle specific problem features, but also its ability to handle a high number of objectives (e.g., θ-DEA on WFG2 and SDE on DTLZ7). Another noteworthy finding is that, for certain problems, the impact of increasing the number of objectives can vary among different algorithms (e.g., NSGA-III on WFG1). A third significant discovery is the robust performance of θ-DEA, NSGA-III, and GrEA across most of the problem instances studied in this chapter, showcasing their strong competitiveness. θ-DEA may face challenges in dealing with problems featuring high-dimensional convex disconnected PFs, such as the 15-objective WFG2. NSGA-III may encounter difficulties in solving biased problems with mixed PFs, particularly those with

Table 2.14 Average HV values for θ-DEA, NSGA-III, and SDE on large-scale DTLZ2 and WFG7 problems.

Problem	m	MaxGen	θ-DEA	NSGA-III	SDE
DTLZ2	3	250	0.605706	0.576772[a]	**0.681272**
	5	350	1.194953	1.033459[a]	**1.270122**
	8	500	1.819000	1.193003[a]	**1.955069**
	10	750	2.474082	2.228702[a]	**2.492587**
	15	1000	**4.100986**	3.382835[a]	4.070196[a]
WFG7	3	400	0.664099	0.656173[a]	**0.711816**
	5	750	**1.240632**	1.225887[a]	1.224485[a]
	8	1500	**1.916811**	1.903908[a]	1.716448[a]
	10	2000	**2.472800**	2.462653[a]	2.232295[a]
	15	3000	**4.107807**	4.105074[a]	3.574938[a]

Best performance is shown in bold.
[a]The result is significantly outperformed by θ-DEA.

relatively low dimensions, such as the 3-, 5-, 8-, and 10-objective WFG1. GrEA may not excel in solving problems with a large number of local PFs, as seen in the cases of DTLZ1 and DTLZ3. Conversely, the other algorithms under consideration demonstrate particular strengths on specific problem instances, which can be summed up as follows.

1. θ-DEA* exhibits exceptional performance on normalized test problems, such as DTLZ1−4.
2. POGA demonstrates remarkable effectiveness in solving problems with disconnected or degenerated PFs, particularly in relatively high dimensions. This is evident in the cases of 8-, 10-, and 15-objective WFG2, as well as 5-, 8-, and 10-objective WFG3.
3. SDE performs well on the majority of problems, and it delivers outstanding results on low-dimensional problems with disconnected and mixed PFs. This is evident in the cases of three- and five-objective DTLZ7.
4. MOEA/D demonstrates strong performance on normalized test problems, such as DTLZ1−3. However, it may not be as effective in addressing problems with strong bias, as seen in the case of DTLZ4.
5. HypE exhibits exceptional performance in solving three-objective problems, and it also performs well in high-dimensional problems with linear and degenerated PFs, particularly in the cases of 8-, 10-, and 15-objective WFG3.
6. MOMBI excels in addressing PFs with irregular geometrical shapes, as observed in the cases of WFG1−3. Moreover, it delivers exceptional performance on biased problems with mixed PFs, particularly on WFG1.

2.5.3 Influence of parameter θ

This section delves into the impact of parameter θ on the performance of the proposed algorithm. The modification of θ can alter the normalization process outlined in Section 2.3.4, consequently affecting the search strategy of θ-DEA. To isolate the impact of θ, we posit that the ideal and nadir points are known beforehand, and accurate normalization can be performed. As a result, we opt to demonstrate the impact of θ by implementing θ-DEA* on the normalized test problems, namely DTLZ1−4. Comparable findings can be deduced from the other test scenarios.

Figs. 2.7 and 2.8 showcase the fluctuations in the performance of θ-DEA* concerning the average IGD and average HV, respectively, as θ is altered across the DTLZ1−4 problems. We experiment with θ values between 0 and 50, with a step size of 5, and we also examine the case where $\theta = 0.1$. Based on these figures, we deduce the following insights.

1. In most cases, setting θ to 0 results in the poorest performance.
2. In general, $\theta = 0.1$ is not an optimal choice and usually results in subpar performance. However, it appears to be the most appropriate setting for the three-objective DTLZ3 problem.

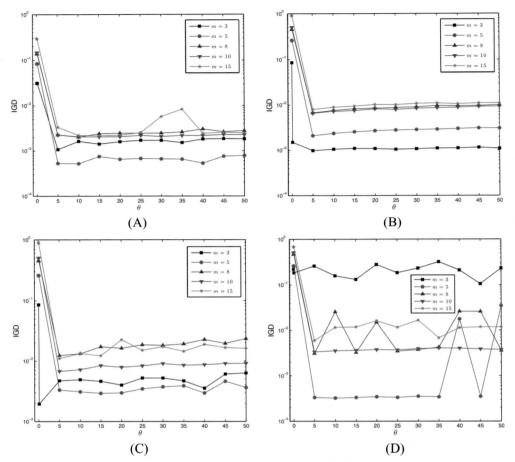

Figure 2.7 Examination of the influence of θ on IGD of θ-DEA* for DTLZ1−4 problems with varying number of objectives m. The figures show the average IGD of 20 independent runs each. (A) DTLZ1. (B) DTLZ2. (C) DTLZ3. (D) DTLZ4.

3. Determining the optimal value of θ is highly dependent on the specific problem instance being tackled.

4. The performance of θ-DEA* remains stable across a broad range of θ values for most of the problem instances, highlighting the practical usability of the proposed algorithm.

It is worth noting that, for the eight-objective DTLZ4 problem, the IGD values exhibit fluctuations as θ increases, whereas the corresponding HV values remain consistent. The methodology we employ to calculate IGD in our experiments renders it a more responsive metric compared to HV. As an instance, if a reference point cannot be appropriately associated with the discovered solutions, it can result in significantly higher IGD values, while the corresponding HV may only decrease marginally in such a scenario.

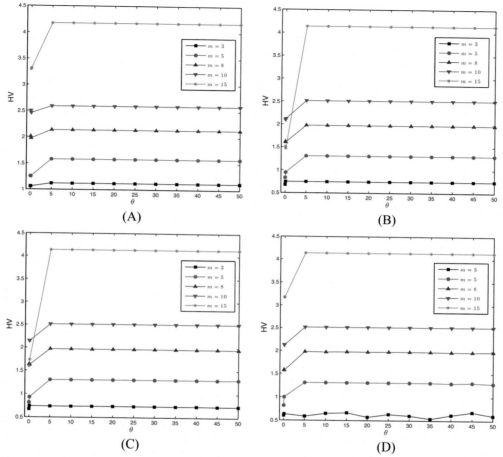

Figure 2.8 Examination of the influence of θ on HV of θ-DEA* for DTLZ1—4 problems with varying number of objectives **m**. The figures show the average HV of 20 independent runs each. (A) DTLZ1. (B) DTLZ2. (C) DTLZ3. (D) DTLZ4.

It is intriguing to explore the performance of θ-DEA* as θ approaches positive infinity. Under this circumstance, the environmental selection phase of θ-DEA* prioritizes only the proximity of each solution to its corresponding reference points, resulting in a search strategy that resembles that of NSGA-III. To explore this extreme scenario, we assign a large value of 10^6 to θ. Table 2.15 presents a comparison of the average IGD and average HV values between θ-DEA* ($\theta = 5$) and θ-DEA* ($\theta = 10^6$). It is evident that, in terms of reference points, $\theta = 5$ typically strikes a better trade-off between convergence and diversity than $\theta = 10^6$.

Table 2.15 Performance comparison between θ-DEA* ($\theta = 5$) and θ-DEA* ($\theta = 10^6$) in terms of average IGD and HV values.

Problem	m	MaxGen	IGD		HV	
			θ-DEA* ($\theta = 5$)	θ-DEA* ($\theta = 10^6$)	θ-DEA* ($\theta = 5$)	θ-DEA* ($\theta = 10^6$)
DTLZ1	3	400	**1.250E − 03**	1.876E − 03	1.118329	1.117384
	5	600	**5.163E − 04**	9.613E − 04	**1.577892**	1.577693
	8	750	**2.172E − 03**	3.422E − 03	2.137998	**2.138139**
	10	1000	**2.235E − 03**	3.282E − 03	2.592696	**2.592832**
	15	1500	**3.626E − 03**	6.688E − 03	4.175713	**4.176786**
DTLZ2	3	250	**9.735E − 04**	1.573E − 03	**0.744320**	0.743924
	5	350	**2.135E − 03**	4.461E − 03	**1.307368**	1.304332
	8	500	**6.902E − 03**	1.549E − 02	**1.978469**	1.969621
	10	750	**6.725E − 03**	1.576E − 02	**2.514485**	2.508654
	15	1000	**8.670E − 03**	1.993E − 02	**4.137766**	4.132136
DTLZ3	3	1000	3.519E − 03	5.202E − 03	0.738977	0.736557
	5	1000	**2.565E − 03**	4.723E − 03	**1.305846**	1.302989
	8	1000	**1.290E − 02**	3.094E − 02	**1.970805**	1.954208
	10	1500	**6.361E − 03**	1.541E − 02	**2.514027**	2.508178
	15	2000	**1.102E − 02**	9.510E − 02	**4.136332**	3.989831
DTLZ4	3	600	2.396E − 01	2.282E − 01	0.602951	0.603710
	5	1000	**3.134E − 04**	1.809E − 02	**1.308934**	1.299265
	8	1250	**1.443E − 02**	1.527E − 02	**1.977231**	1.976809
	10	2000	**3.375E − 03**	4.251E − 03	**2.515468**	2.515248
	15	3000	**5.729E − 03**	2.206E − 02	**4.138225**	4.135672

The performance that is significantly better than the other is shown in bold.

2.6 Conclusion

This chapter introduced a novel evolutionary algorithm, θ-DEA, designed specifically for many-objective optimization. The environmental selection mechanism of θ-DEA is based on θ dominance, a unique approach to dominance relation that emphasizes both convergence and diversity in the proposed algorithm. θ-DEA is designed to leverage the strengths of both NSGA-III and MOEA/D, with the aim of enhancing the convergence ability of NSGA-III in high-dimensional objective space. By incorporating the aggregation function-based fitness evaluation scheme from MOEA/D, θ-DEA seeks to achieve a more balanced compromise between convergence and diversity in many-objective optimization. In pursuit of this objective, we introduced a novel dominance relation, θ dominance, into the proposed algorithm. This approach places equal emphasis on both convergence and diversity, thereby enabling θ-DEA to achieve a more balanced and effective optimization performance.

Through our experimental investigation of θ-DEA, we have demonstrated the algorithm's robustness with regards to the crucial parameter, θ. Our experimental results have confirmed that, as a reference point-based algorithm, θ-DEA generally outperforms NSGA-III and MOEA/D in the search for Pareto-optimal solutions that are in close proximity to the given reference points. Furthermore, we have observed that the integrated normalization procedure enhances the ability of θ-DEA to tackle scaled problems with greater efficacy.

To showcase the exceptional competitiveness of θ-DEA, we conducted a comprehensive experimental comparison with eight cutting-edge algorithms from five distinct technology categories. We selected multiple renowned benchmark problems to evaluate the diverse capabilities of the algorithms in question. Our comparative analysis demonstrates that, across nearly all problem instances examined in this chapter, the proposed θ-DEA delivers highly satisfactory results and compares favorably with state-of-the-art many-objective optimization algorithms. Nevertheless, we have noted that none of the algorithms managed to outperform all the others across all problem instances, highlighting the need for a judicious selection of algorithms when tackling a many-objective optimization task.

References

[1] Ishibuchi H, Tsukamoto N, Nojima Y. Evolutionary many-objective optimization: a short review. In: Proceedings of the 10th IEEE congress on evolutionary computation. IEEE; 2008. p. 2419−26.
[2] Wagner T, Beume N, Naujoks B. Pareto-, aggregation-, and indicator-based methods in many-objective optimization. In: Proceedings of the 4th evolutionary multi-criterion optimization; 2007. p. 742−56.
[3] Zhang Q, Li H. MOEA/D: a multiobjective evolutionary algorithm based on decomposition. IEEE Transactions on Evolutionary Computation 2007;11(6):712−31.

[4] Li H, Zhang Q. Multiobjective optimization problems with complicated Pareto sets, MOEA/D and NSGA-II. IEEE Transactions on Evolutionary Computation 2008;13(2):284—302.

[5] Deb K, Pratap A, Agarwal S, et al. A fast and elitist multiobjective genetic algorithm: NSGA-II. IEEE Transactions on Evolutionary Computation 2002;6(2):182—97.

[6] Deb K, Agrawal RB. Simulated binary crossover for continuous search space. Complex Systems 1995;9(2):115—48.

[7] Kukkonen S, Deb K. Improved pruning of non-dominated solutions based on crowding distance for bi-objective optimization problems. In: Proceedings of the 8th IEEE international conference on evolutionary computation. IEEE; 2006. p. 1179—86.

[8] Deb K, Jain H. An evolutionary many-objective optimization algorithm using reference-point-based non-dominated sorting approach, part I: solving problems with box constraints. IEEE Transactions on Evolutionary Computation 2013;18(4):577—601.

[9] Das I, Dennis JE. Normal-boundary intersection: a new method for generating the Pareto surface in nonlinear multicriteria optimization problems. SIAM Journal on Optimization 1998;8(3):631—57.

[10] Murata T, Ishibuchi H, Gen M. Specification of genetic search directions in cellular multi-objective genetic algorithms. In: Proceedings of the 1st evolutionary multi-criterion optimization; 2001. p. 82—95.

[11] Purshouse RC, Fleming PJ. On the evolutionary optimization of many conflicting objectives. IEEE Transactions on Evolutionary Computation 2007;11(6):770—84.

[12] Adra SF, Fleming PJ. Diversity management in evolutionary many-objective optimization. IEEE Transactions on Evolutionary Computation 2010;15(2):183—95.

[13] Deb K, Goldberg DE. An investigation of niche and species formation in genetic function optimization. In: Proceedings of the 3rd international conference on genetic algorithms; 1989. p. 42—50.

[14] Deb K, Miettinen K. A review of nadir point estimation procedures using evolutionary approaches: a tale of dimensionality reduction. In: Proceedings of the multiple criterion decision making (MCDM-2008) conference; 2009. p. 1—14.

[15] Deb K, Miettinen K, Chaudhuri S. Toward an estimation of nadir objective vector using a hybrid of evolutionary and local search approaches. IEEE Transactions on Evolutionary Computation 2010;14(6):821—41.

[16] Deb K, Thiele L, Laumanns M, et al. Scalable multi-objective optimization test problems. In: Proceedings of the 4th congress on evolutionary computation, vol. 1. IEEE; 2002. p. 825—30.

[17] Huband S, Hingston P, Barone L, et al. A review of multiobjective test problems and a scalable test problem toolkit. IEEE Transactions on Evolutionary Computation 2006;10(5):477—506.

[18] Gómez RH, Coello CAC. MOMBI: a new metaheuristic for many-objective optimization based on the R2 indicator. In: Proceedings of the 15th IEEE congress on evolutionary computation. IEEE; 2013. p. 2488—95.

[19] Zitzler E, Thiele L, Laumanns M, et al. Performance assessment of multiobjective optimizers: an analysis and review. IEEE Transactions on Evolutionary Computation 2003;7(2):117—32.

[20] Yang S, Li M, Liu X, et al. A grid-based evolutionary algorithm for many-objective optimization. IEEE Transactions on Evolutionary Computation 2013;17(5):721—36.

[21] Li M, Yang S, Liu X, et al. A comparative study on evolutionary algorithms for many-objective optimization. In: Proceedings of the 7th evolutionary multi-criterion optimization; 2013. p. 261—75.

[22] Li M, Yang S, Liu X. Shift-based density estimation for Pareto-based algorithms in many-objective optimization. IEEE Transactions on Evolutionary Computation 2013;18(3):348—65.

[23] Bader J, Zitzler E. HypE: an algorithm for fast hypervolume-based many-objective optimization. Evolutionary Computation 2011;19(1):45—76.

[24] Ishibuchi H, Akedo N, Nojima Y. Behavior of multiobjective evolutionary algorithms on many-objective knapsack problems. IEEE Transactions on Evolutionary Computation 2014;19(2):264—83.

[25] Zitzler E, Thiele L. Multiobjective evolutionary algorithms: a comparative case study and the strength Pareto approach. IEEE Transactions on Evolutionary Computation 1999;3(4):257—71.

[26] Auger A, Bader J, Brockhoff D, et al. Theory of the hypervolume indicator: optimal μ-distributions and the choice of the reference point. In: Proceedings of the 10th ACM SIGEVO workshop on foundations of genetic algorithms; 2009. p. 87—102.

[27] Ishibuchi H, Hitotsuyanagi Y, Tsukamoto N, et al. Many-objective test problems to visually examine the behavior of multiobjective evolution in a decision space. In: Proceedings of 9th international conference on parallel problem solving from nature; 2010. p. 91—100.

[28] Zou X, Chen Y, Liu M, et al. A new evolutionary algorithm for solving many-objective optimization problems. IEEE Transactions on Systems, Man, and Cybernetics, Part B (Cybernetics) 2008;38 (5):1402—12.

[29] While L, Bradstreet L, Barone L. A fast way of calculating exact hypervolumes. IEEE Transactions on Evolutionary Computation 2011;16(1):86—95.

[30] Di Pierro F, Khu ST, Savic DA. An investigation on preference order ranking scheme for multiobjective evolutionary optimization. IEEE Transactions on Evolutionary Computation 2007;11(1):17—45.

[31] Storn R, Price K. Differential evolution—a simple and efficient heuristic for global optimization over continuous spaces. Journal of Global Optimization 1997;11(4):341.

[32] Martínez SZ, Coello CAC. A multi-objective particle swarm optimizer based on decomposition. In: Proceedings of the 13th annual conference on genetic and evolutionary computation; 2011. p. 69—76.

[33] Kennedy J, Eberhart R. Particle swarm optimization. In: Proceedings of the 5th international conference on neural networks, vol. 4. IEEE; 1995. p. 1942—8.

[34] Durillo JJ, Nebro AJ. jMetal: a Java framework for multi-objective optimization. Advances in Engineering Software 2011;42(10):760—71.

[35] Wilcoxon F. Individual comparisons by ranking methods. New York: Springer; 1992.

[36] Ishibuchi H, Akedo N, Nojima Y. A study on the specification of a scalarizing function in MOEA/ D for many-objective knapsack problems. In: Proceedings of the 7th learning and intelligent optimization: 7th international conference. Springer; 2013. p. 231—46.

[37] Antonio LM, Coello CAC. Use of cooperative coevolution for solving large scale multiobjective optimization problems. In: Proceedings of the 15th IEEE congress on evolutionary computation. IEEE; 2013. p. 2758—65.

CHAPTER 3

Balancing convergence and diversity in decomposition-based many-objective optimizers

Contents

3.1 Introduction

Numerous multiobjective evolutionary algorithms (MOEAs) have been suggested to efficiently tackle multiobjective optimization problems (MOPs). However, although optimization problems involving a plethora of objectives are widespread in real-world applications [1–3], most of these algorithms have only been evaluated and applied to MOPs featuring two or three objectives [4,5]. In the literature, these MOPs with more than three objectives are commonly referred to as many-objective optimization

Intelligent Evolutionary Optimization
DOI: https://doi.org/10.1016/B978-0-443-27400-8.00003-4

problems (MaOPs) [6,7]. It's worth noting that the existing algorithms' inability to handle MaOPs hinders their practical applicability, thus highlighting the need for developing algorithms that can address MOPs with a higher number of objectives.

Alas, both empirical and analytical findings [8,9] have revealed that the conventional MOEAs, particularly the prominent Pareto-dominance-based MOEAs, would encounter formidable challenges when dealing with MaOPs. The fundamental reason for this is that the population's proportion of non-dominated solutions undergoes an exponential increase as the number of objectives grows. This phenomenon, in turn, results in a significant drop in the Pareto-dominance-based selection pressure toward the Pareto front (PF). As a result, the existing MOEAs fail to sustain the desired level of effectiveness when addressing MaOPs.

This chapter is primarily dedicated to exploring the decomposition-based MOEAs that employ aggregation functions to facilitate convergence in many-objective optimization. Our contributions to this area can be outlined as follows:

1. Our significant contribution to the field of decomposition-based many-objective optimization is the introduction of an improved balance between convergence and diversity. This is achieved by utilizing the perpendicular distance between a solution and the weight vector in the objective space.
2. We have applied this idea to MOEA/D and epsilon front ranking (EFR) to enhance their performance on MaOPs. This resulted in two improved algorithms: MOEA/D-DU, which is a variant of MOEA/D with a distance-based updating strategy, and EFR-RR.
3. We have included an optional online normalization procedure that can be seamlessly integrated into MOEA/D-DU and EFR-RR to effectively address scaling issues.
4. For the first time, we have synergistically combined various existing concepts into a single MOEA.
5. Drawing on the results of our experimental investigations, we have put forward a novel approach for conducting fair and reasonable comparisons of MOEAs when dealing with benchmark problems—regardless of whether they utilize sophisticated normalization techniques or not.

3.2 Preliminaries and background

This section commences with an overview of the fundamental concepts underpinning multiobjective optimization. Following this, we provide a brief overview of several recent proposals that exhibit similarities to our approach and have been documented in the literature.

A MOP can be mathematically defined as

$$\min \quad \mathbf{f}(\mathbf{x}) = (f_1(\mathbf{x}), f_2(\mathbf{x}), \ldots, f_m(\mathbf{x}))^{\mathrm{T}}$$

$$\text{subject to} \quad \mathbf{x} \in \Omega \subseteq \mathbb{R}^n \tag{3.1}$$

Here, we define $\mathbf{x} = (x_1, x_2, \ldots, x_n)^T$ as an n-dimensional decision variable vector within the decision space Ω. The objective vector, denoted as $\mathbf{f} : \Omega \to \Theta \subseteq \mathbb{R}^m$, is comprised of m objective functions that map the n-dimensional decision space Ω to an m-dimensional attainable objective space Θ in R^m.

Definition 3.1:

A vector, $\mathbf{u} = (u_1, u_2, \ldots, u_k)^T$, is considered to dominate another vector, $\mathbf{v} = (v_1, v_2, \ldots, v_k)^T$, represented by $\mathbf{u} \preccurlyeq \mathbf{v}$, if and only if $\forall i \in \{1, 2, \ldots, k\}$, $u_i \leq v_i$ and $\exists i \in \{1, 2, \ldots, k\}$, $u_j < v_j$.

Definition 3.2:

In the context of a given MOP, a decision vector, $\mathbf{x}^* \in \Omega$, is considered Pareto optimal if there exists no $\mathbf{x} \in \Omega$ such that $\mathbf{f}(\mathbf{x})\mathbf{f}(\mathbf{x}^*)$.

Definition 3.3:

In the case of a given MOP, we define the Pareto set, PS, as follows:

$$PS = \{\mathbf{x} \in \Omega \,|\, \mathbf{x} \text{ is Pareto optimal}\} \tag{3.2}$$

Definition 3.4:

In the context of a given MOP, we define PF as:

$$PF = \{\mathbf{f}(\mathbf{x}) \in \Theta \,|\, \mathbf{x} \in PS\} \tag{3.3}$$

Definition 3.5:

In the context of a given MOP, the ideal point, $\mathbf{z}^*$, is a vector expressed as $\mathbf{z}^* = (z_1^*, z_2^*, \ldots, z_m^*)^T$, where z_i^* represents the infimum of f_i for all $i \in \{1, 2, \ldots, m\}$.

Definition 3.6:

In the context of a given MOP, the nadir point, $\mathbf{z}^{nad}$, is a vector denoted as $\mathbf{z}^{nad} = (z_1^{nad}, z_2^{nad}, \ldots, z_m^{nad})^T$, where z_i^{nad} represents the supremum of f_i over the Pareto set (PS) for every $i \in \{1, 2, \ldots, m\}$.

The primary objective of multiobjective optimization is to identify a collection of objective vectors that are non-dominated and situated close to the PF, this is referred to as convergence. Additionally, these objective vectors should be well-distributed over the PF, thus promoting diversity.

3.3 Basic idea

The Tchebycheff function is a popular type of aggregation function that is frequently utilized in decomposition-based MOEAs. In this chapter, we implement a modified variant of the Tchebycheff function. To be more specific, let $\lambda_j = \left(\lambda_{j,1}, \lambda_{j,2}, \ldots, \lambda_{j,m}\right)^{\mathrm{T}}$ represent a set of uniformly distributed weight vectors, and z^* denote the ideal point. The function for the jth subproblem can be expressed as:

$$\mathcal{F}_j(\mathbf{x}) = \max_{k=1}^{m} \left\{ \frac{1}{\lambda_{j,\ k}} |f_k(\mathbf{x}) - z_k^*| \right\} \tag{3.4}$$

Here, $\lambda_{j,k}$ denotes a non-negative value for all $k \in \{1, 2, \ldots, m\}$, with the constraint that $\sum_{k=1}^{m} \lambda_{j,k} = 1$. If $\lambda_{j,k} = 0$, we set $\lambda_{j,k}$ to a very small value, specifically 10^{-6}, to avoid any potential issues.

The modified Tchebycheff function utilized in our approach offers two distinct advantages over the original variant [10]. First, the utilization of uniformly distributed weight vectors results in uniformly distributed search directions within the objective space. This enhances the ability of the algorithm to explore different regions of the objective space. Second, each weight vector corresponds to a unique solution located on the PF. This ensures that the solutions obtained are of high quality and diverse, thus alleviating the difficulty often encountered with preserving diversity. A detailed proof of these advantages can be found in [11].

However, it is worth noting that even the modified Tchebycheff function outlined in Eq. (3.4) is not without its limitations in practice. In theory, obtaining the optimal solution for each $\mathcal{F}_j$ defined in Eq. (3.4) would lead to the most desirable level of diversity, this is not always the case for MOEA/D and EFR. In practice, the solutions generated by these algorithms often tend to be near-optimal rather than fully optimal, which may limit the diversity of the final population. For instance, Fig. 3.1 provides a visualization of the distribution of solutions (A−E) obtained with the aid of five weight vectors $(\boldsymbol{\lambda}_1, \boldsymbol{\lambda}_2, \ldots, \boldsymbol{\lambda}_5)$ in a bi-objective space, where the contour lines of subproblems decomposed by Eq. (3.4) are depicted using dashed lines. It is evident from Fig. 3.1 that the solutions obtained do not distribute as well as the weight vectors. This can be attributed to the fact that although solutions B and D perform well on $\mathcal{F}_2$ and $\mathcal{F}_4$, respectively, they deviate significantly from their corresponding directions ($\boldsymbol{\lambda}_2$ and $\boldsymbol{\lambda}_4$). Moreover, a more pressing issue arises during the evolutionary process, where the selection of solutions can be potentially misleading if it relies solely on aggregation function values. For instance, in Fig. 3.1, there is another solution F, which is marginally worse than B in terms of $\mathcal{F}_2$ value. In MOEA/D, F may be replaced by B in the updating procedure, while in EFR, F may be eliminated in the environmental selection due to B achieving a better ranking on $\mathcal{F}_2$. However, it is worth noting that F is preferable to the weight vector $\boldsymbol{\lambda}_2$. Notably, in the early stages of evolution, the solutions are typically distant from the PF, thereby increasing the likelihood of misleading selection, which can restrict the search to only a portion of the PF.

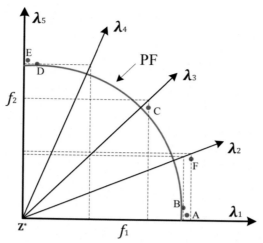

Figure 3.1 Illustration of the distribution of solutions in the two-dimensional objective space.

The two aforementioned situations can be primarily attributed to the fact that a solution that is far from the weight vector λ_j can still achieve a relatively high value on $\mathcal{F}_j$. This issue arises due to the contour lines of Eq. (3.4), which can create a mismatch between the direction of λ_j and the position of the optimal solution. This problem is further exacerbated in high-dimensional objective spaces due to the sparse distribution of solutions and the exponential growth of hypervolume (HV).

Considering the issues discussed above, we propose a novel approach in MOEA/D and EFR that takes into account not only the aggregation function value of a solution but also its distance to the corresponding weight vector. This approach is expected to compel solutions to remain close to the weight vectors while explicitly maintaining the desired distribution of solutions throughout the evolutionary process, thereby achieving a better balance between convergence and diversity in many-objective optimization. It is worth noting that the penalty-based boundary intersection function [10] partially addresses the proximity issue by implicitly considering the closeness of a solution to the weight vector. However, it still possesses the problem mentioned above. In this chapter, we focus on the modified Tchebycheff function outlined in Eq. (3.4), as it serves as a generic and effective approach for addressing the proximity issue without loss of generality.

Let us assume that $\mathbf{f}(\mathbf{x}) = (f_1(\mathbf{x}), f_2(\mathbf{x}), ..., f_m(\mathbf{x}))^{\mathrm{T}}$ represents the objective vector of solution $\mathbf{x}$. We also consider a line L that passes through $\mathbf{z}^*$ with direction λ_j, and $\mathbf{u}$ represents the projection of $\mathbf{f}(\mathbf{x})$ on L. To compute the perpendicular distance from solution $\mathbf{x}$ to the weight vector λ_j in the objective space, we utilize the notation $d_{j,2}(\mathbf{x})$

$$d_{j,2}(\mathbf{x}) = \|\mathbf{f}(\mathbf{x}) - \mathbf{z}^* - d_{j,1}(\mathbf{x})\big(\lambda_j / \|\lambda_j\|\big)\| \tag{3.5}$$

We can calculate the distance between $\mathbf{z}^*$ and $\mathbf{u}$ using the notation $d_{j,1}(\mathbf{x})$. The formula to obtain $d_{j,1}(\mathbf{x})$ is as follows:

$$d_{j,1}(\mathbf{x}) = \|(\mathbf{f}(\mathbf{x}) - \mathbf{z}^*)^{\mathrm{T}} \boldsymbol{\lambda}_j\| / \|\boldsymbol{\lambda}_j\| \qquad (3.6)$$

Fig. 3.2 provides a visualization of the perpendicular distance $d_{j,2}(\mathbf{x})$ in a two-dimensional objective space. Moving forward, we will elaborate on how to leverage $d_{j,2}(\mathbf{x})$ to improve the performance of MOEA/D and EFR.

3.4 Proposed algorithms

This section delves into the specifics of two enhanced algorithms, namely MOEA/D-DU and EFR-RR.

3.4.1 Enhancing MOEA/D

Algorithm 3.1 outlines the framework of the proposed MOEA/D-DU. The initial step involves generating a set of uniformly spread weight vectors $\Lambda = \boldsymbol{\lambda}_1, \boldsymbol{\lambda}_2, ..., \boldsymbol{\lambda}_N$, where each $\boldsymbol{\lambda}_j$ corresponds to the jth subproblem, i.e., $\mathcal{F}_j$. To ensure diversity, MOEA/D-DU employs Das and Dennis's systematic approach [12], which is similar to that used in NSGA-III [13]. Subsequently, a population of N solutions $\mathbf{x}_1, \mathbf{x}_2, ..., \mathbf{x}_N$ is initialized, where $\mathbf{x}_j$ represents the current solution to the jth subproblem. In step 3, the ideal point $\mathbf{z}^*$ is initialized. However, it is often computationally expensive to compute the exact z_i^* value. As such, MOEA/D-DU approximates z_i^* by using the minimum value found thus far for objective f_i, which is updated during the

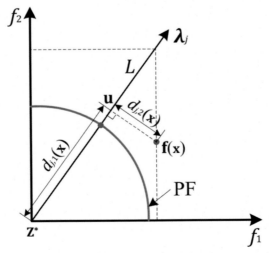

Figure 3.2 Illustration of the perpendicular distance from the solution to the weight vector in the two-dimensional objective space.

search process. The MOEA/D-DU maintains the same mating restriction scheme as its predecessor [14] for generating child solutions, which results in the determination of the neighborhood $B(i)$ for each subproblem f_i in steps 4−6. Steps 7−18 are iterated until the termination criterion is satisfied. During each iteration, for solution $\mathbf{x}_i$, a mating solution $\mathbf{x}_k$ is selected from the neighborhood $B(i)$ with a probability δ or from the entire population with a probability of $1 - \delta$, as depicted in steps 9−12 of Algorithm 3.1. These selected solutions undergo genetic operators, such as simulated binary crossover (SBX) and polynomial mutation [15], to generate a novel solution $\mathbf{y}$. Subsequently, $\mathbf{y}$ is utilized to update the ideal point and the current population.

Algorithm 3.1: Framework of MOEA/D-DU.

1: Generate a set of weight vectors $\Lambda \leftarrow \{\boldsymbol{\lambda}_1, \boldsymbol{\lambda}_2, ..., \boldsymbol{\lambda}_N\}$
2: Initialize the population $P \leftarrow \{\mathbf{x}_1, \mathbf{x}_2, ..., \mathbf{x}_N\}$
3: Initialize the ideal point $\mathbf{z}^* \leftarrow (z_1^*, z_2^*, ..., z_m^*)^{\mathrm{T}}$
4: **for** $i \leftarrow 1$ to N **do**
5:     $B(i) \leftarrow \{i_1, i_2, ..., i_T\}$, where $\boldsymbol{\lambda}_{i_1}, \boldsymbol{\lambda}_{i_2}, ..., \boldsymbol{\lambda}_{i_T}$ are T closest weight vectors to $\boldsymbol{\lambda}_i$
6: **end for**
7: **while** the termination criterion is not satisfied **do**
8:         **for** $i \leftarrow 1$ to N **do**
9:                 **if** $rand() < \delta$ **then**
10:                 $E \leftarrow B(i)$
11:         **else**
12:                 $E \leftarrow \{1, 2, ..., N\}$
13:         **end if**
14:         Randomly select an index $k \in E$ and $k \neq i$
15:         $\mathbf{y} \leftarrow$ Genetic Operators $(\mathbf{x}_i, \mathbf{x}_k)$
16:         Update Ideal Point $(\mathbf{y}, \mathbf{z}^*)$
17:         Update Current Population $(\mathbf{y}, \mathbf{z}^*, \Lambda, P, K)$
18:         **end for**
19: **end while**
20: **return** all the non-dominated solutions in P

The updating strategy outlined in step 17 of Algorithm 3.1 is a key feature of MOEA/D-DU that distinguishes it from the original MOEA/D. This strategy is presented in detail in Algorithm 3.2, which operates as follows:

Once a new solution y is generated, its perpendicular distances to each weight vector $\boldsymbol{\lambda}_j$, i.e., $d_{j,2}(\mathbf{y}), j = 1, 2, ..., N$, are computed. Subsequently, K minimum distances are selected from the N distances, where $K \ll N$ is a parameter. These K minimum distances are denoted as $d_{j_1,2}(\mathbf{y}), d_{j_2,2}(\mathbf{y}), ..., d_{j_K,2}(\mathbf{y})$ and are arranged in nondecreasing order, i.e., $d_{j_1,2}(\mathbf{y}) \leq d_{j_2,2}(\mathbf{y}) \leq ... \leq d_{j_K,2}(\mathbf{y})$.

The proposed MOEA/D-DU algorithm employs a steady-state approach, where only one solution in the current population can be replaced by a newly generated solution $\mathbf{y}$. Upon generating a new solution $\mathbf{y}$, it is compared to solutions $\mathbf{x}_{j_1}, \mathbf{x}_{j_2}, ..., \mathbf{x}_{j_K}$ in a sequential manner. If a solution $\mathbf{x}_{j_k}$, $k \in \{1, 2, ..., K\}$, satisfies the condition that $\mathcal{F}_{j_k}(\mathbf{x}_{j_k})$ is greater than $\mathcal{F}_{j_k}(\mathbf{y})$, then solution $\mathbf{x}_{j_k}$ is replaced by solution y, and the updating procedure is terminated.

Algorithm 3.2: Update Current Population ($\mathbf{y}$, $\mathbf{z}^*$, Λ, P, K).

1: **for** $j \leftarrow 1$ to N **do**
2:     Compute the perpendicular distance from $\mathbf{y}$ to the weight vector λ_j, i.e., $d_{j,2}(\mathbf{y})$
3: **end for**
4: Select K minimum distances from N distances $d_{j,2}(\mathbf{y}), j = 1, 2, ..., N$ and obtain
   $d_{j_1,2}(\mathbf{y}) \leq d_{j_2,2}(\mathbf{y}) \leq \cdots \leq d_{j_K,2}(\mathbf{y})$
5: **for** $k \leftarrow 1$ to K **do**
6:         **if** $\mathcal{F}_{j_k}(\mathbf{y}) < \mathcal{F}_{j_k}(\mathbf{x}_{j_k})$ **then**
7:             $\mathbf{x}_{j_k} \leftarrow \mathbf{y}$
8:             **return**
9:     **end if**
10: **end for**

3.4.2 Enhancing epsilon front ranking

The EFR algorithm [16] employs the generational scheme and is built upon the NSGA-II framework. However, it differs significantly in the environmental selection phase.

In EFR, at the tth generation, the parent population P_t (of size N) and the offspring population Q_t (of size N) are combined to form a population $U_t = P_t \cup Q_t$ (of size $2N$). Subsequently, the top N solutions are selected from U_t to form the next population. Each solution $\mathbf{x}$ in U_t is associated with N different fitness values $\mathcal{F}_1(x), \mathcal{F}_2(x), ..., \mathcal{F}_N(\mathbf{x})$.

Each fitness function $\mathcal{F}_j$ is used to sort all solutions in U_t in ascending order based on their respective function values. Consequently, each solution is assigned its unique ranking position. With N fitness functions in consideration, each solution $\mathbf{x}$ is assigned N ranking positions represented as the vector $\mathbf{R}(\mathbf{x}) = (r_1(\mathbf{x}), r_2(\mathbf{x}), ..., r_N(\mathbf{x}))^{\mathrm{T}}$, where $r_j(\mathbf{x})$ denotes ranking position of $\mathbf{x}$ on the fitness function $\mathcal{F}_j$. To determine the overall rank $R_g(\mathbf{x})$ of each solution $\mathbf{x}$, an ensemble ranking method is employed, based on $\mathbf{R}(\mathbf{x})$. Yuan et al. [16] provides three alternative ensemble ranking schemes, but only the maximum ranking will be examined here. This approach computes $R_g(\mathbf{x})$ as:

$$R_9(\mathbf{x}) = \min_{j=1}^{N} r_j(\mathbf{x}) \tag{3.7}$$

Based on the global rank R_g, the merged population U_t can be segregated into several sets of solutions denoted as $\{F_1, F_2, ...\}$ (comparable to "fronts" in NSGA-II), where F_i comprises of solutions having the ith lowest R_g value. Unlike NSGA-II, EFR randomly selects solutions from the most recently accepted front.

The aforementioned description indicates that every solution in U_t will be ranked based on each of the fitness functions. Nevertheless, as stated in Section 3.3, this approach may result in the erroneous selection of solutions. To mitigate this issue, we present a novel variant of EFR, referred to as EFR-RR, which incorporates a ranking restriction mechanism. In other words, a solution can only be ranked on fitness functions whose corresponding weight vectors are proximate to it in the objective space. The step-by-step procedure is outlined below. To mitigate the misinterpretation of solutions that can potentially arise when all solutions are ranked on all fitness functions, EFR-RR introduces a ranking restriction scheme. For each solution $\mathbf{x}$ in U_t, we define a set $B(\mathbf{x})$ consisting of the K (where $K \ll N$) closest weight vectors to $\mathbf{x}$, based on their perpendicular distance as given in Eq. (3.5). Solution $\mathbf{x}$ is then only ranked on the fitness functions $\mathcal{F}_j$ that correspond to the weight vectors contained in $B(\mathbf{x})$. Consequently, each solution $\mathbf{x}$ has K ranking positions, and each fitness function assigns ranks to only a subset of solutions. The global rank of solution x in EFR-RR is determined as follows:

$$R_g(\mathbf{x}) = \min_{j \in B(\mathbf{x})} r_j(\mathbf{x}) \tag{3.8}$$

Algorithm 3.3 outlines the steps involved in the maximum ranking approach implemented in EFR-RR. Additionally, Algorithm 3.4 provides a comprehensive summary of the entire procedure followed in EFR-RR.

Algorithm 3.3: Maximum Ranking ($\boldsymbol{U_t}$, $\boldsymbol{K}$).

1: $\{L_1, L_2, \ldots, L_N\} \leftarrow \{\varnothing, \varnothing, \ldots, \varnothing\}$
2: **for** each solution $\mathbf{x} \in U_t$ **do**
3:    $R_g(\mathbf{x}) \leftarrow +\infty$
4:    Compute the set $B(\mathbf{x})$
5:    **for** each $j \in B(\mathbf{x})$ **do**
6:       $L_j \leftarrow L_j \cup \mathbf{x}$
7:    **end for**
8: **end for**
9: **for** $j \leftarrow 1$ to N **do**
10:    Sort L_j according to $\mathcal{F}_j$ in nondecreasing order
11:    **for** $k \leftarrow 1$ to $|L_j|$ **do**
12:       $\mathbf{x} \leftarrow L_j[k]$
13:       **if** $k < R_g(\mathbf{x})$ **then**
14:          $R_g(\mathbf{x}) \leftarrow k$
15:       **end if**
16:    **end for**
17: **end for**
18: return R_g

Algorithm 3.4: Framework of EFR-RR.

1: Generate a set of weight vectors $\Lambda \leftarrow \{\boldsymbol{\lambda}_1, \boldsymbol{\lambda}_2, ..., \boldsymbol{\lambda}_N\}$
2: Initialize the population $P_0 \leftarrow \{\mathbf{x}_1, \mathbf{x}_2, ..., \mathbf{x}_N\}$
3: Initialize the ideal point $\mathbf{z}^* \leftarrow (z_1^*, z_2^*, ..., z_m^*)^{\mathrm{T}}$
4: $t \leftarrow 0$
5: **while** the termination criterion is not met **do**
6:        $Q_t \leftarrow$ Make Off spring Population (P_t)
7:        $U_t \leftarrow P_t \cup Q_t$
8:        $R_g \leftarrow$ Maximum Ranking (U_t, K)
9:        $\{F_1, F_2, ...\} \leftarrow$ Get Fronts (U_t, R_g)
10:        $P_{t+1} \leftarrow \varnothing$
11:        $i \leftarrow 1$
12:        **while** $|P_{t+1}| + |F_i| < N$ **do**
13:                $P_{t+1} \leftarrow P_{t+1} \cup F_i$
14:                $i \leftarrow i + 1$
15:        **end while**
16:        Randomly shuffle F_i
17:        $P_{t+1} \leftarrow P_{t+1} \cup F_i[1 : (N - |P_{t+1}|)]$
18:        $t \leftarrow t + 1$
19: **end while**

3.4.3 Optional normalization procedure

Normalizing objective values is a valuable technique for algorithms aimed at solving problems with a PF that contains objective values with varying scales. Zhang and Li [10] demonstrated that even a simple normalization procedure can substantially enhance the efficacy of MOEA/D on scaled test problems. The fundamental objective of normalization is to estimate the values of $\mathbf{z}^*$ and $\mathbf{z}^{\mathrm{nad}}$, which can be used to replace the objective function $f_i(\mathbf{x})$ with Eq. (3.9) during normalization.

$$\tilde{f}_i(\mathbf{x}) = \frac{f_i(\mathbf{x}) - z_i^*}{z_i^{\mathrm{nad}} - z_i^*} \tag{3.9}$$

In general, determining the value of z_i^* can be accomplished by utilizing the best objective function value attained thus far for f_i. Conversely, estimating $\mathbf{z}^{\mathrm{nad}}$ is a considerably more intricate undertaking, as it requires comprehensive information regarding the entire PF [17].

In this chapter, we introduce an online normalization approach that is similar to the one implemented in NSGA-III and can be integrated into the proposed algorithms to handle scaled test problems. Our normalization method differs slightly from that of NSGA-III in terms of the achievement scalarizing function used to identify extreme points. Given a population S_t to be normalized, we identify the extreme point on the objective axis f_j by identifying the solution $\mathbf{x} \in S_t$ that minimizes the following achievement scalarizing function with weight vector $\mathbf{w}_j = (w_{j,1}, w_{j,2}, ..., w_{j,m})^{\mathrm{T}}$ representing the axis direction:

$$\mathrm{ASF}(\mathbf{x}, \mathbf{w}_j) = \max_{i=1}^{m} \left\{ \frac{1}{w_{j,i}} \left| \frac{f_i(\mathbf{x}) - z_i^*}{z_i^{\mathrm{nad}} - z_i^*} \right| \right\} \tag{3.10}$$

Here, $j \in \{1, 2, ..., m\}$, and $w_{j,i} = 0$ when $i \neq j$, while $w_{j,i} = 1$ when $i = j$. Within Eq. (3.10), we substitute a small value of 10^{-6} in place of $w_{j,i} = 0$. Additionally, z_i^{nad} refers to the intercept of the constructed hyperplane with the ith objective axis in the previous generation.

It should be noted that m extreme points may not always form an m-dimensional hyperplane. Furthermore, even if a hyperplane is constructed, it may result in negative intercepts in certain axis directions. The original study on NSGA-III [13] did not provide a solution for handling such situations. In our normalization approach, we assign z_i^{nad} to the highest value of fi found in the non-dominated solutions of St for each $i \in \{1, 2, ..., m\}$ if these cases arise. For additional information regarding the normalization process, please refer to [13].

3.4.4 Computational complexity

The primary computational overhead for MOEA/D-DU is in the updating process presented in Algorithm 3.2. To compute $d_{j,2}(\mathbf{y})$ for $j = 1, 2, ..., N$ in Steps 1−3, $O(mN)$ calculations are necessary. In Step 4, $O(N \log K)$ computations are required to select the K smallest distances and sort them. At most, Steps 8−13 need $O(mK)$ calculations. As a result, the overall complexity of MOEA/D-DU for creating N trial solutions in a single generation is $O(mN^2)$, as m is typically greater than $\log K$ for many-objective optimization.

In the case of EFR-RR, the primary computation expenses are associated with the determination of global ranks. The calculation of perpendicular distances necessitates $O(mN^2)$ computations. The calculation of $B(\mathbf{x})$ for each solution $\mathbf{x}$ requires $O(N^2 \log K)$ computations in total. Suppose C_j represents the number of solutions involved in the ranking of the aggregation function $\mathcal{F}_j$. The ranking on all the aggregation functions requires $O\left(\sum_{j=1}^{N} C_j \log C_j\right)$ computations. Given that $\sum_{j=1}^{N} C_j \log C_j < N^2 \log N$ and $m > \log N$ in most many-objective scenarios, the overall worst-case complexity is $O(mN^2)$.

3.4.5 Discussion

Having elucidated the intricacies of MOEA/D-DU and EFR-RR, we aim to explore the primary similarities and differences between our proposed algorithms and others. It is imperative to note that all of these algorithms utilize a collection of weight vectors to steer the search process.

1. MOEA/D-DU and MOEA/D-AWA both ensure that uniformly distributed weight vectors guide the exploration process in the objective space, but they utilize different approaches to achieve this objective. MOEA/D-AWA adopts a novel approach to initializing weight vectors, while MOEA/D-DU modifies the aggregation function. Moreover, MOEA/D-AWA periodically adjusts the weights to enhance the uniformity of solutions on complex PFs, whereas MOEA/D-DU maintains a balance between convergence and diversity by employing a fixed set of weight vectors. Essentially, MOEA/D-AWA focuses on a weight adjustment strategy, while MOEA/D-DU emphasizes a new population updating strategy.

2. MOEA/D-DU and MOEA/D-STM both utilize a modified version of the Tchebycheff function and employ $d_{j,2}(\mathbf{x})$ to balance convergence and diversity. However, they differ significantly in their implementation mechanisms. In MOEA/D-STM, the aggregation function value and $d_{j,2}(\mathbf{x})$ are treated as preferences of two types of agents (subproblem and solution), respectively. A deferred acceptance procedure is then employed to establish a stable matching of preferences between subproblems and solutions, resulting in the selection of half of the solutions from the combined population. Conversely, MOEA/D-DU achieves a compromise between the aggregation function value and $d_{j,2}(\mathbf{x})$ in a more straightforward manner. The newly generated solution initially selects its K closest weight vectors based on $d_{j,2}(\mathbf{x})$, and it only competes with the solutions associated with these K weight vectors. Furthermore, MOEA/D-STM employs a generational scheme, while MOEA/D-DU is a steady-state algorithm.

3. MOEA/D-DU and I-DBEA both enhance MOEA/D through significant modifications to the updating procedure and require the computation of $d_{j,2}(\mathbf{x})$ during the evolutionary process. Additionally, they both adopt the steady-state form. However, the core idea of MOEA/D-DU differs considerably from that of I-DBEA. I-DBEA employs $d_{j,1}(\mathbf{x})$ in addition to $d_{j,2}(\mathbf{x})$ for solution selection, but the precedence of $d_{j,2}(\mathbf{x})$ over $d_{j,1}(\mathbf{x})$ means that $d_{j,1}(\mathbf{x})$ is rarely used, as $d_{j,2}(\mathbf{x})$ is a real value and can nearly always differentiate between two solutions. As a result, similar to NSGA-III, I-DBEA emphasizes solutions that are non-dominated and close to the reference lines. Unlike I-DBEA, MOEA/D-DU does not rely on Pareto dominance, as the original MOEA/D, but rather moves the population toward the PF by minimizing multiple aggregation functions simultaneously. Additionally, $d_{j,2}(\mathbf{x})$ serves different purposes in MOEA/D-DU and I-DBEA. In I-DBEA, $d_{j,2}(\mathbf{x})$ is employed as a metric for directly comparing solutions. On the other hand, in MOEA/D-DU, $d_{j,2}(\mathbf{x})$ is utilized to select solutions that have the potential to be replaced by the newly generated solution, and the solutions are still evaluated based on aggregation function values.

4. Both MOEA/D-DU and MOEA/D-GR employ a selective replacement strategy to determine which solutions can be replaced by the newly generated solution. However, the two algorithms have different original intentions. MOEA/D-GR aims to identify the most appropriate subproblem for the newly generated solution, and the neighborhood concept of subproblems defined in MOEA/D is still utilized in the replacement scheme of MOEA/D-GR. In contrast, MOEA/D-DU no longer employs the subproblem neighborhood in the updating procedure. Instead, it takes a purely geometric approach and employs $d_{j,2}(\mathbf{x})$ to prevent the preservation of solutions that achieve a good aggregation function value but are far from the region represented by the corresponding weight vector, to maintain the desired distribution of solutions in a high-dimensional objective space.

5. EFR-RR and NSGA-III both utilize the generational scheme and divide the combined population into a series of "fronts" to select solutions. However, there are significant differences between them in terms of how solutions are ranked during the environmental selection phase. NSGA-III still employs Pareto dominance to promote convergence, and a niche-preservation operator aided by a set of weight vectors is utilized to select solutions in the last accepted front, aiming to maintain population diversity. In contrast to NSGA-III, EFR-RR promotes convergence through aggregation functions, rather than Pareto dominance. Notably, EFR-RR also employs a niching procedure with the aid of weight vectors, with each weight vector serving the dual purpose of promoting both convergence and diversity. In contrast, each weight vector in NSGA-III is primarily used to emphasize diversity. Even when it comes to niching methodology, there is a distinction between NSGA-III and EFR-RR. Each solution in NSGA-III can only be associated with a single weight vector, whereas in EFR-RR, each solution can be linked to multiple weight vectors.

3.5 Experimental design

This section focuses on designing experiments to evaluate the effectiveness of MOEA/D-DU and EFR-RR. Initially, we present the test problems and performance metrics employed in the experiments. Next, we outline eight MOEAs used to validate the proposed algorithms. Lastly, we describe the experimental configurations used in this chapter.

3.5.1 Test problems

To enable effective comparison, we select test problems from the DTLZ [18] and WFG [19] test suites. These problems are grouped into two distinct categories.

The initial set of problems consists entirely of normalized test problems, comprising DTLZ1−4, DTLZ7, and WFG1−9. It is worth noting that the objective values of the original DTLZ7 and WFG1−9 problems are scaled differently. To facilitate accurate analysis, we adjust their objective functions to ensure their true PFs are known.

$$f_i \leftarrow \frac{f_i - z_i^*}{z_i^{\text{nad}} - z_i^*}, i = 1, 2, ..., m \tag{3.11}$$

Therefore, the ideal point and the nadir point for each normalized DTLZ7 and WFG 1−9 problem are set to 0 and 1, respectively, ensuring known true PFs. This collection of problems is used to evaluate the performance of the algorithms without requiring an explicit normalization procedure. We provide a summary of the key characteristics of these problems in Table 3.1.

The next set of issues involves a series of test problems that have been scaled for evaluation purposes. These include modified versions of the DTLZ1 and DTLZ2 problems, known as scaled DTLZ1 and scaled DTLZ2, as well as the original WFG4 to WFG9 problems [13]. The scaled DTLZ1 and DTLZ2 have been adjusted from their original versions to better suit the evaluation criteria. For instance, when the scaling factor is 10^i, the objective functions in the original DTLZ1 problem are altered to create a modified version called scaled DTLZ1.

$$f_i \leftarrow 10^{i-1} f_i, i = 1, 2, \ldots, m \tag{3.12}$$

Table 3.1 Features of the test problems.

Problem	Features
DTLZ1	Linear, multi-modal
DTLZ2	Concave
DTLZ3	Concave, multi-modal
DTLZ4	Concave, biased
DTLZ7	Mixed, disconnected, multi-modal
WFG1	Mixed, multi-modal
WFG2	Convex, disconnected, multi-modal, non-separable
WFG3	Linear, degenerate, non-separable
WFG4	Concave, multi-modal
WFG5	Concave, deceptive
WFG6	Concave, non-separable
WFG7	Concave, biased
WFG8	Concave, biased, non-separable
WFG9	Concave, biased, multi-modal, deceptive, non-separable

This set of test problems is employed to evaluate how effectively algorithms with normalization procedures can handle objective values that are scaled differently.

Each of these problems has the flexibility to be scaled to accommodate any number of objectives and decision variables. However, in this chapter, we focus on the range of objectives with m values of 2, 5, 8, 10, and 13. For DTLZ problems, the number of decision variables is determined by the formula $n = m + k - 1$, with k set to 5 for DTLZ1, 10 for DTLZ2 to DTLZ6, and 20 for DTLZ7. The number of decision variables for all WFG problems is fixed at 24, and the position-related parameter is determined by the value $m - 1$. Table 3.2 displays the scaling factors utilized for scaled DTLZ1 and DTLZ2 problems with varying objective numbers.

3.5.2 Performance metrics

To appraise the effectiveness of the algorithms under consideration, performance metrics are required. Among the most commonly utilized metrics in multiobjective settings is the inverted generational distance (IGD) [20]. This metric offers a comprehensive evaluation of both convergence and diversity of a solution set. When dealing with high-dimensional objective spaces, an extensive number of uniformly distributed points on the PF are necessary to accurately compute the IGD metric [21]. In this chapter, we employ the HV [4] metric as the primary comparison criterion, which is a widely used and popular performance metric in multiobjective optimization. The HV metric is strictly Pareto-compliant [20], and its excellent theoretical properties make it a fair and reliable metric [22]. The HV metric is capable of evaluating both the convergence and diversity of a set of solutions in a meaningful way.

When computing the HV metric, the selection of an appropriate reference point is a critical consideration. In our experiments, we adopt the recommendation put forth in [23] and [24] and set the reference point to $1.1\mathbf{z}^{\mathrm{nad}}$, where $\mathbf{z}^{\mathrm{nad}}$ is calculated analytically for each test problem. Furthermore, as per the approach utilized in [7] and [25], any solutions that fail to dominate the reference point are not considered in the HV calculation. When dealing with scaled problems, the objective values of the solution set obtained and the reference point are initially normalized using $\mathbf{z}^{\mathrm{nad}}$ and $\mathbf{z}^*$

Table 3.2 Scaling factors for scaled DTLZ1 and DTLZ2 problems.

Number of objectives (m)	Scaling factor DTLZ1	DTLZ2
2	10^i	10^i
5	10^i	10^i
8	3^i	3^i
10	2^i	3^i
13	1.2^i	2^i

(which is zero for all the test problems used) before computing the HV. In our experiments, the HV metric ranges between 0 and $1.1^m - V_m$ for an m-objective problem. Here, V_m represents the HV of the region enclosed by the normalized PF and the coordinate axes. For problems with no more than ten objectives, the HV metric is computed exactly using the WFG algorithm recently introduced in [26]. Regarding problems with 13 objectives, the HV is estimated using a Monte Carlo simulation method proposed in [27]. To guarantee accuracy, a total of 10 million sampling points are utilized in the simulation.

In addition, we utilize two supplementary performance metrics, namely the generational distance (GD) [28] and diversity comparison indicator (DCI) [29]. These metrics provide additional insights into the convergence and diversity of the solution set under evaluation. The GD metric measures the proximity of the obtained solution set to the true PF and solely reflects the convergence of the algorithm being evaluated. A smaller GD value is indicative of a better convergence of the algorithm, as it implies a closer proximity to the true PF. The diversity comparison indicator (DCI) is a recently proposed metric used to evaluate the diversity of PF approximations in many-objective optimization. The DCI metric ranges between 0 and 1, and only has a relative interpretation, with a larger value indicating better diversity of the solution set. To compute the DCI, a parameter called div (the number of divisions) is necessary to establish a grid-based environment. As per the recommendations outlined in [29], we set the value of div according to the values specified in Table 3.3.

3.5.3 MOEAs for comparison

To evaluate the performance of MOEA/D-DU and EFR-RR, we assess their performance against eight different MOEAs, of which four belong to the MOEA/D family.

The initial MOEA/D variant examined is a slightly altered form of MOEA/D-DE [14]. To ensure a fair comparison, we substitute the differential evolution (DE) operator in MOEA/D-DE with the recombination schemes utilized in MOEA/D-DU. One of the reasons for making this substitution is that the outcomes reported in [13] have suggested that the differential evolution (DE) operator may not be the most appropriate choice for addressing MaOPs. For our experiments, we refer to this MOEA/D version as simply "MOEA/D," which serves as the foundation of MOEA/D-DU.

Three additional MOEA/D variants are compared in our study, namely MOEA/D-STM [30], MOEA/D-GR [31], and I-DBEA [32]. These algorithms are selected for comparison due to their similarities with MOEA/D-DU. Similar to the rationale

Table 3.3 Setting of div in DCI.

Number of objectives (m)	5	8	10	13
div	10	6	5	5

explained earlier, we substitute the differential evolution (DE) operator in MOEA/D-STM and MOEA/D-GR with the recombination schemes utilized in MOEA/D-DU.

We also include the original version of the EFR algorithm [16] in our comparative analysis, as it serves as the precursor to EFR-RR.

Furthermore, we incorporate two alternative MOEAs into our comparative analysis, which do not rely on the decomposition-based approach used in MOEA/D-DU and EFR-RR. The first of these algorithms is the grid-based evolutionary algorithm (GrEA) [33], which was specifically designed to address MaOPs and has demonstrated favorable performance in comparison with several other cutting-edge many-objective optimizers. The second algorithm is the shift-based density estimation (SDE) method [34], which also does not employ a decomposition-based strategy and has been shown to perform competitively against existing state-of-the-art many-objective optimization techniques. In our analysis, we focus on the SPEA2 + SDE version of the SDE algorithm, which demonstrated the most promising overall performance among the three versions evaluated (NSGA-II + SDE, SPEA2 + SDE, and PESA-II + SDE) in [34].

Except for MOEA/D-STM and I-DBEA, none of the seven MOEAs mentioned previously utilize any explicit normalization techniques in their original publications. MOEA/D-STM employs a straightforward normalization procedure, while I-DBEA utilizes a more sophisticated normalization approach. The primary focus of this chapter is not on the normalization procedures themselves. Thus, to ensure a fair comparison among the MOEAs being evaluated, we omit the normalization procedures employed in MOEA/D-STM and I-DBEA from our analysis. By utilizing normalized test problems, we aim to eliminate the potential impact of varying objective value scales and different normalization procedures on the performance of the MOEAs under evaluation. This approach allows us to more accurately assess the effectiveness of the proposed strategies in isolation.

To assess the performance of MOEA/D-DU and EFR-RR on scaled test problems, we incorporate the normalization procedure outlined in Section IV-C into both algorithms. We then compare the performance of these normalized versions of MOEA/D-DU and EFR-RR with that of NSGA-III [13] in Section VII-B. NSGA-III is known for its clever normalization procedure, which enables it to effectively handle objective values that are scaled differently from one another.

Except for GrEA and SDE, all of the MOEAs considered in our evaluation employ the approach proposed in [12] to generate structured weight vectors. Specifically, MOEA/D, MOEA/D-STM, MOEA/D-GR, MOEA/D-DU, EFR, and EFR-RR all utilize a modified version of the Tchebycheff function.

We implement all of the MOEAs being evaluated, including MOEA/D-DU and EFR-RR, using the Metal framework [35]. These algorithms are executed on a computing system equipped with an Intel Core i7 2.9 GHz processor and 8 GB of RAM.

3.5.4 Experimental settings

Our experimental design encompasses two types of settings: general settings and parameter settings. The general settings are outlined below.

1. We execute each algorithm 30 times on each test instance to obtain a robust estimate of its performance. The average metric values are recorded across these independent runs. The algorithm is terminated once it has completed 20,000 times the number of objectives in the problem being solved function evaluations per run.

2. In some cases, we conduct a statistical analysis to assess whether any observed differences in performance between two competing algorithms are statistically significant. To do so, we employ the Wilcoxon signed-rank test [36] at a significance level of 5%. This test allows us to determine whether any observed differences in metric values between the two algorithms are statistically significant.

Moving on to the parameter settings, we begin by listing several commonly used parameters.

1. Population Size: In all of the algorithms under consideration, except for GrEA and SDE, the population size is set equal to the number of weight vectors. For GrEA and SDE, however, the generation mode of weight vectors necessitates a specific population size, which is controlled by a parameter denoted as H. Specifically, the population size for these algorithms is determined by the expression $N = C_{H+m-1}^{m-1}$. In contrast to the other algorithms being evaluated, GrEA and SDE do not have any constraints on their population size. In contrast to the other algorithms being evaluated, GrEA and SDE do not have any constraints on their population size. These algorithms allow for the population size to be set to any positive integer value. Table 3.4 lists the population sizes used for the different target number questions. To prevent the algorithms from generating weight vectors that are solely located on the boundary of the objective space, we utilize a two-layer approach to generate weight vectors for problems with more than five objectives [13].

2. Parameter for Crossover and Mutation: To generate new candidate solutions, each of the algorithms being evaluated employs the SBX crossover and polynomial mutation operators. The specific settings for these operators are documented in Table 3.5. Notably, EFR, EFR-RR, I-DBEA, and NSGA-III utilize a larger distribution index for crossover ($\eta_c = 30$), as recommended in [13], [16], and [32].

Table 3.4 Setting of the population size.

Number of objectives (m)	Divisions (H)	Population size (N)
2	99	100
5	5	210
8	3, 3	240
10	3, 2	275
13	2, 2	182

Table 3.5 Parameter settings for crossover and mutation.

Parameter	Value
Crossover probabilityp (p_c)	1.0
Mulation probability (p_m)	1 / n
Distribution index for crossover (η_c)	20
Distribution index for mutation (η_m)	20

3. Neighborhood Size T and Probability δ: For MOEA/D, MOEA/D-STM, MOEA/D-GR, and MOEA/D-DU, we set the parameter T equal to 20 and δ equal to 0.9.
4. Parameter K in MOEA/D-DU and EFR-RR: We set the value of K equal to 5 for MOEA/D-DU and 2 for EFR-RR. We will explore the impact of varying the value of K on the performance of the algorithms.

Each of the MOEAs being evaluated, including MOEA/D, MOEA/D-GR, GrEA, and SDE, has its own unique set of parameters. For MOEA/D, we set the maximum number of solutions that can be replaced by each newly generated child solution (n_r) to 1. For MOEA/D-GR, we specify the size of the replacement neighborhood (T_r) as 5, and we allow only one solution to be replaced by each newly generated child solution. In the case of GrEA, the number of grid segments (DIVs) used by each instance is shown in Table 3.6, which is adjusted according to the suggestions in [33]. For SDE, we set the archive size equal to the population size.

3.6 Analysis of the performance of enhanced algorithms

We delve into the performance of our enhanced optimization algorithms. Our first order of business is to analyze the impact of the parameter K on the performance of MOEA/D-DU and EFR-RR. We will investigate the ability of our proposed algorithms to strike a balance between convergence and diversity in the context of many-objective optimization.

3.6.1 Influence of parameter K

The parameter K plays a pivotal role in balancing the trade-off between convergence and diversity in the context of MOEA/D-DU and EFR-RR. To assess the sensitivity of these algorithms to variations in K, we conducted a comprehensive study that involved testing K values within the range of [1,20] with a step size of 1, using all of the normalized problem instances. All other parameters, except for K, were kept constant and consistent with those used in Section 3.5.4.

Table 3.6 Setting of grid division in GRE.

Problem	Number of objectives (*m*)	Grid division (*div*)
DTLZ1	2, 5, 8, 10, 13	18, 15, 14, 16, 19
DTLZ2	2, 5, 8, 10, 13	19, 11, 12, 15, 10
DTLZ3	2, 5, 8, 10, 13	19, 19, 19, 19, 20
DTLZ4	2, 5, 8, 10, 13	19, 10, 13, 15, 14
DTLZ7	2, 5, 8, 10, 13	20, 13, 12, 11, 9
WFG1	2, 5, 8, 10, 13	18, 17, 15, 13, 10
WFG2	2, 5, 8, 10, 13	19, 16, 18, 20, 16
WFG3	2, 5, 8, 10, 13	20, 19, 16, 16, 12
WFG4	2, 5, 8, 10, 13	18, 13, 12, 11, 9
WFG5	2, 5, 8, 10, 13	19, 12, 13, 15, 10
WFG6	2, 5, 8, 10, 13	20, 12, 13, 12, 10
WFG7	2, 5, 8, 10, 13	19, 12, 13, 14, 9
WFG8	2, 5, 8, 10, 13	20, 14, 12, 12, 14
WFG9	2, 5, 8, 10, 13	19, 13, 13, 15, 10

As a result of space constraints, the figure presented in Fig. 3.3 only displays the changes in HV values across all K values for a subset of the normalized problems, namely DTLZ4, DTLZ7, WFG3, and WFG9, with 5, 8, 10, and 13 objectives. From Fig. 3.3, we can observe the following.

1. We found that K has a consistent and comparable impact on the performance of both MOEA/D-DU and EFR-RR across each of the test instances.
2. the most suitable value of K is not only influenced by the specific problem being addressed, but also by the number of objectives that the problem involves.
3. We found that for certain problems, such as DTLZ4, the performance of both MOEA/D-DU and EFR-RR is relatively insensitive to variations in the value of K. Specifically, these algorithms were found to exhibit stable and consistent performance across a wide range of K values for this particular problem.
4. We observed that for certain problems, such as WFG3 and WFG9, adjusting the value of K may only result in minor fluctuations in the performance of the algorithms.
5. In contrast, we found that for certain problems, such as DTLZ7, a more careful and deliberate selection of K is essential to achieving optimal performance. In such cases, even slight variations in the value of K can have a significant impact on the overall performance of MOEA/D-DU and EFR-RR.

Our experiments indicate that while the performance of MOEA/D-DU and EFR-RR can be affected by different values of K, these algorithms can achieve an optimal balance between convergence and diversity with the appropriate setting of K. Our findings suggest that it may be beneficial to adjust K within the range of [1,8], as this range typically yields optimal or near-optimal performance for both algorithms.

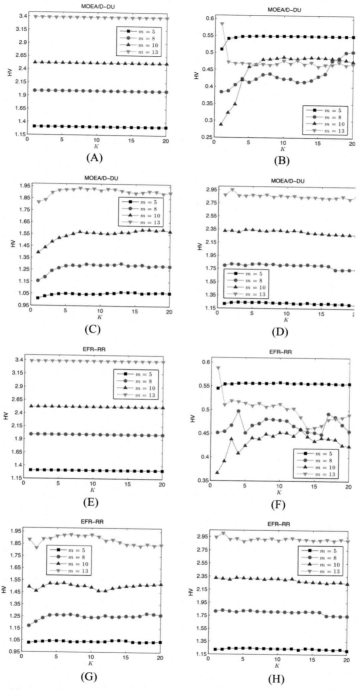

Figure 3.3 Examination of the influence of K on the performance of MOEA/D-DU, EFR-RR for the normalized (A) and (E) DTLZ4, (B) and (F) DTLZ7, (C) and (G) WFG3, and (D) and (H) WFG9 test problems with varying number of objectives m. The figures show the average HV of 30 independent runs each.

When tuning K for a given problem instance, we recommend considering the convergence and diversity of the solutions. If the solutions do not converge well, a larger value of K may be more suitable. Conversely, if the diversity of solutions is not desirable, a smaller value of K is recommended. By carefully tuning the value of K, these algorithms can effectively balance the trade-off between convergence and diversity, ultimately leading to the discovery of high-quality solutions.

3.6.2 Investigation of convergence and diversity

This segment is dedicated to examining the convergence and variety of the suggested techniques through the utilization of GD and DCI measurements, correspondingly. At this juncture, our focus is solely on normalized DTLZ1-DTLZ4 and WFG4-WFG9 quandaries. The rationale behind this decision is that the PFs of these predicaments constitute regular geometries, which allows for a straightforward analytical determination of the GD value without the need for point sampling on the PF. DTLZ1 has a PF structure that resembles a hyperplane, in contrast to the other quandaries whose PF structure takes the form of a hypersphere.

In the context of multiple objectives, we have opted to draw a comparison between MOEA/D-DU and EFR-RR, and their respective precursors (MOEA/D and EFR). The mean GD and DCI outcomes are presented in Table 3.7. With regard to convergence, MOEA/D-DU has emerged as the overall superior performer compared to MOEA/D, as evidenced by its superior GD results in the majority of the cases. Furthermore, EFR-RR has proven to be a strong contender to EFR in terms of convergence, with both techniques displaying better average GD results across various problem instances. One noteworthy observation is that, when compared to EFR, EFR-RR has demonstrated significantly inferior GD and DCI outcomes in the case of five-objective DTLZ3, which is characterized by an extensive collection of local PFs. The precise explanations for EFR-RR's suboptimal performance in this particular instance are a subject for future inquiry.

To visually depict the dispersion of solutions in a high-dimensional objective space in a more intuitive manner, Fig. 3.4 employs parallel coordinates to plot the ultimate non-dominated solutions attained by MOEA/D-DU, MOEA/D, EFR-RR, and EFR in a single run on the 10-objective WFG4 instance. This specific execution is linked with a result that is closest to the mean HV value. As can be inferred from Fig. 3.4, MOEA/D-DU and EFR-RR can discover solutions that are broadly dispersed throughout the range of $f_i \in [0, 1]$ for all ten objectives, while simultaneously demonstrating a superior balance among them, as evidenced by the plot. In contrast, both MOEA/D and EFR fall short of capturing a significant portion of the intermediate solutions.

In light of the aforementioned comparisons, it can be inferred that MOEA/D-DU and EFR-RR, on the whole, are capable of achieving a superior balance between convergence and diversity as compared to their respective predecessors.

Table 3.7 Comparison between MOEA/D-DU and MOEA/D (EFR-RR and EFR) in terms of average GD and DCI values on normalized test problems.

Problem	m	GD				DCI			
		MOEA/D-DU	MOEA/D	EFR-RR	EFR	MOEA/D-DU	MOEA/D	EFR-RR	EFR
DTLZ1	5	**0.000020**	0.004803	0.000668	0.000188	**0.969315**	0.896647	0.943488	0.920854
	8	0.000136	**0.000048**	0.000170	**0.000073**	0.992567	0.972053	**0.989848**	0.949016
	10	0.000022	**0.000004**	**0.000215**	0.000579	0.991502	0.959821	0.988164	0.922184
	13	**0.000029**	0.000084	0.000173	**0.000039**	0.992594	0.936280	**0.994281**	0.945934
DTLZ2	5	**0.000023**	0.000054	**0.000052**	0.000105	0.939564	0.836140	0.933494	0.854702
	8	0.000199	**0.000103**	0.000429	**0.000211**	0.985478	0.968888	**0.985609**	0.925318
	10	0.000087	**0.000059**	0.000573	0.000148	0.976237	0.930026	0.978438	0.876171
	13	**0.000218**	0.000328	0.000354	0.000286	0.990947	0.942113	0.998750	0.964441
DTLZ3	5	0.011119	**0.009032**	0.312651	**0.002989**	0.814999	0.701524	0.007747	**0.995126**
	8	0.003099	**0.000492**	**0.003595**	0.031573	0.982177	0.945281	0.985280	0.926237
	10	0.001925	**0.000282**	0.005250	**0.001787**	0.961370	0.914810	0.984499	0.857481
	13	**0.001035**	0.001727	**0.000481**	0.019179	0.975368	0.804104	0.997120	0.939957
DTLZ4	5	**0.000016**	0.000027	**0.000024**	0.000027	0.957419	0.934750	0.955842	0.946478
	8	**0.000026**	0.000041	**0.000034**	0.000048	0.982202	0.980584	0.986258	**0.990275**
	10	**0.000014**	0.000021	**0.000022**	0.000030	0.998616	0.981274	0.998315	0.995138
	13	**0.000020**	0.000037	**0.000019**	0.000023	0.993399	0.952210	0.995285	0.993149
WFG4	5	**0.000036**	0.000108	0.000098	**0.000058**	0.958943	0.237922	0.960109	0.286770
	8	**0.000488**	0.000632	**0.000457**	0.000663	0.993236	0.951922	0.985042	0.931296
	10	**0.000131**	0.000199	0.000192	0.000208	0.989878	0.907584	0.998226	0.848858
	13	**0.000217**	0.000229	0.000214	0.000226	0.991063	0.934429	0.996185	0.967426
WFG5	5	**0.001296**	0.001421	**0.001341**	0.001361	0.883937	0.771605	0.816306	0.735464
	8	**0.001131**	0.001155	**0.001180**	0.001283	0.998100	0.962539	0.987310	0.925904
	10	**0.000703**	0.000832	**0.000792**	0.000878	0.986966	0.934614	0.998997	0.841463
	13	**0.000879**	0.000861	**0.000907**	0.000949	0.996643	0.982889	0.998150	0.964958

(*Continued*)

Table 3.7 (Continued)

Problem	m	GD		DCI		GD		DCI	
		MOEA/D-DU	MOEA/D	MOEA/D-DU	MOEA/D	EFR-RR	EFR	EFR-RR	EFR
WFG6	5	0.001173	**0.001152**	**0.926435**	0.315379	0.001284	**0.001275**	**0.974729**	0.187833
	8	**0.001263**	0.001637	**0.998935**	0.970405	**0.001310**	0.001522	**0.989279**	0.927994
	10	**0.000789**	0.000937	**0.993133**	0.932979	**0.000910**	0.001007	**0.999700**	0.819165
	13	**0.001172**	0.001184	**0.996104**	0.962610	**0.001171**	0.001207	**0.999021**	0.961705
WFG7	5	**0.000066**	0.000136	**0.899289**	0.480338	0.000099	**0.000064**	**0.945729**	0.332050
	8	**0.000552**	0.000966	**0.996412**	0.965031	**0.000271**	0.000445	**0.989559**	0.930570
	10	**0.000128**	0.000168	**0.975515**	0.954160	**0.000096**	0.000186	**0.999086**	0.838123
	13	**0.000786**	0.002391	**0.974228**	0.759269	0.000374	**0.000372**	**0.992426**	0.924018
WFG8	5	**0.003256**	0.014374	**0.982783**	0.125524	**0.003480**	0.006584	**0.990924**	0.095518
	8	0.005102	**0.005095**	**0.959361**	0.819171	0.005643	**0.005110**	**0.968154**	0.830303
	10	0.005566	**0.003776**	**0.988397**	0.717678	0.006110	**0.004606**	**0.996009**	0.756254
	13	0.004611	**0.001271**	**0.981147**	0.665580	0.003793	**0.001848**	**0.989844**	0.677784
WFG9	5	**0.000704**	0.001363	**0.980032**	0.152752	0.001065	**0.001042**	**0.978193**	0.190482
	8	0.001224	**0.001114**	**0.997196**	0.963975	0.001212	**0.001026**	**0.990183**	0.922299
	10	**0.000668**	0.000675	**0.997815**	0.927091	0.000927	**0.000584**	**0.998744**	0.880118
	13	**0.000945**	0.001150	**0.994202**	0.947416	**0.000961**	0.001285	**0.996398**	0.955634

The better average result for each instance is highlighted in boldface.

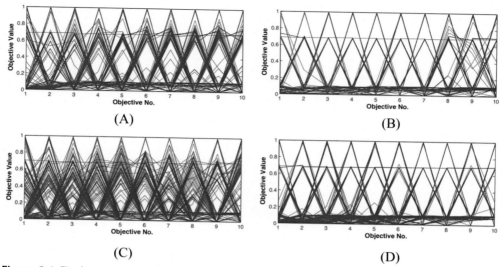

Figure 3.4 Final non-dominated solution set of (A) MOEA/D-DU, (B) MOEA/D, (C) EFR-RR, and (D) EFR on the normalized 10-objective WFG4 instance, shown by parallel coordinates.

3.7 Comparison with state-of-the-art algorithms

Within this segment, we undertake a comparative analysis of the proposed MOEA/D-DU and EFR-RR against several state-of-the-art MOEAs.

3.7.1 Comparison of normalized test problems

This section is devoted to the comparison of algorithms that lack explicit normalization with respect to the first set of problems, namely the normalized test problems. Table 3.8 presents a comparative analysis of nine algorithms in relation to the HV metric across the normalized DTLZ test problems, while Table 3.9 does the same for the normalized WFG test problems. To arrive at statistically reliable conclusions, we have conducted a significance test between MOEA/D-DU (EFR-RR) and each of the remaining seven algorithms. Within the two tables, results that were significantly bettered by MOEA/D-DU, EFR-RR, or both have been annotated using distinct symbols for each. The summary of the significance test pertaining to the HV outcomes across all 70 test instances, comparing the proposed MOEA/D-DU (EFR-RR) against the other algorithms, is presented in Table 3.10. Within Table 3.10, the comparison between Alg_1 and Alg_2 is denoted by the symbols "B" and "W," which signify the number of instances in which the results of Alg_1 are significantly better or worse than

Table 3.8 Performance comparison on normalized WFG problems with respect to the average HV values.

Problem	m	MOEA/D-DU	EFR-RR	MOEA/D	MOEA/D-STM	MOEA/D-GR	I-DBEA	EFR	GrEA	SDE
DTLZ1	2	0.704279	0.704371	0.703886[b]	0.703975[b]	**0.704426**	0.667992[a]	0.703793[a]	0.678608[a]	0.70298[a]
	5	**1.577413**	1.573057	1.561594[a]	1.553199[a]	1.577212	1.572915[a]	1.568136[a]	1.378445[a]	1.545282[a]
	8	2.131065	**2.137607**	2.095140[a]	2.072317[a]	2.094544[a]	2.136977	2.072935[a]	2.121597[a]	2.105726[a]
	10	2.591995	2.592416	2.587703[a]	2.584714[a]	2.587288[a]	**2.592680**	2.573180[a]	2.560445[a]	2.561582[a]
	13	3.389976	3.450434	3.280537[a]	3.198809[a]	3.387834[c]	**3.450678**	3.376324[a]	2.189600[a]	3.396960[c]
DTLZ2	2	**0.420129**	0.420127	0.420128	0.420122[b]	0.420128	0.418982[a]	0.420128[b]	0.406731[a]	0.419984[a]
	5	**1.307144**	1.306897	1.279784[a]	1.256106[a]	1.305507[a]	1.305292[a]	1.285600[a]	1.303783[a]	1.298814[a]
	8	1.950643	1.980951	1.880637[a]	1.802214[a]	1.799788[a]	1.972858[c]	1.780040[a]	**2.008651**	1.995382
	10	2.499082	2.503177	2.469220[a]	2.437519[a]	2.428536[a]	2.506564	2.384168[a]	**2.518827**	2.505607
	13	3.123026	3.323667	3.009885[a]	2.951134[a]	2.984305[a]	3.379538	3.122809[c]	3.306616[c]	**3.380496**
DTLZ3	2	0.396144	**0.411314**	0.351672[c]	0.404385[c]	0.394502[c]	0.002024[a]	0.394373[c]	0.366298[a]	0.391238[c]
	5	1.224940	0.054759	1.211052[b]	1.220319	1.023841[b]	0.496700[b]	1.274197	1.158907	**1.294771**
	8	1.927300	1.981563	1.777357[a]	1.731227[a]	1.820582[a]	1.831474[a]	1.760750[a]	1.601322[a]	**1.994729**
	10	2.451253	2.484752	2.388250[a]	2.377550[a]	2.304133[a]	2.405593[c]	2.326901[a]	2.304258[a]	**2.503337**
	13	3.089054	3.343837	2.844142[a]	2.609725[a]	3.035628[a]	3.350566	3.100067[c]	2.359130[a]	**3.370061**
DTLZ4	2	0.420128	0.420128	0.378778	0.409783	**0.420128**	0.420005[a]	0.420128[b]	0.347491[a]	0.295993[a]
	5	**1.308070**	1.307969	1.300444[a]	1.304319	1.307972[b]	1.302482[a]	1.305789[a]	1.306873[a]	1.302604[a]
	8	1.990879	1.992482	1.987187[c]	1.980209[a]	1.985272[a]	1.980485[a]	1.990668	**2.013161**	1.998266
	10	2.519895	**2.521704**	2.518763[a]	2.517569[a]	2.519728[c]	2.514036[a]	2.521234[c]	2.519544[c]	2.501111[a]
	13	**3.388281**	3.388239	3.371633[a]	3.340614[a]	3.384074[a]	3.384292[a]	3.386687	3.359210[a]	3.376911[a]
DTLZ7	2	0.491624	0.543805	**0.543950**	0.543948	0.495961[c]	0.495626[c]	0.543947	0.534730[c]	0.542912[c]
	5	0.548057	0.554015	0.549165[c]	0.548522[c]	0.535319[a]	0.486780[a]	0.552953	**0.584698**	0.560808
	8	0.412756	0.454187	0.390231[a]	0.409169[c]	0.469486	0.460563	0.426755[c]	**0.618048**	0.491885
	10	0.458421	0.391554	0.459661	0.460771	0.316704[a]	0.457378	0.369927[a]	**0.674957**	0.451083
	13	0.467171	0.510667	0.451700[a]	0.452945[a]	0.501658	0.482824[c]	0.470118[c]	**0.612042**	0.464647[c]

The best average HV value for each instance is highlighted in bold.

[a] The result is significantly outperformed by both MOEA/D-DU and EFR-RR.

[b] The result is significantly outperformed by MOEA/D-DU.

[c] The result is significantly outperformed by EFR-RR.

Table 3.9 Performance comparison on normalized WFG problems with respect to the average HV values.

Problem	m	MOEA/D-DU	EFR-RR	MOEA/D	MOEA/D-STM	MOEA/D-GR	I-DBEA	EFR	GrEA	SDE
WFG1	2	0.562230	0.581095	0.593810	**0.641743**	0.568671	0.426905[a]	0.573331	0.623764	0.561651[b]
	5	1.001123	1.242156	1.306573	**1.349242**	0.465755[a]	0.882835[a]	1.236781	1.136911[b]	1.212965[b]
	8	1.410532	1.562607	1.766691	**1.935880**	1.482641[b]	1.711815	1.782913	1.631993	1.898297
	10	1.666437	2.178243	**2.442026**	2.439172	1.292318[a]	2.416167	2.396391	2.156655	2.399104
	13	3.167303	3.125288	3.125818[c]	2.975475[a]	3.024708[a]	**3.179508**	3.156495	3.158010[c]	3.170219
WFG2	2	0.740281	0.758307	0.761351	0.760855	0.742650[b]	0.713250[a]	0.762530	0.758330	**0.762608**
	5	1.600169	**1.601199**	1.571654[a]	1.589303[a]	1.464050[a]	1.584469[a]	1.546560[a]	1.565527[a]	1.581520[b]
	8	**2.139066**	2.135469	2.119648[a]	2.121209[a]	2.107631[a]	2.108573[a]	2.116394[a]	2.111040[a]	2.118015[a]
	10	**2.591736**	2.589398	2.578580[a]	2.583832[a]	2.589241[c]	2.573491[a]	2.576869[a]	2.562607[a]	2.573589[a]
	13	3.431186	**3.442014**	3.406848[a]	3.386077[a]	3.430181[b]	3.428283[b]	3.414637[a]	3.414581[a]	3.431470[b]
WFG3	2	0.700664	0.699118	0.700160	0.700704	0.700284	0.677166[a]	0.699375[c]	0.682771[a]	**0.700997**
	5	**1.050757**	1.034773	0.867282[a]	0.866017[a]	0.906913[a]	1.037868[c]	0.852188[a]	1.045229[c]	0.994442[a]
	8	1.280380	1.204763	1.222794[c]	1.227956[c]	1.136276[a]	1.244489[c]	1.213499[c]	**1.416407**	1.247331[c]
	10	1.532371	1.460729	1.458075[a]	1.460352[c]	1.489880[c]	1.528830	1.454140[c]	**1.726470**	1.518089
	13	1.920702	1.816198	1.671833[a]	1.642120[a]	1.736590[a]	1.922486	1.754964[a]	**2.284531**	1.925885
WFG4	2	0.417000	**0.418377**	0.416908[b]	0.417200[b]	0.417183[b]	0.405476[a]	0.418244	0.406336[a]	0.418255[b]
	5	1.285940	1.287692	0.920686[a]	0.962506[a]	0.792782[a]	1.254008[a]	0.961821[a]	1.253821[a]	1.247417[a]
	8	1.934635	**1.965264**	1.679865[a]	1.659225[a]	1.715845[a]	1.860717[a]	1.724350[a]	1.930146[b]	1.905486[a]
	10	2.468681	**2.491699**	2.231219[a]	2.247558[a]	2.369648[a]	2.435737[a]	2.194736[a]	2.405230[a]	2.347108[a]
	13	3.008914	3.337246	2.900558[a]	2.777046[a]	3.030456[b]	**3.339312**	3.085706[b]	3.119742[b]	3.247644[b]
WFG5	2	0.378917	**0.379074**	0.373096[a]	0.378518[b]	0.378374	0.374261[a]	0.379034	0.366330[a]	0.377682[a]
	5	**1.216121**	1.207217	1.173121[a]	1.175929[a]	0.798748[a]	1.208029[c]	1.186556[a]	1.213000[c]	1.210585[c]
	8	1.809546	1.853939	1.523779[a]	1.499358[a]	1.610531[a]	1.811091[b]	1.572135[a]	**1.868017**	1.840307[b]
	10	2.288982	2.338790	2.044104[a]	2.111802[a]	2.110555[a]	2.327699[b]	1.988422[a]	**2.338894**	2.285479[b]
	13	2.685390	3.077929	2.629138[a]	2.599395[a]	2.629734[a]	**3.135248**	2.802878[b]	2.945444[b]	3.118274

(Continued)

Table 3.9 (Continued)

Problem	m	MOEA/D-DU	EFR-RR	MOEA/D	MOEA/D-STM	MOEA/D-GR	I-DBEA	EFR	GrEA	SDE
WFG6	2	0.386121	0.387136	0.388269	0.388159	0.386992	0.371930[a]	0.386763	0.375526[a]	**0.388339**
	5	1.203532	1.202838	0.932134[a]	0.989178[a]	0.745472[a]	1.198173[c]	0.814322[c]	**1.209398**	1.204154
	8	1.792582	1.845513	1.524041[a]	1.514136[a]	1.632452[a]	1.788382[b]	1.568782[a]	**1.860831**	1.823996[b]
	10	2.264165	**2.318441**	1.973321[a]	2.019177[a]	2.106371[a]	2.288335[b]	1.942445[a]	2.291735[b]	2.281144[b]
	13	2.694571	3.028384	2.632777[a]	2.577972[a]	2.703796[b]	**3.057529**	2.797318[b]	2.947601[b]	3.048374
WFG7	2	0.419219	0.419127	0.419264	0.419271	0.419270	0.403176[a]	0.419119[c]	0.406740[a]	**0.419480**
	5	1.278119	1.280956	1.119326[a]	1.134063[a]	0.843455[a]	1.269955[a]	1.032286[a]	**1.294253**	1.280318
	8	1.926683	1.987161	1.657222[a]	1.640169[a]	1.741279[a]	1.917133[a]	1.704069[a]	**1.998229**	1.953074[b]
	10	2.458886	**2.509162**	2.329332[a]	2.319595[a]	2.315842[a]	2.475375[b]	2.162850[a]	2.491561[b]	2.421732[a]
	13	3.080436	3.350532	2.792831[a]	2.760968[a]	2.918742[a]	**3.353342**	3.106133[b]	3.198467[b]	3.320231[b]
WFG8	2	0.380438	0.379809	0.379589	0.380673	0.380463	0.354848[a]	0.380610	0.374610[a]	**0.381698**
	5	1.174365	**1.179315**	0.620310[a]	0.606449[a]	0.687016[a]	1.165600[a]	0.614472[a]	1.160200[a]	1.153417[a]
	8	1.753599	1.739425	1.426568[a]	1.416873[a]	1.545540[a]	1.686752[a]	1.443098[a]	**1.760000**	1.682100[a]
	10	2.227371	2.192016	1.770687[a]	1.781845[a]	1.925330[a]	2.228087	1.789877[a]	**2.235939**	2.079279[a]
	13	2.668338	3.070900	2.465452[a]	2.451922[a]	2.766640[b]	**3.073486**	2.535248[a]	2.990715[b]	3.036104[b]
WFG9	2	0.395282	0.393623	0.400667	0.387581[b]	0.388456	0.378018[a]	0.407289	0.382390[a]	**0.409947**
	5	**1.237722**	1.223673	0.658931[a]	0.674282[a]	0.677244[a]	1.176343[a]	0.789826[a]	1.226696[c]	1.228754[c]
	8	1.819899	1.830079	1.628043[a]	1.623609[a]	1.639324[a]	1.744089[a]	1.682517[a]	**1.870276**	1.848786
	10	**2.341604**	2.314426	2.062388[a]	2.074169[a]	2.134863[a]	2.293407[c]	2.096066[a]	2.327689[c]	2.296196[a]
	13	2.871460	3.003053	2.722066[a]	2.711396[a]	2.842311[a]	3.045041	2.811748[b]	2.941058[b]	**3.082909**

The best average HV value for each instance is highlighted in boldface.

[a]The result is significantly outperformed by both MOEA/D-DU and EFR-RR.

[b]The result is significantly outperformed by EFR-RR.

[c]The result is significantly outperformed by MOEA/D-DU.

Table 3.10 Summary of the significance test of HV between the proposed algorithms and the other algorithms.

		MOEA/D-DU	EFR-RR	MOEA/D	MOEA/D-STM	MOEA/D-GR	I-DBEA	EFR	GrEA	SDE
MOEA/D-DU vs	B	—	21	52	50	46	40	43	32	26
	W	—	41	8	8	6	21	15	34	32
	E	—	8	10	12	18	9	12	4	12
EFR–RR vs	B	41	—	52	52	54	45	48	41	39
	W	21	—	11	11	8	16	7	24	27
	E	8	—	7	7	8	9	15	5	5

those of Alg_2, respectively. In addition, the symbol "E" denotes the number of instances where no statistically significant difference was observed between the results of Alg_1 and Alg_2.

Based on the above results, the following observations can be made for the proposed MOEA/D-DU and EFR-RR.

1. MOEA/D-DU has decisively surpassed MOEA/D. Specifically, MOEA/D-DU has demonstrated significantly superior performance as compared to MOEA/D in 52 out of the 70 instances, whereas MOEA/D has only emerged as the victor in eight instances, half of which pertain to the 2-objective problems. The data strongly suggests that the updating strategy employed by MOEA/D-DU is more efficacious than the original strategy used in MOEA/D when it comes to solving MaOPs.

2. MOEA/D-DU has exhibited certain advantages over the three other MOEA/D variants, namely MOEA/D-STM, MOEA/D-GR, and I-DBEA. To be more specific, MOEA/D-DU has demonstrated substantially superior performance as compared to both MOEA/D-STM and MOEA/D-GR across the vast majority of the instances. In comparison to I-DBEA, MOEA/D-DU has generally exhibited significantly better performance on the 2, 5, and 8-objective instances, while remaining a very strong contender on the 10-objective instances. However, it is worth noting that on the 13-objective instances, I-DBEA has generally demonstrated superior performance. These outcomes serve as a validation of the fact that the selection mechanism employed by MOEA/D-DU is on par with, or even superior to, the other available selection mechanisms used in state-of-the-art MOEA/D variants.

3. EFR-RR has demonstrated a marked improvement over EFR in the many-objective scenario. Specifically, among the 56 instances where the number of objectives exceeds 3, EFR-RR has achieved significantly better performance in 46 instances, while EFR has only achieved superior performance in 5 instances. When it comes to the 2-objective instances, no significant performance discrepancy has been observed between EFR-RR and EFR. These outcomes serve as a clear testament to the efficacy of the ranking restriction scheme utilized by EFR-RR when it comes to addressing MaOPs.

4. Both MOEA/D-DU and EFR-RR have emerged as highly competitive alternatives to two non-decomposition-based MOEAs that have been specifically designed for many-objective optimization, namely GrEA and SDE. In fact, each of the four algorithms has demonstrated superior performance in certain specific problem instances.

Building upon the extensive outcomes presented earlier, we have introduced the performance score [27] as an additional metric to help quantify the overall performance of the compared algorithms, thereby making it easier to gain valuable insights into the behavior of these algorithms. For a given problem instance, let Alg_1, Alg_2,..., Alg_l denote the l algorithms that are being compared. Let $\delta_{i,j}$ be equal to 1 if Alg_j significantly outperforms

Alg$_i$ in terms of the HV metric, and 0 otherwise. Then, for each algorithm Alg$_l$, the performance score $P(\text{Alg}_i)$ is determined based on the following equation:

$$P(\text{Alg}_i) = \sum_{\substack{j=1 \\ j \neq i}}^{l} \delta_{i,j} \qquad (3.13)$$

The performance score indicates the number of algorithms that have demonstrated significantly superior performance as compared to Alg$_i$ on the given problem instance. Consequently, a lower value indicates better performance on the part of Alg$_i$. Fig. 3.5 provides an overview of the average performance score across various problem instances, grouped by the number of objectives and the test problems employed.

Based on the insights provided by Fig. 3.5A, it is evident that both MOEA/D–DU and EFR–RR have performed exceedingly well in the context of MaOPs. In terms of the 2-objective problems, the overall performance of MOEA/D–DU has been slightly better than that of MOEA/D, while EFR–RR has fared slightly worse than EFR. One interesting observation to be made is that GrEA and I-DBEA, despite exhibiting competitive performance in the context of MaOPs, have not demonstrated strong performance when it comes to two–objective problems. On the other hand, MOEA/D, MOEA/D-STM, and MOEA/D-GR, which have demonstrated satisfactory performance in the context of 2-objective problems, have not scaled well when it comes to MaOPs. In addition, I-DBEA has shown a notable characteristic in its search behavior, namely that it tends to be more competitive on problems with a larger number of objectives.

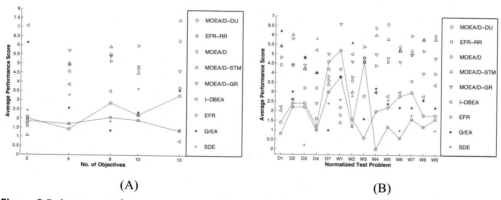

(A)   (B)

Figure 3.5 Average performance score over all (A) normalized test problems for a different number of objectives and (B) dimensions for different normalized test problems, namely DTLZ(Dx) and WFG (Wx). The smaller the score, the better the PF approximation in terms of the HV metric. The values of proposed MOEA/D-DU and EFR-RR are connected by a solid line to easier assess the score.

Based on the insights provided by Fig. 3.5B, EFR-RR has emerged as the top performer across 10 out of the 14 test problems and has secured the second position for the WFG9 problem. However, EFR-RR has not demonstrated the same level of exceptional performance when it comes to WFG1 and WFG3. In contrast, MOEA/D-DU has achieved the best overall performance on WFG3 and has secured the second position in eight instances, with EFR-RR being the top performer in all those cases. Nonetheless, MOEA/D-DU may face challenges when it comes to DTLZ7 and WFG1, where it has only outperformed MOEA/D-GR in terms of overall performance.

Table 3.11 has been compiled to provide an overview of the average performance score for the nine algorithms across all 70 problem instances, along with the overall rank assigned to each algorithm based on the score. EFR-RR and MOEA/D-DD have secured the top two positions in the rankings, followed by SDE and GrEA, as per Table 3.11. However, it is important to note that this evaluation is solely based on the performance of the algorithms across the problem instances considered in this chapter. It is important to recognize that no single algorithm can outperform all other algorithms across all possible problem instances. Rather, each algorithm has its strengths and weaknesses, and some algorithms may be better suited to solving certain types of problems. For instance, I-DBEA may demonstrate certain advantages over the other algorithms when it comes to problems that feature a very high number of objectives. It is worth noting that the exceptional overall performance of GrEA in our experiments has been achieved by carefully tuning the div parameter for each of the test instances. Consequently, GrEA has been able to take advantage of the strengths of the other compared algorithms to achieve its outstanding performance.

As GrEA and SDE have emerged as two highly competitive alternatives to MOEA/D-DU and EFR-RR in the context of many-objective optimization, we have provided an overview of the average CPU time for each of the four algorithms across 2100 runs (i.e., 70 problem instances $\times$ 30 independent runs) in Table 3.12. Given that all four

Table 3.11 Ranking in the average performance score over all normalized test instances for the nine algorithms.

Algorithm	Score	Rank
MOEA/D-DU	2.36	2
EFR-RR	1.79	1
MOEA/D	4.71	9
MOEA/D-STM	4.70	8
MOEA/D-GR	4.47	7
I-DBEA	3.49	5
EFR	4.27	6
GrEA	3.20	4
SDE	2.53	3

The smaller the score, the better the overall performance in terms of HV metric.

Table 3.12 Performance comparison on scaled test problems with respect to the average HV values.

Problem	m	MOEA/D-DU	EFR-RR	NSGA-III
DTLZ1	2	**0.704179**	0.704174	0.701746*
	5	**1.576914**	1.563334	1.571783[†]
	8	2.130914	**2.137705**	2.129752[‡]
	10	2.591432	**2.592426**	2.585756[‡]
	13	3.386799	3.450218	**3.450789**
DTLZ2	2	**0.420127**	0.420115	0.419951[‡]
	5	**1.307157**	1.306985	1.297456[‡]
	8	1.952661	**1.983739**	1.970329*
	10	2.499967	**2.506082**	2.505281
	13	3.135602	3.349935	**3.379670**
WFG4	2	0.416934	**0.418212**	0.417910*
	5	**1.287030**	1.286825	1.265777[‡]
	8	1.937218	**1.971430**	1.879845[‡]
	10	2.472125	**2.499611**	2.442636[‡]
	13	3.039460	**3.359619**	3.316773*
WFG5	2	0.378437	**0.379066**	0.378669*
	5	**1.216065**	1.206244	1.213641[†]
	8	1.812500	**1.858908**	1.820270*
	10	2.291171	**2.341408**	2.327403*
	13	2.792708	3.103004	**3.134267**
WFG6	2	**0.386738**	0.386458	0.386413
	5	**1.205599**	1.204359	1.201132[†]
	8	1.788193	**1.847898**	1.803972*
	10	2.262895	**2.324245**	2.300161*
	13	2.691167	3.057463	**3.067444**
WFG7	2	**0.419193**	0.419167	0.418768[‡]
	5	1.278789	**1.282254**	1.278558*
	8	1.927311	**1.989183**	1.920527[‡]
	10	2.459857	**2.511870**	2.474063*
	13	3.115259	**3.370701**	3.347897*
WFG8	2	0.379874	**0.379964**	0.379504
	5	1.166643	**1.178156**	1.163539[‡]
	8	**1.774488**	1.773226	1.679544[‡]
	10	2.243801	**2.264483**	2.214018[‡]
	13	2.587436	**2.993202**	2.947889*
WFG9	2	0.395017	**0.403498**	0.401294*
	5	**1.239003**	1.229890	1.179849[‡]
	8	1.834668	**1.850715**	1.728561[‡]
	10	**2.352997**	2.336695	2.274673[‡]
	13	2.961438	**3.095129**	2.978443*

The best average HV value for each instance is highlighted in boldface.
*Results are significantly worse than EFR-RR.
[†]Results are significantly worse than MOEA/D-DU.
[‡]Results are significantly worse than MOEA/D-DU and EFR-RR.

algorithms have been implemented within the same framework and have been run on identical computing environments, the data presented in Table 3.12 can offer us a general idea of the relative speed of each algorithm in a fairly equitable manner. The outcomes of the experiments indicate that even though GrEA and SDE have demonstrated satisfactory overall performance, their efficiency falls short of that of MOEA/D-DU and EFR-RR, necessitating significantly greater computational resources.

3.7.2 Comparison of scaled test problems

This section introduces a novel approach to improving the proposed MOEA/D-DU and EFR-RR algorithms by integrating the normalization procedure. Furthermore, we have conducted a comprehensive comparative analysis of the performance of these enhanced algorithms against NSGA-III on the second group of test problems, which are the scaled test problems.

The average HV results for MOEA/D-DU, EFR-RR, and NSGA-III have been presented in Table 3.13. Based on the observations made from this table, it is evident that EFR-RR has a clear edge over NSGA-III. In particular, it is important to note that EFR-RR has demonstrated significantly superior performance to NSGA-III across 30 out of the 40 instances considered in the evaluation. In contrast, NSGA-III has only been able to achieve superior performance to EFR-RR on five instances, which include the 5- and 13-objective DTLZ1, 13-objective DTLZ2, and 5- and 13-objective WFG5 problems. Regarding the performance of MOEA/D-DU, it has emerged as the superior algorithm to NSGA-III on problems with two, five, and eight objectives. When it comes to 10-objective problems, MOEA/D-DU and NSGA-III have comparable performance, with each algorithm outperforming the other on half of the instances. However, it is worth noting that MOEA/D-DU has not demonstrated the same level of performance as NSGA-III on problems featuring 13 objectives. NSGA-III has emerged as the superior algorithm in seven of these instances.

The performance of MOEA/D-DU, EFR-RR, and NSGA-III on the eight-objective WFG9 instance has been visualized in Fig. 3.6, which presents the evolutionary trajectories of HV as a function of generation numbers. Based on the observations made from Fig. 3.6, it is apparent that all three algorithms exhibit a steady increase in HV as generation numbers elapse. However, MOEA/D-DU and EFR-RR converge to the PF at a faster rate than NSGA-III, ultimately leading to higher HV values.

In light of the foregoing results, it can be inferred that either MOEA/D-DU or EFR-RR, when equipped with an effective normalization procedure, represents a highly competitive or even superior alternative to NSGA-III when it comes to solving scaled problems.

Table 3.13 Performance comparison on scaled test problems with respect to the average HV values.

Problem	m	MOEA/D-DU	EFR-RR	NSGA-III
DTLZ1	2	**0.704179**	0.704174	0.701746[a]
	5	**1.576914**	1.563334	1.571783[b]
	8	2.130914	**2.137705**	2.129752[c]
	10	2.591432	**2.592426**	2.585756[c]
	13	3.386799	3.450218	**3.450789**
DTLZ2	2	**0.420127**	0.420115	0.419951[c]
	5	**1.307157**	1.306985	1.297456[c]
	8	1.952661	**1.983739**	1.970329[a]
	10	2.499967	**2.506082**	2.505281
	13	3.135602	3.349935	**3.379670**
WFG4	2	0.416934	**0.418212**	0.417910[a]
	5	**1.287030**	1.286825	1.265777[c]
	8	1.937218	**1.971430**	1.879845[c]
	10	2.472125	**2.499611**	2.442636[c]
	13	3.039460	**3.359619**	3.316773[a]
WFG5	2	0.378437	**0.379066**	0.378669[a]
	5	**1.216065**	1.206244	1.213641[b]
	8	1.812500	**1.858908**	1.820270[a]
	10	2.291171	**2.341408**	2.327403[a]
	13	2.792708	3.103004	**3.134267**
WFG6	2	**0.386738**	0.386458	0.386413
	5	**1.205599**	1.204359	1.201132[b]
	8	1.788193	**1.847898**	1.803972[a]
	10	2.262895	**2.324245**	2.300161[a]
	13	2.691167	3.057463	**3.067444**
WFG7	2	**0.419193**	0.419167	0.418768[c]
	5	1.278789	**1.282254**	1.278558[a]
	8	1.927311	**1.989183**	1.920527[c]
	10	2.459857	**2.511870**	2.474063[a]
	13	3.115259	**3.370701**	3.347897[a]
WFG8	2	0.379874	**0.379964**	0.379504
	5	1.166643	**1.178156**	1.163539[c]
	8	**1.774488**	1.773226	1.679544[c]
	10	2.243801	**2.264483**	2.214018[c]
	13	2.587436	**2.993202**	2.947889[a]
WFG9	2	0.395017	**0.403498**	0.401294[a]
	5	**1.239003**	1.229890	1.179849[c]
	8	1.834668	**1.850715**	1.728561[c]
	10	**2.352997**	2.336695	2.274673[c]
	13	2.961438	**3.095129**	2.978443[a]

The best average HV value for each instance is highlighted in boldface.
[a]The result is significantly outperformed by EFR-RR.
[b]The result is significantly outperformed by MOEA/D-DU.
[c]The result is significantly outperformed by both MOEA/D-DU and EFR-RR.

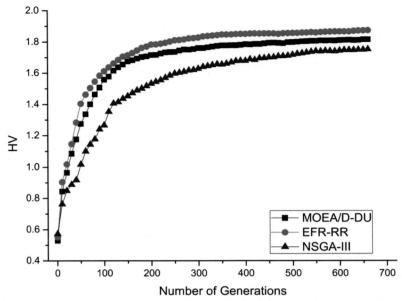

Figure 3.6 Evolutionary trajectories of HV over generations for MOEA/D-DU, EFR-RR, and NSGA-III on the eight-objective WFG9 instance.

3.8 Conclusion

This chapter outlines two new approaches, MOEA/D-DU and EFR-RR, that are tailored specifically for the task of many-objective optimization. These methods build upon two decomposition-based MOEA/D and EFR, respectively. The fundamental concept behind these methods is to actively preserve the distribution of solutions throughout the evolutionary process by leveraging the perpendicular distance between a given solution and its associated weight vector within the objective space. MOEA/D-DU employs a specific updating process that involves identifying the K weight vectors that are closest to a newly generated solution within the objective space based on their perpendicular distances. Once these K weight vectors have been identified, the new solution is only permitted to attempt to replace those existing solutions that correspond to the identified weight vectors. To determine whether a replacement should occur, the aggregation function values are compared between the new solution and the existing solutions being considered for replacement. Within the context of EFR-RR, we posit that each solution may perform better in relation to a subset of aggregation functions as opposed to all of them. Importantly, the selection of these aggregation functions is facilitated by taking into account the perpendicular distance between solutions and weight vectors within the objective space.

Throughout our experimental investigations, we examined the impact of the critical parameter K on the performance of MOEA/D-DU and EFR-RR. Based on our findings, we offer several recommendations with respect to setting the value of K appropriately. Our research has demonstrated that, on the whole, MOEA/D-DU and EFR-RR outperform their predecessors in terms of striking a balance between convergence and diversity within the domain of many-objective optimization. To showcase the efficacy of MOEA/D-DU and EFR-RR, we conducted comparative analyses of their performance against seven leading-edge MOEAs. The comparative evaluation involved a comprehensive analysis of 70 normalized problem instances drawn from the DTLZ and WFG test suites. The results of our experimentation highlight the significant advantages offered by both MOEA/D-DU and EFR-RR over their predecessors in the realm of many-objective optimization. Notably, both of these algorithms were found to outperform their peer counterparts across a range of performance metrics, further underscoring their effectiveness and competitiveness within the field. In addition, we integrated a sophisticated online normalization procedure into both MOEA/D-DU and EFR-RR and conducted a comparative analysis of their performance against NSGA-III on a range of scaled test problems. Our findings provided strong confirmation of the effectiveness of MOEA/D-DU and EFR-RR in addressing multiobjective optimization challenges across a range of objective scales when the normalization procedure was applied.

References

[1] Fleming PJ, Purshouse RC, Lygoe RJ. Many-objective optimization: an engineering design perspective. Proceedings of the 2nd evolutionary multi-criterion optimization; 2005. Vol. 5, p. 14–32.

[2] Herrero JG, Berlanga A, López JMM. Effective evolutionary algorithms for many-specifications attainment: application to air traffic control tracking filters. IEEE Transactions on Evolutionary Computation 2008;13(1):151–68.

[3] Harman M, Yao X. Software module clustering as a multi-objective search problem. IEEE Transactions on Software Engineering 2010;37(2):264–82.

[4] Zitzler E, Thiele L. Multiobjective evolutionary algorithms: a comparative case study and the strength Pareto approach. IEEE transactions on Evolutionary Computation 1999;3(4):257–71.

[5] Yuan Y, Xu H. Multiobjective flexible job shop scheduling using memetic algorithms. IEEE Transactions on Automation Science and Engineering 2013;12(1):336–53.

[6] Ishibuchi H, Tsukamoto N, Nojima Y. Evolutionary many-objective optimization: a short review. Proceedings of the 10th IEEE congress on evolutionary computation. IEEE; 2008. p. 2419–26.

[7] Wagner T, Beume N, Naujoks B. Pareto-, aggregation-, and indicator-based methods in many-objective optimization. Proceedings of the 4th evolutionary multi-criterion optimization; 2007. p. 742–56.

[8] Ikeda K, Kita H, Kobayashi S. Failure of Pareto-based MOEAs: does non-dominated really mean near to optimal? Proceedings of the 14th congress on evolutionary computation. IEEE; 2001. Vol. 2, p. 957–62.

[9] Khare V, Yao X, Deb K. Performance scaling of multi-objective evolutionary algorithms. Proceedings of the 2nd evolutionary multi-criterion optimization; 2003. p. 376–90.

[10] Zhang Q, Li H. MOEA/D: a multiobjective evolutionary algorithm based on decomposition. IEEE Transactions on Evolutionary Computation 2007;11(6):712–31.

[11] Qi Y, Ma X, Liu F, et al. MOEA/D with adaptive weight adjustment. Evolutionary Computation 2014;22(2):231–64.

[12] Das I, Dennis JE. Normal-boundary intersection: a new method for generating the Pareto surface in nonlinear multicriteria optimization problems. SIAM Journal on Optimization 1998;8 (3):631–57.

[13] Deb K, Jain H. An evolutionary many-objective optimization algorithm using reference-point-based nondominated sorting approach, part I: solving problems with box constraints. IEEE Transactions on Evolutionary Computation 2013;18(4):577–601.

[14] Li H, Zhang Q. Multiobjective optimization problems with complicated Pareto sets, MOEA/D and NSGA-II. IEEE Transactions on Evolutionary Computation 2008;13(2):284–302.

[15] Deb K, Agrawal RB. Simulated binary crossover for continuous search space. Complex Systems 1995;9(2):115–48.

[16] Yuan Y, Xu H, Wang B. Evolutionary many-objective optimization using ensemble fitness ranking. Proceedings of the 16th annual conference on genetic and evolutionary computation; 2014. p. 669–76.

[17] Deb K, Miettinen K, Chaudhuri S. Toward an estimation of nadir objective vector using a hybrid of evolutionary and local search approaches. IEEE Transactions on Evolutionary Computation 2010;14(6):821–41.

[18] Deb K, Thiele L, Laumanns M, et al. Scalable multi-objective optimization test problems. Proceedings of the 4th congress on evolutionary computation. IEEE; 2002. Vol. 1, p. 825–30.

[19] Huband S, Hingston P, Barone L, et al. A review of multiobjective test problems and a scalable test problem toolkit. IEEE Transactions on Evolutionary Computation 2006;10(5):477–506.

[20] Zitzler E, Thiele L, Laumanns M, et al. Performance assessment of multiobjective optimizers: an analysis and review. IEEE Transactions on Evolutionary Computation 2003;7(2):117–32.

[21] Ishibuchi H, Akedo N, Nojima Y. Behavior of multiobjective evolutionary algorithms on many-objective knapsack problems. IEEE Transactions on Evolutionary Computation 2014;19(2): 264–83.

[22] Beume N, Naujoks B, Emmerich M. SMS-EMOA: multiobjective selection based on dominated hypervolume. European Journal of Operational Research 2007;181(3):1653–69.

[23] Ishibuchi H, Hitotsuyanagi Y, Tsukamoto N, et al. Many-objective test problems to visually examine the behavior of multiobjective evolution in a decision space. Proceedings of the 9th international conference on parallel problem solving from nature; 2010. p. 91–100.

[24] Auger A, Bader J, Brockhoff D, et al. Theory of the hypervolume indicator: optimal μ-distributions and the choice of the reference point. Proceedings of the 10th ACM SIGEVO workshop on foundations of genetic algorithms; 2009. p. 87–102.

[25] Zou X, Chen Y, Liu M, et al. A new evolutionary algorithm for solving many-objective optimization problems. IEEE Transactions on Systems, Man, and Cybernetics, Part B (Cybernetics) 2008;38 (5):1402–12.

[26] While L, Bradstreet L, Barone L. A fast way of calculating exact hypervolumes. IEEE Transactions on Evolutionary Computation 2011;16(1):86–95.

[27] Bader J, Zitzler E. HypE: an algorithm for fast hypervolume-based many-objective optimization. Evolutionary Computation 2011;19(1):45–76.

[28] Van Veldhuizen DA. Multiobjective evolutionary algorithms: classifications, analyses, and new innovations. Dayton: Air Force Institute of Technology; 1999.

[29] Li M, Yang S, Liu X. Diversity comparison of Pareto front approximations in many-objective optimization. IEEE Transactions on Cybernetics 2014;44(12):2568–84.

[30] Li K, Zhang Q, Kwong S, et al. Stable matching-based selection in evolutionary multiobjective optimization. IEEE Transactions on Evolutionary Computation 2013;18(6):909–23.

[31] Wang Z, Zhang Q, Gong M, et al. A replacement strategy for balancing convergence and diversity in MOEA/D. Proceedings of the 16th IEEE congress on evolutionary computation. IEEE; 2014. p. 2132–9.

[32] Asafuddoula M, Ray T, Sarker R. A decomposition based evolutionary algorithm for many objective optimization with systematic sampling and adaptive epsilon control. Proceedings of the 7th evolutionary multi-criterion optimization; 2013. p. 413–27.

[33] Yang S, Li M, Liu X, et al. A grid-based evolutionary algorithm for many-objective optimization. IEEE Transactions on Evolutionary Computation 2013;17(5):721–36.

[34] Li M, Yang S, Liu X. Shift-based density estimation for Pareto-based algorithms in many-objective optimization. IEEE Transactions on Evolutionary Computation 2013;18(3):348–65.

[35] Durillo JJ, Nebro AJ. Metal: a Java framework for multi-objective optimization. Advances in Engineering Software 2011;42(10):760–71.

[36] Wilcoxon F. Individual comparisons by ranking methods. New York: Springer; 1992.

CHAPTER 4

Objective reduction in many-objective optimization: evolutionary multiobjective approaches and comprehensive analysis

Contents

Intelligent Evolutionary Optimization
DOI: https://doi.org/10.1016/B978-0-443-27400-8.00004-6

4.1 Introduction

Despite recent advancements in many-objective optimization algorithms, their efficacy in handling many-objective optimization problems (MaOPs) with more than approximately 15 objectives remains questionable [1,2]. Therefore their effectiveness on real-world problems necessitates further investigation. Furthermore, despite the enhancements made to multiobjective evolutionary algorithms (MOEAs), the challenge of visualizing the high-dimensional Pareto front remains a significant obstacle in selecting optimal solutions in many-objective optimization [2].

Objective reduction techniques aim to alleviate the complexity of the problem by reducing the number of objectives during the search process and/or the decision-making stage, rather than focusing on improving the scalability of current MOEAs [2–5]. The rationale behind this approach is that, for many problems with m objectives, there exists a subset of k (where $k < m$) conflicting objectives that can create the same Pareto front as the original problem, with the minimum possible cardinality. In this context, the k objectives are typically considered essential, while all the other objectives are regarded as redundant [3].

It should be noted that, in accordance with prior research [3–6], objective reduction in this chapter pertains specifically to selecting a subset of predetermined objectives that most accurately represent the original multiobjective optimization problem (MOP). This approach bears some resemblance to feature selection, although it is important to recognize that there is another related research avenue that strives to identify a small set of arbitrary objectives for the original MOP, akin to feature transformation techniques commonly employed in visualizing many-objective solution sets [7,8].

The global search capabilities of evolutionary computation (EC) techniques have garnered significant interest in feature selection [9], owing to the vast search spaces involved in such problems. To the best of our knowledge, no prior research has explored the application of EC for objective reduction in the context of feature selection. It is noteworthy that despite the δ-minimum objective subset problem (δ-MOSS) and k-EMOSS problems [6] that arise from objective reduction having been demonstrated to be non-deterministic polynomial hard (NP-hard), and the infeasibility of exact algorithms for handling larger instances of practical significance [6], no prior research has explored the potential of EC for objective reduction in the context of feature selection. Furthermore, the majority of current objective reduction algorithms [3,10–12] only produce a single reduced objective set as the output in a single simulation run, without taking into account conflicting requirements such as the desired number of objectives and the acceptable error tolerance. As a consequence, their rigidity precludes the provision of essential adaptability to the user in terms of decision support, as noted in reference [13]. In light of this premise, the current chapter introduces an original investigation into the use of evolutionary multiobjective techniques for objective reduction. This investigation leverages the global search capabilities of EC and the decision support properties of multiobjective optimization. To be more precise, we put forth three distinct multiobjective formulations of the objective reduction problem. Each formulation employs a different type of error measure (δ, η, and γ), with the first two measures taking into account the Pareto dominance structure and the last measure centering on the correlation structure. Subsequently, we utilize nondominated sorting genetic algorithm II (NSGA-II) as a proficient solver for the three MOPs that were formulated, resulting in the development of three evolutionary multiobjective methodologies (NSGA-II-δ, NSGA-II-η, and NSGA-II-γ) for objective reduction.

A notable aspect of this chapter is the thorough examination of current objective reduction algorithms, which can be broadly classified into two categories: those based on the dominance structure and those based on correlation, as noted in references [3,6,10]. The impetus for this research stems from the observation that while each of the two approaches to objective reduction (dominance structure-based and correlation-based) has its strengths and limitations, previous investigations have not adequately scrutinized their performance characteristics. This chapter represents an all-encompassing analysis of the two categories of objective reduction approaches. Through a theoretical examination of the subject matter, we aim to provide an explicit delineation of the general advantages and disadvantages of each category. The objective of this research is to enhance the comprehension of users of these algorithms regarding the underlying principles of their operation, as well as the circumstances under which they are most suitable. Furthermore, we anticipate that our analysis will yield further insights that can be utilized to develop more efficacious objective reduction algorithms in the future.

To affirm the effectiveness of the proposed multiobjective methodologies and to comprehensively analyze the two categories of objective reduction approaches, we carry out a series of experiments using benchmark problems. Our experiments entail detailed comparisons with present-day state-of-the-art algorithms. The experimental outcomes not only confirm the advantages of our proposed algorithms but also align well with our theoretical analysis. Additionally, we employ the proposed multiobjective methodologies in two real-world scenarios and showcase their effectiveness in optimization, visualization, and decision-making.

4.2 Preliminaries and background

4.2.1 Multi and many-objective optimization

A mathematical representation of a typical MOP can be expressed as

$$
\begin{aligned}
&\min \mathbf{f}(\mathbf{x}) = (f_1(\mathbf{x}), f_2(\mathbf{x}), \ldots, f_m(\mathbf{x}))^{\mathrm{T}} \\
&\text{subject to } g_i(\mathbf{x}) \leq 0, i = 1, 2, \ldots, u \\
&h_j(\mathbf{x}) = 0, j = 1, 2, \ldots, v \\
&\mathbf{x} \in \Omega
\end{aligned}
\tag{4.1}
$$

The decision vector, denoted as $\mathbf{x} = (x_1, x_2, \ldots, x_n)^{\mathrm{T}}$, is an n-dimensional element of the decision space Ω. On the other hand, the objective vector $f{:}\Omega \to \Theta \subseteq \mathbb{R}^m$ is composed of m objective functions that map the n-dimensional decision space Ω to the m-dimensional attainable objective space Θ. In MaOPs, where $m > 3$, the objective vector consists of more than three objective functions. The constraints can be classified into two types: inequality constraints denoted by $g_i(\mathbf{x}) \leq 0$, and equality constraints represented by $h_j(\mathbf{x}) = 0$.

In general, an MOP does not possess a solution that can minimize all objective functions simultaneously. As a result, the primary focus is on achieving an approximation of the Pareto front which signifies the optimal trade-offs among the objectives. Outlined below are some fundamental concepts related to MOPs.

1. **Weak Pareto dominance:** A vector $\mathbf{u} = (u_1, u_2, \ldots, u_k)^{\mathrm{T}}$ is considered to weakly dominate another vector $\mathbf{v} = (v_1, v_2, \ldots, v_k)^{\mathrm{T}}$, indicated by the notation $\mathbf{u} \preccurlyeq \mathbf{v}$, if for every $i \in \{1, 2, \ldots, k\}$, it holds that $u_i \leq v_i$.
2. **Pareto dominance:** A vector $\mathbf{u} = (u_1, u_2, \ldots, u_k)^{\mathrm{T}}$ is considered to dominate another vector $\mathbf{v} = (v_1, v_2, \ldots, v_k)^{\mathrm{T}}$, indicated by the notation $\mathbf{u} \prec \mathbf{v}$, if for every $i \in \{1, 2, \ldots, k\}$, $u_i \leq v_i$ and there exists at least one $j \in \{1, 2, \ldots, k\}$ such that $u_j \leq v_j$.
3. **Pareto front:** The Pareto front of an MOP is characterized by $PF{:}= \{\mathbf{f}(\mathbf{x}^*) \in \Theta \mid \nexists \mathbf{x} \in \Omega, \mathbf{f}(\mathbf{x}) \prec \mathbf{f}(\mathbf{x}^*)\}$.
4. **Weak ϵ-dominance** [14]: A vector $\mathbf{u} = (u_1, u_2, \ldots, u_k)^{\mathrm{T}}$ is considered to weakly ϵ-dominate another vector $\mathbf{v} = (v_1, v_2, \ldots, v_k)^{\mathrm{T}}$, indicated by the notation $\mathbf{u} \preccurlyeq^{\epsilon} \mathbf{v}$, if $\forall i \in \{1, 2, \ldots, k\}{:}u_i - \epsilon \leq v_i$.

Broadly speaking, the objective of MOEAs is to achieve the optimal approximation of the Pareto front. This entails obtaining nondominated objective vectors that are both proximal to the Pareto front (convergence) and well-dispersed along the Pareto front (diversity).

4.2.2 Basic concepts in objective reduction

In the absence of any specific instructions to the contrary, the MOP that is intended for objective reduction is invariably represented using the formulation specified in Eq. (4.1). Additionally, the original (or universe) objective set is identified as $\mathcal{F}_0 = \{f_1, f_2, \ldots, f_m\}$.

The notation PF_0 is reserved for the Pareto front of the original MOP. To simplify matters, the notation $\mathbf{u}^{(\mathcal{F})}$ is employed to indicate the subvector of u that corresponds to a nonempty subset $\mathcal{F}$ of the objectives. For instance, if $\mathbf{u} = (f_1(\mathbf{x}), (f_2(\mathbf{x}), (f_3(\mathbf{x}))^{\mathrm{T}}$ and $\mathcal{F}$ is defined as the objective subset $\{f_1, f_3\}$, then $\mathbf{u}^{(\mathcal{F})} = (f_1(\mathbf{x}), (f_3(\mathbf{x}))^{\mathrm{T}}$.

Objective reduction is fundamentally aimed at determining a fundamental objective set [3] for a given MOP. The definition and associated concepts of this objective set are provided below:

Definition 1:

If the Pareto front that corresponds to $\mathcal{F}' = \mathcal{F}_0 \backslash \mathcal{F}$ is equivalent to $\mathcal{F}_0$, an objective subset $\mathcal{F} \subset \mathcal{F}_0$ is deemed to be redundant.

Definition 2:

A nonempty objective set $\mathcal{F}$ is designated as an essential objective set if $\mathcal{F}_0 \backslash \mathcal{F}$ is a redundant objective subset with the maximum cardinality.

Definition 3:

The dimensionality of a given MOP or PF_0 is the size of an essential objective set, specified as its cardinality.

The definitions provided above are demonstrated in Fig. 4.1, which depicts the Pareto front of the WFG3 problem [15,16] with three objectives. The Pareto front is a linear segment connecting the points $(0, 0, 6)^T$ and $(1, 2, 0)^T$. As depicted in Fig. 4.1, the objective sets f_1 and $\{f_2\}$ are both considered redundant. Conversely, there are two essential objective sets, namely $\{f_1, f_3\}$ and $\{f_2, f_3\}$, which are responsible for determining the dimensionality of this problem, set at 2. The illustrations demonstrate that there could be multiple essential objective sets for a given MOP. The term "redundant" pertains to $\mathcal{F}_0$, and the removal of two redundant objective sets may not always be carried out at the same time.

"Nonconflicting" is another frequently encountered term in objective reduction. Its definition is as follows:

Definition 4:

Two objectives f_i and f_j, both of which belong to $\mathcal{F}_0$, are considered nonconflicting if for all $\mathbf{u}, \mathbf{v} \in PF_0$, the following holds true: $\mathbf{u}^{(\{f_i\})} \leq \mathbf{v}^{(\{f_i\})}$ if and only if $\mathbf{u}^{(\{f_j\})} \leq \mathbf{v}^{(\{f_j\})}$.

The concept of nonconflict is related to the notion of redundancy as follows: if f_i and f_j are nonconflicting, then both $\{f_i\}$ and $\{f_j\}$ are considered redundant.

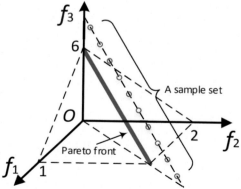

Figure 4.1 The Pareto front and a sample set of the three-objective WFG3 problem.

This is illustrated in Fig. 4.1 by the objectives f_1 and f_2. The supplementary material provides a proof of this relationship.

The magnitude of conflict between two objectives can be estimated through their correlation. Typically, objectives with a more negative correlation are deemed to be more conflicting, while objectives with a more positive correlation are generally considered to be more nonconflicting.

4.2.3 Pareto front-representation and misdirection

Objective reduction techniques generally function on a collection of nondominated objective vectors derived from an MOEA. This set is subsequently referred to as the sample set. In the context of objective reduction, it is not imperative for the sample set to be an excellent Pareto front-approximation. Instead, it should be a good Pareto front-representation that conforms to the dominance or correlation structure of the Pareto front. Saxena et al. [3] have provided a detailed explanation of the distinction between "approximation" and "representation."

The sample set depicted in Fig. 4.1 serves as an ideal representation of the Pareto front for the 3–objective WFG3 problem. This is because the dominance/correlation structure of the sample set is entirely in line with that of the Pareto front. Specifically, the objectives f_1 and f_2 do not conflict with each other, and either of them is entirely conflicting with f_3. With the sample set available, an objective reduction algorithm that utilizes either dominance or correlation can accurately and dependably recognize the essential objectives. It is essential to note that this set is not an excellent Pareto front-approximation as it is considerably distant from the actual Pareto front.

In real-world scenarios, the sample set is usually not a flawless Pareto front-representation, and there is typically a certain degree of deviation [3,13] in it. The term "misdirection" in this context refers to the contrast between the dominance or correlation structure of the Pareto front and the sample set [13]. To provide further clarification, Fig. 4.2 illustrates a sample set

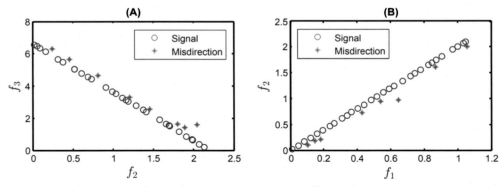

Figure 4.2 The illustration of misdirection using a sample set of three-objective WFG3. (A) Visualization in f_2-f_3 subspace; (B) visualization in f_1-f_2 subspace.

of the 3-objective WFG3 problem, projected onto the $f_2 - f_3$ and $f_1 - f_2$ objective subspaces. As depicted in Fig. 4.2A, the dominance structure of this sample set exhibits some variation from that of the Pareto front. This deviation is due to some solutions being dominated in relation to the $f_2 - f_3$ objective subspace; these solutions that are dominated contribute to the disparity between the sample set and the Pareto front, which can be deemed as misdirection. The remaining solutions can be considered as the signal. The correlation structure of the Pareto front is also somewhat disrupted by this sample set, as depicted in Fig. 4.2B. Specifically, there is a slight deviation in the degree of positive correlation between f_1 and f_2. A well-crafted objective reduction algorithm is anticipated to function effectively, even when there is a certain level of misdirection present [3].

4.2.4 Existing approaches to objective reduction

Over the past few years, a multitude of objective reduction algorithms have been introduced in the literature. As previously stated, these algorithms can be primarily grouped into two categories: those that are based on dominance structure and those that are based on correlation. Approaches based on dominance structure aim to conserve the dominance structure to the maximum extent possible after objectives have been removed. In contrast, correlation-based approaches leverage the correlation among pairs of objectives and strive to retain the most conflicting objectives while eliminating those that are nonconflicting with other objectives. Here, we draw attention to two exemplary studies that fall under the categories of dominance structure-based and correlation-based approaches, respectively.

4.2.4.1 Dominance relation preservation

The objective reduction method operates by maintaining the weak Pareto dominance relationships. When evaluating a specific subset of objectives $\mathcal{F} \subseteq \mathcal{F}_0$, the technique examines each solution pair $\mathbf{u}, \mathbf{v} \in \mathcal{N}$ that satisfies $\mathbf{u}^{(\mathcal{F})} \preccurlyeq \mathbf{v}^{(\mathcal{F})}$, and calculates the minimum nonnegative ϵ value that guarantees $\mathbf{u} \preccurlyeq^{\epsilon} \mathbf{v}$ for every pair. After analyzing all feasible solution pairs in $\mathcal{N}$, the maximum recorded ϵ value is considered the error. The error is represented by δ, which can serve as a criterion for quantifying the extent of conflict between $\mathcal{F}$ and $\mathcal{F}_0$. Utilizing this criterion, two objective reduction problems are formulated as follows:

1. **δ-MOSS Problem:** Given a sample set N and a $\delta_0 \geq 0$, the problem entails determining the smallest subset $\mathcal{F} \subseteq \mathcal{F}_0$ that satisfies the condition whereby its corresponding δ value is less than or equal to δ_0.
2. **k-EMOSS Problem:** Given a sample set $\mathcal{N}$ and $k_0 \in \mathbb{N}^+$, the problem involves identifying the objective subset $\mathcal{F} \subseteq \mathcal{F}_0$ that has the minimum δ value under the condition that $\mathcal{F} \leq k_0$.

Brockhoff and Zitzler [6] presented a precise algorithm for solving both the δ-MOSS and k-EMOSS problems. Since both problems are NP-hard, three greedy algorithms were also developed for addressing large instances of δ-MOSS and k-EMOSS, respectively.

4.2.4.2 *Principal component analysis and maximum variance unfolding*

This study introduced two algorithms, namely L-principal component analysis (PCA) and NL-maximum variance unfolding (MVU)-PCA, for linear and nonlinear objective reduction, respectively. These algorithms are founded on two widely recognized dimensionality reduction techniques, namely PCA and MVU. The main concept is to identify the minimum subset of conflicting objectives while maintaining the correlation structure within the provided sample set, this is done by eliminating objectives that do not conflict with each other along the important eigenvectors of the correlation matrix (for L-PCA) or the kernel matrix (for NL-MVU-PCA). The experiments evaluated the performance of L-PCA and NL-MVU-PCA in identifying the crucial objective set, in comparison to the exact and greedy algorithms presented in [6].

In addition to the works mentioned above, there are several other notable contributions to objective reduction. Jaimes et al. [17] proposed an unsupervised feature selection approach, where the objective set is partitioned into neighborhoods of fixed size around each objective based on the correlation strength. Singh et al. [10] put forward a Pareto corner search evolutionary algorithm (PCSEA), which concentrates on exploring only the corners of the Pareto front, rather than the whole Pareto front. After obtaining the population using PCSEA, the objective reduction process is conducted based on the assumption that removing a crucial objective can significantly impact the number of nondominated solutions. To detect possibly redundant objectives, Guo et al. [11] advocated using a k-medoids clustering algorithm to combine highly correlated objectives into a single cluster. The clustering process relies on a metric that integrates mutual information and correlation coefficients. Duro et al. [13] expanded the framework presented in [3] to encompass analysis similar to δ-MOSS and k-EMOSS, which could function as decision support for decision-makers. The concept of aggregation trees was introduced by De Freitas et al. [18] to visualize the outcomes of MaOPs, and it was also utilized as a technique for objective reduction. According to Guo et al. [19], the corners utilized in PCSEA do not adequately represent the complete Pareto front. Consequently, they devised an algorithm that employs the representative nondominated solutions instead. Wang and Yao [12] utilized nonlinear correlation information entropy to evaluate both the linear and nonlinear correlation between objectives. They then employed a straightforward approach to identify the most conflicting objectives.

It is noteworthy that several investigations [20–24] have concentrated on integrating objective reduction algorithms into MOEAs. This integration simplifies the search process. The term "online objective reduction" is frequently employed to describe this paradigm. The main focus of this chapter is on the objective reduction algorithms themselves, with a particular emphasis on offline objective reduction. Table 4.1 provides a comprehensive summary of the reviewed studies on objective reduction in each category.

It is crucial at this point to differentiate between two distinct aspects of objective reduction algorithms: (1) δ-MOSS and k-EMOSS analysis; (2) Identification of the

Table 4.1 Summary of the studies reviewed in this chapter.

Algorithm category	References
Dominance structure-based approaches	[6,10,18−20]
Correlation-based approaches	[3,11−13,17,21,24]

crucial objective set. Certain prior investigations, such as [6,17], exclusively focus on the first aspect and do not explicitly address the second aspect. In contrast, other studies, such as [3,10], solely concentrate on the second aspect. Algorithms designed for the first aspect can offer decision support to users by analyzing δ-MOSS problems with various δs and k-EMOSS problems with different ks. The selected objective subset may not necessarily be a crucial objective set, but rather a desirable one that aligns with the user's preferences in a specific application context. The second aspect, on the other hand, solely hinges on the specific MaOP at hand and has no connection to the user's preference. It's worth noting that an algorithm designed for the first aspect can be readily employed for the second aspect by solving a δ-MOSS problem with an adequately small δ value [3]. This chapter introduces multiobjective approaches that effectively address the first aspect, which is deemed more practical. Nevertheless, it seems challenging to conduct an experimental assessment and comparison of the impact of objective reduction concerning this aspect. Thus, when evaluating the strengths and limitations of objective reduction, the proposed multiobjective approaches are employed to address the second aspect.

4.3 Proposed multiobjective approaches

In this section, we provide a detailed overview of the proposed multiobjective approaches. Initially, we expound on how the objective reduction problem can be formulated as an MOP.

4.3.1 Dominance structure-based multiobjective formulation

The objective reduction problem is posed with the original objective set $\mathcal{F}_0$ and sample set $\mathcal{N}$ as inputs and its potential solution is represented as an objective subset $\mathcal{F}$.

The first multiobjective formulation for objective reduction, referred to as δ-OR, consists of two objectives: minimizing the number of selected objectives k (where $k = |\mathcal{F}|$), and reducing the δ error as proposed in [6]. The δ value can be mathematically expressed in the following manner:

$$\delta = \max\left\{\left\{\min_{\substack{\epsilon > 0 \\ u \preceq_\epsilon v}} \epsilon \,|\, u, v \in \mathcal{N}, u^{(\mathcal{F})} \preceq v^{(\mathcal{F})}\right\} \cup \{0\}\right\} \quad (4.2)$$

The parameter δ serves as a gauge for gauging the extent of changes in the dominant structure between $\mathcal{F}$ and $\mathcal{F}_0$. However, there is some tension between k and δ. Typically, δ decreases as k increases, and when k reaches the maximum value possible (i.e., $k = |\mathcal{F}_0|$), the minimum value of δ (i.e., $\delta = 0$) is attained. The –OR formulation aims to uncover a range of objective subsets on the Pareto front through objective reduction.

It should be noted that for the δ error to be effective, all objective values must be measured on the same scale to enable comparison of ϵ values across objectives [6]. Furthermore, the δ error may not provide accurate results if the objective functions differ in terms of nonlinearity [13]. To circumvent these issues, we have devised an alternative error metric, referred to as η, which is inspired by the R parameter definition presented in [10]. Unlike δ, η is not subject to the aforementioned drawbacks and can be used to measure changes in the dominance structure effectively.

To determine the η error for a given objective subset $\mathcal{F} \subseteq \mathcal{F}_0$, a sample set $\mathcal{N}$ is partitioned into two distinct sets: $\mathcal{N}_{NS}$ and $\mathcal{N}_{DS}$. Specifically, $\mathcal{N}_{NS}$ comprises all elements $\mathbf{u} \in \mathcal{N}$ such that there exists no other element $\mathbf{v} \in \mathcal{N}$ satisfying the condition $\mathbf{u}^{(\mathcal{F})} \prec \mathbf{v}^{(\mathcal{F})}$. On the other hand, $\mathcal{N}_{DS}$ is the set of remaining elements in $\mathcal{N}$ after $\mathcal{N}_{NS}$ has been removed. The η error can then be computed as follows:

$$\eta = \frac{|\mathcal{N}_{DS}|}{|\mathcal{N}|} \tag{4.3}$$

It's worth highlighting that the η error metric has a distinct advantage over δ in that it falls within the interval $[0, 1)$, independent of the problem being considered. This range corresponds to the proportion of objective vectors in the sample set $\mathcal{N}$ that are dominated (with respect to $\mathcal{F}$).

The second multiobjective formulation of objective reduction, referred to as η –OR, can be obtained by substituting the δ error with the η error in δ-OR. The relationship between k and η is akin to that between k and δ, with the maximum value of k (i.e., $k = |\mathcal{F}_0|$) also resulting in the minimum possible value of η, which is 0. This is because the objective vectors in the sample set $\mathcal{N}$ are nondominated with respect to $\mathcal{F}_0$.

4.3.2 Correlation-based multiobjective formulation

In this subsection, we present a novel multiobjective formulation of objective reduction called γ-OR, which differs from δ-OR and η-OR in that it focuses on correlation rather than dominance structure. While Section 4.2.4 outlines several objective reduction algorithms that rely on correlation analysis, none of them provide a ready-made criterion for evaluating a given objective subset based on such analysis. To address this gap, we introduce a new criterion, denoted as γ, which draws inspiration from the objective reduction techniques presented in [17].

To compute γ, it's necessary to account for the correlation between every pair of objectives in $\mathcal{F}_0$. However, instead of relying on Pearson's correlation coefficient, which only captures linear relationships between variables, we use Kendall's rank correlation coefficient [25]. This is because Kendall's coefficient measures the degree to which one variable tends to increase as the other increases, irrespective of the functional form of the relationship. This property aligns closely with the objective of correlation analysis in objective reduction, which is to determine whether enhancing one objective could lead to a decline or enhancement in another [26].

We use Kendall's rank correlation coefficient to determine the degree of correlation between any two objectives f_i and f_j in $\mathcal{F}_0$, which can be computed using the sample set $\mathcal{N}$. Specifically, we denote the coefficient as $r_T(i,j)$, where values closer to 1 (or -1) indicate stronger positive (or negative) monotonic relationships between the objectives. We define the distance between f_i and f_j as $d(i,j) = (1 - r_T(i,j))/2$, which falls within the range $[0, 1]$. A value of 0 (or 1) signifies that f_i and f_j are fully positively (or negatively) correlated. It's worth noting that $d(i,j) = d(j,i)$ since $r_T(i,j)$ is symmetric.

To compute γ for a given objective subset $\mathcal{F} = \{f_{i_1}, f_{i_2}, ..., f_{i_k}\} \subseteq \mathcal{F}_0$, we follow these steps. First, we partition $\mathcal{F}$ into k distinct clusters, denoted as $C_1, C_2, ..., C_k$, with f_{i_j} serving as the centroid of C_j for $j = 1{:}k$. Next, every objective $f_l \in \mathcal{F}_0 \backslash \mathcal{F}$ is assigned to the cluster whose centroid is closest to it in terms of distance. The clustering process is explained in Algorithm 4.1. After clustering is completed, every objective in $\mathcal{F}_0$ is associated with a single cluster, and the γ criterion can be computed using the following:

$$\gamma = \max_{j=1:k} \max_{f_l \in C_j} d(i_j, l) \qquad (4.4)$$

The γ criterion provides a measure of the extent to which the correlation structure between $\mathcal{F}$ and $\mathcal{F}_0$ has changed. If an important objective is omitted from $\mathcal{F}$, it's common for two conflicting objectives to be clustered together, resulting in a suboptimal γ value. Thus, γ serves as an indicator of how well a given objective subset $\mathcal{F}$ captures the correlation structure in $\mathcal{F}_0$.

Algorithm 4.1: Clustering ($\mathcal{F}$, $\mathcal{F}_0$).

Input: an objective subset $\mathcal{F} = \{f_{i_1}, f_{i_2}, ..., f_{i_k}\} \subseteq \mathcal{F}_0$; the original objective set $\mathcal{F}_0 = \{f_1, f_2, ..., f_m\}$
Output: k objective set clusters $C_1, C_2, ..., C_k$
for $j = 1$ **to** k **do**
   $C_j \leftarrow \{f_{i_j}\}$;
for each objective f_l in $\mathcal{F}_0 \backslash \mathcal{F}$ **do**
   $\min \leftarrow d(l, i_1)$;
   $c \leftarrow 1$;
   for $j = 2$ **to** k **do**
      if $d(l, i_1) < \min$ **then**
         $\min \leftarrow d(l, i_j)$;
         $c \leftarrow j$;
   $C_c \leftarrow C_c \cup f_l$;

The objective of γ-OR is to simultaneously minimize the number of selected objectives k and the γ value, with γ falling within the interval [0,1] due to the range of $d(i,j)$. As with δ-OR and η-OR, the two objectives of γ-OR may conflict with each other to some degree. Moreover, according to Eq. (4.4), the maximum value of k (i.e., $k = |\mathcal{F}_0|$) corresponds to the minimum possible value of γ (i.e., $\gamma = 0$). This implies that selecting all objectives in $\mathcal{F}_0$ would result in the optimal γ value, while choosing fewer objectives may lead to a higher γ value.

4.3.3 Using multiobjective evolutionary algorithms

To apply MOEAs to solve the MOP formulated by δ-OR, η-OR, or γ-OR, it's necessary to represent the candidate solutions as chromosomes and encode them accordingly. In this chapter, we use a binary string with m bits to represent the solution, where m is the size of the original objective set $|\mathcal{F}_0|$. Fig. 4.3 illustrates the chromosome representation, with each binary bit encoding a single objective. A value of "1" indicates that the objective is selected, while a value of "0" implies that it's excluded from the solution.

Using the representation described previously, any MOEA can generate Pareto optimal objective subsets for each of the three formulated MOPs. In this study, we employ a popular MOEA called NSGA-II [27]. The objective reduction process using NSGA-II can be summarized as follows: starting with the original objective set $\mathcal{F}_0$, the sample set $\mathcal{N}$, and the formulated MOP (δ-OR, η-OR, or γ-OR), the algorithm generates an initial population of N chromosomes randomly. These chromosomes are then evaluated based on their fitness, and the nondominated solutions are selected as parents for the next generation. The algorithm then applies genetic operators, such as crossover and mutation, to create a new population. This process is repeated until the termination criteria are met, and the resulting Pareto front represents the optimal objective subset for the given MOP. By using NSGA-II for objective reduction, we can efficiently identify the most important objectives while minimizing computational complexity.

The algorithm proceeds through a series of iterations until the maximum number of generations specified by the stopping criterion is reached. At each generation g, the current population P_g undergoes binary tournament selection [27], single-point crossover [28], and bit flip mutation [28] to produce offspring population Q_g. The best N chromosomes from the union population U_g are then selected as the next population

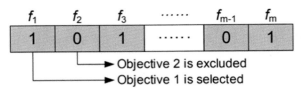

Figure 4.3 Representation of chromosome as a binary string.

$P_g + 1$ using fast nondominated sorting and crowding distance. Additionally, it's important to note that $k = 0$ holds no significance in objective reduction. Therefore, when $k = 0$ for a chromosome in the proposed multiobjective approaches, its two objective values are immediately set to $+\infty$. This ensures that such chromosomes are easily eliminated during elitist selection, streamlining the objective reduction process.

To distinguish between the NSGA-II-based objective reduction algorithms resulting from the δ-OR, η-OR, and γ-OR formulations, we refer to them as NSGA-II-δ, NSGA-II-η, and NSGA-II-γ, respectively. This naming convention helps to differentiate between the different algorithms and ensures clarity in discussions and comparisons.

4.3.4 Why multiobjective approaches

The advantages of employing multiobjective approaches for objective reduction stem from two primary factors. Firstly, objective reduction is inherently a multiobjective task, and reducing the number of objectives is typically a desirable outcome. Secondly, multiobjective approaches enable the consideration of multiple criteria or objectives simultaneously, which can provide a more comprehensive understanding of the problem and lead to improved decision-making.

Reducing the number of objectives comes with a trade-off between computational efficiency and the risk of losing problem information since the given sample set is only an approximation of the Pareto front. Therefore, when determining a reduced objective set, the user must make a compromise between these conflicting aspects. This application scenario can be naturally modeled as an MOP. In each of our multiobjective formulations, the first objective (k) represents the size of the objective subset, while the second objective (δ, η or γ) measures the degree of risk in a specific way.

In addition to reducing the number of objectives, multiobjective approaches can also provide a set of estimated Pareto optimal objective subsets. By analyzing these subsets, the user can gain a deeper understanding of the objective reduction problem and make more informed decisions when selecting a final reduced objective set. To illustrate this further, we establish the relationship between NSGA-II-δ and the work presented in [6] using the following theorem.

Theorem 1:
Assuming a sample set $\mathcal{N}$, let $PF_\delta = \{(k_j, \delta_j)^T \mid j = 1{:}\kappa\}$ represent the Pareto front of the δ-OR problem. From this, we can derive the following solutions:

The δ-MOSS problem has a solution denoted by δ_0, which corresponds to any objective subset that can be represented by $(k_\mu, \delta_\mu)^T$, where

$$\mu = \operatorname*{argmax}_{j} \left\{ \delta_j \mid \delta_j \leq \delta_0, j = 1{:}\kappa \right\} \tag{4.5}$$

The k-EMOSS problem has a solution denoted by k_0, which corresponds to any objective subset that can be represented by $(k_\nu, \delta_\nu)^T$, where

$$\nu = \underset{j}{\mathrm{argmax}} \left\{ k_j \mid k_j \le k_0, j = 1{:}\kappa \right\} \tag{4.6}$$

Theorem 1 suggests that NSGA-II-δ can derive solutions for all conceivable δ-MOSS and k-EMOSS problems associated with a given sample set $\mathcal{N}$ in a single simulation run. This implies that NSGA-II-δ can provide the essential information for decision support in one fell swoop, potentially saving time and resources. In contrast to [6], where a simulation run of the algorithm is focused on a single δ-MOSS problem (given by δ_0) or k-EMOSS problem (given by k_0), and where heuristic algorithms are used to address these problems separately, NSGA-II-δ can obtain solutions for all possible δ-MOSS and k-EMOSS problems related to a given sample set $\mathcal{N}$ in a single simulation run.

It's worth noting that Theorem 1, along with the definitions of δ-MOSS and k-EMOSS, can be extended to other types of errors, such as η and γ. However, for the sake of simplicity, the terms "δ-MOSS" and "k-EMOSS" are still used regardless of the type of error being used.

4.4 Analysis of dominance structure- and correlation-based approaches

In this section, we introduce a series of theorems related to objective reduction. Using these theorems, we analyze the dominance structure-based and correlation-based approaches to identifying the essential objective set. It's worth noting that this analysis also applies to the proposed multiobjective approaches, since they are fundamentally based on the dominance structure or correlation.

4.4.1 Theoretical foundations

To effectively reduce objectives, it is crucial to have a thorough understanding of both the original Pareto front and the corresponding Pareto front associated with a given objective subset. The following theorem establishes the connection between these two fronts, providing valuable insights into the objective reduction process.

Lemma 1:
Let PF' be the Pareto front corresponding to an objective subset $\mathcal{F}' \subseteq \mathcal{F}_0$, then $PF' \subseteq \{\mathbf{u}^{(\mathcal{F}')} \mid \mathbf{u} \in PF_0\}$.

This principle enables the determination of whether a given objective subset is redundant or not.

Theorem 2:
An objective subset $\mathcal{F} \subset \mathcal{F}_0$ is redundant, if $\nexists \mathbf{u}, \mathbf{v} \in PF_0 : \mathbf{u}^{(\mathcal{F}')} < \mathbf{v}^{(\mathcal{F}')}$, where $\mathcal{F}' := \mathcal{F}_0 \backslash \mathcal{F}$.

The relationship between two objective subsets can be used to determine whether a given subset is redundant, as shown by Theorem 3. It should be noted that the condition provided in Theorem 3 is sufficient but not necessary for "redundancy," which differs from the condition in Theorem 2. This means that if subset F is redundant, there may not exist an objective subset $\mathcal{F}'$ satisfying $\forall \mathbf{u}, \mathbf{v} \in PF_0: \mathbf{u}^{(\mathcal{F}')} \preccurlyeq \mathbf{v}^{(\mathcal{F}')} \Rightarrow \mathbf{u}^{(\mathcal{F})} \preccurlyeq \mathbf{v}^{(\mathcal{F})}$.

Theorem 3:

Given two nonempty objective subsets $\mathcal{F}$, $\mathcal{F}' \subset \mathcal{F}_0$ and $\mathcal{F} \cap \mathcal{F}' = \varnothing$, if $\forall \mathbf{u}, \mathbf{v} \in PF_0: \mathbf{u}^{(\mathcal{F}')} \preccurlyeq \mathbf{v}^{(\mathcal{F}')} \Rightarrow \mathbf{u}^{(\mathcal{F})} \preccurlyeq \mathbf{v}^{(\mathcal{F})}$ then $\mathcal{F}$ is redundant.

The relationship between "nonconflicting" and "redundant" concepts can be established through a corollary derived from Theorem 3.

Corollary 1:

Given two objectives $f_i, f_j \in \mathcal{F}_0$, if f_i and f_j are nonconflicting, then $\{f_i\}$ and $\{f_j\}$ are both redundant.

In Section 4.4.3, the principle and limitation of correlation-based approaches will be demonstrated through the use of Theorem 3 and Corollary 1.

We present a theorem regarding the multiobjective formulation η-OR, which will be utilized to showcase the effectiveness of dominance structure-based approaches at a later stage.

Theorem 4:

Given a sample set $\mathcal{N}:=PF_0$ and $|PF_0| < +\infty$, PF_η denotes the Pareto front of η-OR problem. Then $k^* \in \mathbb{N}: (k^*, 0)^T \in PF_\eta$ and any objective subset corresponding to $(k^*, 0)^T$ is an essential objective set for the given MOP.

4.4.2 Strengths and limitations of dominance structure-based approaches

The examination of the dominance relation in the sample set with respect to every objective subset can reveal an essential objective set, as implied by Theorem 2. Dominance structure-based approaches utilize this characteristic to guide the algorithm design. The main difference among these approaches lies in the method used to measure the degree of violation of the condition in Theorem 2. This allows for algorithm mechanisms that are well-suited to the nature of objective reduction. In theory, a basic dominance structure-based algorithm can accurately identify the essential objective set on all problems given sufficient computation time, as long as the sample set $\mathcal{N}$ provides a perfect Pareto front-representation. For example, in the case of η-OR, Theorem 4 ensures that the vector $(k^*, 0)^T$, corresponding to an essential objective, is included in PF_η under the most ideal condition where N is equal to the Pareto front PF_0.

It is often unrealistic to expect $\mathcal{N}$ to provide a perfect Pareto front-representation, which can cause dominance structure-based approaches to fail in capturing the true dimensionality of PF_0. This is primarily because it is challenging to determine whether some solutions represent misdirection by only relying on the mutual dominance relationship. To elaborate on this further, let us examine the criteria δ and η. Consider the following scenario where $\mathcal{N} = \{\mathbf{u}_0, \mathbf{u}_1, \ldots, \mathbf{u}_{2n-1}, \mathbf{u}_{2n}\}$ for the criterion δ, where

$$
\mathbf{u}_i = \begin{cases}
\left(10^{-6}, 2n, 0\right)^{\mathrm{T}}, & i = 0 \\
(i, 2n - i, i)^{\mathrm{T}}, & i = 1:n \\
(i, 2n - i, 3n - i)^{\mathrm{T}}, & i = n + 1:2n - 1 \\
(0, 2n, +\infty)^{\mathrm{T}} & i = 2n
\end{cases}
\tag{4.7}
$$

In this case, the solution $\mathbf{u}_{2n}$ may represent misdirection as it is an outlier. Ignoring $\mathbf{u}_{2n}$ would lead to the identification of $\{f_1, f_2\}$ as a unique essential objective set, since the dominance structure remains unchanged with respect to the $f_1 - f_2$ objective subspace. However, the computation of δ cannot automatically ignore $\mathbf{u}_{2n}$ and involves all solutions in N. This results in the δ error of $\{f_1, f_2\}$ tending toward positive infinity by considering the dominance relation between $\mathbf{u}_0$ and $\mathbf{u}_{2n}$, disqualifying $\{f_1, f_2\}$ from becoming an essential objective set. Regarding criterion η, let us consider the 3-objective WFG3 as an example. The projections of a sample set $\mathcal{N}$ (including $\mathcal{N}_{NS}$ and $\mathcal{N}_{DS}$) onto the $f_2 - f_3$ objective space is shown in Fig. 4.4. The value of η for $\{f_2, f_3\}$ is 0.52, which is a significant proportion. This suggests that it is not safe to assume that the solutions in $\mathcal{N}_{DS}$ represent misdirection due to the large η error. Consequently, $\{f_2, f_3\}$ would not be identified as an essential objective set, which contradicts the intuition presented in Fig. 4.4. The issue stems from the fact that although $\mathcal{N}_{DS}$ constitutes a significant proportion of $\mathcal{N}$, most of its objective vectors are very close to those in $\mathcal{N}_{NS}$ and can be interpreted as misdirection. In summary, a major limitation of dominance structure-based approaches is their inability to effectively handle varying degrees of misdirection in the sample set.

A limitation of dominance structure-based approaches is their tendency to oversimplify the objectives if the sample set $\mathcal{N}$ does not adequately cover the Pareto front PF_0. This occurrence is more probable when the dimensionality of PF_0 is 15 and the

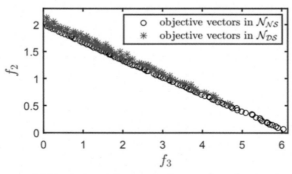

Figure 4.4 The projection of $\mathcal{N}$ (including $\mathcal{N}_{NS}$ and $\mathcal{N}_{DS}$) on $f_2 - f_3$ objective three-objective WFG3.

size and diversity of $\mathcal{N}$ are limited, leading to its distribution being confined to only a portion of PF_0. Because of the insufficient representation of PF_0, the solutions in $\mathcal{N}$ may also be mutually nondominated in an objective subset $\mathcal{F}$ that corresponds to a lower-dimensional (e.g., 10-dimensional) objective subspace. As a result, the associated error (e.g., δ or η) of $\mathcal{F}$ may have already reached its minimum value of 0, and since the size of F ($|\mathcal{F}|$) is less than 15, the dominance structure-based approaches may prioritize selecting $\mathcal{F}$ as the essential objective set, resulting in an unsuccessful identification.

Furthermore, the computational complexity of dominance structure-based approaches is primarily determined by the analysis of the dominance relationship between each pair of solutions. In contrast, correlation-based approaches primarily rely on leveraging the correlation relationship between objective pairs to determine computational complexity. Because the number of solutions ($|\mathcal{N}|$) is typically much greater than the number of objectives (m), dominance structure-based approaches are generally much more computationally expensive than correlation-based approaches.

4.4.3 Strengths and limitations of correlation-based approaches

Compared to dominance structure-based approaches, correlation-based approaches are better equipped to handle misdirection in a sample set. This is because correlation only considers the overall trend between objectives, without taking into account the relationship between specific solutions, which is what dominance structure-based approaches do. As a result, correlation-based approaches can effectively neutralize the impact of misdirection. An example of this can be seen in the computation of Kendall's rank correlation matrix based on $\mathcal{N}$ shown in Fig. 4.4 is computed as follows:

$$r_\tau = \begin{pmatrix} 1 & 0.901 & -0.943 \\ 0.901 & 1 & -0.952 \\ -0.943 & -0.952 & 1 \end{pmatrix} \qquad (4.8)$$

Upon examining the correlation matrix, it can be inferred that there exists a strong positive correlation between f_1 and f_2, signifying their nonconflicting nature. However, both f_1 and f_2 display a strong negative correlation with f_3, indicating a conflicting relationship between these objectives. Therefore we can deduce that $\{f_1\}$ and $\{f_2\}$ are redundant, while $\{f_2, f_3\}$ and $\{f_1, f_3\}$ are both essential objective sets. This conclusion is in agreement with the actual Pareto front of the three-objective WFG3 problem. Remember that it is challenging to use the η criterion to identify an essential objective set in this scenario. This emphasizes the effectiveness of correlation-based methods in dealing with the misguidance issue. Given their superior computational efficiency, coupled with the aforementioned advantage, correlation-based techniques seem to be a more favorable option compared to dominance structure-based methods for implementing online objective reduction in MOEA iterations. Unlike dominance structure-based methods, correlation-based methods not only identify the essential objective set but also determine which objectives are conflicting and nonconflicting. This additional information can be valuable for decision-makers.

The primary constraint of correlation-based methods is that they may not be entirely consistent with the original objective reduction objectives when reducing objectives using correlation analysis. Correlation-based techniques utilize correlation coefficients to evaluate the degree of conflict between each pair of objectives and to retain highly conflicting objectives while eliminating nonconflicting ones. Corollary 1 provides support for the validity of correlation-based methods in this regard. However, Theorem 3 indicates that an objective's redundancy may be caused by its relationship with a subset of objectives rather than a single objective. Nevertheless, conflict or correlation can only capture the relationship between two objectives. To exemplify this, we append a third objective $f_3 = f_1 + f_2$ to the widely used 2-objective DTLZ2 [29] problem and obtain an almost perfect sample set for this modified problem using NSGA-II. Fig. 4.5 illustrates the sample set projections on the objective subspaces $f_1 - f_2, f_1 - f_3$, and $f_2 - f_3$.

Using this sample set, the Kendall's rank correlation matrix is computed as follows:

$$r_\tau = \begin{pmatrix} 1 & -1 & -0.016 \\ -1 & 1 & 0.016 \\ -0.016 & 0.016 & 1 \end{pmatrix} \tag{4.9}$$

Eq. (4.9) indicates that f_1 and f_2 exhibit strong conflict, whereas f_3 appears to be neither conflicting nor nonconflicting with either of them since $r_\tau(1, 3)$ and $r_\tau(2, 3)$ are both very close to zero. Therefore correlation analysis cannot safely eliminate f_3. Nevertheless, by utilizing $f_3 = f_1 + f_2$ and Theorem 3, it can be established that $\{f_3\}$ is

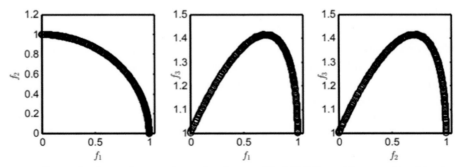

Figure 4.5 The projections of a sample set for the modified DTLZ2 problem on the objective subspaces $f_1 - f_2, f_1 - f_3$ and $f_2 - f_3$.

actually redundant. In fact, by examining Fig. 4.5 and utilizing Theorem 2, it can be deduced that $\{f_3\}$ is the only redundant objective set, and $\{f_1,f_2\}$ is the sole essential objective set for this problem.

Saxena et al. [3] pointed out that in certain cases, correlation-based approaches may produce inaccurate results when the misdirection interpreted is the signal. To illustrate this issue, they created an artificial problem depicted in Fig. 4.6, where f_1 and f_3 are globally correlated but locally conflicting, and the latter is not significant enough. Nonetheless, this potential side effect is not an inherent limitation of correlation-based approaches, as any algorithm capable of handling misdirection would inevitably encounter this problem. To mitigate this issue, one approach is to set a lower error tolerance. For instance, in the case of objectives f_1 and f_3 in Fig. 4.6, assuming that two objectives are considered nonconflicting only when the correlation coefficient is greater than 0.7, accurate results can still be obtained, albeit at the expense of sacrificing some of the ability to handle misdirection. The correlation coefficient r_τ (1,3) = 0.652 for the objectives f_1 and f_3 in Fig. 4.6.

To sum up, while correlation-based approaches may not be able to precisely identify the essential objective set on all problems, their aforementioned advantages have contributed to their popularity in objective reduction. This is evidenced by the fact that most of the existing studies, as illustrated in Table 4.1, have focused on correlation-based methods.

4.5 Benchmark experiments

This section begins by outlining several experimental design conditions, such as the benchmark problems employed, the generation of sample sets, and the algorithms utilized for comparison purposes. Following this, comprehensive experiments and comparisons are performed on various benchmark problems, with a focus on three distinct facets.

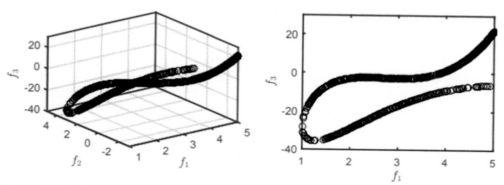

Figure 4.6 A high-quality sample set obtained for the spline problem: $f_1 = x^2 + 1$, $f_2 = -x^2 + x + 3$ and $f_3 = -(f_1 + f_2{}^3)$, where $x \in [-2,2]$, and its projection on the $f_1 - f_3$ objective subspace.

4.5.1 Benchmark problems

To evaluate how objective reduction algorithms perform, we use five distinct test problems in our experiments, each with different numbers of objectives and dimensions. These problems consist of three established benchmark problems, namely DTLZ5(I,m) [3,30], WFG3(m) [15,16], and DTLZ2(m) [29], as well as two newly created problems based on DTLZ2(m), specifically POW-DTLZ2(p,m) and SUM-DTLZ2(m). Detailed descriptions of each problem can be found below.

1. DTLZ5(I,m) is a problem that was developed from the scalable DTLZ5(m) [29]. In DTLZ5(I,m), I is the dimensionality of the Pareto front, while m represents the original number of objectives for the problem. The first $m - I + 1$ objectives over the Pareto front are free from conflicts with each other. An essential objective set for the problem can be defined as $\mathcal{F}_\mathcal{T} = \{f_l, f_{m-I+2}, \ldots, f_m\}$, where l is an integer belonging to the set $\{1, 2, \ldots, m - I + 1\}$.

2. WFG3(m) is a problem in multiobjective optimization that involves m objectives, and its corresponding Pareto front has a dimensionality of 2. All of the objectives over the Pareto front, except for f_m, are independent of one another and do not interfere with each other's optimization. Consequently, a crucial set of objectives can be defined as $\mathcal{F}_\mathcal{T} = \{f_l, f_m\}$, where l is an integer belonging to the set $\in \{1, 2, \ldots, m - 1\}$. This set comprises f_m, which is dependent on the other objectives, and a single independent objective from the set of nonconflicting objectives.

3. DTLZ2(m) is a problem with m objectives that is nonredundant, and every objective is essential. Therefore the essential objective set can be defined as $\mathcal{F}_\mathcal{T} = \{f_1, f_2, \ldots, f_m\}$, which includes all m objectives.

4. The purpose of utilizing POW-DTLZ2(p,m) is to evaluate the effectiveness of objective reduction algorithms in dealing with significant nonlinearity. The problem is created by incorporating m new objectives into DTLZ2(m), resulting in a total of $2m$ objectives. The initial m objectives are the same as those in DTLZ2(m), while the following m objectives are expressed as $f_{m+j} = f_j^p$, where $j = 1{:}m$. An essential objective set can be defined as $\mathcal{F}_\mathcal{T} = \{f_{l_1}, f_{l_2}, \ldots, f_{l_m}\}$, where l_j belongs to the set $\{j, m + j\}$ for $j = 1{:}m$.

5. SUM-DTLZ2(m) is developed to uncover any potential constraints of utilizing correlation-based methods, while also highlighting the advantages of utilizing dominance structure-based approaches in specific scenarios. As with POW-DTLZ2(p,m), the initial m objectives of this problem are derived from DTLZ2(m). The remaining $(m(m - 1))/2$ objectives are generated by taking the sum of each pair of distinct objectives in $\{f_1, f_2, \ldots, f_m\}$. Therefore the total number of objectives in SUM-DTLZ2(m) is $(m(m + 1))/2$. The essential objective set for this problem is defined as $\mathcal{F}_\mathcal{T} = \{f_1, f_2, \ldots, f_m\}$.

For all problems, except for WFG3(m), the number of decision variables is determined by a parameter p, where $n = m + p - 1$. To ensure consistency with the recommendations in [29], we have set the parameter p to 10 for all problems, except for WFG3(m). For WFG3(m), we have set the number of decision variables to 28, and the position-related parameter is defined as $m - 1$.

4.5.2 Generation of sample sets

The performance of these algorithms is significantly influenced by the quality of the sample set used. Despite its importance, the impact of sample set quality on objective reduction has not yet received significant attention in the literature, except for Saxena et al.'s [3] work. In this study, the performance of the proposed algorithms was evaluated using four distinct sample sets, each with varying levels of quality. For our experimental analysis, we utilized two distinct sample sets, $\mathcal{N}_1$ and $\mathcal{N}_2$, for each test instance. Each of these sample sets comprises 30 different sets, which were generated using a SPEA2 variant known as SPEA2-SDE [31]. The sample sets were generated using the same number of generations for each of the 30 independent repetitions conducted. Generating sample set $\mathcal{N}_2$ requires significantly more computational resources, with a requirement of 2000 generations, as compared to $\mathcal{N}_1$, which only requires 200 generations. However, $\mathcal{N}_2$ generates a high-quality Pareto front-representation, while $\mathcal{N}_1$ is associated with more challenges due to the misdirection that stems from its lower quality. Therefore the algorithms must overcome greater difficulties when working with $\mathcal{N}_1$. It is worth noting that, unlike in [3], we did not analyze a randomly generated sample set or a sample set that was uniformly distributed across the actual Pareto front, as the implications of these scenarios are self-evident.

Similar to [3], we evaluated the quality of $\mathcal{N}_1$ and $\mathcal{N}_2$ using the problem parameter g (convergence, except for WFG3) and the normalized maximum spread indicator I_s (diversity) [32]. A value of g closer to 0 and a value of I_s closer to 1 indicate better convergence and diversity, respectively. For $\mathcal{N}_1$ and $\mathcal{N}_2$, we obtained the following average values for g and I_s: (1) $\mathcal{N}_1$: g = 0.213 and $I_s = 1.636$; (2) $\mathcal{N}_2$: $g = 0.019$ and $I_s = 1.044$. As can be observed, the average g value of $\mathcal{N}_1$ is significantly larger than that of $\mathcal{N}_2$, indicating a clear difference in the quality of these sample sets.

4.5.3 Algorithms in comparison

In addition to the proposed multiobjective approaches, we also compared several other objective reduction algorithms. Table 4.2 presents their respective short names, categories, and brief descriptions. All of the algorithms were implemented in Java and executed on an Intel 3.20 GHz Xeon processor with 16.0 GB of RAM.

Table 4.2 List of other algorithms in comparison.

Name	Category	Description
ExactAlg [6]	C1	An exact algorithm for both δ-MOSS and k-EMOSS
Greedy-δ [6]	C1	A greedy algorithm for δ-MOSS
Greedy-k [6]	C1	A greedy algorithm for k-EMOSS
L-PCA [3]	C2	An algorithm based on principal component analysis
NL-MVU-PCA [3]	C2	An algorithm based on maximum variance unfolding

C1: Dominance structure-based approaches.
C2: Correlation-based approaches.

Table 4.3 Parameters in the proposed multiobjective approaches (NSGA-II-δ, NSGA-II-η, and NSGA-II-γ).

Parameter	Value
Population size	$5m$
Maximum	$\lfloor 2.5m \rfloor$
Crossover probability	0.9
Mutation probability	$1/m$

Due to its unsuitability for large-scale instances, ExactAlg was unable to produce results for some of the experiments. In [6], two greedy algorithms were proposed for solving the k-EMOSS problem. In this study, Greedy-k refers to the algorithm that operates by omitting objectives. For the proposed multiobjective approaches, we have utilized the parameter values listed in Table 4.3. In this table, m represents the number of objectives present in the problem to be reduced. It should be noted that an exhaustive search approach could be employed for smaller instances, where $m \leq 10$. However, for the sake of consistency, we chose to apply the evolutionary multiobjective search to all instances considered in this study.

Before executing ExactAlg, Greedy-δ, Greedy-k, and NSGA-II-δ, we first normalized the objective values of the sample set to fall within the range of [0, 1] in each dimension. This is because one of the underlying assumptions of δ error is that all objective values are on the same scale [6].

4.5.4 Investigation of the behavior of multiobjective approaches

The objective reduction problem is tackled using multiobjective approaches that yield multiple nondominated objective subsets, each accompanied by its respective errors. These subsets can be instrumental in aiding decision-making, thereby providing valuable decision support to the user. As an illustration, Table 4.4 displays the outcome obtained by NSGA-II-δ when applied to a sample set of DTLZ5(3, 20) that corresponds to $\mathcal{N}_1$. The data presented in Table 4.4 indicates that reducing the size of the

Table 4.4 The result of NSGA-II-δ for a sample set of DTLZ5(3, 20) corresponding $\mathcal{N}_1$.

k	δ	Objective set
1	1	$\{f_i\}, i = 6, 13, 15, 16, 19, 20$
2	0.997	$\{f_{19}, f_{20}\}$
3	0.255	$\{f_{13}, f_{19}, f_{20}\}$
4	0.133	$\{f_{11}, f_{16}, f_{19}, f_{20}\}$
5	0.053	$\{f_{11}, f_{15}, f_{16}, f_{19}, f_{20}\}$
6	0	$\{f_9, f_{13}, f_{15}, f_{16}, f_{19}, f_{20}\}$
6	0	$\{f_{11}, f_{15}, f_{16}, f_{18}, f_{19}, f_{20}\}$
6	0	$\{f_9, f_{13}, f_{16}, f_{17}, f_{19}, f_{20}\}$

objective set results in a larger error. Therefore users must weigh the pros and cons when selecting a preferred objective set. For instance, when opting for $\{f_{13}, f_{19}, f_{20}\}$ as the reduced objective set, the user must take into account whether an error of $\delta = 0.225$ is acceptable or not, given the specific context of the application.

Fig. 4.7 offers a more lucid representation of how the error diminishes as the number of objectives increases, as observed in the results obtained by NSGA-II-δ, NSGA-II-η, and NSGA-II-γ. To illustrate this point, we have utilized four DTLZ5(I, 20) instances, and the obtained results are presented for both $\mathcal{N}_1$ and $\mathcal{N}_2$. Each chart in Fig. 4.7 plots the number of selected objectives (k) against the corresponding error value ($\delta, \eta,$ or γ) obtained from the k–EMOSS problem. The error values are averaged across 30 sample sets in $\mathcal{N}_1$ or $\mathcal{N}_2$ and are directly obtained from the results of the multiobjective approaches, as specified in Theorem 1. The horizontal axis represents k, while the vertical axis represents the error value.

Drawing insights from Fig. 4.7 can help gain a better understanding of the multiobjective approaches' behavior. The following observations can be made:

1. The behavior of error variations differs across NSGA-II-δ, NSGA-II-η, and NSGA-II-γ. This discrepancy is expected, given that the three types of errors carry distinct implications.

2. In most scenarios, all three multiobjective approaches obtain a relatively small error value when $k = |\mathcal{F}_T|$. This observation lends some support to the validity of the three error types.

3. In the case of $\mathcal{N}_2$, the error values displayed by the multiobjective approaches generally exhibit a steep decline at $k = |\mathcal{F}_T| - 1$, and eventually reach a very small value at $k = |\mathcal{F}_T|$. This characteristic can be exploited to identify the essential objective set with ease. However, in the case of $\mathcal{N}_1$, this phenomenon is not as apparent, indicating that identifying the essential objective set would be relatively more challenging.

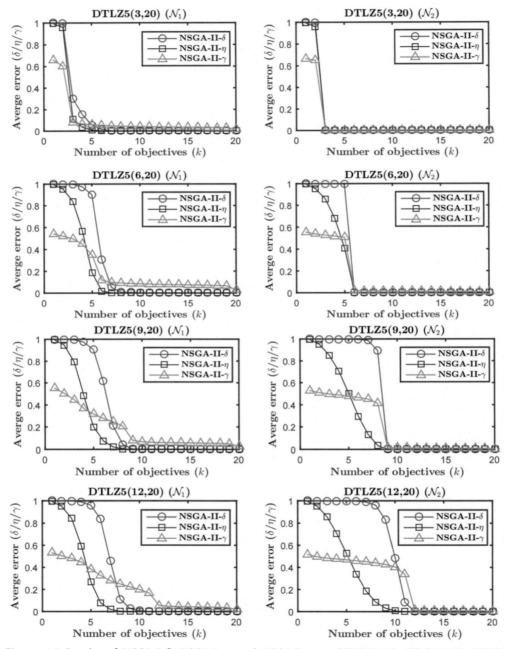

Figure 4.7 Results of NSGA-II-δ, NSGA-II-η, and NSGA-II-γ on DTLZ5(3,20), DTLZ5(6,20), DTLZ5 (9,20), and DTLZ5(12,20), corresponding to $\mathcal{N}_1$ and. $\mathcal{N}_2$. The error for each point is averaged over 30 sample sets in $\mathcal{N}_1$ or $\mathcal{N}_2$.

4. Except for DTLZ5(3, 20), the error value η in NSGA-II-η decreases almost exponentially to 0 as k increases. Furthermore, in most cases, the error value has already fallen to a sufficiently small value before k reaches $|\mathcal{F}_T|$. This behavior is markedly different from the other two types of errors. One possible explanation for this behavior is that, as the dimensionality of the problem increases, the number of nondominated solutions in the sample set grows exponentially. Consequently, the cardinality of $\mathcal{N}_{DS}$ may become insufficient in capturing the actual degree of dominance structure change in the Pareto front. Given this observation, we recommend that the tolerable value for the error η should be smaller for larger k values, to mitigate the effects of the curse of dimensionality.

Table 4.5 displays the average computation time for each run of NSGA-II-δ, NSGA-II-η, and NSGA-II-γ. The results indicate that the dominance structure-based algorithms, NSGA-II-δ and NSGA-II-η, require significantly more computational effort than the correlation-based algorithm, NSGA-II-γ.

4.5.5 Effectiveness of evolutionary multiobjective search

NSGA-II-δ, ExactAlg, and Greedy-δ (also known as Greedy-k) are algorithms that use the δ error metric to evaluate changes in dominance structure. However, each algorithm differs in its search methods. In this section, we conduct a comparative analysis of NSGA-II-δ, ExactAlg, and Greedy-δ (Greedy-k) in solving δ-MOSS or k-EMOSS problems to demonstrate the efficacy of evolutionary multiobjective search.

As an example, we will continue to use the four test cases that were utilized in Section 4.5.4 for illustration. To conduct our analysis, we select one sample set from a pool of 30 in $\mathcal{N}_1$ for each test case. The sample set chosen corresponds to the result that is closest to the average convergence metric. We then proceed to vary the value of δ_0 from 0 to 0.6, with an increment of 0.05, and k_0 from 1 to 20, with an increment of 1. This results in a total of 13 δ-MOSS problems and all related k-EMOSS problems being considered.

The comparison results for the considered algorithms on both the δ-MOSS problems and k-EMOSS problems are presented in Fig. 4.8. From the observations made in Fig. 4.8, it can be seen that the results obtained by NSGA-II-δ match perfectly with those of ExactAlg. This implies that NSGA-II-δ has successfully obtained optimal solutions for all the considered δ-MOSS and k-EMOSS problems. In terms of performance, the greedy algorithms (Greedy-δ and Greedy-k) are unable to obtain optimal

Table 4.5 The average computation time (in seconds) for each run on four considered DTLZ5(i, 20) instances.

NSGA-II-δ	NSGA-II-η	NSGA-II-γ
4.45	4.59	0.12

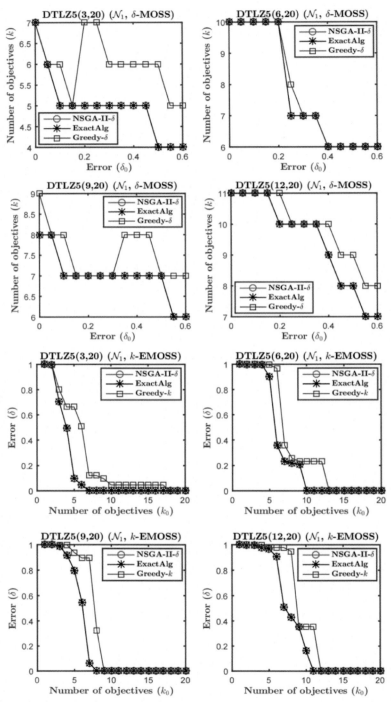

Figure 4.8 Comparison of NSGA-II-δ, ExactAlg, and Greedy-δ (Greedy-**k**) for the δ-MOSS or **k**-EMOSS problem.

solutions in certain scenarios and consistently underperform when compared to NSGA-II-δ in other cases. A specific instance where the performance of Greedy-k is inferior to NSGA-II-δ can be observed in the results obtained for the sample set of DTLZ5(3, 20). Out of the total of 20 k-EMOSS problems, Greedy-k produces worse δ values than NSGA-II-δ in 15 of them and only matches the results achieved by NSGA-II-δ in the remaining 5 cases. In addition, when addressing the δ-MOSS problem, it is expected that the number of objectives obtained should not increase as the value of δ_0 increases. However, this is not always the case for Greedy-δ, as it may only converge to a locally optimal solution that is dependent on the given δ_0. This highlights the importance of conducting a global search, as is done in NSGA-II-δ.

Table 4.6 presents the computation times required by NSGA-II-δ, ExactAlg, and Greedy-k for solving all the related k-EMOS problems. Additionally, it provides the average computation time required by Greedy-δ to solve a particular δ-MOSS problem. The results presented in Table 4.6 indicate that NSGA-II-δ requires significantly less time than ExactAlg to solve all four sample sets of the test instances considered. The computation time required by ExactAlg may not be practical, as it can take up to 4 h to solve the sample set of DTLZ5(12,20). When compared to Greedy-k, NSGA-II-δ also demonstrates a shorter computation time, usually taking only a few seconds less, across all test instances. Although Greedy-δ requires less time than NSGA-II-δ, it is important to note that Greedy-δ only solves a specific δ-MOSS problem in this context, while NSGA-II-δ is capable of providing solutions to all δ-MOSS problems (which are infinite in number) in a single run.

Based on the observations made above, it can be concluded that evolutionary multiobjective search algorithms can achieve results that are comparable to those obtained with global exact search, but with a significant advantage in terms of computational efficiency. Moreover, these algorithms demonstrate superior performance when compared to greedy search, achieving better results in both effectiveness and efficiency.

4.5.6 Comparison in identifying the essential objective set

The effectiveness of the proposed multiobjective approaches is demonstrated by comparing them with ExactAlg, Greedy-δ, L-PCA, and NL-MVU-PCA in identifying

Table 4.6 Comparison of the computational time (in seconds) of (NSGA-II-δ, exactalg, Greedy-k, and Greedy-δ.

Test instance	NSGA-II-δ[a]	ExactAlg[a]	Greedy-k[a]	Greedy-δ[b]
DTLZ5(5,20)	3.19	5280.79	7.16	0.17
DTLZ5(6,20)	3.80	1533.35	7.55	0.21
DTLZ5(9,20)	4.71	11,588.49	7.59	0.20
DTLZ5(12,20)	5.15	14,491.03	7.12	0.26

[a]The computational time for all related k-EMOSS problems.
[b]The average computational time for a specific δ-MOSS problem.

the essential objective set. The multiobjective approaches are capable of providing several nondominated objective subsets that can aid in decision-making. However, for comparison, a single objective subset must be chosen as the essential objective set. In practical applications, the obtained Pareto front of objective subsets for a specific problem can be visually examined to identify the most suitable objective subset. For the sake of simplicity, we select the solution to a given δ-MOSS problem, where the error threshold (δ_0, η_0, or γ_0) is predetermined and kept constant for all the test instances. This approach avoids the need for visual inspection and allows for a more straightforward comparison between the different algorithms. The value of η_0 is reduced by an empirical factor of $\sqrt{3}$ as k increases from 2. This adjustment is made to counteract the effect of the exponentially increasing number of nondominated solutions in higher-dimensional objective spaces.

Determining the appropriate threshold value is a crucial issue. If the threshold value is set too low, the algorithm may not possess the necessary capability to handle misdirection. An example of the consequences of setting the threshold value too low can be observed in [3]. In this case, the value of δ for ExactAlg and Greedy-δ is fixed at 0, resulting in poor performance on sample sets with misdirection, as reported by Saxena et al. [3]. On the other hand, if the threshold value is set too high, we may inadvertently omit essential objectives in many scenarios. For instance, if we set γ_0 to 0.3, it would imply that two objectives can be deemed nonconflicting once the correlation coefficient between them reaches 0.4. Such a high threshold value is unreliable and may result in the exclusion of important objectives. Drawing from our experience with a variety of problems and sample sets of varying quality, we recommend using threshold values within the range of [0.1, 0.2]. This range of values is typically effective in enabling the algorithm to handle moderate levels of misdirection while also enabling reliable identification in various scenarios. Fig. 4.9 examines the impact of $\delta_0/\eta_0/\gamma_0 \in [0.1, 0.2]$ on the performance of multiobjective approaches. The performance is measured in terms of the frequency of successful identification of the essential objective set out of 30 runs. The graphical representation in Fig. 4.9 suggests that the performance of each algorithm displays a noteworthy level of stability. Furthermore, the relative superiority or inferiority of the algorithms appears to remain consistent across the entire range of threshold values under consideration. It is important to note that only four cases are presented in Fig. 4.9 due to space constraints. However, similar trends are observed in the other cases as well. Additionally, we have discovered that the algorithms' performance becomes much less sensitive to the threshold values in the case of $\mathcal{N}_2$. To ensure a fair comparison among the three multiobjective algorithms, ExactAlg, and Greedy-δ, we have set the same threshold value of 0.15 for all these algorithms in the subsequent experiments. Regarding L-PCA and NL-MVU-PCA, we have set the variance threshold θ to 0.997. Additionally, the correlation threshold T_{cor} has been determined using an empirical formula as recommended in [3].

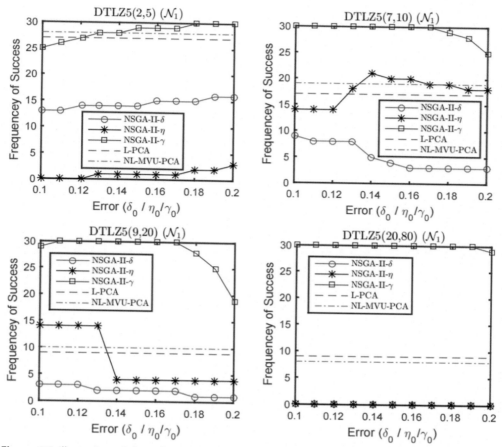

Figure 4.9 Illustration of the influence of $\delta_0/\eta_0/\gamma_0$ on the performance of the proposed multiobjective approaches in identifying the essential objective set. The performance of L-PCA and NL-MVU-PCA is provided as a reference.

The outcomes of all the algorithms are presented in Table 4.7, indicating the frequency of successful identification out of 30 runs. Each run corresponds to a unique sample set in $\mathcal{N}_1(\mathcal{N}_2)$. Table 4.7 provides a basis for examining the performance of the dominance structure-based approaches, which include NSGA-II-δ, NSGA-II-η, ExactAlg, and Greedy-δ.

The presence of misdirection within the sample set. Insufficient coverage of the high–dimensional Pareto front by the sample set. In the presence of the first difficulty, the dominance structure–based approaches may tend to select an excessive number of objectives. Conversely, the second difficulty may lead to over–reduction of objectives by these approaches. By considering the two aforementioned

Table 4.7 The frequency of success in identifying the essential objective set $\mathcal{F}_T$ out of 30 runs, corresponding to $\mathcal{N}_1$ and $\mathcal{N}_2$.

Test instance	$\mathcal{N}_1$							$\mathcal{N}_2$						
	NSGA-II-δ	NSGA-II-η	NSGA-II-γ	Exact Alg	Greedy-δ	L-PCA	NL-MVU-PCA	NSGA-II-δ	NSGA-II-η	NSGA-II-γ	Exact Alg	Greedy-δ	L-PCA	NL-MVU-PCA
D5(2,3)	23	0	30	23	23	30	30	30	30	30	30	30	30	30
D5(2,5)	14	1	29	14	14	27	28	30	30	30	30	30	30	30
D5(3,5)	7	6	30	7	3	29	30	30	30	30	30	30	30	30
D5(3,10)	10	19	29	10	5	28	28	29	30	30	29	28	30	30
D5(5,10)	0	4	28	0	0	28	29	30	30	30	30	29	30	28
D5(7,10)	4	20	30	4	6	17	19	30	30	30	30	27	30	22
D5(3,20)	10	16	25	10	2	26	26	30	30	30	30	28	30	30
D5(6,20)	3	13	29	3	0	4	5	29	29	29	29	27	30	29
D5(9,20)	2	4	30	2	4	9	10	29	29	29	29	29	20	16
D5(12,20)	0	0	25	—	0	3	6	5	5	5	—	7	19	14
D5(5,50)	0	9	30	—	0	28	28	30	30	30	—	30	30	30
D5(8,50)	14	4	30	—	6	1	0	30	30	30	—	29	27	26
D5(10,50)	0	0	30	—	3	13	2	29	29	29	—	29	28	28
D5(15,50)	0	0	30	—	1	9	13	12	12	12	—	16	26	23
D5(25,50)	0	0	29	—	0	29	9	0	0	0	—	0	23	22
D5(5,80)	2	25	30	—	0	0	29	30	30	30	—	25	30	29
D5(10,80)	1	1	28	—	4	2	0	30	29	30	—	29	24	23
D5(15,80)	0	0	30	—	0	9	3	11	11	11	—	16	25	22
D5(20,80)	0	0	30	—	0	16	8	2	2	2	—	5	25	22
D5(30,80)	0	0	30	0	0	30	16	0	0	0	30	0	27	27
W3(5)	0	0	29	—	0	30	30	30	30	30	0	22	30	30
W3(15)	0	0	30	—	0	30	30	30	30	30	—	23	30	30
W3(25)	0	0	30	30	0	30	30	30	30	30	30	30	30	30
D2(5)	30	30	30	30	30	30	30	4	4	4	30	30	30	30
D2(15)	0	0	30	—	0	30	28	0	0	0	—	6	30	28
D2(25)	0	0	30	30	0	30	29	0	0	0	30	0	30	28
P2(3,5)	30	30	30	30	30	3	0	30	30	30	30	30	0	30
P2(3,10)	10	10	30	—	13	0	0	23	23	23	—	23	0	21
P2(8,5)	30	30	30	30	30	0	0	30	30	30	30	30	0	1
P2(8,10)	6	6	30	—	9	0	0	27	27	27	—	28	0	1
S2(3)	30	30	0	30	0	0	0	30	30	0	30	0	0	0
S2(5)	30	30	0	30	0	0	0	30	30	0	30	0	0	0

The best frequencies are shown in bold. For brevity, DTLZ5(l,m), WFG3(m), DTLZ2(m), POW-DTLZ2(p,m), and SUM-DTLZ2(m) are abbreviated as D5(l,m), W3(m), D2(m), P2(p,m), and S2(m), respectively; "—" means the corresponding data is not available.

difficulties, we can offer a sound explanation for the outcomes of these algorithms. This will be demonstrated through the following three scenarios:

1. When the dimensionality of the objective space, denoted by $|\mathcal{F}_T|$, is relatively low (i.e., $|\mathcal{F}_T| \leq 6$), the primary challenge encountered by these algorithms is the first difficulty, particularly in the case of $\mathcal{N}_1$. Table 4.8 presents some of these instances separately and also reports the average number of objectives identified by NSGA-II-δ, NSGA-II-η, and Greedy-δ for $\mathcal{N}_1$. The results are not included in Table 4.8 as they are consistently identical to those obtained using NSGA-II-δ. Based on the outcomes presented in Tables 4.7 and 4.8, the algorithms considered in this study display suboptimal performance in such instances for $\mathcal{N}_1$ and typically select more than $|\mathcal{F}_T|$ objectives on average. This is primarily due to their limitations in effectively handling misdirection. Conversely, in the case of $\mathcal{N}_2$, the algorithms display significantly better performance and attain optimal or near-optimal results in all instances. This can be attributed to the fact that there is significantly less misdirection in $\mathcal{N}_2$ compared to $\mathcal{N}_1$, which leads to a notable mitigation of the first difficulty encountered by these algorithms.

2. In instances where the dimensionality of the objective space, denoted by $|\mathcal{F}_T|$, is moderately high ($7 \leq |\mathcal{F}_T| \leq 10$), these algorithms encounter both of the aforementioned difficulties in the case of $\mathcal{N}_1$. Table 4.9 presents the average number of objectives identified by NSGA-II-δ, NSGA-II-η, and Greedy-δ in such instances for $\mathcal{N}_1$. Table 4.7 indicates that their performance is generally unsatisfactory on instances that correspond to $\mathcal{N}_1$. This can be attributed to the combined effect of two difficulties. On the other hand, Table 4.9 reveals that the number of objectives can differ from $|\mathcal{F}_T|$, depending on which difficulty has a greater influence on the

Table 4.8 The average number of objectives identified per run by NSGA-II-δ, NSGA-II-η and Greedy-δ on the test instances with the dimensionality $|\mathcal{F}_T| \leq 6$ corresponding to $\mathcal{N}_1$.

Test instance	NSGA-II-δ	NSGA-II-η	Greedy-δ
DTLZ5(2,3)	2.23	3.00	2.23
DTLZ5(2,5)	2.70	3.37	2.70
DTLZ5(3,5)	3.83	3.83	4.03
DTLZ5(3,10)	3.93	3.53	4.43
DTLZ5(5,10)	6.80	6.10	6.97
DTLZ5(3,20)	4.23	3.93	4.77
DTLZ5(6,20)	7.07	6.73	7.53
DTLZ5(5,50)	6.50	5.70	7.40
DTLZ5(5,80)	6.13	5.17	6.63
WFG3(5)	3.63	3.57	3.90
WFG3(15)	7.10	14.57	7.90
WFG3(25)	10.07	18.73	10.90

Table 4.9 The average number of objectives identified per run by NSGA-II-δ, NSGA-II-η and Greedy-δ on the test instances with the dimensionality $7 \leq |\mathcal{F}_T| \leq 10$, corresponding to $\mathcal{N}_1$.

Test instance	NSGA-II-δ	NSGA-II-η	Greedy-δ
DTLZ5(7,10)	6.10	7.27	6.30
DTLZ5(9,20)	7.70	8.20	8.00
DTLZ5(8,50)	7.77	9.73	8.10
DTLZ5(10,50)	8.73	8.50	9.07
DTLZ5(10,80)	8.90	8.60	9.40
POW-DTLZ2(3,10)	9.30	9.23	9.43
POW-DTLZ2(3,10)	9.20	9.03	9.30

Table 4.10 The average number of objectives identified per run by NSGA-II-δ, NSGA-II-η and Greedy-δ on the test instances with the dimensionality $|\mathcal{F}_T| \geq 12$, corresponding to $\mathcal{N}_1$ and $\mathcal{N}_2$.

Test instance	$\mathcal{N}_1$			$\mathcal{N}_2$		
	NSGA-II-δ	NSGA-II-η	Greedy-δ	NSGA-II-δ	NSGA-II-η	Greedy-δ
D5(12,20)	8.37	8.30	8.77	10.77	10.77	11.00
D5(15,50)	12.67	12.60	12.97	14.23	14.23	14.53
D5(25,50)	14.03	14.03	14.93	15.63	15.67	16.23
D5(15,80)	12.50	12.43	13.00	14.23	14.23	14.43
D5(20,80)	13.23	13.27	14.07	17.90	17.90	18.47
D5(20,80)	15.67	15.50	16.57	15.70	15.67	16.50
D2(3,10)	11.50	11.50	12.13	13.33	13.33	13.73
D2(3,10)	11.87	11.83	12.73	13.80	13.80	14.77

For brevity, DTLZ5(*I,m*) and DTLZ2(*m*) are abbreviated as D5(*I,m*) and D2(*m*), respectively.

algorithm. Regarding $\mathcal{N}_2$, they achieve outstanding results, with most of them achieving the maximum frequency of 30. One can deduce that, the superior quality of $\mathcal{N}_2$ can effectively address both difficulties associated with these algorithms. Specifically, it can significantly reduce misdirection while also improving the coverage of the Pareto front to a satisfactory level.

3. With an escalation in the dimensionality of $|\mathcal{F}_T|$ ($|\mathcal{F}_T| \geq 12$), the second difficulty starts to exert a more significant influence over the behavior of these algorithms in relation to $\mathcal{N}_1$. What's intriguing is that despite showing some degree of performance enhancement, their performance in such instances of $\mathcal{N}_2$ remains subpar. To delve deeper into this matter, Table 4.10 presents a breakdown of these instances, displaying the average number of objectives achieved per run for $\mathcal{N}_1$ and $\mathcal{N}_2$ separately. Table 4.10 reveals that the issue of over-reduction of objectives is present in all instances of concern for both $\mathcal{N}_1$ and $\mathcal{N}_2$. From this, we can infer that even though $\mathcal{N}_2$ almost completely eliminates the first difficulty, the second difficulty remains a significant obstacle for these algorithms. Achieving satisfactory

coverage of the Pareto front in a high–dimensional (i.e., $|\mathcal{F}_T| \geq 12$) objective space is inherently challenging for sample sets, which results in the persistence of this difficulty and its negative impact on these algorithms.

Apart from the shared characteristics mentioned earlier, we can derive additional insights from Table 4.7 by contrasting the four algorithms that are based on dominance structures:

1. In 21 out of 32 instances, both NSGA-II-η and NSGA-II-δ produce identical results for $\mathcal{N}_1$. In the case of $\mathcal{N}_2$, NSGA-II-η performs similarly to NSGA-II-δ on all instances except for a minor variation in DTLZ5(3,5). Therefore it can be inferred that NSGA-II-η generally offers comparable performance to NSGA-II-δ.

2. In both $\mathcal{N}_1$ and $\mathcal{N}_2$, NSGA-II-δ consistently produces identical results to ExactAlg (when available). This is because NSGA-II-δ possesses a robust capability to attain optimal solutions for the δ-MOSS problems, which has been thoroughly corroborated in previous studies.

3. It is intriguing to note that despite their superior performance in solving δ-MOSS problems, NSGA-II-δ and ExactAlg are not entirely dominant over Greedy-δ in determining the fundamental objective set. Upon closer examination, it becomes evident that Greedy-δ may outperform NSGA-II-δ and ExactAlg in instances with relatively high dimensionality. This can also be ascribed to the insufficient representation of the Pareto front by the provided sample set. Under such circumstances, NSGA-II-δ and ExactAlg are prone to excessively simplifying the objectives, as previously demonstrated. In other words, they often produce an objective subset with a size of $k_1 < |\mathcal{F}_T|$ for a specified δ_0. However, owing to its inferior search capability, Greedy-δ may generate an objective subset with a larger size $k_2 > k_1$ by addressing the same δ-MOSS problem, thereby increasing the likelihood of encompassing $|\mathcal{F}_T|$. However, it would be illogical to consider the accidental success of Greedy-δ as an advantage. The overall performance of NSGA-II-δ and ExactAlg is still superior to that of Greedy-δ, as evidenced by their prominent performance on the SUM-DTLZ2(m) instances.

Table 4.7 facilitates a comparative analysis of the correlation-based techniques, namely NSGA-II-γ, L-PCA, and NL-MVU-PCA. Our evaluation has led to the following observations regarding their performance:

1. NSGA-II-γ demonstrates impressive performance on all test instances, except for SUM-DTLZ2(m), for both $\mathcal{N}_1$ and $\mathcal{N}_2$. These outcomes indicate that NSGA-II-γ possesses significant and consistent capabilities in handling varying degrees of misdirection in the sample set. To visually illustrate NSGA-II-γ's strength, we display a sample set of DTLZ5(2, 5) corresponding to $\mathcal{N}_1$ and $\mathcal{N}_2$, respectively, in Fig. 4.10, and we employ a parallel coordinate plot to exhibit a sample set of an instance with higher dimensionality, i.e., DTLZ5(6, 20), for $\mathcal{N}_1$ and $\mathcal{N}_2$, respectively, in Fig. 4.11. From the two figures, we can observe that $\mathcal{N}_1$ displays features

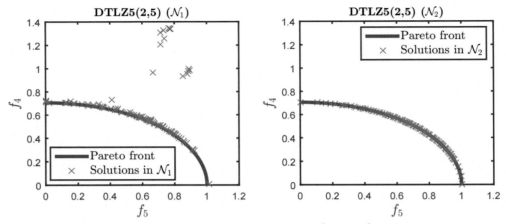

Figure 4.10 DTLZ5(2, 5): a randomly selected sample set in $\mathcal{N}_1$ and $\mathcal{N}_2$ respectively, corresponding to $\mathcal{F}_{\mathcal{T}} = \{f_4, f_5\}$.

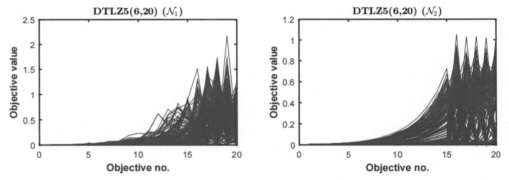

Figure 4.11 DTLZ5(6, 20): the parallel coordinate plots for a randomly selected sample set in $\mathcal{N}_1$ and $\mathcal{N}_2$ respectively.

that are evidently affected by misdirection, in contrast to $\mathcal{N}_2$. For DTLZ5(2, 5), a fraction of solutions in $\mathcal{N}_1$ are far from the true Pareto front, while for DTLZ5(6, 20), some solutions in $\mathcal{N}_1$ exhibit conflicts between f_i and f_j, where $i, j \in [1, 15]$.

2. L-PCA and NL-MVU-PCA exhibit favorable performance on DTLZ5(I,m) instances with a relatively low dimensionality and all WFG3(m) instances, such as DTLT5(5, 50) and WFG3(25), for both $\mathcal{N}_1$ and $\mathcal{N}_2$. This suggests that they possess a certain capability to effectively handle misdirection. However, it appears that their effectiveness significantly deteriorates on problems with redundancy at higher dimensionality, such as DTLZ5(10, 50) and DTLZ5(20, 80). This conclusion is drawn from the observation that L-PCA and NL-MVU-PCA produce inferior outcomes in such instances for $\mathcal{N}_1$ but still demonstrate decent performance on

them for $\mathcal{N}_2$. Additionally, it is noteworthy that both algorithms can adequately address the nonredundant problem, i.e., DTLZ2(m), in all considered scenarios.

3. NSGA-II-γ generally outperforms or at least performs comparably to L-PCA and NL-MVU-PCA. Notably, NSGA-II-γ exhibits a significant advantage over both L-PCA and NL-MVU-PCA on instances with very strong nonlinearity between redundant objectives, such as POW-DTLZ2(8, 5) and POW-DTLZ2(8, 10). Therefore it can be safely concluded that in comparison to L-PCA and NL-MVU-PCA, NSGA-II-γ has a stronger ability to handle not only misdirection but also nonlinearity in these problems.

4. As a whole, NL-MVU-PCA outperforms L-PCA for $\mathcal{N}_1$, indicating that NL-MVU-PCA may be more effective at dealing with misdirection than L-PCA. However, L-PCA generally exhibits slightly better performance than NL-MVU-PCA for DTLZ5(I,m) instances corresponding to $\mathcal{N}_2$. This is reasonable because there is only a linear relationship between redundant objectives over the Pareto front of DTLZ5(I,m), and there is less misdirection in $\mathcal{N}_2$. Additionally, it is noteworthy that NL-MVU-PCA successfully addresses POW-DTLZ2(3, 5) and POW-DTLZ2(3, 10) for $\mathcal{N}_2$, whereas L-PCA fails to identify the essential objective set in all trials. Therefore it can be inferred that NL-MVU-PCA is superior to L-PCA in terms of handling nonlinearity, although it cannot match NSGA-II-γ in this regard.

Using Table 4.7 as a reference, comparing the considered dominance structure-based approaches and correlation-based approaches provides us with the following insights:

1. In all cases, the three correlation-based algorithms perform poorly for SUM-DTLZ2(m) due to their inherent limitation as discussed in Section 4.4.3. However, NSGA-II-δ, NSGA-II-η, and ExactAlg are capable of perfectly addressing the two SUM-DTLZ2(m) instances of interest.

2. Except for SUM-DTLZ2(m), NSGA-II-γ outperforms or performs comparably to all four dominance structure-based algorithms for both $\mathcal{N}_1$ and $\mathcal{N}_2$, owing to its ability to effectively handle misdirection.

3. Comparing L-PCA (NL-MVU-PCA) with dominance structure-based algorithms is considerably more intricate, primarily due to the decreased ability of L-PCA (NL-MVU-PCA) to handle misdirection at higher dimensionality, as previously mentioned. However, in general, disregarding SUM-DTLZ2(m), for problems with very low or very high dimensionality, L-PCA and NL-MVU-PCA tend to perform better, while for problems with medium dimensionality, the four dominances structure-based algorithms typically exhibit an advantage.

4. To summarize, if the user possesses a high-quality sample set and has knowledge that the true dimensionality is not very high, dominance structure-based approaches are generally a more suitable choice since they apply to all problem types under such conditions. Conversely, if the true dimensionality is unknown or may be high, correlation-based approaches are recommended for objective reduction.

Lastly, it is noteworthy that although NSGA-II-δ and NSGA-II-η demonstrate comparable performance in our experiments, NSGA-II-δ requires execution on a normalized sample set. As normalization can be challenging in the presence of outliers, NSGA-II-η appears to be a better option from this perspective.

4.6 Applications to real-world problems

This section delves deeper into the evaluation of the suggested multiobjective approaches to two real-world problems: the water resource problem [33] and the car side-impact problem [22,34].

4.6.1 Water resource problem

The water resource problem pertains to optimal planning for a storm drainage system [33], and it entails five objectives and seven constraints. To facilitate the analysis, a sample set is initially generated by running SPEA2-SDE with a population size of 200 and 2000 generations.

Table 4.11 presents the comprehensive outcomes of the proposed multiobjective approaches. Based on this table, it is reasonable to determine the reduced objective set as $\{f_2, f_3, f_5\}$ for both NSGA-II-δ and NSGA-II-η. On the other hand, for NSGA-II-γ, two objective sets, namely $\{f_1, f_2, f_4, f_5\}$ and $\{f_2, f_3, f_4, f_5\}$, result in the same error of 0.109 and seem to be the most optimal choices for the reduced objective set.

Table 4.11 The results of NSGA-II-δ, NSGA-II-η and NSGA-II-γ for the water resource problem.

Algorithm	k	$\delta/\eta/r$	Objective set
NSGA-II-δ	1	1	$\{f_i\}, i = 1, 2, 3, 4, 5$
	2	0.789	$\{f_3, f_4\}$
	3	0.078	$\{f_2, f_3, f_5\}$
	4	0	$\{f_2, f_3, f_4, f_5\}$
NSGA-II-η	1	0.995	$\{f_i\}, i = 1, 2, 3, 4, 5$
	2	0.51	$\{f_3, f_4\}$
	3	0.03	$\{f_2, f_3, f_5\}$
	4	0	$\{f_2, f_3, f_4, f_5\}$
NSGA-II-γ	1	0.7	$\{f_i\}, i = 2, 5$
	2	0.388	$\{f_i, f_4\}, i = 1, 3$
	3	0.313	$\{f_2, f_3, f_4\}$
	3	0.313	$\{f_1, f_2, f_4\}$
	3	0.313	$\{f_2, f_3, f_5\}$
	4	0.109	$\{f_1, f_2, f_5\}$
	4	0.109	$\{f_2, f_3, f_4, f_5\}$
	5	0	$\{f_1, f_2, f_3, f_4, f_5\}$

To verify the outcomes, Fig. 4.12 utilizes parallel coordinate plots to depict the nondominated solution acquired by executing SPEA2-SDE on the original objective set and the three reduced objective sets, where the objective values are scaled by constant factors recommended in [35] to facilitate visualization. As evidenced by Fig. 4.12, the parallel coordinate plot for each of the three reduced objective sets closely corresponds to that obtained using the original objective set, thereby affirming that any of the three reduced objective sets are adequate for producing a reliable estimate of the Pareto front for this problem.

4.6.2 Car side-impact problem

The car side-impact problem is converted into a many-objective problem that involves 11 objectives and 10 constraints [22]. Similar to the previous problem, the sample set is produced using SPEA2-SDE with a population size of 200 and 2000 generations.

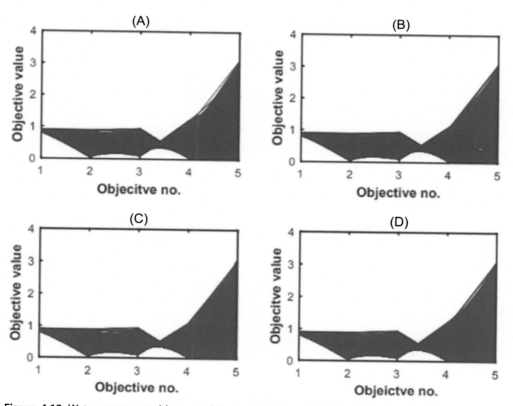

Figure 4.12 Water resource problem: parallel coordinate plots for the nondominated solutions obtained by running SPEA2-SDE. (A) On the original objective set. (B) On the reduced objective set $\{f_2, f_3, f_5\}$. (C) On the reduced objective set $\{f_1, f_2, f_4, f_5\}$. (D) On the reduced objective set $\{f_2, f_3, f_4, f_5\}$.

Fig. 4.13 illustrates how the error decreases in the results of the three multiobjective approaches for the car side-impact problem as the number of objectives increases. According to Fig. 4.13, the best trade-off for NSGA-II-δ is obtained at $k = 6$, while the best trade-off for NSGA-II-η or NSGA-II-γ is less apparent and is dependent on the user's preference. Using the same threshold as in Section 4.5.6 for η and γ errors, $\{f_1, f_4, f_5, f_9, f_{10}, f_{11}\}$ or $\{f_1, f_4, f_5, f_8, f_9, f_{11}\}$ is determined as the reduced objective set for both NSGA-II-δ and NSGA-II-η, whereas $\{f_1, f_2, f_5, f_6, f_8, f_9, f_{11}\}$ is selected for NSGA-II-γ. Fig. 4.14 presents the parallel coordinate plots that correspond to the nondominated solutions obtained by executing SPEA2-SDE on the original objective set and three reduced objective sets, respectively. As depicted by Fig. 4.14, the four parallel coordinate plots are highly similar, indicating that any of the three reduced objective sets is sufficient for attaining a reliable estimate of the Pareto front for this problem.

4.6.3 Discussion

The outcomes suggest that the three multiobjective algorithms are capable of diminishing the number of objectives for the two real-world problems. Notably, the objective sets produced by NSGA-II-δ and NSGA-II-η are identical, but differ from those obtained by NSGA-II-γ. Since the true Pareto front of the two real-world problems is unknown, it is challenging to draw a definitive conclusion on which outcome is superior. However, the objective sets produced by NSGA-II-δ (NSGA-II-η) are smaller in size and have been verified to be sufficient for representing the original objective set, making them more likely to constitute the essential objective set. One possible explanation for the discrepancy is that the correlation analysis in the correlation-based approaches, such as NSGA-II-γ, may not adequately capture the intricate relationship between objectives in the two real-world problems, despite its general effectiveness in existing benchmark problems.

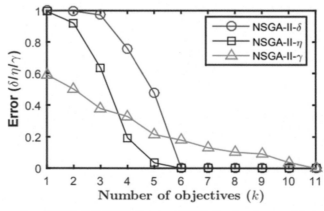

Figure 4.13 The results of NSGA-II-δ, NSGA-II-η, and NSGA-II-γ for the car side-impact problem.

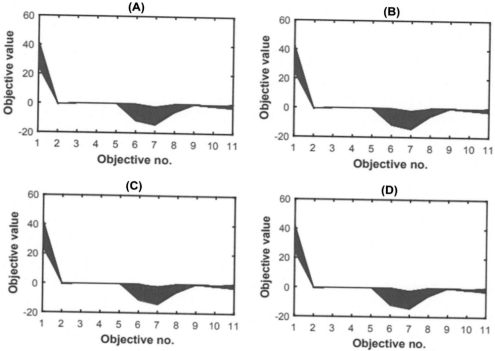

Figure 4.14 Car side-impact problem: parallel coordinate plots for the nondominated solutions obtained by running SPEA2-SDE. (A) On the original objective set. (B) On the reduced objective set $\{f_1, f_4, f_5, f_9, f_{10}, f_{11}\}$. (C) On the reduced objective set $\{f_1, f_4, f_5, f_8, f_9, f_{11}\}$. (D) On the reduced objective set $\{f_1, f_2, f_5, f_6, f_8, f_9, f_{11}\}$.

Table 4.12 Essential objective sets obtained for the water resource problem in different studies.

Reference	Essential objective set
[3]	$\{f_2, f_3, f_4, f_5\}$ or $\{f_1, f_2, f_4, f_5\}$
[10]	$\{f_1, f_2, f_5\}$ or $\{f_2, f_3, f_5\}$
[19]	$\{f_3, f_4\}$
[11,22]	$\{f_2, f_3, f_4, f_5\}$

Furthermore, it is intriguing to note that the essential objective sets identified for the two real-world problems often differ across various studies. Table 4.12 illustrates the outcomes obtained from five prior studies on the water resource problem. Given that these algorithms can reliably determine the essential objective set for numerous benchmark problems, it is possible to infer that the two real-world problems examined in this study may pose a greater challenge to existing objective reduction algorithms, particularly the correlation-based approaches.

Lastly, it is important to note that the validation method used in this section to confirm the obtained reduced objective set follows the approach taken in [3,10,19]. This validation method is reasonable given that the Pareto fronts of real-world problems are often unknown. However, one limitation of this method is that it relies on an evolutionary many-objective optimizer, which is a stochastic algorithm and may not possess adequate optimization capability. To overcome this limitation, we utilized a high-performing algorithm (SPEA2-SDE) to generate a nondominated solution set for the parallel coordinate plot by executing it for a large number of generations until convergence. Despite Figs. 4.12 and 4.14 display the results of a single simulation run, numerous repetitions were carried out in practice, and the parallel coordinate plots observed were almost identical.

4.7 Benefits of the proposed approaches

The objective of this section is to examine the advantages of the proposed objective reduction algorithms in optimization, visualization, and decision-making, along with providing illustrative examples.

4.7.1 On objective reduction-assisted optimization

Objective reduction techniques can generally aid optimization in two ways. The first approach, known as subsequent optimization in this chapter, is simplistic: once an objective reduction algorithm obtains a reduced objective set, an MOEA continues to operate on the reduced set for a specific number of generations and produces the obtained nondominated solutions. The second approach, which is more commonly used, is referred to as online objective reduction [20,21], where the objective reduction algorithm is integrated into the iterations of the MOEA. In the following sections, we employ both techniques based on NSGA-II-γ to demonstrate the advantages of the proposed objective reduction approaches in optimization.

Regarding subsequent optimization, we initiated the process by executing a many-objective algorithm, SPEA2-SDE, for 100 generations. Then, the set of nondominated solutions obtained was fed into NSGA-II-γ for objective reduction, and subsequently, we ran SPEA2-SDE on the reduced objective set for 300 generations. For ease of reference, we refer to this optimization mode as SDE_{so}. Concerning online objective reduction, we utilized SPEA2-SDE as the underlying optimizer, and NSGA-II-γ was incorporated into SPEA2-SDE utilizing the integration scheme detailed in [6]. The resulting online objective reduction algorithm is labeled as SDE_{online}. To demonstrate the effectiveness of the proposed approaches, we compare SDE_{so} and SDEonline with SPEA2-SDE without any objective reduction, which we denote as SDE_{ref}. Additionally, we include A-NSGA-III [36] in the comparison, which is a decomposition-based algorithm that employs reference vector adaptation and aims to address MaOPs with nonuniformly distributed Pareto fronts more effectively. To ensure a fair comparison, we set the optimization iterations to 400 generations for SDE_{online}, SDE_{ref}, and A-NSGA-III, and maintain the same population size for all algorithms. The other parameters for SPEA2-SDE and A-NSGA-III align with the original studies [31,36].

For illustrative purposes, we utilize a benchmark problem, specifically the 15-objective WFG3. We use the inverted generational distance (IGD) [37] as the performance metric, and sample 1,000 points uniformly on the true Pareto front to generate the reference set. Initially, A-NSGA-III employs two-layered reference vectors with two divisions in both boundary and inside layers, resulting in a population size of 240. Table 4.13 presents the average IGD (including the standard deviation) and the average computational time over 30 runs by four algorithms for comparison. Our results demonstrate that SDE_{so} and SDE_{online} outperform SDE_{ref} in terms of both effectiveness and efficiency, highlighting the usefulness of NSGA-II-γ in facilitating the effect of many-objective optimization. A-NSGA-III, on the other hand, performs poorly, as evidenced by the large IGD, indicating its inability to approach the Pareto front. This observation also suggests that reference vector adaptation may not be sufficiently strong to locate a lower-dimensional front from a high-dimensional objective space. Fig. 4.15 further compares the convergence curves of the average IGD with the number of generations, where it can be seen that the proposed objective reduction algorithm in SDE_{so} and SDE_{online} promotes the convergence of the many-objective optimizer.

Subsequently, we examine a real-world problem, specifically, the water resource problem, for which the Pareto front is unknown. To evaluate the performance, we utilize the hypervolume (HV) [38] as the performance metric, which is computed in the same manner as in [1]. Table 4.14 presents the average HV, along with the standard deviation and the average computational time. Our results indicate that the two objective reduction-assisted optimization algorithms, SDE_{so} and SDE_{online}, achieve significant improvements in performance over SDE_{ref} in terms of HV. In contrast to the 15-objective WFG3, A-NSGA-III performs well on this problem and even outperforms SDE_{so} and SDE_{online}. Given that the water resource problem may have only one or two redundant objectives, as depicted in Section 4.6.1, the

Table 4.13 The average IGD (including the standard deviation in the bracket) and the average computation time (in seconds) over 30 runs on 15-objective WFG3.

	SDE_{ref}	SDE_{so}	SDE_{online}	A-NSGA-III
IGD	0.2820 (0.1044)	0.1466 (0.0662)	0.1098 (0.0475)	7.3570 (2.6868)
Time	52.32	27.50	22.99	44.39

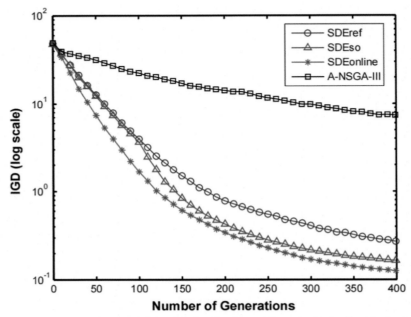

Figure 4.15 Convergence curves of the average IGD (over 30 runs) obtained with the number of generations for SDE$_{ref}$, SDE$_{so}$, SDE$_{online}$ and A-NSGA-III on 15-objective WFG3.

Table 4.14 The average HV (including the standard deviation in the bracket) and the average computation time (in seconds) over 30 runs on the water resource problem.

	SDE$_{ref}$	SDE$_{so}$	SDE$_{online}$	A-NSGA-III
HV	0.4200	1.0030	1.0377	1.0537
	(0.0376)	(0.0435)	(0.0157)	(0.0036)
Time	35.41	31.25	31.87	30.64

reason for this could be that the reference vector adaptation in A–NSGA–III can effectively handle a slight degree of degeneration of the Pareto front in this problem.

Based on the results presented in Tables 4.13 and 4.14, the proposed objective reduction algorithm can effectively reduce the overall optimization time, albeit at the expense of additional computational costs. This benefit is particularly evident when dealing with a HV–based MOEA as the underlying optimizer or when the objective computations of the MaOP are resource-intensive. The former scenario is illustrated in the study by Brockhoff and Zitzler [20], while the latter is exemplified in a recent work by Carreras et al. [39].

While the experiments have demonstrated the effectiveness of objective reduction-assisted optimization, it is important to acknowledge its limitations. Namely, if the objective reduction algorithm fails to operate effectively, the elimination of essential objectives during optimization can potentially bias the search process. This risk is more significant in subsequent optimization, as the removed objectives are not considered again. Nonetheless, based on our experimental findings and those in the literature (e.g., [23,30,40]), combining objective reduction with MOEAs remains a valuable approach in practical many-objective optimization, particularly for MaOPs with redundant objectives. Decomposition-based algorithms with reference vector adaptation [36,41–43] may provide a competitive alternative for redundant MaOPs, but based on our experimental study of A-NSGA-III, such techniques do not demonstrate a clear advantage over objective reduction-assisted optimization algorithms. In the future, additional experimental comparisons between the two methodologies are necessary to gain a deeper understanding of their respective strengths and weaknesses.

4.7.2 On visualization and decision-making

Visualizing Pareto front approximations is crucial in many-objective optimization, as it allows the user to gain a better understanding of the nondominated solutions obtained and make an informed final selection. Several many-objective visualization methods, such as parallel coordinate plots, heatmaps, and bubble charts, have been proposed in the literature. For more details, interested readers can refer to [7,8]. While these techniques can be useful, their representation can quickly become confusing when the number of objectives or nondominated solutions increases. To address this issue, objective reduction approaches can be employed to remove redundant objectives and reduce the problem's dimensionality. In some cases, the number of objectives can be reduced to two or three, making the visualization more intuitive. In other cases, objective reduction can help the visualization method to consider fewer objectives and a lower number of nondominated solutions, resulting in a simpler and more manageable visualization for the user.

To illustrate the effectiveness of the proposed NSGA-II-γ, we employ it along with the parallel coordinate plots visualization method on the DTLZ5(6, 20) problem, which has a high number of objectives. To cover the high-dimensional Pareto front with sufficient diversity, a relatively large population size, such as 500, is typically used. After running an optimizer, such as SPEA2-SDE, the user obtains a nondominated set, which can be visualized using parallel coordinate plots, as shown in Fig. 4.16A. However, due to the high number of objectives, Fig. 4.16A can be very difficult for the user to analyze visually, and the nonconflicting relationships between objectives are not obvious in this figure. To address this issue, NSGA-II-γ is used to identify an essential objective set

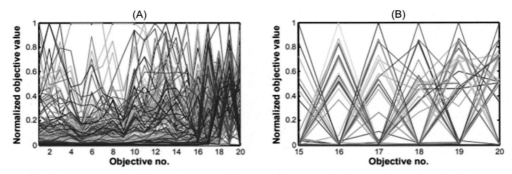

Figure 4.16 Comparison of the parallel coordinate plots obtained before and after objective reduction.

$\{f_{15}, f_{16}, f_{17}, f_{18}, f_{19}, f_{20}\}$ with a γ error of 0.11, while the remaining objectives are considered to behave in a nonconflicting manner. By using NSGA-II-γ, the user can infer that the true dimensionality of DTLZ5(6, 20) is much lower than 20, and can thus use a nondominated set with a much smaller size, such as 50, for better coverage. To achieve this, the user can first use environmental selection in SPEA2-SDE to choose 50 diverse and well-distributed solutions from the nondominated set in Fig. 4.16A, and then refine them by optimizing the essential objectives identified by NSGA-II-γ. The resultant nondominated set is shown in Fig. 4.16B, which is much easier for the user to comprehend and reveals good trade-offs.

In many-objective optimization problems with redundant objectives, objective reduction approaches can assist users in making decisions regarding the final solution in a similar manner to visualization techniques. It should be noted that NSGA-II-η and NSGA-II-γ, the proposed objective reduction methods, do not require each objective of the nondominated solution set to be normalized to the same range. However, it is highly recommended to normalize the objectives before making decisions based on the essential objectives identified using NSGA-II-η or NSGA-II-γ to avoid difficulties in comparing objectives with different scales. In decision-making using dominance structure-based objective reduction algorithms, it is possible for two solutions to be nondominated to each other in the reduced objective space, yet exhibit significant differences in some of the objectives that have been removed. In such cases, the user may be concerned about simply dropping these objectives, as they may be relevant to the decision-making process. To address this issue, we propose aggregating the removed objectives into a single objective using a preferred aggregation function. This aggregated objective, along with the identified essential objectives, can be presented to the user for consideration. This approach seeks to strike a balance between the effect of objective reduction and the user's concerns about significant differences in the removed objectives.

4.8 Conclusion

This chapter aims to explore evolutionary multiobjective approaches for objective reduction. Our approach involves treating objective reduction as a multiobjective search problem and introducing three distinct multiobjective formulations. These formulations are tailored to preserve either the dominance or correlation structure of the sample set provided. For each formulation, we consider two conflicting objectives: the number of objectives selected (k) and the error (δ, η, or γ) resulting from removing the unselected objectives. To address this multiobjective problem, we develop a multi-objective objective reduction algorithm (NSGA-II-δ, NSGA-II-η, or NSGA-II-γ) that employs NSGA-II to strike a balance between the two objectives and generate a set of nondominated objective subsets that can assist the user in making decisions. Furthermore, we conduct a thorough analysis of dominance structure- and correlation-based approaches using several theorems to provide a clear understanding of the general benefits and drawbacks of these two key objective reduction techniques. To validate the effectiveness of our proposed multiobjective approaches, we perform extensive experiments and comparisons on a diverse set of problems. Our findings reveal the characteristics of the algorithms studied, which align with our theoretical analysis.

References

[1] Yuan Y, Xu H, Wang B, et al. A new dominance relation-based evolutionary algorithm for many-objective optimization. IEEE Transactions on Evolutionary Computation 2015;20(1):16−37.
[2] Deb K, Jain H. An evolutionary many-objective optimization algorithm using reference-point-based nondominated sorting approach, part I: solving problems with box constraints. IEEE Transactions on Evolutionary Computation 2013;18(4):577−601.
[3] Saxena DK, Duro JA, Tiwari A, et al. Objective reduction in many-objective optimization: linear and nonlinear algorithms. IEEE Transactions on Evolutionary Computation 2012;17(1):77−99.
[4] Ishibuchi H, Tsukamoto N, Nojima Y. Evolutionary many-objective optimization: a short review. Proceedings of the 10th IEEE congress on evolutionary computation. IEEE; 2008. p. 2419−26.
[5] López Jaimes A, Coello Coello CA. Some techniques to deal with many-objective problems. Proceedings of the 11th annual conference companion on genetic and evolutionary computation conference: late breaking papers; 2009. p. 2693−6.
[6] Brockhoff D, Zitzler E. Objective reduction in evolutionary multiobjective optimization: theory and applications. Evolutionary Computation 2009;17(2):135−66.
[7] Walker DJ, Everson RM, Fieldsend JE. Visualizing mutually nondominating solution sets in many-objective optimization. IEEE Transactions on Evolutionary Computation 2012;17(2):165−84.
[8] Tušar T, Filipič B. Visualization of Pareto front approximations in evolutionary multiobjective optimization: a critical review and the prosection method. IEEE Transactions on Evolutionary Computation 2014;19(2):225−45.
[9] Xue B, Zhang M, Browne WN, et al. A survey on evolutionary computation approaches to feature selection. IEEE Transactions on evolutionary computation 2015;20(4):606−26.
[10] Singh HK, Isaacs A, Ray T. A Pareto corner search evolutionary algorithm and dimensionality reduction in many-objective optimization problems. IEEE Transactions on Evolutionary Computation 2011;15(4):539−56.

[11] Guo X, Wang Y, Wang X. Using objective clustering for solving many-objective optimization problems. Mathematical Problems in Engineering 2013;2013(pt.5):133−74.

[12] Wang H, Yao X. Objective reduction based on nonlinear correlation information entropy. Soft Computing 2016;20:2393−407.

[13] Duro JA, Saxena DK, Deb K, et al. Machine learning based decision support for many-objective optimization problems. Neurocomputing 2014;146:30−47.

[14] Laumanns M, Thiele L, Deb K, et al. Combining convergence and diversity in evolutionary multi-objective optimization. Evolutionary Computation 2002;10(3):263−82.

[15] Huband S, Hingston P, Barone L, et al. A review of multiobjective test problems and a scalable test problem toolkit. IEEE Transactions on Evolutionary Computation 2006;10(5):477−506.

[16] Ishibuchi H, Masuda H, Nojima Y. Pareto fronts of many-objective degenerate test problems. IEEE Transactions on Evolutionary Computation 2015;20(5):807−13.

[17] López Jaimes A, Coello Coello CA, Chakraborty D. Objective reduction using a feature selection technique. Proceedings of the 10th annual conference on genetic and evolutionary computation; 2008. p. 673−80.

[18] De Freitas ARR, Fleming PJ, Guimaraes FG. Aggregation trees for visualization and dimension reduction in many-objective optimization. Information Sciences 2015;298:288−314.

[19] Guo X, Wang Y, Wang X. An objective reduction algorithm using representative Pareto solution search for many-objective optimization problems. Soft Computing 2016;20:4881−95.

[20] Brockhoff D, Zitzler E. Improving hypervolume-based multiobjective evolutionary algorithms by using objective reduction methods. Proceedings of the 9th IEEE congress on evolutionary computation. IEEE; 2007. p. 2086−93.

[21] López Jaimes A, Coello CAC, Urías Barrientos JE. Online objective reduction to deal with many-objective problems. Proceedings of the 5th evolutionary multi-criterion optimization; 2009. p. 423−37.

[22] Sinha A, Saxena DK, Deb K, et al. Using objective reduction and interactive procedure to handle many-objective optimization problems. Applied Soft Computing 2013;13(1):415−27.

[23] Bandyopadhyay S, Mukherjee A. An algorithm for many-objective optimization with reduced objective computations: a study in differential evolution. IEEE Transactions on Evolutionary Computation 2014;19(3):400−13.

[24] Min B, Park C, Jang I, et al. Development of Pareto-based evolutionary model integrated with dynamic goal programming and successive linear objective reduction. Applied Soft Computing 2015;35:75−112.

[25] Kendall MG. A new measure of rank correlation. Biometrika 1938;30(1/2):81−93.

[26] Purshouse RC, Fleming PJ. Conflict, harmony, and independence: relationships in evolutionary multi-criterion optimisation. Proceedings of the 2nd evolutionary multi-criterion optimization; 2003. p. 16−30.

[27] Deb K, Pratap A, Agarwal S, et al. A fast and elitist multiobjective genetic algorithm: NSGA-II. IEEE Transactions on Evolutionary Computation 2002;6(2):182−97.

[28] Golberg DE. Genetic algorithms in search, optimization, and machine learning. Addion Wesley 1989;1989(102):36.

[29] Deb K, Thiele L, Laumanns M, et al. Scalable multi-objective optimization test problems. Proceedings of the 4th congress on evolutionary computation. IEEE; 2002. Vol. 1, p. 825−30.

[30] Deb K, Saxena D. Searching for Pareto-optimal solutions through dimensionality reduction for certain large-dimensional multi-objective optimization problems. Proceedings of the 8th world congress on computational intelligence; 2006. p. 3352−60.

[31] Li M, Yang S, Liu X. Shift-based density estimation for Pareto-based algorithms in many-objective optimization. IEEE Transactions on Evolutionary Computation 2013;18(3):348−65.

[32] Adra SF, Fleming PJ. Diversity management in evolutionary many-objective optimization. IEEE Transactions on Evolutionary Computation 2010;15(2):183−95.

[33] Musselman K, Talavage J. A tradeoff cut approach to multiple objective optimization. Operations Research 1980;28(6):1424−35.

[34] Gu L, Yang RJ, Tho CH, et al. Optimisation and robustness for crashworthiness of side impact. International Journal of Vehicle Design 2001;26(4):348–60.

[35] Ray T, Tai K, Seow KC. Multiobjective design optimization by an evolutionary algorithm. Engineering Optimization 2001;33(4):399–424.

[36] Jain H, Deb K. An evolutionary many-objective optimization algorithm using reference-point based nondominated sorting approach, part II: handling constraints and extending to an adaptive approach. IEEE Transactions on evolutionary computation 2013;18(4):602–22.

[37] Van Veldhuizen DA, Lamont GB. Multiobjective evolutionary algorithm research: a history and analysis. Technical Report TR-98-03, Department of Electrical and Computer Engineering, Graduate School of Engineering, Air Force Institute of Technology, Wright-Patterson AFB, Ohio; 1998.

[38] Beume N, Naujoks B, Emmerich M. SMS-EMOA: multiobjective selection based on dominated hypervolume. European Journal of Operational Research 2007;181(3):1653–69.

[39] Carreras J, Pozo C, Boer D, et al. Systematic approach for the life cycle multi-objective optimization of buildings combining objective reduction and surrogate modeling. Energy and Buildings 2016;130:506–18.

[40] Copado-Méndez PJ, Pozo C, Guillén-Gosálbez G, et al. Enhancing the ϵ-constraint method through the use of objective reduction and random sequences: application to environmental problems. Computers & Chemical Engineering 2016;87:36–48.

[41] Siwei J, Zhihua C, Jie Z, et al. Multiobjective optimization by decomposition with Pareto-adaptive weight vectors. Proceedings of the 7th international conference on natural computation. IEEE; 2011. Vol. 3, p. 1260–4.

[42] Qi Y, Ma X, Liu F, et al. MOEA/D with adaptive weight adjustment. Evolutionary Computation 2014;22(2):231–64.

[43] Cheng R, Jin Y, Olhofer M, et al. A reference vector guided evolutionary algorithm for many-objective optimization. IEEE Transactions on Evolutionary Computation 2016;20(5):773–91.

CHAPTER 5

Expensive multiobjective evolutionary optimization assisted by dominance prediction

Contents

5.1 Introduction

A commonly used group of surrogate-assisted algorithms for expensive multiobjective optimizations involve concepts from the single-objective efficient global optimization (EGO) [1]. Bayesian optimization [2] is another term for this optimization approach.

There is another notable group of surrogate-assisted algorithms for expensive multiobjective optimization that utilizes existing multiobjective evolutionary algorithms (MOEAs). The typical approach adopted by these algorithms is to construct a single surrogate model for each objective. In MOEAs, a diverse array of machine learning models, including Kriging, neural networks, and support vector machine (SVM), have been employed to develop such surrogate models.

Intelligent Evolutionary Optimization
DOI: https://doi.org/10.1016/B978-0-443-27400-8.00005-8

While constructing a separate surrogate model for each objective is a simple method for developing surrogate-assisted MOEAs, the accuracy of the optimization process as a whole may be negatively impacted by the cumulative approximation errors stemming from each metamodel [3,4]. Furthermore, as the number of objectives increases, this method of constructing surrogates results in escalated computational costs. To address these limitations, an alternative research approach for surrogate-assisted MOEAs that has received less attention involves creating a unified surrogate model that encompasses all objectives.

Since dominance comparisons plays a crucial role in numerous MOEAs, the classification-based mono-surrogate approach would seamlessly integrate with a machine learning model that can precisely predict the dominance relationship between two solutions. It is striking that, despite its significance, the literature has given limited consideration to dominance prediction.

One significant limitation of the approach proposed in [5], as well as the preliminary work conducted by Guo et al. [6], is that they do not explore efficient methods for integrating surrogate models based on dominance prediction with a MOEA for costly multiobjective optimization. It is possible that relying solely on Pareto dominance prediction might not be sufficient for establishing an effective surrogate-assisted MOEA. Given the aforementioned restrictions in current research about the prediction of dominance relations, we offer the following contributions:

1. Our proposed approach considers dominance prediction as a challenge of imbalanced classification and utilizes modern deep learning techniques to capture complex, nonlinear dominance relationships more accurately. Moreover, using deep neural networks as surrogates provides the advantage of enabling online model updates through mini-batch gradient descent, which is especially valuable in expensive optimization scenarios where solutions are obtained sequentially.

2. Our exploration involves the investigation of the notion of dominance prediction about an extra type of dominance relation known as θ-dominance, as detailed in [7] and [8]. θ-Dominance is characterized by its ability to explicitly maintain diversity, and its efficacy in exerting moderate selection pressure, even in cases involving high-dimensional objective spaces, thus compensating for the constraints of Pareto dominance.

3. Our novel surrogate-assisted MOEA, named θ-DEA-DP, is proposed for expensive MOPs. Our approach combines dominance prediction-based surrogates with θ-DEA [8]. θ-DEA-DP utilizes a two-stage preselection approach that employs both Pareto dominance and θ-dominance prediction to achieve an optimal balance between convergence and diversity preservation within the objective space.

5.2 Preliminaries and background

In this section, we provide fundamental concepts and background information that is essential for the content covered in this chapter.

5.2.1 Multiobjective optimization

A formal way to express a multiobjective optimization problem (MOP) is as follows:

$$\min \mathbf{f}(\mathbf{x}) = (f_1(\mathbf{x}), f_2(\mathbf{x}), \ldots, f_m(\mathbf{x}))^{\mathrm{T}}$$
$$\text{subject to} \quad \mathbf{x} \in \Omega \subseteq \mathbb{R}^n \tag{5.1}$$

The decision vector, $\mathbf{x}$, represents an n-dimensional element from the decision space, Ω. Meanwhile, the objective vector, $\mathbf{f}:\Omega \rightarrow \Theta \subseteq \mathbb{R}^m$, is composed of m objective functions and maps Ω to the feasible objective space, Θ. If $m > 3$, the term many-objective optimization problem (MaOP) [9,10] is used in the literature to refer to a MOP.

(1) *Pareto dominance*: If a solution, $\mathbf{u} \in \Omega$, satisfies the condition $\forall i \in \{1, 2, \ldots, m\}$: $f_i(\mathbf{u}) \leq f_i(\mathbf{v})$, and $\exists j \in \{1, 2, \ldots, m\}$: $f_j(\mathbf{u}) < f_j(\mathbf{v})$, for some other solution, $\mathbf{v} \in \Omega$, then $\mathbf{u}$ is deemed to dominate $\mathbf{v}$ inby the definition of Pareto dominance, denoted by $\mathbf{u} \prec \mathbf{v}$.

In general, the objectives of an MOP are in conflict with each other, making it impossible for a single solution to Pareto dominate all others. As a result, a set of solutions with equal Pareto dominance, known as the Pareto set (PS), exists instead. These solutions are considered to be equally optimal according to the Pareto dominance criterion.

(2) *Pareto set*: The PS for a given MOP is defined as the set of solutions $PS := \{x^* \in \Omega | \nexists x \in \Omega, x \prec x^*\}$ that is not dominated by any other solution in the decision space.

The process of transforming the PS into the objective space is commonly known as the Pareto front (PF) mapping, and can be characterized by the following definition:

(3) *Pareto front*: Given a specific MOP, the PF is defined as $PF := \{\mathbf{f}(x^*) | x^* \in PS\}$. The primary objective of multiobjective optimization is typically to obtain an approximation of the PF that is as close as possible to the true PF.

In multiobjective optimization, the primary objective is to achieve an approximation of the PF that is as accurate as possible. Achieving the primary objective of multiobjective optimization necessitates that the objective vectors obtained possess two key attributes: proximity to the PF (convergence), and a uniform distribution across it (diversity).

5.2.2 θ-Dominance

θ-Dominance [7,8] is a novel approach to dominance that incorporates the principles of decomposition. Under this framework, a set of N uniformly distributed weight vectors must be predetermined in order to apply θ-dominance. (also referred to as reference vectors), let $\mathbf{w}_1, \mathbf{w}_2, \ldots, \mathbf{w}_N$ denote the set of uniformly distributed weight vectors. For a given solution $\mathbf{x} \in \Omega$, we can denote its representation in the normalized objective space as P, and its projection onto the direction of $\mathbf{w}_i$ as H. By following a prescribed methodology, we can calculate two distances that correspond to $\mathbf{w}_i$, we can evaluate two distances that correspond to $\mathbf{w}_i$, namely, $d_{i,1}(\mathbf{x}) = |OH|$ and $d_{i,2}(\mathbf{x}) = |PH|$, where the symbol O is used to represent the point of origin. In addition, the penalty boundary intersection (PBI) function [11] is incorporated as $\mathcal{F}_i(\mathbf{x}) = d_{i,1}(\mathbf{x}) + \theta d_{i,2}(\mathbf{x})$, where the penalty parameter θ is utilized. Essentially, $\mathcal{F}_i(\mathbf{x})$ serves to assess the proximity of a given solution, $\mathbf{x}$, to the PF with respect to the direction of $\mathbf{w}_i$. Fig. 5.1A depicts $d_{i,1}$ and $d_{i,2}$ in a two-dimensional space representing the objectives.

The θ-dominance approach involves using N weight vectors to partition the space of objectives into N clusters, denoted as $\mathcal{C}_1, \mathcal{C}_2, \ldots, \mathcal{C}_N$. The perpendicular distance between the weight vectors and each solution is used to assign it to a distinct cluster (i.e., $d_{i,2}$). Mathematically, $\mathbf{x} \in \mathcal{C}_j$ if and only if $j = \operatorname{argmin}_{i=1}^{N} d_{i,2}(\mathbf{x})$. Fig. 5.1B provides an illustration of how objective space is divided using $N = 4$ weight vectors. For example, $\mathcal{C}_2$ is the cluster to which point E belongs, as it has the shortest distance with respect to the perpendicular distance from $\mathbf{w}_2$.

Through the utilization of both the PBI function and clustering operator, the definition of θ-dominance is as follows:

(4) $\boldsymbol{\theta}$-*Dominance*: If there exists a $j \in \{1, 2, \ldots, N\}$ such that $\mathbf{u}$ and $\mathbf{v}$ belong to the same cluster, $\mathcal{C}_j$, and $\mathcal{F}_j(\mathbf{u}) < \mathcal{F}_j(\mathbf{v})$, then solution $\mathbf{u} \in \Omega$ is considered to θ-dominate solution $\mathbf{v} \in \Omega$, denoted as $\mathbf{u} \prec_\theta \mathbf{v}$.

The main objective of θ-dominance is to differentiate solutions that belong to the same cluster. For example, in Fig. 5.1B, due to their membership in different clusters, solutions B and F do not θ-dominate each other, whereas solution B θ-dominates solution E owing to their shared membership in cluster $\mathcal{C}_2$ and the better PBI function value of solution B concerning $\mathbf{w}_2$.

Like Pareto dominance, θ-dominance creates a rigorous partial ordering of solutions [8]. A possible approach to conduct nondominated sorting through θ-dominance

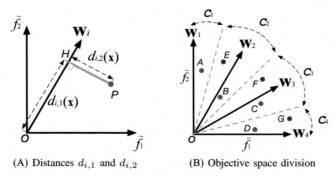

(A) Distances $d_{i,1}$ and $d_{i,2}$ (B) Objective space division

Figure 5.1 Illustration of θ-dominance in the normalized objective space.

is to rank the solutions within each cluster C_j by $\mathcal{F}_j$. Subsequently, the top solutions from each cluster form the initial θ-nondomination tier, followed by the second-best solutions, and so on. It is important to highlight that, in contrast to Pareto dominance, θ-dominance emphasizes the importance of convergence and diversity. Thus, during the process of survival selection, solutions belonging to the last θ-nondomination tier can be selected randomly instead of depending on a secondary measure such as a measure like crowding distance [12]. As indicated in Fig. 5.1B, the first θ-nondomination tier includes solutions A, B, C, and D, while the second θ-nondomination tier comprises solutions E, F, and G.

It is worth noting that θ-dominance is noncompliant with the principles of Pareto dominance. This highlights the rationale behind our strategy of predicting both Pareto and θ-dominance within the scope of this chapter. Furthermore, because of its use of the PBI function, in multiobjective optimization problems with numerous objectives, θ-dominance frequently applies greater selection pressure on the PF than Pareto dominance [8].

5.2.3 Deep feedforward neural networks

Feedforward neural networks (FNNs) are a widespread type of deep learning model, which are designed to approximate the function that links an input $\mathbf{x}$ to an output $\mathbf{y}$, based on a training set $\mathbb{T} = \{(\mathbf{x}^{(1)}, \mathbf{y}^{(1)}), (\mathbf{x}^{(2)}, \mathbf{y}^{(2)}), ..., (\mathbf{x}^{(M)}, \mathbf{y}^{(M)})\}$. To fulfill this objective, the FNN specifies a function with adjustable parameters and an architecture, illustrated in Fig. 5.2. An FNN of depth D consists of an input layer (i.e., the 0-th layer) that is responsible for receiving the input data, $\mathbf{x}$, and an output layer (i.e., the D-th layer) that produces the output, $\mathbf{y}$. Between these two layers, a total of D-1 hidden layers are present. At each layer l ($1 \leq l \leq D$), the previous layer's output $\mathbf{a}^{[l-1]}$, ($l-1$)-th is utilized as input, and a nonlinear transformation $\mathbf{a}^{[l]} = h(W^{[l]}\mathbf{a}^{[l-1]} + \mathbf{b}^{[l]})$ is applied to generate the output $\mathbf{a}^{[l]}$. The initial value of a is set to $\mathbf{x}$, and the weight and bias parameters for the l-th layer are denoted by $W^{[l]}$ and $\mathbf{b}^{[l]}$, respectively.

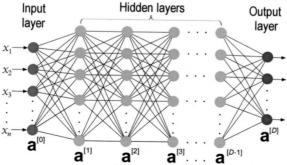

Figure 5.2 The fully connected deep feedforward neural network.

Additionally, $h(\cdot)$ represents a nonlinear activation function that is applied to the data. The objective of the learning process is to find the parameters $W^{[l]}$ and $\mathbf{b}^{[l]}$, for $l = 1, 2, ..., D$, through the training set $\mathbb{T}$.

FNNs are widely utilized for multiclass classification tasks. In such cases, the output layer has K units, where K is the number of classes, and the softmax function is applied to $\mathbf{a}^{[D]} = (a_1^{[D]}, a_2^{[D]}, ..., a_K^{[D]})^{\mathsf{T}}$ to generate a discrete probability distribution that corresponds to K different classes. $p_k(\mathbf{x}) = \exp\left(a_k^{[D]}\right) / \sum_{k=1}^{K} \exp(a_K^{[D]})$, where $k = 1, 2, ..., K$. In the context of multiclass classification, the target $\mathbf{y}^{(i)}, i = 1, 2, ..., M$ within the training set $\mathbb{T}$ is frequently depicted as a one-hot vector $\mathbf{y}^{(i)} = (y_1^{(i)}, y_2^{(i)}, ..., y_K^{(i)})$, where $y_k^{(i)} = 1$ if $\mathbf{x}^{(i)}$ is a member of class k, and $y_k^{(i)} = 0$ otherwise, for $k = 1, 2, ..., K$. In order to determine the values of the parameters $(W^{[1]}, W^{[2]}, ..., W^{[D]})$ and $\mathbf{b} = (\mathbf{b}^{[1]}, \mathbf{b}^{[2]}, ..., \mathbf{b}^{[D]})$, the backpropagation algorithm is utilized to minimize the cross-entropy loss function for $\mathbb{T}$, as proposed in [13].

$$J(W, \mathbf{b}) = -\frac{1}{M} \sum_{i=1}^{M} \sum_{k=1}^{K} y_k^{(i)} \log\left(p_k(\mathbf{x}^{(i)})\right) \tag{5.2}$$

After learning the parameters, FNNs can predict the class of a new input $\mathbf{x}$ by $t(\mathbf{x}) = \text{argmax}_{k=1}^{K} p_k(\mathbf{x})$. Furthermore, the FNN can also provide the probability (or confidence) that the forecasted category for $\mathbf{x}$ is determined by $p(\mathbf{x}) = \max_{k=1}^{K} p_k(\mathbf{x})$.

During the era of deep learning, the rectified linear unit (ReLU) has become the most widely used nonlinear activation function. Compared to the tanh or sigmoid functions, ReLU can often accelerate the learning process [14]. In addition, a variety of advanced techniques have been developed to enable the effective training of deep neural networks. These include methods for parameter initialization (e.g., Kaiming initialization [15]), regularization (e.g., dropout [16]), and gradient-based optimization (e.g., Adam optimizer [17]).

5.3 The proposed algorithm

5.3.1 Overview

Algorithm 5.1 outlines the framework of the proposed θ-DEA-DP. The first step involves generating a set of N structured weight vectors, following the same approach as in θ-DEA [8]. Next, we utilize Latin hypercube sampling, as described in ParEGO [18], to produce a set of initial solutions $\mathbb{P}$ in Step 2. To determine the size of $\mathbb{P}$, the number of solutions is specified as $11n - 1$, where n represents the total number of decision variables. In Steps 3–9, every solution in $\mathbb{P}$ is evaluated and subsequently added to an external archive $\mathbb{A}$. This data structure is utilized to maintain a record of all the assessed solutions up to the present moment.

Algorithm 5.1: Framework of the Proposed θ-DEA-DP

1: $\{\mathbf{w}_1, \mathbf{w}_2, \ldots, \mathbf{w}_N\} \leftarrow$ Initialize Weight Vectors (m)
2: $\mathbb{P} \leftarrow$ LatinHypercube (n)
3: *evals* $\leftarrow 0$
4: $\mathbb{A} \leftarrow \varnothing$
5: **for** $\mathbf{x} \in \mathbb{P}$ **do**
6: Evaluate $(\mathbf{x})$
7:    *evals* $\leftarrow$ *evals* $+ 1$
8:    $\mathbb{A} \leftarrow \mathbb{A} \cup \mathbf{x}$
9: **end for**
10: p-net $\leftarrow$ Initiate-Pareto-Net $(\mathbb{A})$
11: θ-net $\leftarrow$ Initiate-θ-Net $(\mathbb{A})$
12: $\{\mathbf{x}_1^*, \mathbf{x}_2^*, \ldots, \mathbf{x}_N^*\} \leftarrow$ Get-θ-Reps $(\mathbb{A})$
13: $\{\mathbf{y}_1^*, \mathbf{y}_2^*, \ldots, \mathbf{y}_N^*\} \leftarrow$ Get-Pareto- Reps $(\mathbb{A})$
14: $\mathbb{P} \leftarrow$ TruncatePopulation $(\mathbb{P}, N)$
15: **while** *evals* $<$ MaxEval **do**
16:    $j \leftarrow$ ChooseTargetClusterIndex (N)
17:    $\mathbb{Q} \leftarrow$ GenerateOffsprings $(\mathbb{P}, N^*)$
18:    $\mathbf{z}^* \leftarrow$ TwoStagePreSelection $(\mathbb{Q}, \mathbf{x}_j^*, \mathbf{y}_j^*,$ p-net, θ-net$)$
19:    Evaluate $(\mathbf{z}^*)$
20:    *evals* $\leftarrow$ *evals* $+ 1$
21:    $\mathbb{A} \leftarrow \mathbb{A} \cup \mathbf{z}^*$
22:    Update-Pareto-Net (p-net, $\mathbb{A}$)
23:    Update-θ-Net (θ-net, $\mathbb{A}$))
24:    Update-θ-Reps $(\{\mathbf{x}_1^*, \mathbf{x}_2^*, \ldots, \mathbf{x}_N^*\}, \mathbb{A})$
25:    Update-Pareto-Reps $(\{\mathbf{y}_1^*, \mathbf{y}_2^*, \ldots, \mathbf{y}_N^*\}, \mathbb{A})$
26:    $\mathbb{P} \leftarrow$ TruncatePopulation $(\mathbb{P} \cup \mathbf{z}^*, N)$
27: **end while**

At Step 10, we establish Pareto-Net by training a neural network for Pareto dominance prediction, using the solutions stored in $\mathbb{A}$. Once Pareto-Net has been trained, it can determine the predicted Pareto dominance relation between any two solutions, $\mathbf{u}$ and $\mathbf{v}$ (i.e., $\mathbf{u} \prec \mathbf{v}$, $\mathbf{v} \prec \mathbf{u}$ or $\mathbf{u} \simeq \mathbf{v}$), together with the likelihood of being a member of the predicted dominance relationship. This is accomplished without any awareness of their objective values. In a similar vein, in Step 11, we commence the training of θ-Net, an additional neural network, to predict θ-dominance.

Section 5.2.2 provides an overview of the process by which N weight vectors partition the objective space into N distinct clusters, denoted as $\mathcal{C}_1, \mathcal{C}_2, \ldots, \mathcal{C}_N$. Steps 12−13 involve the identification of both the θ-representative solution, $\mathbf{x}_j^*$, and the Pareto-representative solution, $\mathbf{y}_j^*$, for each cluster $\mathcal{C}_j$. It is important to note that the selection of both $\mathbf{x}_j^*$ and $\mathbf{y}_j^*$ are made exclusively from the set $\mathbb{A}$. A detailed explanation of the concepts of θ and Pareto representative solutions will be provided at a later stage.

For θ-DEA-DP, the population size is established as N, matching the number of weight vectors. However, it's worth noting that the initial population size, $\mathbb{P}$, may exceed N, as it is initially determined as $11n - 1$. If the number of solutions exceed N (where N is a predetermined number), then Step 14 involves employing nondominated sorting via θ-dominance to identify the top N elite solutions.

The process comprising Steps 15–27 is repeated until the maximum number of evaluations (MaxEval) has been attained. During each iteration, the first step entails the selection of a cluster C_j to be evaluated (i.e., Step 16). Nevertheless, to ensure impartiality, we randomize the sequence of the clusters in every round.

In Step 17, we generate a new population $\mathbb{Q}$, containing N^* individuals, from the current population $\mathbb{P}$, utilizing simulated binary crossover (SBX) and polynomial mutation [19]. Consistent with θ-DEA, we apply random mating selection. It's worth noting that $N^* \gg N$, ensuring that $\mathbb{Q}$ includes a high probability of good candidate solutions.

At this stage, we have a designated cluster, C_j, and a collection of candidate solutions, $\mathbb{Q}$. At Step 18, we employ a two-stage preselection strategy, supported by the trained Pareto-Net and θ-Net, to choose a single solution, $\mathbf{z}^*$, from $\mathbb{Q}$ for evaluation. The anticipated outcome is that $\mathbf{z}^*$ will yield significant improvements over the θ-representative solution, $\mathbf{x}_j^*$, and the Pareto-representative solution, $\mathbf{y}_j^*$.

Following the evaluation of the newly generated solution, $\mathbf{z}^*$, it is possible to generate supplementary training instances for Pareto-Net and θ-Net. In Steps 22 and 23, the Pareto-Net and the θ-Net are both updated by incorporating new training samples in conjunction with those from previous iterations, by merging them with the existing training examples. Furthermore, as $\mathbf{z}^*$ is present, the θ and Pareto representative solutions must be updated at Steps 24 and 25, respectively. Ultimately, we re-establish the population size to N through θ-nondominated sorting in Step 26.

It's worth noting that θ-DEA-DP does not utilize a distinct normalization procedure. At present, the normalization of objective functions at the outset of optimization for θ-DEA-DP is conducted via the same approach utilized in ParEGO [18].

5.3.2 Representative solutions

In the context of a cluster, C_j, its θ-representative solution, $\mathbf{x}_j^*$, is defined as the solution that satisfies $\mathbf{x}_j^* \in \mathbb{A} \cap C_j$ and $\nexists \mathbf{x} \in \mathbb{A}, \mathbf{x} \prec_\theta \mathbf{x}_j^*$. It is noteworthy that $\mathbf{x}_j^*$ is the solution that attains the lowest value of $\mathcal{F}_j$ relative to all the solutions located in $\mathbb{A} \cap C_j$. Bear in mind that $\mathbf{x}_j^*$ may be void if there exists no solution in $\mathbb{A}$ that falls within C_j (i.e., $\mathbb{A} \cap C_j = \varnothing$).

Assuming that we have successfully obtained all the θ-representative solutions $\{\mathbf{x}_1^*, \mathbf{x}_2^*, \ldots, \mathbf{x}_N^*\}$, we can subsequently determine the Pareto nondominated solutions among this set, excluding any null solutions. The resulting indices of these

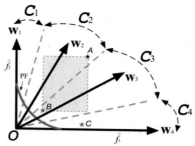

Figure 5.3 Illustration of θ and Pareto representative solutions.

solutions are then allocated to $\mathbb{I} = \{i_1, i_2, \ldots, i_N\}$. In the event that $j \in \mathbb{I}$ for a given cluster, $\mathcal{C}_j$, its Pareto-representative solution, $\mathbf{y}_j^*$, is identical to its θ-representative solution, $\mathbf{x}_j^*$. Conversely, if $j \notin \mathbb{I}$ and $\mathbf{x}_j^*$ is nonnull, we can definitively identify an index, i, from $\mathbb{I}$ such that $\mathbf{x}_i^* \prec \mathbf{x}_j^*$.

We then select $\mathbf{y}_j^*$ to be $\mathbf{x}_i^*$. If $\mathbb{I}$ contains several indices of this nature, we choose the one that results in the smallest Euclidean distance between $\mathbf{w}_i$ and $\mathbf{w}_j$. In the event that $\mathbf{x}_j^*$ is a null solution, $\mathbf{y}_j^*$ is also considered to be null.

Fig. 5.3 elaborates on representative solutions. Specifically, this figure shows that there is no representative solution for $\mathcal{C}_1$; however, A, B, and C serve as the θ-representative solutions for $\mathcal{C}_2$, $\mathcal{C}_3$, and $\mathcal{C}_4$, correspondingly. Given that B and C are both Pareto nondominated solutions within the set of three θ-representative solutions, they can also be considered as Pareto-representative solutions for $\mathcal{C}_3$ and $\mathcal{C}_4$, respectively. As for $\mathcal{C}_2$, B is designated as its Pareto-representative solution. This decision is based on the fact that B Pareto dominates A and that $\mathbf{w}_2$ is nearer to $\mathbf{w}_3$ than it is to $\mathbf{w}_4$.

5.3.3 Surrogates based on dominance prediction

Given that the processes outlined in this subsection apply to Pareto-Net and θ-Net in the same manner, we have used Pareto-Net to illustrate. In the context of dominance prediction, we have formulated this task as a three-class classification problem, which comprises A dominates B, B dominates A, or neither dominates the other.

(1) *Initiate the surrogates*: Generating a training set, $\mathbb{T}$, from the evaluated solutions contained in archive $\mathbb{A}$ is a prerequisite for initializing the Pareto-Net in Step 10 of Algorithm 5.1. It is assumed that $\mathbb{A}$ is comprised of $\{\mathbf{x}_1, \mathbf{x}_2, \ldots, \mathbf{x}_S\}$, where S signifies the current total number of solutions stored in $\mathbb{A}$. Each training example featured within $\mathbb{A}$ consists of an input vector, $\mathbf{x}_{i,j} = [\mathbf{x}_i, \mathbf{x}_j]$, It involves creating a composite vector by merging any two solutions, $\mathbf{x}_i$ and $\mathbf{x}_j$, from $\mathbb{A}$ ($i \neq j$). The output $\mathbf{y}_{i,j}$ is a one-hot vector that denotes the category to which $\mathbf{x}_{i,j}$ is classified. In this chapter, if $\mathbf{x}_i \prec \mathbf{x}_j$, $\mathbf{x}_{i,j}$ is assigned to class 1, if $\mathbf{x}_j \prec \mathbf{x}_i$, it is assigned to class 2, and if $\mathbf{x}_i \simeq \mathbf{x}_j$, it is

assigned to class 3. By doing this, we can generate a training set, $\mathbb{T}$, comprising of input-output examples that amount to $S(S-1)$.

We utilize a collection of examples to instruct the classifier, also known as Pareto-Net, which is a fully connected FNN presented in Fig. 5.2. To start the FNN parameters, we implement Kaiming initiation [15]. To trim down overfitting, weight decay is employed as a form of regularization. The optimization of FNN parameters is accomplished through utilization of the Adam optimizer [17], which operates using a fixed minibatch size. These methods are considered to be conventional approaches for training deep FNNs and have been integrated within PyTorch [20].

Our primary realization concerning dominance prediction is that it often involves a classification issue with imbalanced classes [21]. To tackle class imbalance, we apply a widely employed approach, which involves assigning a weight factor to each class as a component of the cross-entropy loss function. Eq. (5.2) outlines the formulation of the weighted cross-entropy loss, which is expressed as follows:

$$J(W, \mathbf{b}) = -\frac{1}{M}\sum_{i=1}^{M}\sum_{k=1}^{K}\alpha_k y_k^{(i)}\log\big(p_k(\mathbf{x}^{(i)})\big) \tag{5.3}$$

Here, α_k $(k = 1, 2, \ldots, K)$ refers to the reciprocal of class frequency for class k within the training set.

After concatenating two solutions into a vector $[\mathbf{u}, \mathbf{v}]$, the Pareto-Net is trained to predict the class of $[\mathbf{u}, \mathbf{v}]$ as $t(\mathbf{u}, \mathbf{v})$ and we calculate the probability of being assigned to the anticipated class as $p(\mathbf{u}, \mathbf{v})$. This prediction function exhibits a limitation in that the predicted dominance relation between $\mathbf{u}$ and $\mathbf{v}$ may vary based on whether the input vector is $[\mathbf{u}, \mathbf{v}]$ or $[\mathbf{v}, \mathbf{u}]$, especially when Pareto-Net is unsuccessful in accurately capturing the traits of Pareto dominance. An instance of inconsistency may arise, as illustrated by the output of Pareto-Net, which may yield $t(\mathbf{u}, \mathbf{v}) = 1$ to indicate that $\mathbf{u} \prec \mathbf{v}$, while simultaneously outputting $t(\mathbf{u}, \mathbf{v}) = 3$ to indicate that $\mathbf{u} \simeq \mathbf{v}$. In order to address this issue, we modify the prediction process by utilizing the input vector that generates the highest prediction probability/confidence to establish the dominance relation. Consequently, the predicted class of $[\mathbf{u}, \mathbf{v}]$ and the corresponding prediction probability are then updated as follows:

$$\hat{t}(\mathbf{u}, \mathbf{v}) = \begin{cases} t(\mathbf{u}, \mathbf{v}), & \text{if } p(\mathbf{u}, \mathbf{v}) \geq p(\mathbf{v}, \mathbf{u}) \\ 3 - t(\mathbf{u}, \mathbf{v}), & \text{if } p(\mathbf{u}, \mathbf{v}) < p(\mathbf{v}, \mathbf{u}) \text{ and } t(\mathbf{v}, \mathbf{u}) \neq 3 \\ 3, & \text{if } p(\mathbf{u}, \mathbf{v}) < p(\mathbf{v}, \mathbf{u}) \text{ and } t(\mathbf{v}, \mathbf{u}) = 3 \end{cases} \tag{5.4}$$

We set $\hat{p}(\mathbf{u}, \mathbf{v})$ equal to the maximum value between $p(\mathbf{u}, \mathbf{v})$ and $p(\mathbf{v}, \mathbf{u})$, while $\hat{t}(\mathbf{u}, \mathbf{v})$ and $\hat{p}(\mathbf{u}, \mathbf{v})$ are both specified as 0 in the event that either $\mathbf{u}$ or $\mathbf{v}$ is deemed a null solution, for ease of use.

In a similar manner, the θ-Net provides a prediction function $\hat{t}_\theta(\mathbf{u}, \mathbf{v})$ and a prediction probability $\hat{p}_\theta(\mathbf{u}, \mathbf{v})$. When $\hat{t}_\theta(\mathbf{u}, \mathbf{v}) = 1$, it indicates that $\mathbf{u}$ is predicted to be dominated by $\mathbf{v}$ under θ. On the other hand, when $\hat{t}_\theta(\mathbf{u}, \mathbf{v}) = 2$, $\mathbf{v}$ is predicted to be dominated by $\mathbf{u}$ under θ. Finally, when $\hat{t}_\theta(\mathbf{u}, \mathbf{v}) = 3$, $\mathbf{u}$ and $\mathbf{v}$ are predicted to be incomparable under θ.

(2) *Update the surrogates*: During each iteration, our aim is to revise the Pareto-Net (Step 22 of Algorithm 5.1). If the cardinality of $\mathbb{A}$, denoted by $\mathbb{A}$, is less than $T_{\max}$, we use all the solutions in $\mathbb{A}$ to update the Pareto-Net. However, if $\mathbb{A} \geq T_{\max}$, we solely consider the $T_{\max}$ most recently assessed solutions in A to minimize computational expenses, where $T_{\max}$ is a predetermined parameter.

Imagine that $\mathbf{z}^*$ is a solution that has been newly evaluated and added to $\mathbb{A}$ in Step 21 of Algorithm 5.1. Since it has been added to $\mathbb{A}$, it is certain that $\mathbf{z}^*$ will be taken into account during the updating process. All solutions other than $\mathbf{z}^*$ that are being considered form a set called $\mathbb{A}$, which includes the solutions $\{\mathbf{x}_{i_1}, \mathbf{x}_{i_2}, \ldots, \mathbf{x}_{i_{T'}}\}$. The value of T' is determined by taking the maximum of the cardinality of $\mathbb{A}$ and $T_{\max}$, and then subtracting 1. By using the solutions $\{\mathbf{x}_{i_1}, \mathbf{x}_{i_2}, \ldots, \mathbf{x}_{i_{T'}}\}$ and $\mathbf{z}^*$ as inputs, we can create $2T'$ novel examples that have not been observed by the Pareto-Net. These examples are constructed by pairing $\mathbf{z}^*$ with each solution in $\mathbb{A}$, resulting in the following sequence of input pairs: $[\mathbf{x}_{i_1}, \mathbf{z}^*], [\mathbf{x}_{i_2}, \mathbf{z}^*], \ldots, [\mathbf{x}_{i_{T'}}, \mathbf{z}^*], [\mathbf{z}^*, \mathbf{x}_{i_1}], [\mathbf{z}^*, \mathbf{x}_{i_2}], \ldots, [\mathbf{z}^*, \mathbf{x}_{i_{T'}}]$. In order to assess the present efficacy of the Pareto-Net, we evaluate its performance using the $2T'$ examples. It is worth noting that the presence of class imbalance should be taken into consideration, relying solely on overall accuracy may not provide a meaningful evaluation of performance. To obtain a more comprehensive evaluation of performance, we calculate the accuracy for each individual class, denoted as acc_1, acc_2 and acc_3. We then determine the minimum accuracy across all classes, which is represented as $acc_{\min} = \min_{k=1}^3 acc_k$.

By utilizing $acc_{\min}$, we initially determine if an update should occur. When the accuracy of the minimum performing class, represented as $acc_{\min}$, exceeds a predetermined accuracy threshold denoted as γ, then Pareto-Net is likely performing sufficiently, and no further modification is necessary. However, if $acc_{\min} \leq \gamma$, we proceed with updating the model parameters of the Pareto-Net through continued training. Our goal is to generate a training set by combining any two solutions from the set $\mathbb{A} \cup \mathbf{z}^*$ through pairing. As a result of the training mechanism that relies on gradients, it is not necessary to retrain the Pareto-Net from the very beginning. Rather than that, the parameters of the Pareto-Net at the current stage are employed as the initial values for the Adam optimizer.

The last task in the updating process is to establish the number of training epochs, which is represented as E_{upd}. Let us assume that E_{init} refers to the number of training epochs that were employed during the initialization of the Pareto-Net, we define E_{upd} based on $acc_{\min}$ and E_{init} as follows:

$$E_{\mathrm{upd}} = \left(1 - \frac{acc_{\min}}{\gamma}\right) E_{\mathrm{init}} \tag{5.5}$$

This formula takes into account two factors: (1) in general, we can expect that E_{upd} will be smaller than E_{init}, given that the Pareto-Net has already undergone some training prior to the updating process; and (2) smaller alterations of model parameters are likely required for a higher estimated accuracy value of acc_{min}.

5.3.4 Two-stage preselection strategy

During each iteration, to begin, we select a specific target cluster C_j, and then proceed to sample a group of potential solutions $\mathbb{Q}$ by following Steps 16–17 of Algorithm 5.1. Our objective is to choose a solitary solution from $\mathbb{Q}$ for the purpose of evaluation, aided by both Pareto-Net and θ-Net. To accomplish this, we implement a two-stage preselection approach.

(1) *Comparison with representative solutions*: In the first stage, our objective is to choose a subset of $\mathbb{Q}$ containing solutions that are likely to enhance the current representative solutions. Depending on whether a θ-representative solution $\mathbf{x}_j^*$ is null or not, there are two cases that require separate treatment.

Assuming that $\mathbf{x}_j^*$ is not empty, we assess every solution in $\mathbb{Q}$ with respect to θ-dominance compared to $\mathbf{x}_j^*$, and e then assess the level of Pareto dominance between the selected solution and $\mathbf{y}_j^*$. To be precise, we use the θ-Net and Pareto-Net to calculate $\hat{\iota}_\theta(\mathbf{z}, \mathbf{x}_j^*)$ and $\hat{\iota}(\mathbf{z}, \mathbf{y}_j^*)$, respectively, for every solution $\mathbf{z}$ in the set $\mathbb{Q}$. Based on these values, we can classify the solutions in $\mathbb{Q}$ into four different categories:

1. $\mathbb{Q}_1 = \{\mathbf{z} \in \mathbb{Q} \mid \hat{\iota}_\theta(\mathbf{z}, \mathbf{x}_j^*) = 1 \wedge \hat{\iota}(\mathbf{z}, \mathbf{y}_j^*) = 1\}$
2. $\mathbb{Q}_2 = \{\mathbf{z} \in \mathbb{Q} \mid \hat{\iota}_\theta(\mathbf{z}, \mathbf{x}_j^*) = 1 \wedge \hat{\iota}(\mathbf{z}, \mathbf{y}_j^*) = 3\}$
3. $\mathbb{Q}_3 = \{\mathbf{z} \in \mathbb{Q} \mid \hat{\iota}_\theta(\mathbf{z}, \mathbf{x}_j^*) = 3 \wedge \hat{\iota}(\mathbf{z}, \mathbf{y}_j^*) = 1\}$
4. $\mathbb{Q}_4 = \{\mathbf{z} \in \mathbb{Q} \mid \hat{\iota}_\theta(\mathbf{z}, \mathbf{x}_j^*) = 2 \vee \hat{\iota}(\mathbf{z}, \mathbf{y}_j^*) = 2\}$

The solutions that belong to $\mathbb{Q}_4$ will not be taken into account, as they are all predicted to be either θ-dominated by $\mathbf{x}_j^*$ or Pareto-dominated by $\mathbf{y}_j^*$. Out of $\mathbb{Q}_1$, $\mathbb{Q}_2$ and $\mathbb{Q}_3$, we only choose a single category for additional examination and disregard solutions from the remaining categories. In the proposed algorithm, $\mathbb{Q}_1$ is given the utmost priority, followed by $\mathbb{Q}_2$ and $\mathbb{Q}_3$. We opt to directly choose $\mathbb{Q}_1$ if it is nonempty. $\mathbb{Q}_2$ or $\mathbb{Q}_3$, on the other hand, are only considered when higher-priority categories are devoid of any elements.

In the event that $\mathbf{x}_j^*$ is empty, this suggests that one or more clusters lack assessed solutions. In such a scenario, our objective is to identify a solution from the unexplored cluster to increase diversity. We only focus on solutions in the set $\mathbb{Q}$ that are not dominated by θ during our analysis in relation to all existing nonempty θ-representative solutions. This subset is labeled as category $\mathbb{Q}_5$ and is defined as follows: $\mathbb{Q}_5 = \{\mathbf{z} \in \mathbb{Q} \mid \forall i \in \{1, 2, ..., N\}, \hat{\iota}_\theta(\mathbf{z}, \mathbf{x}_i^*) = 3\}$.

It's worth noting that in both cases, if the number of solutions in the selected category exceeds the Q_{max} parameter, we only keep a maximum of Q_{max} solutions. We accomplish this by computing the total prediction probabilities assigned to every solution $\mathbf{z}$ in the selected category, which is represented as $p_{sum}(\mathbf{z})$. In the first scenario, $p_{sum}(\mathbf{z})$ is defined as the sum of $p_\theta(\mathbf{z}, \mathbf{x}_j^*)$ and $p(\mathbf{z}, \mathbf{y}_j^*)$ for each solution $\mathbf{z}$, while in the second scenario, $p_{sum}(\mathbf{z})$ is defined as the sum of $p_\theta(\mathbf{z}, \mathbf{x}_i^*)$ for i ranging from 1 to N. Following this, we proceed to choose the Q_{max} solutions with the highest $p_{sum}(\mathbf{z})$.

(2) *Comparison within the selected category of solutions*: Let us assume that we have chosen a specific category, $\mathbb{Q}_k = \{\mathbf{z}_1, \mathbf{z}_2, \ldots, \mathbf{z}_Q\}$, for evaluation during the initial stage, where k is an element of $\{1, 2, 3, 5\}$. The second stage of preselection is now responsible for singling out one solution from $\mathbb{Q}_k$ that is likely to produce the greatest enhancement over the representative solutions. Our first step is to utilize the Pareto-Net (θ-Net) to predict the Pareto-dominance (θ-dominance) relationship between every pair of solutions in $\mathbb{Q}_k$. Our next step is to define, for each solution $\mathbf{z}_i$ in $\mathbb{Q}_k$, a metric that we refer to as the expected dominance number (EDN):

$$e(\mathbf{z}_i) = \sum_{j \neq i} I\left(\hat{t}(\mathbf{z}_i, \mathbf{z}_j) = 1\right)\hat{p}(\mathbf{z}_i, \mathbf{z}_j) \tag{5.6}$$

Here, $I(\cdot)$ denotes the indicator function. In essence, this metric computes the likelihood of solution $\mathbf{z}_i$ in $\mathbb{Q}_k$ being Pareto-dominant over other solutions, while also considering the associated probability. In the same vein, we can establish an EDN for solution $\mathbf{z}_i$ in $\mathbb{Q}_k$ with respect to θ-dominance:

$$e_\theta(\mathbf{z}_i) = \sum_{j \neq i} I\left(\hat{t}_\theta(\mathbf{z}_i, \mathbf{z}_j) = 1\right)\hat{p}_\theta(\mathbf{z}_i, \mathbf{z}_j) \tag{5.7}$$

In the end, we sort the solutions within $\mathbb{Q}_k$ based on the total sum $e_{sum}(\mathbf{z}_i) = e(\mathbf{z}_i) + e_\theta(\mathbf{z}_i)$. The solution that achieves the highest $e_{sum}(\mathbf{z}_i)$ value is then chosen for function evaluation.

5.3.5 Discussion

θ-DEA-DP involves the integration of both Pareto and θ-dominance prediction techniques. As elaborated in Section 5.1, relying exclusively on Pareto dominance prediction is deemed undesirable. Similarly, relying solely on θ-dominance prediction may reduce the speed of convergence. To demonstrate this point, consider Fig. 5.3, where our objective in this instance is to leverage the θ-Net to aid in locating a solution within cluster C_2 that θ-dominates the current θ-representative solution, A. It is anticipated that the solution selected for evaluation will be positioned within the shaded area illustrated in Fig. 5.3, and may consequently be Pareto dominated by solution B in another cluster C_3. This implies that newly assessed solutions may not enhance the current set of solutions and may impede progress toward the PF, albeit resulting in a higher quality overall. We make a distinction between Pareto and θ-representative solutions for a cluster, for the same reason.

For instance, if we use A instead of B as the Pareto representative solution for $\mathcal{C}_2$, then a significant number of the solutions identified by the Pareto-Net as promising would be located in the shaded area, offering no contribution to an overall quality improvement. Employing both Pareto-Net and θ-Net lead to a potential benefit of enabling effective optimization guidance, even if one of the two surrogates performs inadequately, resulting in improved optimization robustness.

In θ-DEA-DP, it is crucial to have an adequate number of offsprings N^* to generate a more extensive and superior pool of potential solutions. Nonetheless, if N^* is exceedingly large, there is a risk that the surrogates will be overused for comparing alternatives. This could lead to an excessive amount of approximation noise during the selection process, as surrogates are typically not perfect, making it difficult to identify an excellent solution. Additionally, A substantial N^* can lead to computational costs that are too prohibitive. Due to these factors, a maximum category size Q_{max} must be established in the two-stage preselection process.

As discussed in Section 5.3.3 (1), it is critical to regard dominance prediction as a classification problem that is imbalanced in nature. Regarding Pareto dominance, it is widely recognized that as the number of objectives grows, the vast majority of solutions will cease to be dominated by one another. Regarding θ-dominance, the situation where all the solutions employed in the training set come from a single cluster represents a highly unusual case. In this scenario, there will not be any training instances that are categorized as class 3. Assuming an equal distribution of solutions across N clusters, with L solutions per cluster, we can conclude that each of class 1 and class 2 consists of $L(L-1)N/2$ training examples. Furthermore, class 3 encompasses $N(N-1)L^2$ training examples. It can be deduced that the proportion of training examples in class 3 as compared to class 1 or class 2 is greater than 2N − 1:1. The distribution of classes tends to be severely imbalanced due to the typical range of N falling between tens and hundreds.

Dropout [16] is not utilized when training the Pareto-Net and θ-Net. Despite being a popular regularization technique in deep learning, we observed that dropout often leads to poorer performance of optimization in our experiments. In contrast, a moderate degree of weight decay, when used without dropout, has typically shown to produce superior outcomes. It is worth noting that Snoek et al. [22] reported a comparable finding within the framework of single-objective Bayesian optimization. In forthcoming research, we intend to conduct an investigation into the underlying factors that contribute to this phenomenon.

In the two-stage preselection process, it's natural to prioritize solutions in $\mathbb{Q}_1$ since each solution in this category has the potential to enhance both Pareto and θ-representative solutions based on the surrogates. Furthermore, our objective is to promote convergence while maintaining the diversity preservation mechanism intact. To achieve this, we prioritize $\mathbb{Q}_2$ over $\mathbb{Q}_3$.

The primary distinction between θ-DEA-DP and θ-DEA lies in the method used to choose the offspring solutions to evaluate and include in the survival selection process. In the case of θ-DEA, every offspring solution undergoes an evaluation., while with θ-DEA-DP, only one offspring solution is selected for evaluation using a two-stage preselection aided by dominance prediction.

5.4 Experiments

This section begins by outlining the fundamental parameters used in our experiments. We subsequently assess and verify the efficacy of θ-DEA-DP in handling multiobjective and many-objective optimization problems. Finally, we explore how various components of θ-DEA-DP affect its performance.

5.4.1 Experimental design
5.4.1.1 Test problems
We choose problems for testing from three extensively utilized suites of multiobjective benchmarks.

Within the ZDT [23] benchmark suite, there are six two-objective test problems that Deb [24] has proposed a methodology for addressing evolutionary optimization problems that differ in their degree of complexity. In this context, we specifically focus on four unconstrained problems, denoted as ZDT1, ZDT2, ZDT3, and ZDT4.

The DTLZ [25] benchmark suite provides a collection of problems that can scale to any number of objectives. To align with the approach in [18], we assess the performance of our approach on four distinct optimization problems, specifically DTLZ1, DTLZ2, DTLZ4, and DTLZ7. Additionally, we adopt a suggestion from [18] and replace the value of 20π in the cosine term with 2π for DTLZ1. This adjustment serves to decrease the ruggedness of the function.

The WFG [26] benchmark suite is created by applying a sequence of transformations to decision variables, with each transformation potentially introducing a desirable property (such as nonseparability) to the problem. Similar to DTLZ, each WFG problem can scale according to the number of objectives. In this context, we focus on two problems, namely WFG6 and WFG7, for evaluation, as in ref. [27].

Additional experiments are detailed in the supplementary material, where we present results from evaluations on an additional four WFG problems (namely WFG4, WFG5, WFG8, and WFG9) and four practical problems. Four different design problems, which include a pressure vessel challenge, a two-bar truss challenge, a welded beam challenge, and a conceptual marine challenge, constitute the latter group of problems.

Table 5.1 provides a summary of the MOPs (with two or three objectives) employed in our experiments, which exhibit a range of characteristics. To evaluate the

Table 5.1 Multiobjective test problems used in this study.

Problem	Number of objectives (m)	Number of variables (n)	Features
ZDT1	2	10	Convex
ZDT2	2	10	Concave
ZDT3	2	10	Convex, disconnected
ZDT4	2	10	Concave, multimodal
DTLZ1	2	6	Linear, multimodal
DTLZ2	3	8	Concave
DTLZ4	3	8	Concave, biased
DTLZ7	3	8	Mixed, disconnected
WFG6	3	10	Concave, nonseparable
WFG7	3	10	Concave, biased

performance on MaOPs, we also consider the five and eight-objective versions of DTLZ1, DTLZ2, DTLZ4, DTLZ7, WFG6, and WFG7. In all these cases, the number of decision variables is fixed at 10.

It should be emphasized that defining the position-related parameter is imperative when dealing with WFG6 and WFG7. For our experiments, we adhered to the suggestion presented in [8] and [28] by setting this parameter to $m - 1$, where m denotes the number of objectives being considered.

5.4.1.2 Performance indicator

To assess an algorithm's effectiveness, we adopt the inverted generational distance (IGD) metric. This metric is computed by comparing t objective space, denoted as $\mathbb{S}$, with a set of uniformly distributed points on the PF, denoted as $\mathbb{P}^*$. The IGD value can be calculated using the following formula:

$$\text{IGD}(\mathbb{S},\mathbb{P}^*) = \sum_{\mathbf{v} \in \mathbb{P}^*} \frac{d(\mathbf{v},\mathbb{S})}{|\mathbb{P}^*|} \qquad (5.8)$$

To compute the IGD value, we measure the minimum Euclidean distance $d(\mathbf{v},\mathbb{S})$ between $\mathbf{v}$ and the points contained within $\mathbb{P}^*$ (designated as $\mathbb{S}$). This metric provides a thorough evaluation of the convergence and diversity exhibited by a set of solutions, with smaller IGD values indicating superior performance. To ensure reliable IGD calculations, the value of $|\mathbb{P}^*|$ should be sufficiently large to provide an accurate representation of the PF. In our experiments, in the case of problems involving 2, 3, 5, and 8 objectives, we set the value of $|\mathbb{P}^*|$ to be approximately 500, 10^3, 10^5, and 10^6, correspondingly.

It is worth noting that hypervolume (HV) [29] is another widely utilized metric for evaluating performance in the literature. HV is commonly used in place of IGD when the true PF is not available prior to the optimization process. In the supplemental material, we utilize HV as a metric to assess performance on four practical problems.

5.4.1.3 Algorithms in comparison

We evaluate the efficacy of the proposed θ-DEA-DP by comparing its performance to that of the subsequent applicable algorithms:

(1) θ-DEA [8]: Survival selection of solutions is performed by utilizing a unique algorithm that incorporates both Pareto and θ-nondominated sorting techniques. Although θ-DEA is not officially categorized as a surrogate-assisted MOEA, we have included it as a benchmark for comparison purposes because of its strong similarities to θ-DEA-DP.

(2) ParEGO [18]: In this algorithm, several objective values of a solution are combined into a sole function value through a weight vector that can be parameterized. The selection of the solution for evaluation involves maximizing the expected improvement (EI) standard based on the current aggregation function, which is similar to the approach used in EGO [1]. ParEGO is designed to maintain solution diversity implicitly by selecting a unique weight vector during each iteration.

(3) DomRank [30]: Similar to ParEGO, this algorithm is an extension of EGO and caters to MOPs. Nonetheless, it utilizes a different method of scalarization that relies on Pareto dominance. DomRank determines the value of an aggregation function for a solution by directly correlating it with the number of evaluated solutions that dominate it.

(4) MOEA/D-EGO [31]: The scalarization technique used in this algorithm bears resemblance to that of ParEGO. MOEA/D-EGO evaluates all aggregation functions during each iteration, while ParEGO only evaluates one. Using MOEA/D-DE [32], it generates multiple points for function evaluation by maximizing the corresponding expected improvement (EI) values of these functions concurrently.

(5) CSEA [33]: For this algorithm, a group of reference solutions is chosen from the assessed solutions to establish the classification boundary. This boundary is then used to create a classifier that can categorize the candidate solutions into either good or bad. This classifier is employed to assist in the selection of promising solutions for subsequent function evaluation.

Similar to ParEGO and MOEA/D-EGO, θ-DEA-DP utilizes multiple weight vectors to combine the objectives, and this characteristic is apparent in θ-dominance. θ-DEA-DP utilizes dominance comparisons to rank candidate solutions during the second preselection stage, displaying a resemblance to the DomRank method. θ-DEA-DP, like CSEA, utilizes surrogates based on classification.

The Python implementation of θ-DEA-DP and θ-DEA is developed, with PyTorch [20] used to construct the deep learning models in θ-DEA-DP. The source code for θ-DEA-DP has been made publicly available online to ensure reproducibility in research. We utilize the Python implementation of ParEGO and DomRank by Rahat et al. [30], while for MOEA/D-EGO and CSEA, we employ the Matlab implementation from the PlatEMO [34] platform.

Each test problem is run 21 times independently using each algorithm. The Pareto nondominated set, which encompasses all evaluated solutions, is utilized to compute IGD during each run of the algorithm. To establish statistical significance between two competing algorithms, the IGD outcomes are evaluated using the Wilcoxon rank sum test at a 5% significance level. To account for multiple comparisons, we also utilize the Holm–Bonferroni method.

5.4.1.4 Parameter settings
Latin hypercube sampling is employed by all compared algorithms to generate $11n - 1$ initial points for function evaluation, where n corresponds to the number of decision variables. To ensure fair evaluation, every algorithm employs an identical termination criterion for each execution. The maximum number of function evaluations for two and three-objective problems is 250, according to [18], whereas for five-objective problems, it is set at 300, and for eight-objective problems, it is 400.

The usage of a predetermined set of weight vectors is necessary in θ-DEA-DP, θ-DEA, ParEGO, and MOEA/D-EGO. The strategy employed to generate structured weight vectors is identical to that outlined in [8]. Table 5.2 displays a collection of weight vector arrangements for the problem with diverse numbers of objectives, where H is a parameter that governs the generation of weight vectors. The use of two-layered weight vectors [27] is implemented for issues with five and eight objectives to avoid the creation of exclusively boundary weight vectors.

The PBI function's penalty parameter (θ) is set to 5 for both θ-DEA-DP and θ-DEA, while the population size is equivalent to the number of weight vectors. The population size is identical for CSEA.

Table 5.3 displays the parameter values for different modules in θ-DEA-DP. The hyperparameter setting for Pareto-Net and θ-Net is identical. It is important to note

Table 5.2 Weight vector settings.

Number of objectives (m)	Divisions (H)	Number of weight vectors (N)
3	10	11
3	4	15
5	2, 2	30
8	2, 1	44

Table 5.3 Parameter setting for θ-DEA-DP.

Module	Parameter	Value
Evolution	Crossover probability (p_c)	1.0
	Mutation probability (p_m)	$1/n$
	Distribution index for crossover (η_c)	30
	Distribution index for mutation (η_m)	20
	Number of sampled offsprings (N^*)	7000
Surrogate	Depth of FNN (D)	3
	Number of units in each hidden layer (U)	200
	Weight decay coefficient (λ)	0.00001
	Epochs for initiating FNN (E_{init})	20
	Batch size (B)	32
	Learning rate (ϵ)	0.001
	Maximum size for updating (T_{max})	$11n + 24$
	Accuracy threshold (γ)	0.9
	Maximum category size (Q_{max})	300

that these parameter values have been set to enable θ-DEA-DP to perform reasonably well, but they may not be optimal. A comprehensive parametric analysis will be deferred to future research.

Regarding the residual parameters in CSEA, DomRank, MOEA/D-EGO, ParEGO, and θ-DEA, we embrace the parameter configurations advised by the corresponding original investigations [8,18,30,31,33].

5.4.2 Performance on multiobjective optimization problems

The data presented in Table 5.4 illustrates the outcomes obtained from tackling the multiobjective issues portrayed in Table 5.1, highlighting the superior, middle, and inferior IGD values. Each problem is represented by the symbols $+$, $-$, and $\approx$, which indicate that the corresponding algorithm performs considerably inferior, significantly superior, or comparable to θ-DEA-DP. Table 5.4 reveals that θ-DEA-DP outperforms all the other algorithms in a significant manner for 8 out of 10 problems. The two remaining problems have the next-best algorithm, namely CSEA on DTLZ4 and MOEA/D-EGO on DTLZ7, which are only slightly comparable to $\boldsymbol{\theta}$-DEA-DP in statistical terms. Compared to θ-DEA-DP, θ-DEA exhibits notably inferior performance, which showcases the efficacy of surrogates based on dominance prediction. Additionally, it is noteworthy that θ-DEA-DP typically outperforms the other algorithms under comparison to a considerable extent on ZDT1−ZDT3, DTLZ1, and DTLZ7. For ZDT2 and DTLZ1, θ-DEA-DP obtains median IGD results that are almost ten times lower than those achieved by the highest-performing rivals (specifically, MOEA/D-EGO for ZDT2 and ParEGO for DTLZ1).

Table 5.4 Best, median, and worst IGD values on two and three-objective test problems.

Problem	θ-DEA-DP	θ-DEA	ParEGO	DomRank	MOEA/D-EGO	CSEA
ZDT1	**1.16E−02**	3.46E−01	1.00E−01	1.18E−01	3.52E−02	1.61E−01
	1.61E−02	5.94E−01	1.37E−01	2.47E−01	6.30−02	3.86E−01
	2.28E−02	9.74E−01	2.65E−01	4.37E−01	2.50E−01	7.91E−01
		+	+	+	+	+
ZDT2	**1.49E−02**	7.25E−01	1.61E−01	1.30E−01	3.02E−02	4.09E−01
	1.85E−02	1.30E + 00	2.71E−01	1.80E−01	1.36E−01	1.06E + 00
	2.84E−02	2.04E + 00	4.32E−01	2.81E−01	3.74E−01	1.70E + 00
		+	+	+	+	+
ZDT3	3.82E−01	2.77E−01	7.04E−02	4.21E−02	1.57E−01	1.66E−01
	6.05E−02	4.38E−01	1.03E−01	1.04E−01	2.85E−01	4.12E−01
	1.35E−01	5.91E−01	1.75E−01	1.81E−01	5.85E−01	7.43E−01
		+	+	+	+	+
ZDT4	**1.05E + 01**	2.41E + 01	3.40E + 01	4.38E + 01	6.16E + 01	2.34E + 01
	2.80E + 01	3.53E + 01	5.70E + 01	6.80E + 01	8.46E + 01	4.78E + 01
	3.68E + 01	4.97E + 01	7.54E + 01	8.51E + 01	9.49E + 01	6.66E + 01
		+	+	+	+	+
DTLZ1	**2.15E−02**	4.74E−01	1.93E−01	1.05E + 00	1.55E + 00	2.64E + 00
	5.38E−01	6.26E + 00	4.12E−01	4.61E + 00	4.55E + 00	1.22E + 01
	1.14E−01	1.00E + 01	1.75E + 00	1.66E + 01	1.14E + 01	4.39E + 01
		+	+	+	+	+
DTLZ2	**1.10E−01**	1.46E−01	1.47E−01	1.59E−01	2.24E−01	1.69E−01
	1.23E−01	1.77E−01	1.58E−01	1.82E−01	2.58E−01	2.20E−01
	1.44E−01	2.11E−01	1.70E−01	2.43E−01	2.83E−01	2.85E−01
		+	+	+	+	+
DTLZ4	**1.21E−01**	1.99E−01	3.99E−01	3.92E−01	4.54E−01	1.45E−01
	2.12E−01	3.23E−01	4.78E−01	4.80E−01	5.32E−01	2.25E−01
	3.13E−01	6.01E−01	5.44E−01	5.68E−01	6.31E−01	6.03E−01
		+	+	+	+	≈
DTLZ7	**7.26E−02**	5.93E−01	2.30E−01	1.93E−01	8.09E−02	2.59E−01
	9.43E−02	8.80E−01	2.95E−01	5.02E−01	1.07E−01	8.77E−01
	1.72E−01	1.59E + 00	4.42E−01	1.01E + 00	**1.33E−01**	1.51E + 00
		+	+	+	≈	+
WFG6	**1.51E−01**	1.91E−01	2.31E−01	2.00E−01	2.07E−01	2.01E−01
	2.04E−01	2.19E−01	2.41E−01	2.26E−01	2.22E−01	2.10E−01
	2.30E−01	2.46E−01	2.65E−01	2.57E−01	2.37E−01	2.33E−01
		+	+	+	+	+
WFG7	**1.28E−01**	1.46E−01	1.82E−01	1.64E−01	1.73E−01	1.55E−01
	1.46E−01	1.61E−01	1.94E−01	1.77E−01	1.94E−01	1.77E−01
	1.70E−01	1.86E−01	2.09E−01	1.89E−01	2.01E−01	1.85E−01
		+	+	+	+	+
+ /−/ ≈		10/0/0	10/0/0	10/0/0	9/0/1	9/0/1

The best performance is shown in bold.

The ultimate nondominated solutions acquired from the run with the median IGD value for each surrogate–assisted algorithm on ZDT2, ZDT3, DTLZ1, and DTLZ2 are illustrated in Fig. 5.4, to visualize the distribution of solutions in the objective space. Based on Fig. 5.4, the following observations can be made:

1. For ZDT2, θ-DEA-DP offers an extremely precise estimation of the PF, while ParEGO, DomRank, and MOEA/D-EGO are unable to accurately capture a substantial segment of the PF, which can be attributed to their inability to address diversity concerns. Meanwhile, CSEA encounters difficulties in converging toward the PF.

2. ZDT3's PF is composed of five disjointed components. Although all algorithms evaluated struggle to cover all of these components, in terms of both convergence and diversity, θ-DEA-DP is capable of producing the most satisfactory approximation.

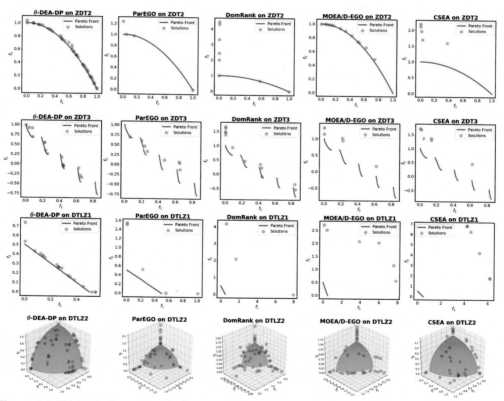

Figure 5.4 Final solution sets with the median IGD values in the objective space on ZDT1, ZDT3, DTLZ1, and DTLZ2.

3. DTLZ1 is formulated with a multimodal g function [18,25], which presents significant challenges in achieving convergence to the PF. Notably, θ-DEA-DP can attain a high level of convergence to the PF of DTLZ1 while simultaneously preserving a favorable dispersion of solutions. Conversely, ParEGO is only capable of generating a few solutions close to the PF. The solutions offered by DomRank, MOEA/D-EGO, and CSEA are significantly far apart from the PF. It is noteworthy that, despite also possessing a multimodal characteristic, the fitness landscape of ZDT4 is exceedingly rugged, with 21^9 local PFs. Consequently, despite attaining a higher solution quality than all other algorithms on ZDT4, θ-DEA-DP still fails to approach the PF, as evidenced by the large IGD values in Table 5.4.

4. In contrast to the other four algorithms, which yield solutions significantly far from the PF, every solution generated by θ-DEA-DP for DTLZ2 is close to the PF.

In Fig. 5.5, the number of function evaluations is graphed against the median IGD values (averaged over 21 runs) for each algorithm on ZDT and DTLZ problems, depicting their evolutionary paths. The data presented in Fig. 5.5 indicates that the surrogates in θ-DEA-DP are remarkably potent, as evidenced by its consistently superior and faster convergence rate in achieving much lower IGD values than θ-DEA. Furthermore, the evolutionary trajectories reveal that θ-DEA-DP maintains highly competitive performance throughout the optimization process relative to all other algorithms under consideration. Such findings suggest that θ-DEA-DP is a versatile optimization approach that can be effectively utilized in various optimization scenarios, even when the number of allowed function evaluations varies. An intriguing discovery

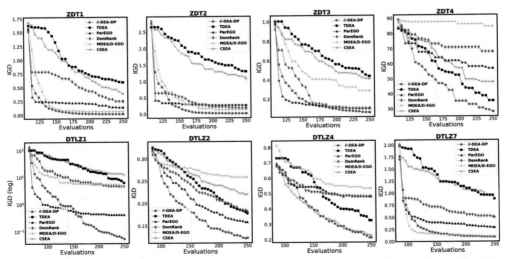

Figure 5.5 Evolution of the median of IGD values (over 21 runs) versus the number of function evaluations on ZDT and DTLZ problems.

is that ParEGO exhibits rapid convergence during the early phases of optimization (and occasionally even surpassing θ-DEA-DP), and some algorithms exhibit better performance, but then eexperience a near-stagnation effect. On ZDT2, ZDT3, and DTLZ1, ParEGO initially outperforms θ-DEA-DP, but is later surpassed by the latter. We postulate that optimization scenarios characterized by a substantially reduced number of function evaluations (e.g., 120) may be better suited for ParEGO.

5.4.3 Performance on many-objective optimization problems

A summary of the optimal, median, and poorest IGD results on five-objective test problems is presented in Table 5.5. It is evident from Table 5.5 that θ-DEA-DP continues to exhibit a decisive advantage over all other algorithms in comparison.

The best performance is shown in bold.

Table 5.5 Best, median and worst IGD values on five-objective test problems.

Problem	θ-DEA-DP	θ-DEA	ParEGO	DomRank	MOEA/D-EGO	CSEA
DTLZ1	**5.38E−01**	1.30E + 01	2.57E + 00	3.57E + 00	1.01E + 01	3.01E + 00
	1.29E + 00	3.78E + 01	4.02E + 00	4.02E + 01	5.43E + 01	1.54E + 01
	6.09E + 00	8.02E + 01	1.85E + 01	1.11E + 02	9.93E + 01	3.34E + 01
		+	+	+	+	+
DTLZ2	**2.46E−01**	3.05E−01	3.59E−01	3.62E−01	3.89E−01	3.45E−01
	2.65E−01	3.41E−01	3.77E−01	4.07E−01	4.41E−01	4.10E−01
	3.01E−01	3.96E−01	4.07E−01	4.48E−01	5.07E−01	4.73E−01
		+	+	+	+	+
DTLZ4	**3.42E−01**	4.43E−01	5.68E−01	6.10E−01	6.32E−01	3.72E−01
	4.45E−01	6.30E−01	6.23E−01	6.64E−01	7.12E−01	**4.10E−01**
	5.57E−01	8.82E−01	7.01E−01	7.62E−01	7.70E−01	**5.48E−01**
		+	+	+	+	≈
DTLZ7	**3.52E−01**	1.05E + 00	4.81E−01	5.63E−01	5.19E−01	1.03E + 00
	6.88E−01	1.18E + 00	**5.37E−01**	8.36E−01	6.47E−01	1.44E + 00
	1.01E + 00	1.76E + 00	**5.73E−01**	1.06E + 00	7.65E−01	1.83E + 00
		+	−	≈	≈	+
WFG6	**2.63E−01**	2.94E−01	3.13E−01	3.33E−01	2.96E−01	2.83E−01
	2.91E−01	3.11E−01	3.28E−01	3.60E−01	3.13E−01	3.18E−01
	3.15E−01	3.46E−01	3.49E−01	3.80E−01	3.23E−01	3.61E−01
		+	+	+	+	+
WFG7	**2.56E−01**	2.64E−01	2.95E−01	2.82E−01	2.93E−01	2.67E−01
	2.69E−01	2.82E−01	3.37E−01	2.97E−01	3.13E−01	2.96E−01
	3.01E−01	3.17E−01	3.54E−01	3.11E−01	3.57E−01	3.47E−01
		+	+	+	+	+
+/ − /≈		6/0/0	5/1/0	5/0/1	5/0/1	5/0/1

Despite the lack of statistical distinctions between the outcomes, the median IGD values generated by CSEA are lower but poorer than those of θ-DEA-DP on the five-objective DTLZ4 problem. The fact that CSEA and θ-DEA-DP demonstrate similar performance on the three-objective DTLZ4 problem suggests that CSEA may possess the ability to effectively navigate search spaces that are predisposed to bias. While θ-DEA-DP is statistically comparable to DomRank and MOEA/D-EGO, it is notably inferior to ParEGO in terms of performance on the five-objective DTLZ7 problem. The underwhelming performance of θ-DEA-DP on the five-objective DTLZ7 problem can be ascribed to the presence of as many as 16 separated PFs that are not connected. As the shape of the PF is not uniform across the problem space, the diversity preservation mechanism utilized by θ-DEA-DP may not function optimally. One feasible solution to this issue is to dynamically regulate the distribution of weight vectors, as proposed in [35].

The IGD results for test problems with eight objectives are presented in Table 5.6. Overall, these problems tend to be better addressed by θ-DEA-DP compared to other

Table 5.6 Best, median and worst IGD values on eight-objective test problems.

Problem	θ-DEA-DP	θ-DEA	ParEGO	DomRank	MOEA/D-EGO	CSEA
DTLZ1	3.21E−01	5.67E−01	6.89E−01	5.95E−01	8.23E−01	4.32E−01
	4.99E−01	2.38E + 00	1.37E + 00	1.31E + 00	6.89E + 00	7.52E−01
	1.28E + 00	7.43E + 00	3.46E + 00	3.79E + 00	2.56E + 01	2.22E + 00
		+	+	+	+	+
DTLZ2	3.90E−01	4.09E−01	5.15E−01	4.75E−01	4.75E−01	5.20E−01
	4.41E−01	4.51E−01	5.48E−01	5.13E−01	5.12E−01	5.82E−01
	4.91E−01	4.97E + 01	5.85E−01	5.52E−01	5.70E−01	6.49E−01
		+	+	+	+	+
DTLZ4	4.95E−01	5.80E−01	6.14E−01	6.38E−01	6.47E−01	4.98E−01
	5.35E−01	6.23E−01	6.30E−01	6.55E−01	6.65E−01	5.63E−01
	6.08E−01	6.98E−01	6.57E−01	6.85E−01	7.12E−01	6.59E−01
		+	+	+	+	+
DTLZ7	1.00E + 00	9.64E−01	6.79E−01	7.14E−01	7.27E−01	1.15E + 00
	1.24E + 00	1.10E + 00	7.18E−01	8.77E−01	8.01E−01	1.33E + 00
	1.38E + 00	1.39E + 00	7.67E−01	1.23E + 00	9.00E−01	1.51E + 00
		≈	−	−	−	≈
WFG6	3.71E−01	4.05E−01	4.60E−01	4.55E−01	4.22E−01	4.56E−01
	4.14E−01	4.46E−01	4.97E−01	4.83E−01	4.37E−01	5.00E−01
	4.75E−01	4.78E−01	5.30E−01	5.29E−01	4.77E−01	5.41E−01
		+	+	+	+	+
WFG7	**4.47E−01**	4.50E−01	5.31E−01	4.50E−01	4.57E−01	4.72E−01
	4.81E−01	**4.71E−01**	5.56E−01	4.82E−01	5.19E−01	5.54E−01
	5.44E−01	5.21E−01	5.84E−01	**5.16E−01**	5.76E−01	6.18E−01
		≈	+	≈	+	+
+/ − /≈		4/0/2	5/1/0	4/1/1	5/1/0	5/0/1

algorithms under evaluation. The subsequent observations are specified in detail below:

1. In the case of eight-objective problems, θ-DEA emerges as a strong competitor to all surrogate-assisted algorithms, including θ-DEA-DP. In comparison to θ-DEA-DP, θ-DEA delivers comparable performance on DTLZ7 and WFG7. This may be because the increased number of objectives makes it significantly more challenging to construct surrogates with high accuracy, resulting in limited guidance provided by the surrogates.

2. In comparison to its performance on five-objective DTLZ7, θ-DEA-DP exhibits reduced competitiveness on eight-objective DTLZ7, in which it is surpassed by three other algorithms to a significant extent. This outcome is unsurprising, considering that DTLZ7 exhibits exponential growth in the number of disconnected PF regions with an increase in the number of objectives.

3. The competitive dynamics between algorithms can be significantly impacted by the number of objectives. For instance, on the eight-objective DTLZ4 problem, θ-DEA-DP outperforms CSEA by a significant margin. However, on the three- and five-objective instances, θ-DEA-DP only exhibits statistical similarity to CSEA. DTLZ1 provides another evident instance of comparison, where CSEA is ranked last among all algorithms compared on the two-objective case, but secures second position for the eight-objective instance, trailing only θ-DEA-DP.

The best performance is shown in bold.

Fig. 5.6 presents the convergence plots of the median IGD values as a function of the number of function evaluations for several five- and eight-objective problems,

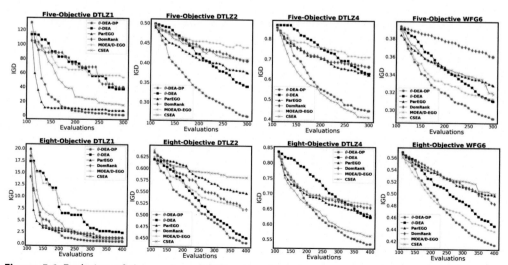

Figure 5.6 Evolution of the median of IGD values (over 21 runs) versus the number of function evaluations on five- and eight-objective test problems.

Table 5.7 The average CPU time consumed in managing surrogates.

	θ-DEA-DP	ParEGO	DomRank
CPU time (min.)	37.74	31.36	41.45

providing additional insight into the optimization process of each algorithm. As illustrated in the plots, θ-DEA-DP typically attains quicker reductions in IGD values compared to the other algorithms.

The three algorithms, θ-DEA-DP, ParEGO, and DomRank, were run in a uniform computing environment throughout our experiments and implemented using Python. Consequently, it is possible to compare the mean CPU times utilized by these three algorithms for handling the surrogates. Table 5.7 exhibits that θ-DEA-DP's surrogate handling time is justifiable in comparison to that of ParEGO and DomRank. This metric is of limited practical significance since function evaluations usually constitute the primary time-consuming aspect of expensive optimization.

5.4.4 Investigations into the components of θ-DEA-DP

Our initial objective is to compare the performance of deep learning with traditional machine learning methods in dominance prediction. To accomplish this, we necessitate the creation of training and test sets. To tackle multiobjective problems, we employ Latin hypercube sampling to produce $11n - 1$ solutions. Following this, 3000 examples are obtained by generating 1000 instances randomly for each category, thus creating the test set. For the sake of comparison, we opted for SVM [36], random forest (RF) [37], and complement naive Bayes (CNB) [38]. The design of CNB is specially aimed at tackling imbalanced classification. We utilized an approach identical to that of Pareto-Net and θ-Net when dealing with class imbalance for SVM and RF. To emphasize the importance of handling imbalance, we investigated modified versions of Pareto-Net and θ-Net, designated as Pareto-Net* and θ-Net*, respectively. The modified models used the standard cross-entropy loss, as opposed to the weighted version. Hyperparameter optimization is an expensive and often impractical procedure for surrogates. Therefore, we did not perform hyperparameter optimization for any of the compared learning algorithms. The hyperparameter settings provided in Table 5.3 were utilized for deep learning algorithms. The default values of hyperparameters provided in scikit-learn [39] were employed for the other learning algorithms.

Table 5.8 presents the standard deviation and median prediction accuracy (averaged over 21 runs) for various algorithms. It is important to note that each training process is performed on a unique set of Latin hypercube samples. The table demonstrates that Pareto-Net (θ-Net) consistently outperforms SVM, RF, and CNB in Pareto (θ) dominance prediction accuracy, underscoring the superiority of deep learning algorithms.

Table 5.8 Comparison of different machine learning models on the dominance prediction problem.

Problem	m	n	Pareto dominance prediction accuracy (%)					θ-Dominance prediction accuracy (%)				
			Pareto-Net	Pareto-Net*	SVM	RF	CNB	θ-Net	θ-Net*	SVM	RF	CNB
ZDT1	2	10	**97.37** (0.54)	96.20 (0.72)$^+$	81.40 (0.63)$^+$	38.33 (1.37)$^+$	63.80 (2.58)$^+$	**67.77** (1.38)	65.70 (1.73)$^+$	66.50 (1.65)$^+$	34.23 (1.48)$^+$	49.10 (2.04)$^+$
ZDT2	2	10	**97.73** (0.37)	97.67 (0.70) $\approx$	85.30 (0.87)$^+$	59.73 (3.83)$^+$	67.03 (1.22)$^+$	79.60 (2.23)	**79.90** (2.31) $\approx$	63.63 (1.27)$^+$	64.93 (3.99)$^+$	51.43 (1.53)$^+$
ZDT3	2	10	**79.93** (1.57)	76.23 (1.94)$^+$	73.27 (1.23)$^+$	40.63 (2.28)$^+$	61.53 (1.92)$^+$	**61.53** (1.73)	57.87 (1.44)$^+$	59.73 (1.26)$^+$	33.37 (0.06)$^+$	44.50 (1.08)$^+$
DTLZ1	2	6	**76.33** (2.65)	70.90 (3.57)$^+$	71.23 (2.78)$^+$	38.50 (2.36)$^+$	34.57 (1.61)$^+$	**70.23** (1.57)	55.60 (2.30)$^+$	56.50 (1.83)$^+$	33.33 (0.00)$^+$	33.50 (1.65)$^+$
DTLZ2	3	8	**65.47** (3.88)	44.37 (2.87)$^+$	56.80 (3.64)$^+$	33.43 (0.42)$^+$	43.87 (1.49)$^+$	**58.03** (1.40)	46.03 (1.34)$^+$	50.13 (1.65)$^+$	33.33 (0.02)$^+$	36.80 (0.81)$^+$
DTLZ4	3	8	**78.87** (2.42)	68.10 (2.82)$^+$	75.63 (1.67)$^+$	41.83 (2.64)$^+$	58.77 (2.85)$^+$	53.67 (2.29)	54.33 (2.06) $\approx$	54.53 (2.40)	**80.87** (4.33)$^-$	37.30 (1.99)$^+$
DTLZ7	3	8	**94.00** (0.78)	89.87 (1.79)$^+$	85.30 (0.80)$^+$	40.10 (2.52)$^+$	63.53 (3.88)$^+$	**63.23** (1.54)	55.03 (2.30)$^+$	58.87 (1.81)$^+$	33.60 (0.61)$^+$	46.23 (0.72)$^+$
WFG6	3	10	**49.10** (3.06)	37.93 (1.39)$^+$	40.87 (1.54)$^+$	33.33 (0.03)$^+$	46.27 (1.56)$^+$	**52.17** (1.62)	46.93 (1.53)$^+$	48.20 (1.04)$^+$	34.77 (3.28)$^+$	40.90 (0.72)$^+$
WFG7	3	10	**62.43** (2.75)	55.53 (2.62)$^+$	59.00 (3.29)$^+$	34.00 (0.56)$^+$	51.53 (1.70)$^+$	**53.30** (2.06)	48.93 (1.98)$^+$	50.13 (1.75)$^+$	34.23 (0.51)$^+$	46.90 (0.92)$^+$

The best performance is shown in bold. Standard deviation is shown in the bracket. $+$, $-$, and $\approx$ indicate that the result is significantly worse, better or comparable compared to that of Pareto-Net (θ-Net), respectively, according to the Wilcoxon rank sum test at a 5% significance level.

When compared to Pareto-Net* (θ-Net*), Pareto-Net (θ-Net) typically demonstrates better performance, highlighting the importance of mitigating the class imbalance challenge in dominance prediction. Moreover, the algorithms typically exhibits reduced precision in forecasting θ-dominance in contrast to Pareto dominance, indicating that θ-dominance connections may be notably more difficult to understand.

While the accuracy of surrogates is not the sole factor influencing the performance of surrogate-assisted MOEAs [40], we have uncovered some intriguing correlations. Notably, Pareto-Net and θ-Net exhibit remarkably high accuracy on ZDT2, which may account for θ-DEA-DP's exceptional performance on this problem, as reflected in its small IGD value.

To explore how different parameters in θ-DEA-DP affect the results, The trajectories of the median IGD for two-objective DTLZ1 under different parameter settings are depicted in Fig. 5.7. This depiction offers the following valuable insights:

1. For U, N^* and Q_{max} to be effective, they must be of adequate size. However, excessively large values may not always be advantageous and can, in fact, impede the final performance.
2. Increasing the values of D and γ can have a positive impact on the ultimate performance. However, it's important to strike a balance as this will also lead to an increase in the computation time required for the surrogates.
3. It is typically more desirable to have a smaller T_{max}, which implies that updating the surrogates should give more weight to the most recently assessed solutions.
4. If the neural networks are overly complex, data limitations may result in overfitting.

5.5 Conclusion

This chapter presents the θ-DEA-DP, a surrogate-based MOEA for expensive optimization problems. The algorithm leverages two deep neural networks, known as Pareto-Net and θ-Net, to predict Pareto dominance and θ-dominance, respectively. Through a two-stage preselection strategy, the surrogates engage in the optimization process by initially comparing each candidate solution with Pareto and θ-representative solutions for the target cluster, followed by the comparison with other surviving candidates. The comparison is based on the predicted dominance relations from Pareto-Net or θ-Net, considering their confidence. The algorithm updates Pareto-Net and θ-Net in an ad-hoc manner based on their estimated accuracy after each function evaluation. By utilizing θ-dominance, the algorithm can retain selection pressure even in objective spaces with high dimensions. At the same time, the algorithm guarantees the intended diversity by explicitly preserving weight vectors that are uniformly distributed.

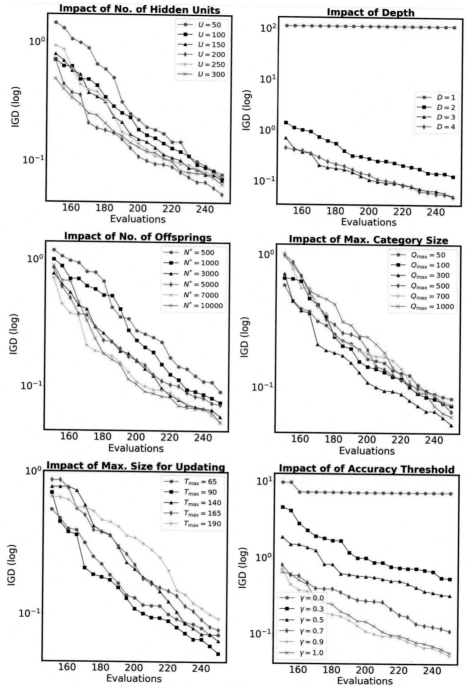

Figure 5.7 Evolution of the median of IGD values (over 21 runs) on two-objective DTLZ1 in the last 100 function evaluations, under various parameter settings.

Experimental results indicate that θ-DEA-DP outperforms several typical surrogate-assisted algorithms across diverse multi/many-objective benchmark problems. It is worth mentioning that θ-DEA-DP presents significant benefits in handling multimodal multiobjective problems, such as DTLZ1. We observed that deep learning algorithms generally outperform traditional learning algorithms for dominance prediction and conducted an analysis of various crucial parameters in θ-DEA-DP. Despite this, the current effectiveness of θ-DEA-DP is insufficient for problems with an extremely large number of objectives (e.g., 10 or more), highlighting the need for further research to improve it. Exploring the use of θ-DEA-DP for costly real-world engineering problems [41,42] would be a valuable avenue of research in the future.

Summary of this part: In the first part of this book, we delve into the field of multiobjective optimization and propose innovative algorithms to address its challenges. Firstly, in Chapter 2, a new evolutionary algorithm is introduced to solve multiobjective optimization problems. This algorithm introduces a novel dominance relation to enhance the convergence and diversity of the nondominated sorting genetic Algorithm III and ranks solutions using a decomposition-based fitness evaluation scheme. Through evaluation on multiple benchmark problems and comparison with other algorithms, the results demonstrate that this algorithm performs well on almost all test functions and exhibits advantages. The approach presented in this chapter achieves better results than existing algorithms by combining convergence and diversity. Chapter 3 proposes a method to address the diversity maintenance problem in high-dimensional objective spaces. By utilizing the perpendicular distance of solutions to weight vectors in the objective space, this method effectively balances convergence and diversity in multiobjective optimization and overcomes limitations of traditional aggregation-based algorithms. Through comparative experimental results, it is shown that this approach achieves a better balance between convergence and diversity and exhibits strong competitiveness in solving multiobjective optimization problems. Chapter 4 discusses the challenges faced by MOEAs while dealing with multiobjective optimization problems and introduces the concept of objective reduction as an important means to address these challenges. Multiple objective reduction algorithms are proposed for different forms of multiobjectives, and their effectiveness and superiority are demonstrated through comprehensive investigation and performance evaluation. Chapter 5 presents an auxiliary agent-based evolutionary algorithm for solving expensive multiobjective optimization problems. By utilizing a classification-based surrogate model and deep learning techniques, this algorithm accurately predicts the Pareto dominance and θ-dominance relationships among solutions. By combining multiobjective evolutionary optimization and a two-stage pre-selection strategy, this algorithm demonstrates superiority within a limited number of function evaluations. In summary, the chapters in the first part introduce several innovative methods for multiobjective optimization. By balancing convergence and diversity, as well as introducing new techniques and algorithms, these methods achieve favorable experimental results and competitiveness. Their application on multiple benchmark problems and real-world scenarios demonstrates their effectiveness and superiority, providing valuable contributions to the research and application of multiobjective optimization.

References

[1] Jones DR, Schonlau M, Welch WJ. Efficient global optimization of expensive black-box functions. Journal of Global optimization 1998;13(4):455.
[2] Shahriari B, Swersky K, Wang Z, et al. Taking the human out of the loop: a review of Bayesian optimization. Proceedings of the IEEE 2015;104(1):148−75.
[3] Loshchilov I, Schoenauer M, Sebag M. Dominance-based Pareto-surrogate for multi-objective optimization. Proceedings of the 8th simulated evolution and learning; 2010. p. 230−9.
[4] Deb K, Hussein R, Roy PC, et al. A taxonomy for metamodeling frameworks for evolutionary multiobjective optimization. IEEE Transactions on Evolutionary Computation 2018;23(1):104−16.
[5] Bandaru S, Ng AHC, Deb K. On the performance of classification algorithms for learning Pareto-dominance relations. Proceedings of the 16th IEEE congress on evolutionary computation. IEEE; 2014. p. 1139−46.
[6] Guo G, Li W, Yang B. et al. Predicting Pareto dominance in multi-objective optimization using pattern recognition. Proceedings of the 2nd international conference on intelligent system design and engineering application. IEEE; 2012. p. 456−9.
[7] Yuan Y, Xu H, Wang B. An improved NSGA-III procedure for evolutionary many-objective optimization. Proceedings of the 16th annual conference on genetic and evolutionary computation; 2014. p. 661−8.
[8] Yuan Y, Xu H, Wang B, et al. A new dominance relation-based evolutionary algorithm for many-objective optimization. IEEE Transactions on Evolutionary Computation 2015;20(1):16−37.
[9] Ishibuchi H., Tsukamoto N., Nojima Y. Evolutionary many-objective optimization: a short review. Proceedings of the 10th IEEE congress on evolutionary computation. IEEE; 2008. p. 2419−26.
[10] Li B, Li J, Tang K, et al. Many-objective evolutionary algorithms: a survey. ACM Computing Surveys 2015;48(1):1−35.
[11] Zhang Q, Li H. MOEA/D: a multiobjective evolutionary algorithm based on decomposition. IEEE Transactions on Evolutionary Computation 2007;11(6):712−31.
[12] Deb K, Pratap A, Agarwal S, et al. A fast and elitist multiobjective genetic algorithm: NSGA-II. IEEE Transactions on Evolutionary Computation 2002;6(2):182−97.
[13] Rumelhart DE, Hinton GE, Williams RJ. Learning representations by back-propagating errors. Nature 1986;323(6088):533−6.
[14] LeCun Y, Bengio Y, Hinton G. Deep learning. Nature 2015;521(7553):436−44.
[15] He K, Zhang X, Ren S, et al. Delving deep into rectifiers: surpassing human-level performance on imagenet classification. Proceedings of the 15th IEEE international conference on computer vision; 2015. p. 1026−34.
[16] Srivastava N, Hinton G, Krizhevsky A, et al. Dropout: a simple way to prevent neural networks from overfitting. The Journal of Machine Learning Research 2014;15(1):1929−58.
[17] Kingma DP, Ba J. Adam: a method for stochastic optimization. Proceedings of the 3rd international conference on learning representations; 2015.
[18] Knowles J. ParEGO: a hybrid algorithm with on-line landscape approximation for expensive multi-objective optimization problems. IEEE Transactions on Evolutionary Computation 2006;10 (1):50−66.
[19] Deb K, Agrawal RB. Simulated binary crossover for continuous search space. Complex Systems 1995;9(2):115−48.
[20] Paszke A, Gross S, Massa F, et al. Pytorch: an imperative style, high-performance deep learning library. Advances in Neural Information Processing Systems 2019;32:8024−35.

[21] He H, Garcia EA. Learning from imbalanced data. IEEE Transactions on Knowledge and Data Engineering 2009;21(9):1263−84.

[22] Snoek J, Rippel O, Swersky K, et al. Scalable bayesian optimization using deep neural networks. Proceedings of the 32nd international conference on machine learning; 2015. p. 2171−80.

[23] Zitzler E, Deb K, Thiele L. Comparison of multiobjective evolutionary algorithms: empirical results. Evolutionary Computation 2000;8(2):173−95.

[24] Deb K. Multi-objective genetic algorithms: problem difficulties and construction of test problems. Evolutionary Computation 1999;7(3):205−30.

[25] Deb K, Thiele L, Laumanns M, et al. Scalable test problems for evolutionary multiobjective optimization. London: Springer; 2005.

[26] Huband S, Hingston P, Barone L, et al. A review of multiobjective test problems and a scalable test problem toolkit. IEEE Transactions on Evolutionary Computation 2006;10(5):477−506.

[27] Deb K, Jain H. An evolutionary many-objective optimization algorithm using reference-point-based nondominated sorting approach, part I: solving problems with box constraints. IEEE Transactions on Evolutionary Computation 2013;18(4):577−601.

[28] Gómez RH, Coello CAC. MOMBI: a new metaheuristic for many-objective optimization based on the R2 indicator. Proceedings of the 15th IEEE congress on evolutionary computation. IEEE; 2013. p. 2488−95.

[29] Zitzler E, Thiele L. Multiobjective optimization using evolutionary algorithms—a comparative case study. Proceedings of the 5th parallel problem solving from nature; 1998. p. 292−301.

[30] Rahat AAM, Everson RM, Fieldsend JE. Alternative infill strategies for expensive multi-objective optimisation. Proceedings of the 19th genetic and evolutionary computation conference; 2017. p. 873−80.

[31] Zhang Q, Liu W, Tsang E, et al. Expensive multiobjective optimization by MOEA/D with Gaussian process model. IEEE Transactions on Evolutionary Computation 2009;14(3):456−74.

[32] Li H, Zhang Q. Multiobjective optimization problems with complicated Pareto sets, MOEA/D and NSGA-II. IEEE Transactions on Evolutionary Computation 2008;13(2):284−302.

[33] Pan L, He C, Tian Y, et al. A classification-based surrogate-assisted evolutionary algorithm for expensive many-objective optimization. IEEE Transactions on Evolutionary Computation 2018;23 (1):74−88.

[34] Tian Y, Cheng R, Zhang X, et al. PlatEMO: a MATLAB platform for evolutionary multi-objective optimization. IEEE Computational Intelligence Magazine 2017;12(4):73−87.

[35] Ma X, Yu Y, Li X, et al. A survey of weight vector adjustment methods for decomposition-based multiobjective evolutionary algorithms. IEEE Transactions on Evolutionary Computation 2020;24 (4):634−49.

[36] Cortes C, Vapnik V. Support-vector networks. Machine Learning 1995;20:273−97.

[37] Breiman L. Random forests. Machine Learning 2001;45:5−32.

[38] Rennie JD, Shih L, Teevan J, et al. Tackling the poor assumptions of naive bayes text classifiers. Proceedings of the 20th international conference on machine learning; 2003. p. 616−23.

[39] Pedregosa F, Varoquaux G, Gramfort A, et al. Scikit-learn: machine learning in Python. Journal of machine Learning research 2011;12:2825−30.

[40] Jin Y. Surrogate-assisted evolutionary computation: recent advances and future challenges. Swarm and Evolutionary Computation 2011;1(2):61−70.

[41] Daniels SJ, Rahat AAM, Everson RM, et al. A suite of computationally expensive shape optimisation problems using computational fluid dynamics. Proceedings of the 15th parallel problem solving from nature; 2018. p. 296−307.

[42] Volz V, Naujoks B, Kerschke P, et al. Single-and multi-objective game-benchmark for evolutionary algorithms. Proceedings of the 21st genetic and evolutionary computation conference; 2019. p. 647−55.

Summary of part I

Since Holland proposed heuristic search methods, with genetic algorithms as representatives, in 1975, heuristic search methods for solving optimization problems have experienced vigorous development. Particularly in the past two decades, algorithms such as nondominated sorting genetic algorithm II (NSGA-II) (2002) for fast low-dimensional multiobjective optimization problems and NSGA-III (2014) for high-dimensional multiobjective optimization, proposed by Deb, have gained wide attention and application in the industry. Building upon this foundation, in 2016, the research team of the authors of this book published theoretical and serialized research results on multiobjective optimization using θ-dominance-based evolutionary algorithm (θ-DEA) in the *IEEE Transactions on Evolutionary Computation* (IEEE TEC), as discussed in the relevant content of the first part of this book. This work received extensive attention and high praise from the academic community both domestically and internationally. Professor Hisao Ishibuchi, an IEEE Fellow and Vice President of the IEEE Computational Intelligence Society (CIS), regarded this method as another milestone in the field of high-dimensional multiobjective evolutionary optimization after NSGA-III (*IEEE CEC 2019, ACM GECCO 2019*). Professor Deb, an IEEE/ASME Fellow and the originator of the NSGA algorithm, believes that our proposed θ-DEA can better maintain a balance between convergence and diversity compared to NSGA-III. Professor Carlos, an IEEE Fellow and the Editor-in-Chief of IEEE TEC, thinks that our θ-DEA algorithm framework introduces a new selection strategy that simultaneously supports the balance of convergence and diversity. The related algorithms have also been integrated into the internationally renowned open-source optimization algorithm library PlatEMO.

The research results of this book have found widespread applications in various fields. The Oak Ridge National Laboratory in the United States utilized θ-DEA and the ensemble fitness ranking with a ranking restriction scheme algorithm (EFR-RR) for optimizing the design of molecular cells related to biocatalysis. Researchers in the Department of Chemistry at Princeton University used θ-DEA to address the problem of quantum robust control, identifying it as one of the worthwhile research directions in the future. The Argonne National Laboratory in the United States applied θ-DEA to solve the economic dispatch of power loads, achieving the economic benefit of reducing costs by \$460 per unit of time and a carbon emission reduction of 1.3 kg. The technology was also applied to energy optimization and distribution in microgrids. The Japan Aerospace Exploration Agency (JAXA) employed θ-DEA for calculating the ideal perigee in the field of aerospace.

Papers presenting the results of the relevant content of this book were selected as one of the top 5 most-contributed papers in *IEEE TEC for 2017—2018*.

Although there has been progress in research on evolutionary multiobjective optimization algorithms, solving large-scale optimization problems in real scenarios remains challenging. In recent years, with the progress in the field of artificial intelligence, especially in deep learning and large model technologies, optimization algorithms based on deep neural networks or large models have gradually demonstrated their potential in problem dimensionality reduction and feasible solution prediction. Particularly, a series of innovative research results have emerged in the past few years at major international conferences in machine learning, including International Conference on Machine Learning (ICML), Conference and Workshop on Neural Information Processing Systems (NIPS), and International Conference on Learning Representations (ICLR), which deserve special attention from researchers in the field. The team of the author will continue to conduct research in this area and promptly present relevant results to the readers.

PART II

Heuristic algorithm for flexible job shop scheduling problem

In Part II, we explore innovative approaches to solve the flexible job shop scheduling problem (FJSP). Our algorithms aim to minimize the makespan and address the challenges of this complex problem. We introduce hybrid harmony search (HHS) and hybrid differential evolution (HDE) algorithms that adapt well to the discrete problem space of the FJSP. In addition, we present a combined search heuristic called hybrid harmony search and large neighborhood search (HHS/LNS), which demonstrates improved performance on large-scale FJSP instances. Finally, we propose memetic

189

algorithms that optimize multiple objectives for the multiobjective flexible job shop scheduling problem (MO-FJSP), outperforming the existing methods. These contributions provide valuable insights and solutions for scheduling optimization and offer a foundation for further research in this field.

CHAPTER 6

Preliminary

Contents

6.1 Dealing with the challenge of scheduling in flexible job-shops with multiple goals

The formal representation of FJSP is as follows: A set of n independent jobs $J = \{J_1, J_2, \ldots, J_n\}$ and a set of m machines $M = \{M_1, M_2, \ldots, M_m\}$. Each job is comprised of a prioritized sequence of operations $O_{i,1}, O_{i,2}, \ldots, O_{i,n_i}$, where job J_i is completed only when all its operations are executed in the given order, denoted as $O_{i,1} \rightarrow O_{i,2} \rightarrow, \ldots, O_{i,n_i}$. Each operation $O_{i,j}$, that is, the jth operation of job J_i, can be executed on any machine selected from a given subset $M_{i,j} \subseteq M$. The processing time of each operation depends on the machine, denoted as $p_{i,j,k}$ for operation $O_{i,j}$ on machine M_k. The scheduling problem involves two subproblems: the routing subproblem of assigning each operation to an appropriate machine and the sequencing subproblem of determining the sequence of all operations on each machine. The objective is to find a schedule that minimizes the makespan, defined as the time required to complete all jobs, denoted as $C_{max} = \max_{1 \leq i \leq u}(C_i)$ where C_i is the completion time of job J_i.

In addition, this chapter makes the following assumptions: all machines are available at time zero; all jobs are released at time zero; each machine can perform only one operation at a time; each operation must be completed without interruption once it starts; the operation sequence for each job is predefined and cannot be changed; and setup times and transition times between operations are negligible.

To provide clarity, Table 6.1 presents an example of FJSP, where rows correspond to operations and columns correspond to machines. Each entry in the input table represents the processing time of the corresponding operation on the respective machine. In this table, the label "—" indicates that the machine is not able to execute the corresponding operation.

Finally, Table 6.2 summarizes some of the commonly used symbols in this chapter.

Intelligent Evolutionary Optimization
DOI: https://doi.org/10.1016/B978-0-443-27400-8.00006-X

Table 6.1 Processing time table for the flexible job-shop scheduling problem example.

Task	Operation	M_1	M_2	M_3
J_1	$O_{1,1}$	2	—	3
	$O_{1,2}$	4	1	3
J_2	$O_{2,1}$	—	2	3
	$O_{2,2}$	6	2	4
	$O_{2,3}$	3	—	—
J_3	$O_{3,1}$	1	5	2
	$O_{3,2}$	3	—	2

Table 6.2 Description of symbols used.

Symbol	Description
J	Set of all jobs
M	Set of all machines
n	Total number of jobs
m	Total number of machines
J_i	The i-th job
n_i	Number of operations in job J_i
M_k	The k-th machine
$O_{i,j}$	The j-th operation of job J_i
$M_{i,j}$	Set of candidate machines for operation $O_{i,j}$
$p_{i,j,k}$	Processing time for operation $O_{i,j}$ on machine M_k
$C_{\max}$	Time required to complete all jobs
d	Total number of operations
$L(j)$	Number of candidate machines for operation j
$\sigma_{i,j}$	Start time of operation $O_{i,j}$ in the schedule
$\mu_{i,j}$	Selected machine for operation $O_{i,j}$ in the schedule.
G	Schedule represented by a disjunctive graph
X_i	The i-th chord vector in the chord progression memory.
$x_i(j)$	The j-th decision variable of chord vector X_i.
$x_{\min}(j)$	Lower bound of decision variable $x_i(j)$.
$x_{\max}(j)$	Upper bound of decision variable $x_i(j)$.
D	Dimension of the chord vector.
$X_{i,1}$	The first half of chord vector X_i
$X_{i,2}$	The second half of chord vector X_i
X_{best}	The best chord vector in the chord progression memory.
X_{worst}	The worst chord vector in the chord progression memory.
X_{new}	A new chord vector obtained through improvisation in the chord search.
X'_{new}	Chord vector obtained after local search.
δ	Constraint factor.
R_i	Machine assignment vector.
$r_i(j)$	The j-th decision variable of machine assignment vector R_i.
S_i	Operation sequence vector.
$s_i(j)$	The j-th decision variable of operation sequence vector S_i.
Ω	Selection of a relaxed set of operations to be performed during large neighborhood search.
γ	Subset of Ω where each operation is fixed on its original machine.

6.2 Research status of multiobjective flexible job-shop scheduling

In the past few decades, the single-objective flexible job-shop scheduling problem (FJSP) has received extensive research attention [1−9], which generally aims to minimize makespan, that is, the time required to complete all jobs. However, compared to single-objective FJSP, research on MO-FJSP is relatively limited. However, many real scheduling problems often involve optimizing several objectives that are mutually conflicting to some extent. Therefore, the MO-FJSP problem is closer to real production environments and should be given sufficient attention. In the past decade, MO-FJSP has attracted increasing attention from scholars, and many new algorithms have been proposed. These algorithms for solving MO-FJSP can be roughly divided into two types: a priori method and a posteriori method In the = priori method, two or more objectives are usually linearly weighted to form a single objective. For example, given n optimization objectives $f_1, f_2, \ldots, f_n$, a linear weight function $f = \sum_{i=1}^{n} w_i f_i$ is used, where $0 \le w_i \le 1$ and $\sum_{i=1}^{n} w_i = 1$, to obtain a single-objective optimization problem. However, linear weighting does not always reflect the trade-off relationship between objectives. Also, setting appropriate weights w_i for each objective is not a simple task. Producers may need to run a priori method multiple times to obtain a satisfactory solution. According to existing literature, early MO-FJSP research mainly focused on priori method. Xia and Wu [10] proposed a hierarchical approach that uses particle swarm optimization (PSO) to assign operations to machines and simulated annealing (SA) to rank the operations on each machine. Liu et al. [11] proposed a metaheuristic method combining PSO and variable neighborhood search (VNS) for MO-FJSP. Zhang et al. [12] combined PSO and tabu search (TS) to handle MO-FJSP, with TS embedded as a local search in PSO. Xing et al. [13] designed an effective search method for MO-FJSP, collecting a set of compromise solutions by using 10 different sets of weights for each problem instance. Li et al. [14] proposed a hybrid TS algorithm for MO-FJSP, with different neighborhood structures designed for machine selection mode and operation sorting mode.

Compared to priori method, posteriori method is more preferable. In this method, solutions are compared based on the Pareto dominance relationship, aiming to find a set of Pareto optimal solutions, rather than seeking a unique optimal solution based on aggregated objectives like a priori methods. A posteriori method does not require prior information and can reflect the trade-off relationship between objectives by the distribution of solutions obtained from a single run. This also helps producers evaluate these solutions and make final decisions. In recent years, researchers have focused more on solving MO-FJSP in a Pareto way. Kacem et al. [15] proposed a hybrid Pareto method for solving MO-FJSP based on fuzzy logic and evolutionary algorithms. Ho and Tay [16] integrated guided local search into evolutionary algorithms and used an elite memory to store all non-dominant solutions found. Frutos et al. [17] proposed a memetic algorithm (MA) based on nondominated sorting genetic algorithm II (NSGA-II), where the local search process uses the SA algorithm. Wang et al. [18] proposed a multiobjective genetic algorithm based on immune and entropy principles for MO-FJSP. Moslehi and Mahnam [19] proposed a new method that combines PSO and local search. Li et al. [20,21] developed a hybrid discrete artificial bee colony (ABC) and a hybrid Shuffled Frog Leaping Algorithm (SFLA), respectively, both of which use the individual evaluation mechanism in NSGA-II. Li et al. proposed a hybrid Pareto-based local search algorithm with an adaptive strategy based on VNS for the same problem. Wang et al. [22] proposed an enhanced Pareto-based ABC algorithm that integrates multiple strategies to ensure the quality and diversity of solutions. Rahmati et al. [23] adapted two existing multiobjective evolutionary algorithms (MOEAs) to solve MO-FJSP and introduced several multiobjective performance indicators to evaluate algorithms for solving MO-FJSP. Rabiee et al. [24] conducted similar research, adapting four existing MOEAs for some MO-FJSP. Xiong et al. [25] developed a hybrid MOEA that combines the key path-based local search. Chiang et al. [26] proposed a new MOEA that uses effective genetic operators and effectively maintains population diversity. Their subsequent research [27] also proposed a multi-objective MA embedded with the variable neighborhood descent search.

Other than the works mentioned in references [11,17,24], the previous discussion on MO-FJSP has primarily focused on three objectives: makespan, total workload, and critical workload. However, reference [11] investigated MO-FJSP problems with the objectives of makespan and flowtime, while references [17] and [24] only considered makespan and total workload as objectives.

Multiobjective flexible job shop scheduling and memetic algorithm are two vastly different algorithms, yet they share some similarities. In multiobjective flexible job shop scheduling, the goal of the algorithm is to maximize the values of multiple objective functions while satisfying various constraints. On the other hand, in MA, the goal of the algorithm is to find the optimal fitness value given a set of memes to determine the best combination of memes. Despite the different goals of the two algorithms, they both involve problem-solving and optimization. Therefore, in practical applications, combining multiobjective flexible job shop scheduling algorithms with memetic algorithms can lead to more optimal solutions.

6.3 Memetic algorithm explained

Extensive research has shown that the memetic algorithm has unique performance advantages in solving combinatorial optimization problems. This book focuses on the research of the FJS problem mainly based on this algorithm framework.

6.3.1 Brief introduction to memetic algorithm

Traditional EAs typically use variation operators such as crossover and mutation, which often lack guidance and have a high degree of randomness, making it difficult to effectively use local information in the problem solution space. To further improve the performance and efficiency of EAs, inspired by the theory of cultural evolution, attempts have been made to introduce local search strategies during the iteration process of EAs (or MOEAs) to achieve self-learning of individuals during their lifecycles. This method has now developed into a new EC paradigm: MAs [28]. MAs are characterized by the use of local search to further improve some individuals after the variation operators. MAs are expected to use this hybrid search mechanism to organically combine global search based on EAs with local search to better balance the relationship between exploration and exploitation in the search process, thus obtaining better solutions with a higher probability. However, the design of MAs is not simple and generally involves the following important issues [29].

1. The probability of a local search for a single individual depends on the specific design of the memetic algorithm and can vary. It is often determined by balancing the global exploration and local exploitation capabilities of the algorithm.
2. The choice of individuals to undergo local search depends on their fitness or other characteristics. Typically, individuals with high fitness or those who have not been subjected to recent local searches are selected.
3. The duration of local search for each individual depends on the specific design of the memetic algorithm. It can be fixed or adaptive and may be determined by factors such as the fitness improvement during the local search process or the number of evaluations.
4. The choice of local search method depends on the specific problem being solved and the characteristics of the individuals being searched. Commonly used local search methods include hill-climbing, SA, TS, and genetic local search. The effectiveness of the local search method may also be enhanced by incorporating domain-specific knowledge or problem-specific heuristics.

The first and second questions concern the selection of initial solutions for local search, which involves determining the set of individuals in the population that will undergo local search. The third question pertains to the computational cost of the algorithm, as local search typically has high complexity. To avoid affecting the overall efficiency of the algorithm, only partial local search processes are executed in MAs, or the intensity of local search is limited through parameters such as the number of iterations. The fourth question concerns the design of the local search neighborhood, which is crucial to the performance of MAs. Generally, the neighborhood design should take into account problem-specific knowledge to give local search strong guidance. Currently, MAs have been highly successful in combinatorial optimization problems [30], mainly because strong local search strategies can be designed based on the characteristics of specific problems, such as JSP.

6.3.2 Memetic algorithm for solving multiobjective combinatorial optimization problems

MAs have demonstrated strong search capabilities in single-objective combinatorial optimization problems (SO-COPs). Many studies [29,31,32] have discussed in detail how to design high-performance MAs for SO-COPs. However, designing efficient MAs for multiobjective combinatorial optimization problems (MO-COPs) will be even more challenging, and this area has not been widely explored.

In designing MAs for solving MO-COPs, not only the four problems mentioned in Section 8.3.1 need to be considered but also additional issues arising from multiple objectives. One particularly unique problem is how to compare solutions during local search. Generally, there are two modes for addressing this problem: one is using aggregation functions, and the other is using Pareto sorting. Research in [33] shows that methods based on aggregation functions achieve better results than those based on Pareto sorting. Among aggregation functions, the weighted sum function is one of the simplest and most commonly used, and its application in MAs can be traced back to the well-known multiobjective genetic local search (MOGLS) [34,35]. Recently, Sindhya et al. [36] provided a comprehensive literature review summarizing the use of different aggregation functions in multiobjective MAs during local search.

If the above-mentioned problems can be effectively addressed, the designed MA can achieve a good balance between development (population-based) and exploration (local improvement) in the search process, thus obtaining good performance. Some work has been devoted to addressing the problems mentioned above. For example, Ishibuchi et al. [35] studied how to balance the relationship between genetic search and local search in MAs for the multiobjective permutation flowshop scheduling problem (MO-PFSP), and their experimental results showed that this balance is particularly important. When this balance is not properly specified, the performance of multiobjective evolutionary algorithms can often be severely degraded due to the mixing of local search. Ishibuchi et al. [37] investigated the effect of specifying the probability of local search on the performance of MAs for solving MO-PFSP and multiobjective 0/1 knapsack problems, and their work showed that dynamically changing the probability of local search is better than specifying a constant probability. In [38], the authors assumed that each objective has a strong heuristic local search process tailored to it, and their idea was to use such heuristic local search in MOGLS for single-objective optimization problems. The results on multiobjective 0/1 knapsack problems showed that this idea can effectively improve the performance of MOGLS. Garrett and Dasgupta [39] performed experimental comparisons of four available strategies in MAs for the multiobjective quadratic assignment problem. These four strategies roughly correspond to "short-term local search for all individuals," "long-term local search for all individuals," "short-term local search for randomly selected individuals," and "long-term local search for randomly selected individuals."

6.4 Conclusion

This chapter begins by introducing the formal representation of the MO-FJSP, which includes basic concepts such as jobs, machines, operations, and processing times. The current research status of the MO-FJSP problem is then outlined, pointing out that compared to the single-objective FJSP, research on MO-FJSP has been relatively limited. However, in the past decade, MO-FJSP has gained increasing attention from scholars and many new algorithms have been proposed. These algorithms can be broadly classified into two types: priori and posteriori methods. Priori methods mainly use linear weighting to transform multiple objectives into a single objective for solving, while posteriori methods consider multiple objectives simultaneously and use different search strategies for solving. This chapter also introduces the basic principles and processes of MA and points out that this algorithm has unique performance advantages in solving combinatorial optimization problems. Finally, a new research direction is proposed in this chapter, which is to integrate the MO-FJSP algorithm with MA to achieve better solutions.

References

[1] Yuan Y, Xu H. Flexible job shop scheduling using hybrid differential evolution algorithms. Computers & Industrial Engineering 2013;65(2):246−60.
[2] Brandimarte P. Routing and scheduling in a flexible job shop by tabu search. Annals of Operations Research 1993;41(3):157−83.
[3] Ho NB, Tay JC, Lai EMK. An effective architecture for learning and evolving flexible job-shop schedules. European Journal of Operational Research 2007;179(2):316−33.
[4] Yuan Y, Xu H, Yang J. A hybrid harmony search algorithm for the flexible job shop scheduling problem. Applied Soft Computing 2013;13(7):3259−72.
[5] Yuan Y, Xu H. An integrated search heuristic for large-scale flexible job shop scheduling problems. Computers & Operations Research 2013;40(12):2864−77.
[6] Jia HZ, Nee AYC, Fuh JYH, et al. A modified genetic algorithm for distributed scheduling problems. Journal of Intelligent Manufacturing 2003;14:351−62.
[7] Pezzella F, Morganti G, Ciaschetti G. A genetic algorithm for the flexible job-shop scheduling problem. Computers & Operations Research 2008;35(10):3202−12.
[8] Bożejko W, Uchroński M, Wodecki M. Parallel hybrid metaheuristics for the flexible job shop problem. Computers & Industrial Engineering 2010;59(2):323−33.
[9] Hmida AB, Haouari M, Huguet MJ, et al. Discrepancy search for the flexible job shop scheduling problem. Computers & Operations Research 2010;37(12):2192−201.
[10] Xia W, Wu Z. An effective hybrid optimization approach for multi-objective flexible job-shop scheduling problems. Computers & Industrial Engineering 2005;48(2):409−25.
[11] Liu H., Abraham A., Choi O., et al. Variable neighborhood particle swarm optimization for multi-objective flexible job-shop scheduling problems. Proceedings of the 6th simulated evolution and learning; 2006. p. 197−204.
[12] Zhang G, Shao X, Li P, et al. An effective hybrid particle swarm optimization algorithm for multi-objective flexible job-shop scheduling problem. Computers & Industrial Engineering 2009;56(4):1309−18.
[13] Xing LN, Chen YW, Yang KW. An efficient search method for multi-objective flexible job shop scheduling problems. Journal of Intelligent Manufacturing 2009;20:283−93.

[14] Li J, Pan Q, Liang YC. An effective hybrid tabu search algorithm for multi-objective flexible job-shop scheduling problems. Computers & Industrial Engineering 2010;59(4):647−62.

[15] Kacem I, Hammadi S, Borne P. Pareto-optimality approach for flexible job-shop scheduling problems: hybridization of evolutionary algorithms and fuzzy logic. Mathematics and Computers in Simulation 2002;60(3−5):245−76.

[16] Ho NB, Tay JC. Solving multiple-objective flexible job shop problems by evolution and local search. IEEE Transactions on Systems, Man, and Cybernetics, Part C (Applications and Reviews) 2008;38(5):674−85.

[17] Frutos M, Olivera AC, Tohmé F. A memetic algorithm based on a NSGAII scheme for the flexible job-shop scheduling problem. Annals of Operations Research 2010;181:745−65.

[18] Wang X, Gao L, Zhang C, et al. A multi-objective genetic algorithm based on immune and entropy principle for flexible job-shop scheduling problem. The International Journal of Advanced Manufacturing Technology 2010;51(5−8):757−67.

[19] Moslehi G, Mahnam M. A Pareto approach to multi-objective flexible job-shop scheduling problem using particle swarm optimization and local search. International Journal of Production Economics 2011;129(1):14−22.

[20] Li JQ, Pan QK, Gao KZ. Pareto-based discrete artificial bee colony algorithm for multi-objective flexible job shop scheduling problems. The International Journal of Advanced Manufacturing Technology 2011;55:1159−69.

[21] Li J, Pan Q, Xie S. An effective shuffled frog-leaping algorithm for multi-objective flexible job shop scheduling problems. Applied Mathematics and Computation 2012;218(18):9353−71.

[22] Wang L, Zhou G, Xu Y, et al. An enhanced Pareto-based artificial bee colony algorithm for the multi-objective flexible job-shop scheduling. The International Journal of Advanced Manufacturing Technology 2012;60:1111−23.

[23] Rahmati SHA, Zandieh M, Yazdani M. Developing two multi-objective evolutionary algorithms for the multi-objective flexible job shop scheduling problem. The International Journal of Advanced Manufacturing Technology 2013;64:915−32.

[24] Rabiee M, Zandieh M, Ramezani P. Bi-objective partial flexible job shop scheduling problem: NSGA-II, NRGA, MOGA and PAES approaches. International Journal of Production Research 2012;50(24):7327−42.

[25] Xiong J, Tan X, Yang K, et al. A hybrid multiobjective evolutionary approach for flexible job-shop scheduling problems. Mathematical Problems in Engineering 2012;2012:857−68.

[26] Chiang TC, Lin HJ. A simple and effective evolutionary algorithm for multiobjective flexible job shop scheduling. International Journal of Production Economics 2013;141(1):87−98.

[27] Chiang TC, Lin HJ. Flexible job shop scheduling using a multiobjective memetic algorithm. Proceedings of the 7th advanced intelligent computing theories and applications; 2012. p. 49−56.

[28] Moscato P. On evolution, search, optimization, genetic algorithms and martial arts: towards memetic algorithms. Caltech concurrent computation program, C3P Report, 1989;826:37.

[29] Krasnogor N, Smith J. A tutorial for competent memetic algorithms: model, taxonomy, and design issues. IEEE transactions on Evolutionary Computation 2005;9(5):474−88.

[30] Neri F, Cotta C. Memetic algorithms and memetic computing optimization: a literature review. Swarm and Evolutionary Computation 2012;2:1−14.

[31] Ong YS, Keane AJ. Meta-Lamarckian learning in memetic algorithms. IEEE Transactions on Evolutionary Computation 2004;8(2):99−110.

[32] Ong YS, Lim MH, Zhu N, et al. Classification of adaptive memetic algorithms: a comparative study. IEEE Transactions on Systems, Man, and Cybernetics, Part B (Cybernetics) 2006;36 (1):141−52.

[33] Ishibuchi H, Narukawa K. Some issues on the implementation of local search in evolutionary multi-objective optimization. Proceedings of the 6th annual conference on genetic and evolutionary computation; 2004. p. 1246−58.

[34] Ishibuchi H, Murata T. A multi-objective genetic local search algorithm and its application to flow-shop scheduling. IEEE Transactions on Systems, Man, and Cybernetics, Part C (Applications and Reviews) 1998;28(3):392−403.

[35] Ishibuchi H, Yoshida T, Murata T. Balance between genetic search and local search in memetic algorithms for multiobjective permutation flowshop scheduling. IEEE Transactions on Evolutionary Computation 2003;7(2):204−23.

[36] Sindhya K, Deb K, Miettinen K. Improving convergence of evolutionary multi-objective optimization with local search: a concurrent-hybrid algorithm. Natural Computing 2011;10:1407−30.

[37] Ishibuchi H., Hitotsuyanagi Y., Nojima Y. An empirical study on the specification of the local search application probability in multiobjective memetic algorithms. Proceedings of the 15th IEEE congress on evolutionary computation; 2007. p. 2788−95.

[38] Ishibuchi H, Hitotsuyanagi Y, Tsukamoto N, et al. Use of heuristic local search for single-objective optimization in multiobjec tive memetic algorithms. Proceedings of the 7th internadtional conference on parallel problem solving from nature; 2008. p. 743−52.

[39] Garrett D, Dasgupta D. An empirical comparison of memetic algorithm strategies on the multiobjective quadratic assignment problem. Proceedings of the 6th IEEE symposium on computational intelligence in multi-criteria decision-making (MCDM). IEEE; 2009. p. 80−87.

CHAPTER 7

A hybrid harmony search algorithm for flexible job shop scheduling problem

Contents

7.1 Introduction

In the majority of manufacturing and production systems and information processing environments, scheduling is an essential decision-making process that plays a significant role [1]. One of the most challenging and significant problems in this field is the classical flexible job shop scheduling problem (FJSP), which has been extensively studied in the research literature [2−5]. The job sequencing problem (JSP) involves processing a set of jobs on a set of machines, where each job is comprised of a sequence of consecutive operations that must be performed in a specific order based on precedence. As per the current problem, each operation is assigned to a specific machine that is available at the beginning of the task and is capable of performing one operation at a time without being disrupted. The objective is to arrange the operations for each machine in a manner that maximizes the performance of a designated metric, such as makespan, which reflects the total amount of time required to finish all jobs.

Intelligent Evolutionary Optimization
DOI: https://doi.org/10.1016/B978-0-443-27400-8.00007-1

The FJSP is a modification of the conventional JSP, which enables operations to be executed on any machine from a pre-determined collection, rather than a single designated machine. The FJSP is more practical in real production environments than the classical JSP; however, it is also more challenging due to the extra decision of assigning each operation to the appropriate machine. As a result, the FJSP is also NP-hard, similar to the classical JSP, which is a well-known NP-hard problem [6].

In recent years, meta-heuristics have become increasingly popular for solving the computationally complex FJSP. In light of the success of existing applications of the harmony search (HS) algorithm, this chapter puts forth a hybrid version of HS, referred to as hybrid harmony search (HHS), which adopts an integrated approach to address the FJSP using a makespan criterion. The HHS algorithm, which is proposed in this chapter, differs from the traditional HS algorithm in that it includes a local search element. By striking a balance between global exploration and local exploitation of the search space, the HHS algorithm can effectively optimize meta-heuristics, an essential consideration [7–9]. The HHS algorithm developed by us represents harmonies using real vectors, and to generate a viable active schedule for the FJSP, we apply converting techniques that map these continuous vectors accordingly. To produce an initial harmony memory (HM) that is both diverse and of high quality, we have deployed an effective initialization scheme that incorporates a blend of heuristic and random strategies. Working in tandem, the global search-based HS and the local search mechanisms collaborate to complete the optimization process. To accelerate the local search process, we have devised the notion of "common critical operations," which concentrates on the critical path and enhances the neighborhood structure. The outcomes derived from our algorithmic calculations and comparisons provide compelling evidence of the effectiveness and efficiency of the approach we have proposed for addressing the FJSP using a makespan criterion.

7.2 The proposed algorithm

In this section, we provide a detailed account of the HHS algorithm, including the algorithmic flow and critical procedures. We introduced some basic notations for better explanation. The HM's ith harmony vector is represented by $X_i = \{x_i(1), x_i(2), \ldots, x_i(n)\}$, where $x_i(j) \in [x_{\min}(j), x_{\max}(j)]$. In this context, $x_{\min}(j)$ and $x_{\max}(j)$ indicate the minimum and maximum limits, correspondingly, for the position value of each dimension j. The HM consists of an assemblage of harmony vectors preserved in the memory, denoted as $HM = \{X_1, X_2, \ldots, X_{HMS}\}$, where HMS denotes the size of the HM. X_{best} and X_{worst} represent the HM's optimal and suboptimal harmony vectors, respectively. The objective function value $f(X)$ for a given harmony vector X represents the makespan in our algorithm, where an improved harmony is indicated by a decreased $f(X)$ value.

7.2.1 Framework

The algorithmic flow for HHS is illustrated in Fig. 7.1, and it is constructed on the HS framework. At the beginning of the optimization process, the parameters and stopping criterion are established. Subsequently, the HM is initialized through a mixture of heuristics and a random procedure. The HM's harmony vectors are evaluated by converting them into a feasible active schedule for FJSP, and selecting the harmony

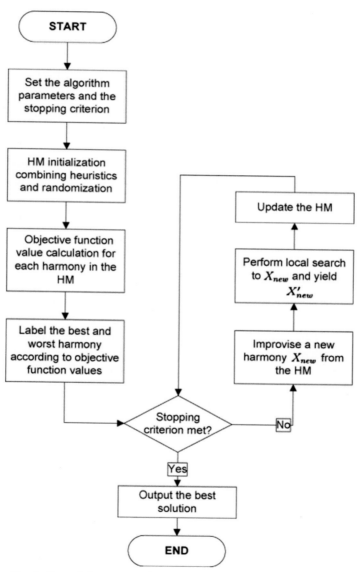

Figure 7.1 Algorithmic flow of the proposed HHS algorithm. *HHS*, Hybrid harmony search.

vectors that are the most optimal and suboptimal in the HM. Following the assessment, a fresh HM is generated from the current HM using memory consideration, pitch adjustment, and random selection. Afterward, a local search algorithm is implemented to enhance the harmony vector generated in the improvisation phase. This stage is distinct from the fundamental HS algorithm. Ultimately, the HM is refreshed by comparing the harmony vector that was enhanced by the local search with the HM's poorest harmony vector. This evolutionary process is reiterated until the stopping criterion is satisfied.

7.2.2 Representation of the harmony vector

In our proposed algorithm, we represent a harmony vector, $X = \{x(1), x(2), \ldots, x(n)\}$, as a vector of n real numbers that adheres to specific constraints based on the particular problem being addressed. When considering the FJSP, the dimension n is equal to twice the number of operations, which is denoted as l. The initial segment of the harmony vector, $X^{(1)} = \{x(1), x(2), \ldots, x(l)\}$, is used to assign operations to machines, while the second half of the vector, $X^{(2)} = \{x(l+1), x(l+2), \ldots, x(2l)\}$, specifies the order of operations on each machine. This approach is consistent with the two-vector code used for the FJSP. Additionally, to simplify the problem, we assign all intervals $[x_{\min}(j), x_{\max}(j)], j = 1, 2, \ldots, n$, uniformly to the range $[-\delta, \delta]$, where $\delta > 0$ in our method.

7.2.3 Evaluation of the harmony vector

This subsection is dedicated to the key obstacle in the HHS algorithm proposed, which centers on the challenge of determining the appropriate evaluation of the objective function value $f(X)$ for a given harmony vector $X = \{x(1), x(2), \ldots, x(n)\}$. To tackle this challenge, we begin by converting the harmony vector X, which is represented as a real number vector, into a two-vector code. We then utilize this two-vector code to derive a viable and efficient schedule for the FJSP and assign $f(X)$ the makespan value associated with this schedule.

7.2.3.1 Two-vector code

Within this chapter, we employ a two-vector code comprised of two distinct vectors: the machine assignment vector and the operation sequence vector. These vectors correspond to the two distinct subproblems present in the FJSP.

Before discussing the details of the two vectors, each operation is assigned a unique identification (ID) based on its position within its respective job and the job number. After the assignment of IDs, every operation can be identified by its distinct ID number. As shown in Fig. 7.2, operation 6 corresponds to $O_{3,1}$.

Operation indicated	$O_{1,1}$	$O_{1,2}$	$O_{2,1}$	$O_{2,2}$	$O_{2,3}$	$O_{3,1}$	$O_{3,2}$
Fixed ID	1	2	3	4	5	6	7

Figure 7.2 Illustration of the numbering scheme for operations.

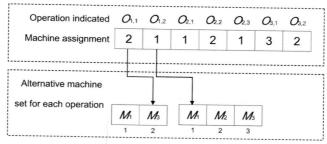

Figure 7.3 Illustration of the machine assignment vector.

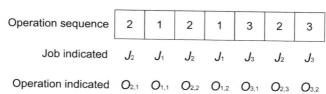

Figure 7.4 Illustration of the operation sequence vector.

The set of l integer values in the machine assignment vector $MA = \{u(1), u(2), ..., u(l)\}$, where l denotes the total number of operations in the FJSP, has an individual element $u(j)$ for each j, such that $1 \leq j \leq l$, indicates the machine selected by operation j from its set of available machines. Fig. 7.3 displays an example machine assignment vector along. For example, $u(1) = 2$ indicates that operation $O_{1,1}$ uses the second machine from its available set of machines, which is machine M_3.

Even though an ID permutation of all operations may appear to be the most direct representation, with regards to the operation sequence vector $OS = \{v(1), v(2), ..., v(l)\}$, it may not always result in a feasible schedule for the FJSP due to the existence of precedence restrictions between operations. Therefore we have adopted the operation-based interpretation [10], which utilizes the same symbol for all operations within a job and understands them based on their order of occurrence in the code's sequence. In contrast to the permutation representation, this code can always be deciphered to produce a viable schedule. Through the utilization of this encoding technique, the job index i, which corresponds to the job J_i, appears exactly n_i times in the operation sequence vector, representing n_i operations $O_{i,1}, O_{i,2}, ..., O_{i,n_i}$ in succession. Fig. 7.4 displays a possible operation sequence vector that can be transformed into a distinct collection of arranged operations: $O_{2,1} \succ O_{1,1} \succ O_{2,2} \succ O_{1,2} \succ O_{3,1} \succ O_{2,3} \succ O_{3,2}$. Operation $O_{2,1}$ is granted the highest precedence and planned initially, succeeded by $O_{1,1}$, and so forth.

7.2.3.2 Converting the harmony vector to the two-vector code

The process of converting a given harmony vector $X = \{x(1), x(2), ..., x(l), x(l+1), x(l+2), ..., x(2l)\}$, where $-\delta \leq x(j) \leq \delta$, $j = 1, 2, ..., 2l$, into the corresponding machine assignment vector $MA = \{u(1), u(2), ..., u(l)\}$ and operation sequence vector $OS = \{v(1), v(2), ..., v(l)\}$ is split into two distinct stages. During the initial stage, $X^{(1)} = \{x(1), x(2), ..., x(l)\}$ is transformed into the machine assignment vector. During the ensuing step, the operation sequence vector is generated by converting $X^{(2)} = \{x(l+1), x(l+2), ..., x(2l)\}$.

In the initial stage of the conversion process, we define $s(j)$ as the size of the alternative machine set for operation j, where $1 \leq j \leq l$. We aim to map the real number $x(j)$ that belongs to the interval $[-\delta, \delta]$ to the integer $u(j)$ that belongs to the interval $[1, s(j)]$. To achieve this, we utilize the following technique: first, we apply a linear transformation to convert $x(j)$ into a real number that falls within the range of $[1, s(j)]$. Subsequently, we assign $u(j)$ the nearest integer value to the converted real number. This process is demonstrated in Eq. (7.1).

$$u(j) = round\left(\frac{1}{2\delta}(s(j) - 1)(x(j) + \delta) + 1\right), 1 \leq j \leq l \qquad (7.1)$$

To round a given number to the closest integer, we employ the function round (x). In cases where $s(j) = 1$, the value of $u(j)$ will always be 1, irrespective of the value of $x(j)$.

During the second stage, we initially apply the largest position value (LPV) rule [11] to construct an ID permutation of operations by arranging them in a descending order based on their position values. Subsequently, we replace each operation ID with its corresponding job number. For example, if we are given a vector $X^{(2)} = \{0.6, 0.3, -0.2, 0.5, 0.7, -0.4, -0.3\}$, Fig. 7.5 shows an instance of the conversion process.

7.2.3.3 Active decoding of two-vector code

Scheduling problems are usually categorized into one of three types of schedules: active schedule, semiactive schedule, and nondelay schedule [1]. Research has shown that the optimal schedule, as per the makespan criterion, must be part of the set of active schedules [12]. Consequently, by decoding the two–vector code, we can generate an active schedule, thereby reducing the overall search space.

Before introducing the concept of an active schedule, it is necessary to discuss the left–shift strategy. This approach is utilized to shift operations to an earlier start time

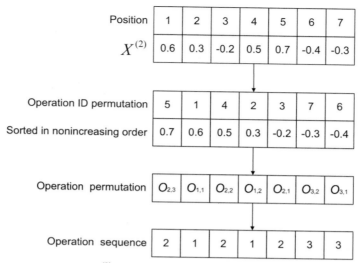

Figure 7.5 The conversion from $X^{(2)}$ to the operation sequence vector.

and minimize the total schedule duration. A left-shift is deemed to be local if it is possible to advance the start time of some operations without altering the operation sequence on each machine. Conversely, the global left-shift, similar to the local left-shift, may impact the operation sequence on each machine. If a schedule cannot be optimized by using local left-shift, it is referred to as semiactive. On the other hand, if global left-shift cannot be applied to a schedule, it is classified as active.

To ensure that the decoded schedule produced by a two-vector code is classified as an active schedule, we adopt the subsequent strategy. While scheduling operation $O_{i,j}$ on machine M_k with processing time $p_{i,j,k}$, we look for the earliest available idle time interval on M_k. In case no such interval is found, the operation is scheduled at the end of M_k. An idle time interval on M_k is represented as $[S_x, E_x]$, and the completion time of operation $O_{i,j}$ is indicated by $c_{i,j}$. The time interval is considered available for $O_{i,j}$ only if the following inequalities are satisfied:

$$\begin{cases} \max\{S_x, c_{i,j-1}\} + p_{i,j,k} \leq E_x, & \text{if } j \geq 2 \\ S_x + p_{i,j,k} \leq E_x, & \text{if } j = 1 \end{cases} \qquad (7.2)$$

Once an available time interval is recognized, we ascertain the starting time $s_{i,j}$ for operation $O_{i,j}$ in the following manner:

$$s_{i,j} = \begin{cases} \max\{S_x, c_{i,j-1}\}, & \text{if } \geq 2 \\ S_x, & \text{if } j = 1 \end{cases} \qquad (7.3)$$

If no available time interval is found, we establish the starting time $s_{i,j}$ according to the following formula, where ET_k denotes the present end time for machine M_k:

$$s_{i,j} = \begin{cases} \max\{ET_k, c_{i,j-1}\}, & \text{if } s(j \geq 2 \\ ET_k, & \text{if } j = 1 \end{cases} \tag{7.4}$$

Once all the operations have been scheduled, we can compute the makespan, which is given by $C_{\max} = \max_{1 \leq k \leq r}(ET_k)$. The decoding process for the two-vector MA and OS is illustrated in Algorithm 7.1.

Algorithm 7.1 The procedure of decoding the two-vector code.

1. Get a triple group $[O_{i,j}, M_k, p_{i,j,k}]$ for each operation $O_{i,j}$ by reading the vector MA
2. Transform OS to a list of ordered operations $\{op_1, op_2, ..., op_l\}$
3. **for** $j = 1$ **to** l **do**
4.   Get the corresponding triple group for operation op_j
5.   Search the earliest available time interval for op_j on its chosen machine
6.   **if** the available time interval is found **then**
7.   the operation op_j is allocated here and its start time is set according to Eq. (7.3)
8.   **else**
9.   the operation op_j is allocated at the end of its selected machine and its start time is set according to Eq. (7.4)
10.   **end if**
11. **end for**
12. **return** the decoded active schedule and the corresponding makespan

7.2.4 Initialize the harmony memory

The initialization strategy plays a crucial role in evolution algorithms as it can impact both the convergence rate and the ultimate solution's quality. To ensure that the initial HM exhibits a certain level of quality and diversity, we generate one harmony vector using a heuristic approach, while the rest are created randomly.

We generate a harmony vector $X = \{x(1), x(2), ..., x(n)\}$ randomly by utilizing the following formula:

$$x(j) = x_{\min}(j) + (x_{\max}(j) - x_{\min}(j)) \times rand(0, 1), \; j = 1, 2, \ldots, n \tag{7.5}$$

For each dimension j, where $x_{\min}(j) = -\delta$ and $x_{\max}(j) = \delta$, we use the random function $rand(0, 1)$ to generate a real number uniformly distributed between 0 and 1.

The generation of the harmony vector using heuristics entails creating a two-vector code using heuristics, which is then translated into the harmony vector X.

7.2.4.1 Generating a two-vector code based on heuristics

To form a schedule for the FJSP, we adopt a two-step methodology to achieve this. Initially, we apply the localization (AL) heuristic, as proposed by [13], to allocate each operation to a suitable machine, considering the processing time of each operation and the workload of each machine. In the AL procedure, we iterate through all the operations, and for each operation, we select the machine with the minimum processing time. Subsequently, we update the processing times of the remaining operations on the selected machine by adding this minimum time. In the second stage, we make use of the widely recognized dispatching rule, most work remaining (MWR), to determine the order in which operations are executed on the machines.

After acquiring the schedule, we transform it into a two-vector code. The machine assignment vector can be readily derived using Eq. (7.6). Subsequently, we utilize the MWR rule to arrange all operations identified by fixed IDs in the order of scheduling, which is represented by $\pi = \{\pi(1), \pi(2), ..., \pi(l)\}$. It is not required to further transform π into OS because the schedule obtained through heuristics is always feasible.

7.2.4.2 Converting the two-vector code to the harmony vector

The first part of the conversion process concerns machine assignment, and it involves an inverse linear transformation of Eq. (7.1). However, when $s(j) = 1$, the case must be treated separately, and $x(j)$ is assigned a random value between $[-\delta, \delta]$. The transformation can be executed by following the steps below:

$$x(j) = \begin{cases} \dfrac{2\delta}{s(j) - 1}(u(j) - 1) - \delta, & s(j) \neq 1 \\ x(j) \in [-\delta, \delta], & s(j) = 1 \end{cases} \tag{7.6}$$

where $1 \leq j \leq l$.

To comply with the LPV rule, we can obtain the latter half of the harmony vector, which is represented as $X^{(2)} = \{x(l+1), x(l+2), ..., x(2l)\}$, by utilizing the vector $\pi = \{\pi(1), \pi(2), ..., \pi(l)\}$ in the following manner:

$$x(\pi(j) + l) = \delta - \dfrac{2\delta}{l-1}(j-1), \ 1 \leq j \leq l \tag{7.7}$$

Assuming that we have $\pi = \{2, 3, 7, 1, 4, 5, 6\}$ and $\delta = 0.6$, we can use Eq. (7.7) to compute $x(9)$ as 0.6, $x(10)$ as 0.4, and so forth. Eventually, we obtain the second half of the harmony vector $X^{(2)}$ as $\{0, 0.6, 0.4, -0.2, -0.4, -0.6, 0.2\}$.

7.2.5 Improvise a new harmony

To produce a novel harmony vector $X_{new} = \{x_{new}(1), x_{new}(2), ..., x_{new}(n)\}$. we utilized three regulations: memory retention, pitch modification, and stochastic selection. In the memory retention phase, any value within the designated *HM* range $x_1(j)$–$x_{HMS}(j)$ can be chosen for each decision variable $x_{new}(j)$ in the novel harmony vector. The *HMCR* is a metric that specifies the likelihood of picking a value from the saved previous values in the *HM* (memory retention), ranging from 0 to 1. Conversely, $(1 - HMCR)$ denotes the likelihood of randomly selecting a value from the possible range of values (random selection), as illustrated in Eq. (7.8).

$$x_{new}(j) = \begin{cases} x_{new}(j) \in \{x_1(j), x_2(j), \dots, x_{HMS}(j)\}, & \text{with probability } HMCR \\ x_{new}(j) \in [x_{min}(j), x_{max}(j)], & \text{with probability } (1 - HMCR) \end{cases}$$
(7.8)

When $x_{new}(j)$ is chosen from the HM, we employ the pitch adjustment rule. This regulation involves the *PAR* parameter, which denotes the rate of pitch adjustment, and can be expressed in the following manner:

$$x_{new}(j) = \begin{cases} x_{new}(j) \pm rand(0,1) \times bw, & \text{with probability } PAR \\ x_{new}(j), & \text{with probability } (1 - PAR) \end{cases}$$
(7.9)

Here, *bw* represents a distance bandwidth with an arbitrary value.

To enhance the adaptability of the HS to the FJSP, the proposed HHS utilizes a modified pitch adjustment rule, represented by Eq. (7.10).

$$x_{new}(j) = \begin{cases} x_{best}(j), & \text{with probability } PAR \\ x_{new}(j), & \text{with probability } (1 - PAR) \end{cases}$$
(7.10)

By incorporating this modification, the algorithm can acquire the outstanding solution structure of X_{best} while reducing the number of necessary parameters.

Algorithm 7.2 outlines the primary steps involved in generating a new harmony using our proposed approach.

Algorithm 7.2 The procedure of improvising a new harmony in the HHS.

---
1. **for** $j = 1$ **to** n **do**
2.   **if** $rand(0,1) < HMCR$ **then**
3. $x_{new}(j) = x_i(j), i \in \{1, 2, \dots, HMS\}$
4.   **if** $rand(0,1) < PAR$ **then**
5. $x_{new}(j) = x_{best}(j)$
6.   **end if**
7.   **else**
8. $x_{new}(j) = x_{min}(j) + (x_{max}(j) - x_{min}(j)) \times rand(0,1)$
9.   **end if**
10. **end for**

7.2.6 Problem-dependent local search

To augment the exploration ability, we integrate a local search mechanism into the HS algorithm to amplify each feasible harmony vector generated during the improvisation phase. In the HHS methodology, the local search is carried out on the timetable depicted by the disjunctive graph, rather than being directly employed on the harmony vector.

7.2.6.1 Disjunctive graph model

The FJSP timetable can be depicted utilizing a disjunctive graph $G = (V, C \cup D)$, where V represents the collection of all nodes, where each node embodies an operation in the FJSP (comprising the opening and concluding dummy operations). C represents the set of all conjunctive arcs that connect adjacent operations within the same job, with their directions indicating the processing order. D represents the set of all disjunctive arcs that link successive operations executed on the same machine, with their directions indicating the order of processing. Ordinarily, the processing duration of each operation is indicated above the corresponding node and is treated as the weight of the node. An example timetable represented by the disjunctive graph is depicted in Fig. 7.6. The graph displays the consecutive processing of $O_{1,1}$, $O_{3,1}$, and $O_{2,3}$ by M_1. In contrast, M_2 successively carries out $O_{1,2}$ and $O_{2,2}$. Lastly, M_3 performs $O_{2,1}$ and $O_{3,2}$ in a sequence.

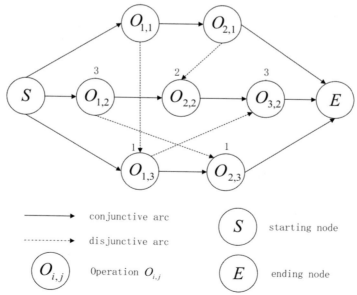

Figure 7.6 Illustration of disjunctive graph.

The disjunctive graph possesses two fundamental and crucial characteristics:

Property 1:
The absence of cyclic paths in the corresponding disjunctive graph indicates the feasibility of a schedule.

Property 2:
If a disjunctive graph is without cycles, the critical path, which is the lengthiest route starting from the initial node S and ending at the terminal node E, denotes the makespan of the respective timetable.

7.2.6.2 Neighborhoods based on common critical operations

Regarding the FJSP, most of the productive neighborhoods for local search are based on the critical path identified in the disjunctive graph [14−16]. Such neighborhoods are established on the premise that relocating an operation on the critical path of the existing disjunctive graph could lead to a decrease in the makespan. The transfer of an operation $O_{i,j}$ transpires in a two-stage process, namely deletion and insertion [15]:

1. First, eliminate all disjunctive arcs in the disjunctive graph that are connected to the node v, which represents $O_{i,j}$, from its current machine sequence. Then, assign a weight of 0 to the node v.
2. Select a machine M_k and designate the position of v in M_k's processing order to accommodate $O_{i,j}$. Next, insert the node v by adding its disjunctive arcs and assigning a weight of $p_{i,j,k}$ to the node v.

Moving an operation along the critical path is advantageous due to the following elementary principle:

Lemma 1:
If P represents a critical path in the current disjunctive graph, then moving an operation $O_{i,j} \notin P$ will not lead to a decrease in the makespan.

This principle can be explained in simple terms: when an operation that is not part of the longest path P in the current schedule is moved, the longest path P remains intact in the disjunctive graph, and therefore, the makespan cannot be decreased.

One of the main advantages of this type of neighborhood is that it avoids unnecessary moves, as indicated by Lemma 1, and reduces the size of neighborhoods effectively compared to moving an arbitrary operation. However, this approach may not be sufficient because the number of operations on a critical path in the current schedule represented by the disjunctive graph is often quite large. As a result, attempting to move many operations to form a new schedule with a shorter makespan can be extremely time-consuming. To accelerate the local search procedure in our proposed algorithm, we have enhanced this type of neighborhood by introducing the concept of common critical operations, which is based on the observation that multiple critical paths usually exist in the disjunctive graph. The notion of common critical operations can be explained through the following definitions:

Definition 1:

An operation can be classified as a critical operation only if its earliest starting time is equivalent to its latest starting time.

Definition 2:

A critical path in the disjunctive graph refers to a path composed entirely of critical operations, running from the starting node S to the ending node E.

Definition 3:

A common critical operation is an operation that is both critical and present on all critical paths of the disjunctive graph. If there is only one critical path, all critical operations are also common critical operations.

An operation's earliest start time corresponds to the earliest point in time at which it can commence execution, whereas its latest start time signifies the latest possible start time that won't cause a delay in the makespan. When determining common critical operations in the disjunctive graph, the following characteristics can be advantageous:

Property 3:

If the processing durations of two critical operations, op_i and op_j, are denoted by the time intervals $[s_i, c_i]$ and $[s_j, c_j]$, and there exists a segment of overlap between the two intervals, then neither op_i nor op_j is considered a common critical operation.

Proof 1:

The op_j is a critical operation, and as such, it appears on a single critical path P. If op_i is believed to be a common critical operation, it must appear on all critical paths, including P. Consequently, op_i and op_j must both appear on the same critical path P, and their processing durations $[s_i, c_i]$ and $[s_j, c_j]$ cannot overlap. This creates a paradox, rendering the assumption that op_i is a common critical operation untenable. Similarly, op_i cannot be a common critical operation either.

The reasoning behind the move strategy in the enhanced neighborhood structure involves relocating common critical operations rather than those present on a single critical path. This approach can be justified through the following explanation:

Corollary 1:

Moving an operation $O_{i,j}$ that is not classified as a common critical operation in the disjunctive graph will not result in a reduction of the makespan.

Proof 2:

As $O_{i,j}$ is not a common critical operation, there must be at least one critical path P without the presence of $O_{i,j}$, i.e., $O_{i,j}\notin P$. This observation is consistent with Lemma 1.

By exclusively relocating common critical operations, additional unnecessary moves can be avoided, and the size of neighborhoods can be reduced. This, in turn, results in a reduction of computational load and an improvement in the efficiency of local search procedures. For instance, consider Fig. 7.6, which contains two critical paths: $S \to O_{1,1} \to O_{1,2} \to O_{2,2} \to O_{2,3} \to E$ and $S \to O_{2,1} \to O_{2,2} \to O_{2,3} \to E$. Nevertheless, solely the operation $O_{2,2}$ is a shared critical operation. In the event where critical path operations were relocated, there would be a minimum of three potential operations to be transferred. Conversely, solely the operation $O_{2,2}$ is considered while relocating shared critical operations.

As demonstrated previously, we have identified the common critical operation that is to be removed. Afterward, we execute the insertion strategy specified in [16] to reintroduce the deleted operation into the timetable, thereby generating a valid neighborhood of the existing schedule. Suppose G' is the disjunctive graph obtained by eliminating the shared critical operation $O_{x,y}$ from G, where $ES'_{x,y}$ and $EC'_{x,y}$ respectively indicate the earliest starting time and the earliest completion time for every remaining operation $O_{x,y}$ in G'. To avoid a rise in the makespan subsequent to the insertion, we treat the makespan of G as the "mandatory" makespan of G', and determine the latest starting time $LS'_{x,y}$ for every operation $O_{x,y}$ based on this makespan. Next, we form the maximum idle time interval $[S_x, E_x]$ for any two adjacent operations $O_{\alpha,\beta}$ and $O_{\mu,\nu}$, on machine M_k, where

$$\begin{cases} S_x = EC'_{\alpha,\beta} = ES'_{\alpha,\beta} + p_{\alpha,\beta,k} \\ E_x = LS'_{\mu,\nu} \end{cases} \quad (7.11)$$

The feasibility of inserting $O_{i,j}$ within the maximum idle time interval $[S_x, E_x]$ can be determined by considering the precedence constraints between the operations.

$$\begin{cases} \max\{S_x, EC'_{i,j-1}\} + p_{i,j,k} < \min\{E_x, LS'_{i,j+1}\}, & j \neq 1, j \neq n_i \\ S_x + p_{i,j,k} < \min\{E_x, LS'_{i,j+1}\}, & j = 1 \\ \max\{S_x, EC'_{i,j-1}\} + p_{i,j,k} < E_x, & j = n_i \end{cases} \quad (7.12)$$

If there are no idle time segments to incorporate any of the shared critical operations, one can eliminate a random operation after eliminating a shared critical operation to generate larger and more idle time segments. These idle time intervals can then be used to insert operations in the same manner as described above. However, this process is more time-consuming and is only executed if an attempt to move a common critical operation fails. In summary, the process of generating an acceptable neighborhood in the local search is outlined in Algorithm 7.3.

Algorithm 7.3 The procedure of generating an acceptable neighborhood.

1. Get all the critical operations in the current disjunctive graph G according to Property 1
2. To pick out all the common critical operations $\{cop_1, cop_2, \ldots, cop_w\}$ To pick out all the common critical operations
3. **for** $i = 1$ **to** w **do**
4.   Delete cop_i from G to yield G'
5.   Calculate all the max idle time intervals in G'
6.   **if** an available time interval is found for cop_i **then**
7.   Insert the operation cop_i to yield G''
8.   **return** the disjunctive graph G''
9.   **end if**
10. **end for**
11. **for** $i = 1$ **to** w **do**
12.   Delete cop_i from G to yield G'
13.   **for** each operation op_i in G' **do**
14.   Delete op_i from G' to yield G''
15.   Calculate all the max idle time intervals in G''
16.   **if** two available time intervals are found for cop_i and op_i **then**
17.   Insert cop_i and op_j to yield G'''
18.   **return** the disjunctive graph G'''
19.   **end if**
20.   **end for**
21. **end for**
22. **return** an empty disjunctive graph

7.2.6.3 Local search procedure

Consider $X = \{x(1), x(2), \ldots, x(l), x(l+1), x(l+2), \ldots, x(2l)\}$ as the harmony vector that requires improvement using local search. At first, the vector X is translated into a timetable illustrated by the disjunctive graph through the two-vector code and decoding. The first step involves the conversion of the vector X into a schedule depicted by the disjunctive graph using the two-vector code and decoding. Ultimately, the timetable attained via this procedure is transformed back into the harmony vector $Y = \{y(1), y(2), \ldots, y(l), y(l+1), y(l+2), \ldots, y(2l)\}$. A comprehensive account of the computational process of the local search algorithm is presented in Algorithm 7.4.

Algorithm 7.4: The procedure of local search in the HHS.

1. Convert the harmony vector X to a two–vector code
2. Decode the two–vector code to a feasible schedule represented by the disjunctive graph G
3. **while** the maximal iterations are not met **do**
4.   To yield G' from G by executing Algorithm 7.3
5.   **if** G' is not empty **then**
6. $G \leftarrow G'$
7.   **else**
8.   Exit the while loop
9.   **end if**
10. **end while**
11. Get the vector $Y^{(1)} = \{y(1), y(2), ..., y(l)\}$ directly from the machine assignment in G according to Eq. (7.6)
12. Sort all the operations in the nondecreasing order of the earliest start time and yield the operation ID permutation $\pi = \{\pi(1), \pi(2), \dots, \pi(l)\}$
13. Rearrange elements in $X^{(2)} = \{x(l+1), x(l+2), \dots, x(2l)\}$ to yield $Y^{(2)} = \{y(l+1), y(l+2), ..., y(2l)\}$ combining π and LPV rule
14. **return** the harmony vector Y

7.2.7 Update harmony memory

In the HHS suggested in this study, the HM is refreshed every time a novel harmony vector $X'_{new} = \{X'_{new}(1), X'_{new}(2), \dots, X'_{new}(n)\}$ is produced by means of local search. In the event where the objective function value of X'_{new} is superior to that of the most inferior harmony X_{worst} in the present HM, then X'_{new} replaces X_{worst} and becomes a new member of the HM. Otherwise, no action is taken. In the event where X'_{new} is included in the HM, it is imperative to consider the update of the labels for the top-most and bottommost harmony vectors in the HM.

7.3 Experimental details

7.3.1 Experimental setup

To evaluate the effectiveness of the proposed HHS in addressing the FJSP, the algorithm was coded in Java and executed on a personal computer with a processing speed of 2.83 GHz and 15.9 GB of RAM. Experimental outcomes are presented and contrasted with those obtained by other researchers. A variety of problem sets were used in our experiment, including:

(1) Kacem data: The dataset used in this study includes three problem instances (8×8, 10×10, and 15×10) sourced from Kacem et al. [13]. The 8×8 problem pertains to a P-FJSP situation that encompasses eight tasks that can be executed on eight machines, with a cumulative count of 27 operations. The 10x10 problem applies to a

T–FJSP situation that features 10 tasks that can be performed on 10 machines, with a total of 30 operations. Finally, the 15×10 problem is a T–FJSP case that comprises 15 tasks that can be processed on 10 machines, with a cumulative count of 56 operations.

(2) Fdata: The dataset utilized in this research comprises 20 problems derived from Fattahi et al.'s work [17]. These problems are segregated into two categories: small–sized flexible job shop scheduling problems (SFJS01: 10) and medium to large–sized flexible job shop scheduling problems (MFJS01: 10). The problems have a job count that varies from 2 to 12, a machine count that ranges from 2 to 8, an operation count per job that fluctuates between 2 and 4, and an overall operation count for all jobs that fluctuates between 4 and 48.

(3) BRdata: The dataset utilized in this study consists of 10 problems sourced from Brandimarte [18]. The problems have a job count that varies from 10 to 20, while the machine count ranges from 4 to 15. The range of flexibility per operation varies between 1.43 and 4.10, and the overall operation count for all jobs fluctuates between 55 and 240.

(4) DPdata: The dataset used for this research comprises 18 problems acquired from Dauzère-Pérès and Paulli [14]. The quantity of jobs in the problems varies between 10 and 20, whereas the number of machines changes between 5 and 10. The variability per operation fluctuates between 1.13 and 5.02, and the overall number of operations for all jobs ranges from 196 to 387.

(5) BCdata: The dataset used in this research consists of 21 problems obtained from Barnes and Chambers [19]. The quantity of jobs in the problems varies between 10 and 15, whereas the number of machines changes between 4 and 15. The variability per operation fluctuates between 1.07 and 1.30, and the overall number of operations for all jobs ranges from 100 to 225.

(6) HUdata: The dataset used for this research comprises 129 problems acquired from Hurink et al. [20]. The problems are classified into three groups, namely Edata, Rdata, and Vdata, based on the typical number of alternate machines accessible for each operation (flexibility). The quantity of jobs in the problems varies between 6 and 30, while the number of machines ranges from 5 to 15. The flexibility per operation ranges from 1.15 to 7.5, and the total number of operations for all jobs ranges from 36 to 300.

To facilitate an all-encompassing performance comparison, we conducted 30 independent iterations for each instance from Kacem data, Fdata, and BRdata, which entail nondeterminacy in the proposed algorithms. To depict the computational outcomes, we captured the following four metrics:

1. BC_{max}: The optimal makespan achieved from multiple runs
2. $AV(C_{max})$: The mean makespan acquired from multiple runs
3. *SD*: The makespan standard deviation derived from multiple runs
4. $AV(CPU)$: The mean solution time, measured in seconds, required to attain the solutions from multiple runs

Table 7.1 Parameters setting of *NI* and *loop*$_{\max}$ for each data set.

Data set	NI	loop$_{\max}$
Kacem data	400	20
Fdata	3000	30
BRdata	5000	200
DPdata	3000	300
BCdata	3000	300
HUdata	3000	300

While $BC_{\max}$ is predominantly used to compare two algorithms in FJSP studies [21–24], we compared AV(CPU) against various algorithms on particular problem instances to showcase the superior effectiveness of our proposed HHS algorithm, for which this metric was also documented. Making comparisons between algorithms is notoriously challenging due to the varying computing hardware, programming platforms, and coding abilities employed in each algorithm [25]. Hence, with respect to AV(CPU), we furnish the CPU's original name, programming language, and computational time associated with the respective algorithm to acquire a general and reasonably fair understanding of the efficiency of the referenced algorithms. We conducted a comprehensive statistical analysis, comparing our HHS algorithm with two previously proposed highly efficient GA algorithms [22,26]. By re-implementing these algorithms, we conducted an in-depth analysis to offer supplementary proof of the superior algorithmic efficacy of HHS concerning solution quality.

The HHS algorithm that we have put forth is composed of various parameters, which consist of harmony memory size (*HMS*), harmony memory considering rate (*HMCR*), pitch adjusting rate (*PAR*), the bound factor (δ), number of improvisations (*NI*), and the maximum iterations of local search (*loop*$_{\max}$). In our experimentation, we maintained a fixed value of 5 for HMS, *HMCR* to 0.95, *PAR* to 0.3, and δ to 1. To achieve satisfactory solutions within a reasonable computational time frame, we adjusted the parameters *NI* and *loop*$_{\max}$ based on the specific characteristics of different datasets. Table 7.1 provides the parameter configurations for each dataset for the two aforementioned parameters.

7.3.2 Computational results and comparisons

The preliminary assessment of the proposed HHS algorithm involved conducting tests on three Kacem data problems, with the corresponding computational outcomes tabulated in Table 7.2. A comparison of our proposed algorithm with five other approaches, namely AL + CGA by Kacem et al. [13], PSO + SA by Xia and Wu [27], PVNS by Yazdani et al. [24], AIA by Bagheri et al. [23], and TSPCB by Li et al. [28], is presented in Table 7.3. In all three problems, our proposed HHS algorithm

Table 7.2 Results of hybrid harmony search (HHS) on Kacem data.

Problem	Proposed HHS			
	BC_{max}	$AV(C_{max})$	SD	AV(CPU)
8×8	14	14	0	0.00
10×10	7	7	0	0.01
15×10	11	11	0	0.42

Table 7.3 Comparison between the proposed hybrid harmony search (HHS) and five existing algorithms on Kacem data.

Problem	AL + CGA	PSO + SA	PVNS	AIA[a]		TSPCB[b]		Proposed HHS[c]	
				BC_{max}	AV (CPU)	BC_{max}	AV (CPU)	BC_{max}	AV (CPU)
8×8	15	15	**14**	**14**	0.76	**14**	4.68	**14**	0.00
10×10	**7**	**7**	**7**	**7**	8.97	**7**	1.72	**7**	0.01
15×10	24	12	12	**11**	109.22	**11**	9.82	**11**	0.42

Note: The best BC_{max} values for each problem are marked in bold.
[a]The CPU time on a 2.0 GHz processor in C++.
[b]The CPU time on a Pentium IV 1.6 GHz processor in C++.
[c]The CPU time on an Intel 2.83 GHz Xeon processor in Java.

outperformed the other algorithms, securing the best results. This is evident from the second to fifth columns of Table 7.3, which display the best makespan outcomes achieved by AL + CGA, PSO + SA, and PVNS, respectively.

The outcomes presented in Table 7.2 indicate that the proposed HHS algorithm displayed exceptional proficiency and stability when tested on Kacem data, as evident from the SD being identical to 0 for each problem. Regarding the best makespan, the AIA and TSPCB algorithms demonstrated comparable performance to HHS. However, it appears that the AIA and TSPCB algorithms required considerably more average CPU time compared to our proposed HHS algorithm. The Gantt Chart as shown in Fig. 7.7 illustrates a solution obtained by using HHS for Problem 15×10.

The second dataset under scrutiny is Fdata, Table 7.4 illustrates the computational results obtained from our proposed HHS algorithm. The opening column of the table designates the problem names, while the second and third columns indicate the number of jobs and machines, respectively. The fourth column displays the lower bound for each problem. The literature on FJSP has recorded that the AIA algorithm [23] exhibits one of the most outstanding performances on Fdata, outperforming all six algorithms introduced in [17]. Table 7.5 presents a comparison between our proposed HHS algorithm and AIA, utilizing the relative deviation criterion (dev). This criterion is defined as follows:

$$dev = \left[\frac{BC_{max}(comp) - BC_{max}(HHS)}{BC_{max}(comp)} \right] \times 100\% \qquad (7.13)$$

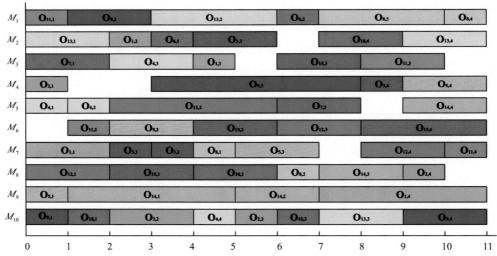

Figure 7.7 Gantt Chart of solution of problem 15 × 10.

Table 7.4 Results of hybrid harmony search (HHS) on Fdata.

Problem	n	m	LB	Proposed HHS			
				BC_{max}	$AV(C_{max})$	SD	AV(CPU)
SFJS01	2	2	66	66	66	0	0.00
SFJS02	2	2	107	107	107	0	0.00
SFJS03	3	2	221	221	221	0	0.00
SFJS04	3	2	355	355	355	0	0.00
SFJS05	3	2	119	119	119	0	0.00
SFJS06	3	3	320	320	320	0	0.00
SFJS07	3	5	397	397	397	0	0.00
SFJS08	3	4	253	253	253	0	0.00
SFJS09	3	3	210	210	210	0	0.00
SFJS10	4	5	516	516	516	0	0.00
MFJS01	5	6	396	468	468	0	0.01
MFJS02	5	7	396	446	447.53	0.86	0.01
MFJS03	6	7	396	466	466.83	1.05	0.12
MFJS04	7	7	496	554	559.87	5.67	0.06
MFJS05	7	7	414	514	514	0	0.02
MFJS06	8	7	469	634	634.4	2.19	0.01
MFJS07	8	7	619	879	879.07	0.37	0.11
MFJS08	9	8	619	884	885.1	0.36	0.08
MFJS09	11	8	764	1055	1065.2	14.24	0.94
MFJS10	12	8	944	1196	1209.07	8.59	0.69

Table 7.5 Comparison between the proposed hybrid harmony search (HHS) and AIA on Fdata.

Problem	n	m	LB	Proposed HHS[a]		AIA[b]		
				BC_{max}	AV(CPU)	BC_{max}	AV(CPU)	dev(%)
SFJS01	2	2	66	**66**	0.00	**66**	0.03	0
SFJS02	2	2	107	**107**	0.00	**107**	0.03	0
SFJS03	3	2	221	**221**	0.00	**221**	0.04	0
SFJS04	3	2	355	**355**	0.00	**355**	0.04	0
SFJS05	3	2	119	**119**	0.00	**119**	0.04	0
SFJS06	3	3	320	**320**	0.00	**320**	0.04	0
SFJS07	3	5	397	**397**	0.00	**397**	0.04	0
SFJS08	3	4	253	**253**	0.00	**253**	0.05	0
SFJS09	3	3	210	**210**	0.00	**210**	0.05	0
SFJS10	4	5	516	**516**	0.00	**516**	0.05	0
MFJS01	5	6	396	**468**	0.01	**468**	9.23	0
MFJS02	5	7	396	**446**	0.01	448	9.35	+0.45
MFJS03	6	7	396	**466**	0.12	468	10.06	+0.43
MFJS04	7	7	496	**554**	0.06	**554**	10.54	0
MFJS05	7	7	414	**514**	0.02	527	10.61	+2.47
MFJS06	8	7	469	**634**	0.01	635	22.18	+0.16
MFJS07	8	7	619	**879**	0.11	**879**	24.82	0
MFJS08	9	8	619	**884**	0.08	**884**	26.94	0
MFJS09	11	8	764	**1055**	0.94	1088	30.76	+3.03
MFJS10	12	8	944	**1196**	0.69	1267	30.94	+5.60

Note: The best BC_{max} values for each problem are marked in bold.
[a]The CPU time on an Intel 2.83 GHz Xeon processor in Java.
[b]The CPU time on a 2.0 GHz processor in C++.

Here, BC_{max}(HHS) denotes the optimal makespan achieved by our algorithm, while BC_{max} (comp) refers to the optimal makespan of the algorithm that we are comparing ours to. Our proposed HHS outperforms the AIA algorithm across all instances of Fdata, discovering six improved solutions for the MFJS02, MFJS03, MFJS05, MFJS06, MFJS09, and MFJS10 instances. The solutions for instances MFJS05, MFJS09, and MFJS10 are notably enhanced. An optimum schedule for the MFJS05 instance, which was obtained using HHS, is illustrated in Fig. 7.8. In terms of efficiency, HHS and AIA prove to be sufficiently efficient for the small instance SFJS01 with virtually zero time consumption. However, when it comes to the medium and large-sized instances of MFJS01, HHS demonstrates evident superiority, consuming significantly less average CPU time than AIA. The HHS algorithm that we have developed surpasses the AIA algorithm in both efficiency and effectiveness when applied to Fdata.

We examined another dataset, BRdata, and presented the results of HHS's performance on this dataset in Table 7.6. The name and size of the problem are listed in the first and second columns, respectively. Furthermore, the third column exhibits the

M_1: $(O_{4,1}$: 0–87$)(O_{2,1}$: 87–301$)$

M_2: $(O_{3,1}$: 0–62$)(O_{5,1}$: 62–185$)(O_{1,2}$: 185–315$)(O_{2,2}$: 315–385$)(O_{5,3}$: 381–481$)$

M_3: $(O_{1,1}$: 0–100$)(O_{7,1}$: 100–245$)(O_{7,2}$: 245–369$)$

M_4: $(O_{6,1}$: 0–154$)(O_{6,2}$: 154–304$)(O_{1,3}$: 315–465$)$

M_5: $(O_{4,2}$: 87–260$)(O_{3,3}$: 260–360$)(O_{7,3}$: 369–514$)$

M_6: $(O_{4,3}$: 260–396$)(O_{2,3}$: 396–491$)$

M_7: $(O_{3,2}$: 62–207$)(O_{5,2}$: 207–293$)(O_{6,3}$: 304–484$)$

Figure 7.8 Scheduling obtained for problem MFJS05.

Table 7.6 Results of hybrid harmony search (HHS) on BRdata.

Problem	$n \times m$	Flex	(LB, UB)	Proposed HHS			
				BC_{max}	$AV(C_{max})$	SD	AV(CPU)
MK01	10×6	2.09	(36, 42)	40	40	0	0.07
MK02	10×6	4.10	(24, 32)	26	26.63	0.49	0.74
MK03	15×8	3.01	(204, 211)	204	204	0	0.01
MK04	15×8	1.91	(48, 81)	60	60.03	0.18	1.04
MK05	15×4	1.71	(168, 186)	172	172.8	0.41	7.47
MK06	10×15	3.27	(33, 86)	58	59.13	0.63	60.73
MK07	20×5	2.83	(133, 157)	139	139.57	0.50	10.59
MK08	20×10	1.43	523	523	523	0	0.02
MK09	20×10	2.53	(299, 369)	307	307	0	0.39
MK10	20×15	2.98	(165, 296)	205	211.13	2.37	373.01

average number of alternate machines for each operation per problem, while the fourth column shows (LB, UB), referring to the lower and upper bounds of the problem.

In the literature, the same set of issues are tackled by GA by Chen et al. [21], GA by Pezzella et al. [22], AIA by Bagheri et al. [23], PVNS by Yazdani et al. [24], TSPCB by Li et al. [28], MA by Raeesi and Kobti [29], and eGA by Zhang et al. [26]. Table 7.7 presents a comparison of the outcomes obtained from the proposed HHS and those of the aforementioned algorithms. Table 7.7 demonstrates that our HHS algorithm performs competitively on BRdata. For BCmax, our HHS algorithm surpasses GA_Chen in 7 out of 10 instances, AIA in 5 out of 10 instances, GA_Pezzella and PVNS in 4 out of 10 instances, and MA and eGA in 2 out of 10 instances. Our HHS is only surpassed by eGA on the MK10 instance. On average, our HHS achieves the best improvement compared to all of the other algorithms mentioned. Our HHS algorithm is much more efficient than AIA in terms of speed. However, TSPCB and eGA sometimes display lower AV(CPU) values than our HHS

Table 7.7 Comparison between the proposed hybrid harmony search (HHS) and existing algorithms on BRdata.

Problem	Proposed HHS[a]		GA_Chen		GA_Pezzell		AIA[b]			PVNS		TSPCB[c]			MA		eGA[d]		
	BC_{max}	AV(CPU)	BC_{max}	dev(%)	BC_{max}	dev(%)	BC_{max}	AV(CPU)	dev(%)	BC_{max}	dev(%)	BC_{max}	AV(CPU)	dev(%)	BC_{max}	dev(%)	BC_{max}	AV(CPU)	dev(%)
MK01	**40**	0.07	**40**	0	**40**	0	**40**	97.21	0	**40**	0	**40**	2.80	0	**40**	0	**40**	1.60	0
MK02	**26**	0.74	29	+10.34	**26**	0	**26**	103.46	0	**26**	0	**26**	19.31	0	**26**	0	**26**	2.60	0
MK03	**204**	0.01	**204**	0	**204**	0	**204**	247.37	0	**204**	0	**204**	0.98	0	**204**	0	**204**	1.30	0
MK04	**60**	1.04	63	+4.76	**60**	0	**60**	152.07	0	**60**	0	62	40.82	+3.23	**60**	0	**60**	6.20	0
MK05	**172**	7.47	181	+4.97	173	+0.58	173	171.95	+0.58	173	+0.58	**172**	20.23	0	**172**	0	173	7.30	+0.58
MK06	**58**	60.73	60	+3.33	63	+7.94	63	245.62	+7.94	63	+3.33	65	27.18	+10.77	59	+1.69	**58**	15.70	0
MK07	**139**	10.59	148	+6.08	**139**	0	140	161.92	+0.71	141	+1.42	140	35.29	+0.71	**139**	0	144	17.30	+3.47
MK08	**523**	0.02	**523**	0	**523**	0	**523**	392.25	0	**523**	0	**523**	4.65	0	**523**	0	**523**	2.20	0
MK09	**307**	0.39	308	+0.32	311	+1.29	312	389.71	+1.60	**307**	0	310	70.38	+0.97	**307**	0	**307**	30.20	0
MK10	205	373.01	212	+3.30	212	+3.30	214	384.54	+4.21	208	+1.44	214	89.83	+4.21	216	+5.09	**198**	36.60	-3.54
Average improvement	+3.31		+1.31		+1.50		+0.68		+1.99	+0.68			+0.05						

Note: The best BC_{max} values for each problem are marked in bold.
[a] The CPU time on an Intel 2.83 GHz Xeon processor in Java.
[b] The CPU time on a 2.0 GHz processor in C++.
[c] The CPU time on a Pentium IV 1.6 GHz processor in C++.
[d] The CPU time on a Pentium IV 1.8 GHz processor in C++.

Table 7.8 Mean relative error (MRE) over best-known lower bound.

Data set	Num	Proposed HHS (%)	GA_Chen (%)	GA_Pezzella (%)	AIA (%)	PVNS (%)
DPdata	18	3.76	7.91	7.63	N/A	5.11
BCdata	21	22.89	38.64	29.56	N/A	26.66
Hurink Edata	43	2.67	5.59	6.00	6.83	3.86
Hurink Rdata	43	1.88	4.41	4.42	3.98	1.88
Hurink Vdata	43	0.39	2.59	2.04	1.29	0.42

Note: N/A means the corresponding data is not available. The best MRE values for each data set are marked in bold.

algorithm. Overall, the efficiency of our HHS algorithm seems to be at least comparable to that of TSPCB and eGA.

The MRE outcomes for three instance categories are summarized in Table 7.8. The first column exhibits the dataset, while the number of instances for each category is displayed in the second column. The next five columns indicate the MRE for each algorithm's best solution, including our HHS, GA by Chen et al. [21], GA by Pezzella et al. [22], AIA by Bagheri et al. [23], and PVNS by Yazdani et al. [24]. The definition of the relative error (RE) is as follows:

$$RE = \left[\frac{BC_{\max} - LB}{LB} \right] \times 100\% \qquad (7.14)$$

Here, it can be observed that our proposed approach outperforms all other relevant methods in terms of the MRE criterion, across all three datasets, with a maximum makespan of $BC_{\max}$ and the best-known lower bound (LB). Additionally, for the Hurink Rdata, PVNS is the only other method that achieves the same top result as our proposed HHS technique.

7.3.3 Further comparisons of hybrid harmony search with other algorithms

This subsection aims to conduct a statistical analysis comparing our HHS method with Pezzella et al.'s GA [22] and Zhang et al.'s eGA [26]. We meticulously re-implemented the GA_Pezzella and eGA algorithms, adhering to the guidelines provided in the original publications. Our implementation of GA_Pezzella produced similar results to those reported in [22]. Despite our efforts to accurately replicate the eGA algorithm described in [26], our implementation did not achieve the level of effectiveness that the authors claimed. We found that when using the population size and number of generations specified in [26], our implementation of eGA did not yield satisfactory computational outcomes. Given that the GA algorithms we used share a similar concept—integrating various initialization strategies—we opted to adopt the parameter settings for eGA outlined in [22]. Accordingly, we set the population size to 5000 and the number of generations to 1000. The remaining parameters for both algorithms were kept consistent with the recommendations provided in their respective original publications.

Table 7.9 presents the statistical outcomes of 30 independent runs for HHS, GA_Pezzella, and eGA on the BRdata. Our HHS method outperformed both GA_Pezzella and eGA, achieving the best $AV(C_{max})$ in 8 out of 10 instances. In contrast, GA_Pezzella and eGA only outperformed our method in two instances. Furthermore, in no instance did our HHS technique yield a worse BC_{max} value than GA_Pezzella or eGA. With respect to efficiency, our HHS method demonstrated superior results in most cases. Nevertheless, GA_Pezzella exhibited superior performance over our algorithm in regards to both makespan and computational time for the MK10 instance. The problems MK03 and MK09 were relatively easy, as all three algorithms were able to solve them optimally within a short period.

To ascertain whether there were any noteworthy distinctions between the outcomes from the HHS algorithm that we have devised and the two GA algorithms that we have implemented, we conducted a significance test. As the makespan values did not exhibit normal distribution or homogeneity of variance, we followed the recommendations in [30] and employed nonparametric tests. The focus of our analysis was to determine if there were no significant variations in the optimization results generated by the three algorithms for each problem instance. To assess the results, we utilized the Wilcoxon signed-rank test. This statistical test is well-suited for comparing paired samples in a nonparametric fashion, allowing for robust analysis of the data. We present the outcomes in Table 7.10, where we utilized a significance level of $\alpha = 0.05$ in all tests. Based on the data provided, it is evident that our HHS method outperformed GA_Pezzella significantly, with the exception of instances MK03, MK08, and MK10. Our analysis revealed that there was no noteworthy difference in performance between HHS and GA_Pezzella on instances MK03 and MK08. However, for instance, MK10, GA_Pezzella outperformed HHS significantly. In contrast, when comparing HHS to eGA, no significant differences were observed in instances MK02, MK03, MK05, and MK08. However, our HHS method demonstrated significantly better performance than eGA in all other instances.

In Fig. 7.9, we present the convergence curves for the average makespan achieved over 30 independent runs by eGA, GA_Pezzella, and HHS on instance MK06. The data indicates that our HHS approach was able to converge more quickly to lower makespan values compared to both GA_Pezzella and eGA.

7.4 Discussion

Through the simulation tests and comparative analysis conducted in Section 7.5, we determined that our proposed HHS technique is a robust, efficient, and effective solution for addressing the makespan criterion in the FJSP. Our approach's effectiveness

Table 7.9 Statistical results of hybrid harmony search (HHS), GA_Pezzella, and eGA over 30 independent runs on BRdata.

Problem	Proposed HHS				Implemented GA_Pezzella				Implemented eGA			
	BC_{max}	$AV(C_{max})$	SD	AV(CPU)	BC_{max}	$AV(C_{max})$	SD	AV(CPU)	BC_{max}	$AV(C_{max})$	SD	AV(CPU)
MK01	40	**40**	0	0.07	40	41.13	0.43	4.62	40	41.33	0.66	0.50
MK02	26	26.63	0.49	0.74	26	27.13	0.43	5.88	26	**26.53**	0.57	8.08
MK03	204	**204**	0	0.01	204	**204**	0	0.21	204	**204**	0	0.00
MK04	60	**60.03**	0.18	1.04	62	63.07	0.69	59.18	64	64.67	0.48	6.19
MK05	172	**172.8**	0.41	7.47	173	173.27	0.52	13.87	173	173	0	19.77
MK06	58	**59.13**	0.63	60.73	61	61.7	0.75	68.68	60	62	0.91	133.32
MK07	139	**139.57**	0.50	10.59	140	140.9	0.66	28.07	140	142	1.34	25.00
MK08	523	**523**	0	0.02	523	**523**	0	0.35	523	**523**	0	0.62
MK09	307	**307**	0	0.39	307	308.77	1.89	169.45	309	309.03	0.18	367.99
MK10	205	211.13	2.37	373.01	205	**209.3**	1.78	232.73	218	220.67	1.12	564.47

Note: The best $AV(C_{max})$ values for each problem are marked in bold.

Table 7.10 Significance tests on the makespan obtained on BRdata instances.

Problem	HHS vs GA_Pezzella			HHS vs eGA		
	R^+	R^-	P-Value	R^+	R^-	P-Value
MK01	0	435	<0.0001	0	378	<0.0001
MK02	0	78	0.0012	63	42	0.2611
MK03	0	0	—	0	0	—
MK04	0	465	<0.0001	0	465	<0.0001
MK05	0	66	0.0018	0	21	—
MK06	0	465	<0.0001	0	435	<0.0001
MK07	0	276	<0.0001	0	351	<0.0001
MK08	0	0	—	0	0	—
MK09	0	120	0.0003	0	465	<0.0001
MK10	259.5	65.5	0.0047	0	465	<0.0001

The P-values are from one sided Wilcoxon signed-rank test. The level of significance α is set to 0.05. *HHS*, Hybrid harmony search.

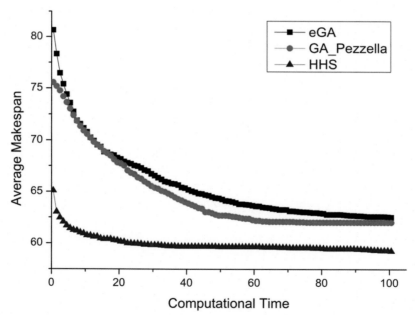

Figure 7.9 Convergence curves in solving the instance MK06 by the eGA, GA_Pezzella, and HHS. *HHS*, Hybrid harmony search.

can be attributed to the emphasis placed on maintaining a balance between exploration and exploitation during the design of the HHS algorithm. Moreover, the high efficiency of our method can be attributed to several factors, including the use of a simple improvisation mechanism and HS's fast convergence, a local search acceleration strategy, and a hybrid initialization scheme.

Compared to other state-of-the-art meta-heuristics designed for the FJSP, HHS has a simpler algorithmic structure that seems more straightforward to implement. Despite its simplicity, however, HHS has displayed a noteworthy level of robust search capability concerning both efficacy and speed. Additionally, due to the presence of fewer parameters, HHS is considered more controllable and potentially more practical. Nevertheless, there is still room for improvement in HHS when it comes to handling large-scale problems, such as the instance MK10 in BRdata where HHS did not obtain the best results among the algorithms used in our study. This limitation could potentially be addressed by developing more effective strategies for escaping local optima during the search process.

It is noteworthy that our proposed HHS methodology provides exceptional adaptability and expandability. The HS and local search components in HHS are not tightly connected, permitting autonomous alterations to one component without influencing the other. Additionally, the conversion strategies devised in HHS can be utilized by other continuous evolutionary algorithms to tackle the FJSP. Finally, the HHS framework can be easily adapted to address other combinatorial optimization problems due to its problem-dependent conversion mechanism and local search.

7.5 Conclusion

Our study represents a novel approach to solving the FJSP using the makespan criterion, as we are the first to employ the HS algorithm for this purpose. Our proposed method utilizes converting techniques to enable the continuous HS to adapt to the discrete FJSP. Through the utilization of the two-vector code and active decoding, we can map a harmony vector to a viable active schedule, leading to a substantial decrease in the search space. Additionally, we have introduced an initialization scheme that combines both heuristic and random strategies to initialize the HM, resulting in a diverse and high-quality HM. To maintain a balance between exploring and exploiting the search space, we have merged the robust global search capability of HS with the local enhancement ability of local search. Furthermore, we have developed an improved neighborhood structure based on common critical operations, which incorporates problem-specific scheduling information and accelerates the local search process.

References

[1] Michael LP. Scheduling: theory, algorithms, and systems. Springer International PU; 2022.
[2] Van Laarhoven PJM, Aarts EHL, Lenstra JK. Job shop scheduling by simulated annealing. Operations Research 1992;40(1):113−25.

[3] Nowicki E, Smutnicki C. A fast taboo search algorithm for the job shop problem. Management Science 1996;42(6):797–813.

[4] Gonçalves JF, de Magalhães Mendes JJ, Resende MGC. A hybrid genetic algorithm for the job shop scheduling problem. European Journal of Operational Research 2005;167(1):77–95.

[5] Lochtefeld DF, Ciarallo FW. Helper-objective optimization strategies for the job-shop scheduling problem. Applied Soft Computing 2011;11(6):4161–74.

[6] Garey MR, Johnson DS, Sethi R. The complexity of flowshop and jobshop scheduling. Mathematics of Operations Research 1976;1(2):117–29.

[7] Ishibuchi H, Yoshida T, Murata T. Balance between genetic search and local search in memetic algorithms for multiobjective permutation flowshop scheduling. IEEE Transactions on Evolutionary Computation 2003;7(2):204–23.

[8] Tan KC, Chiam SC, Mamun AA, et al. Balancing exploration and exploitation with adaptive variation for evolutionary multi-objective optimization. European Journal of Operational Research 2009;197(2):701–13.

[9] Lin JY, Chen YP. Analysis on the collaboration between global search and local search in memetic computation. IEEE Transactions on Evolutionary Computation 2011;15(5):608–23.

[10] Gen M. Solving job-shop scheduling problem using genetic algorithms. Proceedings of the 16th international conference on computer and industrial engineering; 1994.

[11] Wang L, Pan QK, Tasgetiren MF. Minimizing the total flow time in a flow shop with blocking by using hybrid harmony search algorithms. Expert Systems with Applications 2010;37 (12):7929–36.

[12] Baker K. Sequencing and scheduling: an introduction to the mathematics of the job-shop. INFORMS 1983;13(3):94–6.

[13] Kacem I, Hammadi S, Borne P. Approach by localization and multiobjective evolutionary optimization for flexible job-shop scheduling problems. IEEE Transactions on Systems, Man, and Cybernetics, Part C (Applications and Reviews) 2002;32(1):1–13.

[14] Dauzère-Pérès S, Paulli J. An integrated approach for modeling and solving the general multi-processor job-shop scheduling problem using tabu search. Annals of Operations Research 1997;70(0):281–306.

[15] Mastrolilli M, Gambardella LM. Effective neighbourhood functions for the flexible job shop problem. Journal of Scheduling 2000;3(1):3–20.

[16] Wang L, Zhou G, Xu Y, et al. An effective artificial bee colony algorithm for the flexible job-shop scheduling problem. International Journal of Advanced Manufacturing Technology 2012;60 (1–4):303–15.

[17] Fattahi P, Saidi Mehrabad M, Jolai F. Mathematical modeling and heuristic approaches to flexible job shop scheduling problems. Journal of Intelligent Manufacturing 2007;18:331–42.

[18] Brandimarte P. Routing and scheduling in a flexible job shop by tabu search. Annals of Operations Research 1993;41(3):157–83.

[19] Barnes J.W., Chambers J.B. Flexible job shop scheduling by tabu search. Graduate program in operations research and industrial engineering, The University of Texas at Austin, Technical Report Series; 1996.

[20] Hurink J, Jurisch B, Thole M. Tabu search for the job-shop scheduling problem with multi-purpose machines. Operations-Research-Spektrum 1994;15:205–15.

[21] Chen H., Ihlow J., Lehmann C. A genetic algorithm for flexible job-shop scheduling. Proceedings of the 15th IEEE international conference on robotics and automation; 1999. Vol. 2, p. 1120–5.

[22] Pezzella F, Morganti G, Ciaschetti G. A genetic algorithm for the flexible job-shop scheduling problem. Computers & Operations Research 2008;35(10):3202–12.

[23] Bagheri A, Zandieh M, Mahdavi I, et al. An artificial immune algorithm for the flexible job-shop scheduling problem. Future Generation Computer Systems 2010;26(4):533–41.

[24] Yazdani M, Amiri M, Zandieh M. Flexible job-shop scheduling with parallel variable neighborhood search algorithm. Expert Systems with Applications 2010;37(1):678–87.

[25] Beck JC, Feng TK, Watson JP. Combining constraint programming and local search for job-shop scheduling. INFORMS Journal on Computing 2011;23(1):1–14.

[26] Zhang G, Gao L, Shi Y. An effective genetic algorithm for the flexible job-shop scheduling problem. Expert Systems with Applications 2011;38(4):3563−73.

[27] Xia W, Wu Z. An effective hybrid optimization approach for multi-objective flexible job-shop scheduling problems. Computers & Industrial Engineering 2005;48(2):409−25.

[28] Li JQ, Pan QK, Suganthan PN, et al. A hybrid tabu search algorithm with an efficient neighborhood structure for the flexible job shop scheduling problem. The International Journal of Advanced Manufacturing Technology 2011;52:683−97.

[29] Raeesi NMR, Kobti Z. A memetic algorithm for job shop scheduling using a critical-path-based local search heuristic. Memetic Computing 2012;4:231−45.

[30] Demšar J. Statistical comparisons of classifiers over multiple data sets. The Journal of Machine Learning Research 2006;7:1−30.

CHAPTER 8

Flexible job shop scheduling using hybrid differential evolution algorithms

Contents

8.1 Introduction

Recent studies on the flexible job shop scheduling problem (FJSP) have generated growing interest in the exploration of alternative metaheuristic algorithms that go beyond the traditionally employed techniques. For example, Bagheri et al. [1] proposed an artificial immune algorithm (AIA) that incorporates effective rules to enhance search performance. Yazdani et al. [2] suggested the parallel variable neighborhood search (PVNS) algorithm, which employs multiple independent searches to improve the exploration of the search space. Xing et al. [3] introduced

Intelligent Evolutionary Optimization
DOI: https://doi.org/10.1016/B978-0-443-27400-8.00008-3

a knowledge-based ant colony optimization algorithm that integrates the ant colony optimization model with a knowledge model to achieve better-quality solutions. Research on the FJSP has explored a range of metaheuristic algorithms that balance global exploration and local exploitation. Wang et al. [4,5] applied two different approaches, the artificial bee colony (ABC) algorithm and the estimation of distribution algorithm, respectively, to solve the FJSP. In addition to these metaheuristics, constraint programming (CP) techniques have also demonstrated potential in FJSP-solving. Discrepancy search, large neighborhood search, and iterative flattening search (IFS) are examples of CP-based metaheuristics that have been tested on standard benchmarks for the FJSP. Other researchers, such as Ben Hmida et al. [6], Oddi et al. [7], and Pacino and Hentenryck [8], have also conducted studies on the FJSP.

Storn and Price [9] introduced the differential evolution (DE) algorithm as a population-based evolutionary metaheuristic for solving continuous optimization problems. The DE algorithm is a stochastic real-parameter global optimizer that employs simple mutation and crossover operators to generate new candidate solutions. In the selection process, the DE algorithm applies a one-to-one competition scheme to determine which candidate, the new one or its parent, will survive in the next generation. With its simplicity, fast convergence, ease of implementation, and robustness, the DE algorithm has gained considerable attention and found successful applications in various fields. Its popularity stems from its ability to provide high-quality solutions and its versatility in solving a wide range of optimization problems. To the best of our knowledge, there is currently no research that utilizes DE algorithms to solve the FJSP. In this chapter, we propose a hybrid differential evolution (HDE) algorithm to minimize the makespan in FJSP. Our proposed approach for solving the FJSP using HDE algorithms involves several innovative components.

First, we develop a novel conversion mechanism that enables the continuous DE algorithm to solve the discrete FJSP. Second, we incorporate a local search procedure based on the critical path into the global search-based DE algorithm to balance global exploration and local exploitation of the search space. We further enhance the local search phase by presenting two neighborhood structures and a speed-up method to find an acceptable schedule in the neighborhood more quickly. Based on these neighborhood structures, we form two variants of HDE algorithms, HDE-N_1 and HDE-N_2. Our experimental studies demonstrate the effectiveness and efficiency of the proposed algorithms, which outperform state-of-the-art algorithms in terms of solution quality and computation time. The outcomes of these studies underscore the promise of using algorithms to tackle intricate optimization problems.

8.2 Basic differential evolution algorithm

The DE algorithm, introduced by Storn and Price [9], is an evolutionary algorithm that operates on a population of candidate solutions. In DE, a population of NP real-valued parameter vectors is generated for each generation G, with each vector representing a candidate solution, also known as a *chromosome*. The optimization problem is defined as minimizing or maximizing the objective function $f(\vec{X})$, where $\vec{X}=[x_1, x_2, \ldots, x_D]^T$ is a vector of D decision variables. Constraints are placed on the values of each decision variable such that they fall within a defined range $[x_{j,\min}, x_{j,\max}]$. The objective function $f(\vec{X})$, also known as the fitness function, evaluates the quality of each candidate solution and guides the evolution of the population towards better solutions. The lower bound of the range is denoted as $x_{j,\min}$, and the upper bound is denoted as $x_{j,\max}$.

The DE algorithm follows a straightforward cycle of stages to carry out the optimization task until the termination criterion is met. This cycle is illustrated in Fig. 8.1. The stages include mutation, crossover, selection, and so on.

8.2.1 Initialization

In the DE algorithm, the initialization process involves setting the control parameters and generating an initial population of candidate solutions. The control parameters include the population size (NP), The factor of mutation scale (F) is a key control parameter in the DE algorithm that determines the extent of mutation applied to the existing solutions., is an important control parameter in the DE algorithm that determines the likelihood (Cr) of combining existing solutions during the crossover stage.

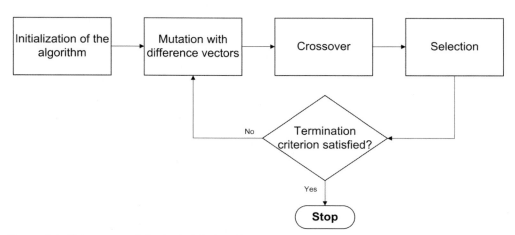

Figure 8.1 Main stages of the basic DE algorithm.

These parameters play a crucial role in determining the success of the DE algorithm in finding an optimal or near-optimal solution. A well-chosen set of control parameters can enhance the algorithm's ability to explore the search space efficiently and converge toward an optimal solution quickly.

In the DE algorithm, the population of candidate solutions evolves over subsequent generations until the termination criterion is met. Each generation of the algorithm is denoted by $G = 0, 1, \ldots, G_{\max}$, where ith vector of the population is the maximum number of generations allowed.

$$\vec{X}_{i,G} = [x_{1,i,G}, x_{2,i,G}, \ldots, x_{D,i,G}]^{\mathrm{T}} \qquad (8.1)$$

To begin with (at generation $G = 0$), vectors are typically created in a random manner, to cover the constrained search space as extensively as possible. As a result, the jth element of the ith vector could be initialized in various ways.

$$x_{j,i,0} = x_{j,\min} + (x_{j,\min} - x_{j,\max}) \times rand(0, 1) \qquad (8.2)$$

The function $rand(0, 1)$ generates a uniformly distributed real number between 0 and 1 in a random manner.

8.2.2 Mutation

During the process of evolution, an individual can be perturbed through a mutation. In the basic DE algorithm, in the current generation, a designated vector is referred to as the target vector, which serves as a parent for generating a new donor vector through mutation. The mutation operator then generates a donor vector, denoted as $V_{i,G} = [v_{1,i,G}, v_{2,i,G}, \ldots, v_{D,i,G}]^{\mathrm{T}}$, which corresponds to the ith target vector $X_{i,G}$. It is important to note that there are multiple mutation schemes available in the DE algorithm. For this chapter, the $DE/best/1$ scheme will be utilized, as illustrated below:

$$\vec{V}_{i,G} = \vec{X}_{\mathrm{best},G} + F \cdot \left(\vec{X}_{r_1^i,G} - \vec{X}_{r_2^i,G} \right) \qquad (8.3)$$

At generation G, the vector $X_{best,G}$ has the lowest objective function value and is considered the fittest vector in the population. To generate a new donor vector, two distinct integers r_1^i and r_2^i are randomly selected from the range $[1, NP]$, with both being different from the base index i. The constant real number F, which is typically less than 1, is used as the scale factor and falls within the range of $[0, 2]$.

The mutation process in DE is distinct from that of traditional genetic algorithms (GAs), as noted earlier. While GA typically involves small modifications to an individual's genes during mutation, DE achieves mutation through individual combinations, according to research by Panduro et al. [10].

8.2.3 Crossover

Crossover is a process that facilitates the exchange of information between individuals in a population. In the basic DE algorithm, the crossover operator generates a trial vector denoted as $U_{i,G}=[u_{1,i,G}, u_{2,i,G}, \ldots, u_{D,i,G}]^{T}$ for the ith target vector $\vec{X}_{i,G}$ by combining components from $\vec{V}_{i,G}$. The equation below outlines the process of generating a trial vector:

$$u_{j,i,G} = \begin{cases} v_{j,i,G}, & \text{if } rand(0,1) \leqslant Cr \quad \text{or} j = q \\ x_{j,i,G}, & \text{otherwise} \end{cases} \tag{8.4}$$

A random integer q is selected from the range $[1, D]$ to ensure that the trial vector $U_{i,G}$ receives at least one component from the donor vector $V_{i,G}$. The crossover probability, denoted as Cr, is a constant real number that falls within the interval of $[0, 1]$.

8.2.4 Selection

In DE, the selection operator plays a critical role in determining whether the trial vector $U_{i,G}$ is selected as an individual from the population is selected to be part of the subsequent generation. This operator essentially decides the fate of the trial vector, based on certain criteria.

$$\vec{X}_{i,G+1} = \begin{cases} \vec{U}_{i,G}, & \text{if} f(\vec{U}_{i,G}) \leqslant f(\vec{X}_{i,G}) \\ \vec{X}_{i,G}, & \text{otherwise} \end{cases} \tag{8.5}$$

The objective function $f(\vec{X})$ is minimized in DE. As a result, if the objective function value of the new trial vector is less than or equal to the objective function value of the corresponding target vector, the trial vector replaces the target vector in the next generation. On the other hand, if the objective function value of the trial vector exceeds the fitness of the target vector, the target vector is preserved in the population.

8.3 Proposed hybrid differential evolution for the flexible job shop scheduling problem

8.3.1 Overview of the hybrid differential evolution

The proposed HDE utilizes the basic DE framework as its foundation but with enhancements and modifications to improve its overall effectiveness. The algorithmic flow of the HDE is presented below:

(1) Step 1: To initialize the HDE algorithm, the following parameters must be set: population size (NP), scale factor (F), cross-over probability (Cr), maximum number of generations (G_{max}), probability of performing a local search P_l, and the maximum number of iterations for local search $iter_{max}$.

(2) Step 2: The HDE algorithm begins by initializing the population and setting the generation counter G to 0.

(3) Step 3: After initializing the population in the HDE algorithm, each chromosome is evaluated to determine its fitness. The chromosome with the best fitness is labeled as $\vec{X}_{best,G}$.

(4) Step 4: In the mutation phase of the HDE algorithm, the mutation operator described in Eq. (8.3) is utilized to generate a set of NP donor vectors, denoted as $\vec{V}_{i,G}$, where i ranges from 1 to NP.

(5) Step 5: During the crossover phase of the HDE algorithm, a set of NP trial vectors denoted as $\vec{U}_{i,G}$, where i ranges from 1 to NP, are generated using the crossover operator specified in Eq. (8.4).

(6) Step 6: In the HDE algorithm, each trial vector $\vec{U}_{i,G}$ undergoes a decision process to determine whether or not to apply a local search procedure. This decision is made by first sampling a random number m from a uniform distribution in the range [0, 1]. If m is less than a predetermined probability value P_l, then a local search is performed on the trial vector $\vec{U}_{i,G}$. Otherwise, the trial vector is evaluated directly.

(7) Step 7: During the selection phase of the HDE algorithm, a set of NP target vectors denoted as $\vec{X}_{i,G+1}$, where i ranges from 1 to NP, are determined for the next generation using a one-to-one selection operator as described in Eq. (8.5). Once the selection phase is complete, the generation counter G is updated to $G+1$, indicating the start of the next generation.

(8) Step 8: In the HDE algorithm, $\vec{X}_{best,G}$ is the best candidate solution encountered at generation G. It represents the individual with the highest fitness value found so far in the search process.

(9) Step 9: If the current generation number G is less than G_{max}, the algorithm proceeds to the next iteration. Otherwise, the algorithm terminates and returns the best candidate solution found, denoted as $\vec{X}_{best,G}$.

As observed, the termination criterion for the HDE is defined by the maximum number of generations. In contrast to the standard DE, the HDE leverages both the DE-based evolutionary search mechanism to explore promising solutions across the entire search space and the advanced local search algorithm to exploit the local regions for improving solutions. The HDE algorithm incorporates a local search step that is applied exclusively to the trial vector $\vec{U}_{i,G}$, rather than the target vector $\vec{X}_{i,G}$. This is a deliberate design choice intended to avoid the possibility of cycling search and getting stuck in a local optimum. The frequency and intensity of the local search are controlled by two key parameters: P_l and $iter_{max}$.

When implementing the HDE algorithm for solving the FJSP, two critical issues must be addressed. The first issue is how to evaluate the fitness of a chromosome, which represents a potential solution to the problem. The second issue is how to effectively apply the local search operator to a chromosome to improve its quality.

When evaluating a chromosome in the context of real-parameter optimization problems, a common approach is to convert the continuous values of the chromosome into a discrete two-vector code. The resulting two-vector code can then be decoded into an active schedule, using techniques such as those described by Pinedo [11]. In the context of optimization problems where the goal is to minimize the makespan (i.e., the total time required to complete all tasks), the fitness of a chromosome is typically defined as the makespan value associated with the corresponding active schedule. This approach is illustrated in Fig. 8.2 of the reference material. It is worth noting that the optimal solution to the optimization problem is always within the collection of operational schedules that minimize the makespan. Therefore, when considering a chromosome, only the corresponding active schedule needs to be evaluated to assess the quality of the solution. This approach can significantly reduce the space to search and improve the efficiency of the search process.

When applying a local search operator to a chromosome in the context of optimization problems, it is often beneficial to first convert the chromosome into an active schedule. This approach is illustrated in Fig. 8.3 of the reference material, which shows the computational flow of the local search algorithm. By applying the local search

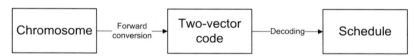

Figure 8.2 The computational flow of the evaluation

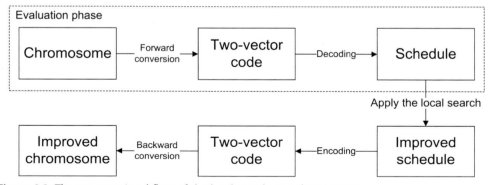

Figure 8.3 The computational flow of the local search to a chromosome

operator directly to the operational schedule that corresponds to the chromosome in question, rather than the chromosome itself, it is possible to incorporate problem-specific knowledge into the search process. When using an evolutionary algorithm to solve optimization problems, a common approach is to first evaluate the fitness of a chromosome (i.e., a potential solution) by converting it into an active schedule. This schedule is then further improved using a local search operator. After the local search operator has been applied to the active schedule, the resulting improved schedule is encoded into a two-vector code. The resulting improved chromosome can then be used to replace the original chromosome in the evolutionary process.

The proposed HDE algorithm for solving the FJSP is implemented in several stages, which are detailed in the following subsections.

8.3.2 Representation and initialization

The proposed HDE algorithm represents a chromosome as a D-dimensional real-parameter vector, denoted as $\vec{X} = [x_1, x_2, \ldots, x_D]^{\mathrm{T}}$. However, the dimensionality of D is constrained by the number of operations in the FJSP that is being solved. Specifically, the dimensionality of the chromosome must satisfy the constraint $D = 2d$, where d is the total number of operations in the FJSP. To accommodate the dual-level decision-making process involving routing and sequencing. involved in the FJSP, the chromosome vector $\vec{X}$ is partitioned into two distinct segments. The first half of the chromosome, denoted as $\vec{X}^{(1)} = [x_1, x_2, \ldots, x_d]^{\mathrm{T}}$, contains information about the assignment of each operation to a particular machine. The second half of the chromosome, denoted as $\vec{X}^{(2)} = [x_{d+1}, x_{d+2}, \ldots, x_{2d}]^{\mathrm{T}}$, contains information about the sequencing of operations on each machine. To simplify the problem and make it more tractable, the range $[x_{j,\min}, x_{j,\max}], j = 1, 2, \ldots, D$, D for decision variables for each element of the chromosome is set to $[-\delta, \delta]$, where δ is a bound factor that is greater than zero. By dividing the chromosome into two separate parts and constraining the search space, the proposed algorithm can effectively explore the solution space and find high-quality solutions to the FJSP.

The proposed HDE algorithm initializes its population randomly and uniformly, similar to the basic DE algorithm. The chromosomes in the population are produced randomly according to Eq. (8.2), where the minimum value of each decision variable is set to $X_{j,\min} = -\delta$ and the maximum value is set to $X_{j,\max} = \delta, j = 1, 2, \ldots, D$.

8.3.3 Two-vector code

This code including two vectors: The two subproblems of the FJSP are addressed using a machine assignment vector and an operation sequence vector, both of which are derived from the chromosome $\vec{X}$.

Table 8.1 Illustration of the numbering scheme for operations.

Operation indicated	$O_{1,1}$	$O_{1,2}$	$O_{2,1}$	$O_{2,2}$	$O_{2,3}$	$O_{3,1}$	$O_{3,2}$
Fixed ID	1	2	3	4	5	6	7

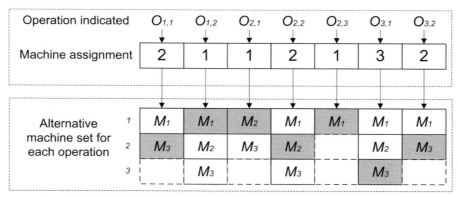

Figure 8.4 Illustration of the machine assignment vector.

To explain these vectors, a fixed ID is assigned to each operation based on its job number and order within the job. Table 8.1 demonstrates the numbering scheme for operations. Once numbered, using a fixed ID, each operation can be identified uniquely. For example, operation 5 can also be depicted in Table 8.1, the operation is denoted as $O_{2,3}$.

8.3.3.1 Machine assignment vector

This vector is represented by an array of d integer values, denoted as $\vec{R}^{(1)} = [r_1, r_2, \ldots, r_d]^{\mathrm{T}}$. Each element in the vector, $r_j, j = 1, 2, \ldots, d$ represents the machine that operation j is assigned to r_jth machine within its alternative machine set. For example, in Fig. 8.4, the operation $O_{3,2}$ is assigned to the second machine in its alternative machine set, which is denoted by $r_7 = 2$ in the machine assignment vector. This corresponds to machine M_3 in the problem instance, which is shaded in the figure.

8.3.3.2 Operation sequence vector

This vector, denoted as $\vec{S} = [s_1, s_2, \ldots, s_d]^{\mathrm{T}}$, corresponds to the ID permutation of operations in the problem instance, where the scheduling priority of each operation is determined by its position in the vector. An example of the operation sequence vector is provided as $\vec{S}=[3, 6, 4, 7, 1, 5, 2]^{\mathrm{T}}$. The sequence vector $\vec{S}$ can be transformed into an ordered list of unique operations straightforwardly: $O_{2,1} \succ O_{3,1} \succ O_{2,2} \succ O_{3,2} \succ O_{1,1} \succ O_{2,3} \succ O_{1,2}$. operation $O_{2,1}$ is possible that an operation with the highest priority is scheduled as the first in the sequence, followed by the operation $O_{3,1}$, and so on. It should be emphasized that the operation sequence vector cannot assume all possible ID permutations. This is because the relative priority order of operations within a job must be maintained in the sequence vector. In other words, the operations belonging to the same job must be arranged in a specific order by their relative priorities in the sequence vector $\vec{S}$.

8.3.3.3 Encoding and decoding

To represent an FJSP schedule using the two-vector code, this approach involves creating two vectors: the machine assignment vector, represented by the vector $\vec{R}$, and the operation sequence vector, represented by the vector $\vec{S}$. The operation sequence vector is obtained by sorting them in ascending order based on their earliest start times. The decoding process is segmented into two parts. The initial phase comprises assigning each operation to the designated machine based on the machine assignment vector, represented by the vector $\vec{R}$. The second stage entails processing the operations sequentially as per their positions in the operation sequence vector, represented by the vector $\vec{S}$. During the process of an operation, it is scheduled to the most optimal available processing time for the associated machine. This ensures that the schedule generated by this process is active, as defined by Cheng et al. [12].

8.3.4 Conversion techniques

8.3.4.1 Forward conversion

This process involves converting a chromosome, which is a real-parameter vector, denoted as $\vec{X}=[x_1, x_2, \ldots, x_d, x_{d+1}, x_{d+2}, \ldots, x_{2d}]^{\mathrm{T}}$, into a two-vector code. They consist of two integer-parameter vectors, denoted as $\vec{R}=[r_1, r_2, \ldots, r_d]^{\mathrm{T}}$ and $\vec{S}=[s_1, s_2, \ldots, s_d]^{\mathrm{T}}$. The process is grouped into two independent parts.

In the first step of the forward conversion process for solving the FJSP using the proposed algorithm, the vector $\vec{X}^{(1)}=[x_1, x_2, \ldots, x_d]^{\mathrm{T}}$ is transformed into a binary vector for machine assignment, $\vec{R}=[r_1, r_2, \ldots, r_d]^{\mathrm{T}}$. This conversion involves the use of a vector $\vec{L}=[l_1, l_2, \ldots, l_d]^{\mathrm{T}}$, where $l_j, j=1, 2, \ldots, d$ indicates the number of potential machines available for operation j. The objective of the conversion process is to transform the continuous value into a numerical representation $x_j \in [-\delta, \delta]$ to the integer $r_j \in [1, l_j]$ for each operation. To accomplish this, a linear transformation is applied to x_j to convert it to a real number within the range

$[1, l_j]$. This ensures that the real number falls within the bounds of the available machines for the operation. Then, the real number is converted into an integer value using the nearest rounding method. is assigned to r_j using the formula described in Eq. (8.6).

$$r_j = round\left(\frac{1}{2\delta}(l_j - 1)(x_j + \delta) + 1\right), \quad j = 1, 2, \ldots, d \tag{8.6}$$

The function $round(x)$ is employed to round a number x to its nearest integer. If $l_j = 1$, the value of r_j is always equal to 1, irrespective of the value of x_j.

In the second step of the forward conversion process for solving the FJSP using the proposed algorithm, the vector $\vec{X}^{(2)} = [x_{d+1}, x_{d+2}, \ldots, x_{2d}]^T$ the sequence of operations is generated from the chromosome vector, $\vec{S} = [s_1, s_2, \ldots, s_d]^T$. The conversion process utilizes the largest position value (LPV) rule, which is a technique that orders the operations in their nonincreasing position value to develop an initial permutation of operation identifiers. However, it is possible that the permutation obtained using the LPV rule may not be feasible for the operation sequence vector $\vec{S}$. To address this issue, the proposed algorithm uses a repair procedure outlined in Algorithm 8.1 to modify the sequencing of operations within a job in the permutation.

Algorithm 8.1: RepairPermutation($\vec{S}$).

---

1. Set $\vec{Q} = [q_1, q_2, \ldots, q_n]^T$
2. $[q_1, q_2, \ldots, q_n]^T \leftarrow [0, 0, \ldots, 0]^T$
3. for $i = 1$ to d **do**
4.   Get the job J_k that the operation s_i belongs to
5. $q_k \leftarrow q_k + 1$
6.   Get the fixed ID op for the operation O_{k,q_k}
7. $s_i \leftarrow op$
8. end for

By following this conversion process, we have successfully transformed the vector $\vec{X}^{(2)} = [0.6, -0.5, 0.4, -0.1, 0.8, 0.2, -0.3]^T$. An example of this conversion process is depicted in Fig. 8.5.

8.3.4.2 Backward conversion
The backward conversion process involves transforming a two-vector code consisting of the machine assignment vector $\vec{R}^{(1)} = [r_1, r_2, \ldots, r_d]^T$ and the operation sequence

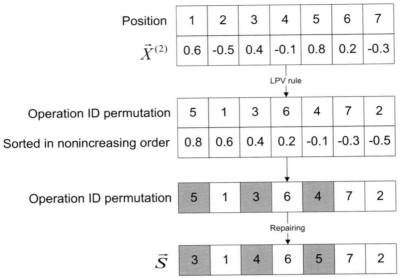

Figure 8.5 The conversion from $\vec{X}^{(2)}$ to the operation sequence vector $\vec{S}$.

vector $\vec{S} = [s_1, s_2, \ldots, s_d]^{\mathrm{T}}$ into a chromosome $\vec{X} = [x_1, x_2, \ldots, x_d, x_{d+1}, x_{d+2}, \ldots, x_{2d}]^{\mathrm{T}}$. This conversion occurs after the local improvement to the schedule, as shown in Fig. 8.3. Similar to the forward conversion, the backward conversion process also consists of two separate parts.

In the first part of the proposed algorithm for solving the FJSP, the machine assignment vector $\vec{R}^{(1)} = [r_1, r_2, \ldots, r_d]^{\mathrm{T}}$ is transformed into the real-value parameter vector $\vec{X}^{(1)} = [x_1, x_2, \ldots, x_d]^{\mathrm{T}}$. This conversion involves applying the inverse of the linear transformation described in Eq. (8.6). However when the value of $l_j = 1$, a special case needs to be considered. In this case, the value of l_j is chosen randomly from the range $[-\delta, \delta]$ when $l_j = 1$. This transformation is performed to ensure that the resulting real-value parameter vector satisfies the constraints of the FJSP.

$$x_j = \begin{cases} \dfrac{2\delta}{l_j - 1}\left(r_j - 1\right) - \delta, & l_j \neq 1 \\ x_j \in [-\delta, \delta], & l_j = 1 \end{cases} \tag{8.7}$$

where $j = 1, 2, \ldots, d$.

In the second stage of the proposed FJSP-solving algorithm, the real-valued parameter vector $\vec{X}^{(2)} = [x_{d+1}, x_{d+2}, \ldots, x_{2d}]^{\mathrm{T}}$ is transformed into a new vector. This transformation involves rearranging the elements of the original $\vec{X}^{(2)}$ according to the

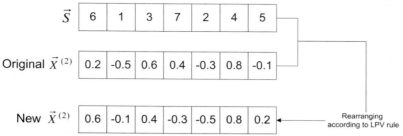

Figure 8.6 The conversion from the operation sequence vector $\vec{S}$ to the $\vec{X}^{(2)}$

LPV rule used during the forward conversion process, resulting in a new vector $\vec{X}^{(2)}$ that corresponds to the $\vec{S}$ a feasible operation sequence vector. Fig. 8.6 depicts a possible conversion process.

8.3.5 Local search algorithm

This section provides a detailed explanation of how local search can be utilized to enhance a schedule. The process begins by introducing the disjunctive graph, which serves as a representation of the schedule. Next, we introduce two neighborhood structures, N_1 and N_2, which are based on the critical path in the disjunctive graph. Finally, we summarize the steps involved in the local search procedure.

8.3.5.1 Disjunctive graph

To represent a schedule for the FJSP, we can utilize a disjunctive graph denoted by $G = (V, C \cup D)$. In this graph, each node corresponds to an operation in the FJSP, including dummy starting and terminating operations S, and forms a set V. The graph also consists of a set of conjunctive arcs denoted by C, which link two consecutive operations within a job and indicate the processing order between them. The set of disjunctive arcs D, in the disjunctive graph links two neighboring operations that are executed on the same machine. The direction of each arc illustrates the order of processing between the two operations. The weight of each node in the graph, which is typically shown above the corresponding operation node, represents the duration of time required for that particular operation to be completed.

An example of a feasible schedule represented by the disjunctive graph can be seen in Fig. 8.7. Specifically, operations $O_{3,1}$, $O_{1,1}$, and $O_{2,3}$ are processed successively on machine M_1, operations $O_{2,1}$ and $O_{1,2}$ are executed consecutively on machine M_2, and operations $O_{3,2}$ and $O_{2,2}$ are performed in sequence on machine M_3. It is important to note that a feasible schedule for the FJSP can only exist in the context of the FJSP, a cyclic path in the corresponding disjunctive graph refers to a series of operations that form a loop with a sequence of disjunctive and conjunctive arcs. In the FJSP, the disjunctive graph is considered acyclic when there are no cyclic paths in the

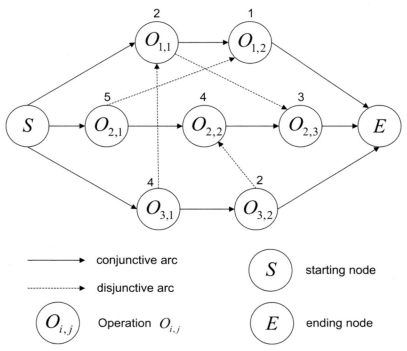

Figure 8.7 Illustration of the disjunctive graph.

graph. In such cases, the longest path from the starting node S to the ending node E is known as the critical path, and its length is used to determine the makespan for the schedule. The operations that belong to the critical path are referred to as critical operations. An example of an acyclic disjunctive graph can be seen in Fig. 8.7, which represents a feasible schedule for the FJSP. The critical path for this schedule is $S \rightarrow O_{3,1} \rightarrow O_{3,2} \rightarrow O_{2,2} \rightarrow O_{2,3} \rightarrow E$, and its length is equal to 13. The operations $O_{3,1}$, $O_{3,2}$, $O_{2,2}$, and $O_{2,3}$ identifying and managing critical operations is critical to achieving optimal scheduling in the FJSP.

8.3.5.2 Neighborhood structures
In the FJSP, the makespan of the schedule is determined by the length of the critical path in the disjunctive graph. The critical path is the longest in the graph and includes all critical operations. As a result, it is not possible to reduce the makespan by moving any noncritical operation. Therefore, to improve the schedule, it is necessary to move critical operations. The insertion step involves finding a new position for the critical operation in the disjunctive graph. The new position must ensure that the operation $O_{i,j}$ is feasible, and no cyclic paths are created in the graph [13].

(1) Step 1: To move a critical operation $O_{i,j}$ in the disjunctive graph, the first step is to delete the corresponding node v from its current position in the machine sequence. To achieve this, all disjunctive arcs associated with node v are removed from the graph, effectively disconnecting it from the sequence. Additionally, the weight of node v is set to 0.

(2) Step 2: After deleting the critical operation $O_{i,j}$ from its original position in the disjunctive graph, the next step is to assign it to a new machine M_k and determine its new position in the processing order. To achieve this, the position of the corresponding node v in the machine sequence is chosen, and the node v is inserted into the graph by adding disjunctive arcs to connect it to the adjacent operations in the sequence. The weight of node v is set to the processing time of the critical operation $p_{i,j,k}$, which indicates the time required to complete the operation on the machine M_k.

Suppose G represents the current schedule in the FJSP and a critical path in G is denoted as $S \rightarrow co_1 \rightarrow co_2 \ldots \rightarrow co_w \rightarrow E$, where S and E represent the starting and ending nodes, respectively, and $co_x, x = 1, 2, \ldots, w$ indicates the x-th critical operation on the path. The neighborhood structure $N_1(G)$ refers to the set of schedules that can be obtained by moving one critical operation in G. This includes both feasible and infeasible schedules. To compute the size of $N_1(G)$, Let us use the notation u_k to represent the total number of operations that have been processed on the machine M_k in the given schedule G.

$$U_{total} = w \cdot \left(\sum_{k=1}^{m}(u_k + 1) - 1 \right) = w \cdot \left(\sum_{k=1}^{m} u_k + m - 1 \right) = w \cdot (d + m - 1) \qquad (8.8)$$

Our local search algorithm for the FJSP involves a process of iteratively searching for an improved schedule by selecting an acceptable schedule G' from the neighborhood structure $N_1(G)$ and setting G' as the new current schedule. A schedule $G' \in N_1(G)$ is considered acceptable if it satisfies G' two criteria: first, it must be acyclic, indicating that there are no cyclic paths in the disjunctive graph; and second, its makespan $C_{max}(G')$ must be less than or equal to the makespan of the current schedule $C_{max}(G)$, which ensures that the new schedule improves the overall performance of the system. However, this process of systematically exploring the neighborhood structure can be time-consuming, as we must check whether each new schedule is cyclic and recalculate its makespan. To speed up this process, we can develop a method to expedite the process of obtaining an acceptable schedule within the neighborhood.

The earliest completion time $ES^G(O_{i,j})$ of an operation $O_{i,j}$ in the schedule, G is calculated by adding its processing time $p_{i,j,k}$ to its earliest start time $ES^G(O_{i,j})$. Similarly, the latest completion time $LC^G(O_{i,j})$ is calculated by adding the same processing time to the latest start time without delaying the makespan $LS^G(O_{i,j})$. In both cases, we assume that the operation is processed on a machine M_k. We can also use the notation $PM(O_{i,j})$ to represent the operation that is processed on the same machine immediately before $O_{i,j}$, and $SM(O_{i,j})$ to represent the operation processed on the same machine right after $O_{i,j}$. Additionally, we use $SJ(O_{i,j}) = O_{i,j+1}$ to represent the operation of job J_i that follows $O_{i,j}$ within the same machine. Suppose we have a scheduling problem where a particular operation (co_x) in the original schedule (G^-) is identified as critical and needs to be moved to optimize the schedule's performance. To achieve the operation co_x in G, we create a new schedule (G^-) by removing this critical operation from the original schedule. To ensure the new schedule does not exceed the maximum makespan $(C_{max}(G))$ of the original schedule, we calculate the latest start time $(LS^{G^-}(O_{i,j}))$ for each operation $(O_{i,j})$ in the new schedule G^- based on the maximum makespan of the original schedule.

Suppose we have a scheduling problem where a critical operation (co_x) needs to be inserted before the operation $O_{i,j}$ on machine M_k in a new schedule (G^-) that satisfies $C_{max}(G') \leq C_{max}(G)$. To ensure that the new schedule G' meets this condition and does not delay the maximum makespan of the original schedule, which is at $ES^{G^-}(PM(O_{i,j}))$ on the same machine. Furthermore, to ensure that delaying the completion time of co_x does not affect the maximum makespan of the original schedule, which is at $LS^{G^-}(O_{i,j})$ without $C_{max}(G)$. If the position before $O_{i,j}$ is available for co_x to insert into, we must ensure that the following equation is satisfied:

$$\max\{EC^{G^-}(PM(O_{i,j})), EC^{G^-}(PJ(co_x))\} + p_{co_x,k} < \min\{LS^{G^-}(O_{i,j}), LS^{G^-}(SJ(cO_x))\}$$

(8.9)

To ensure that the critical operation (co_x) is not the critical operation in the new schedule (G') and to avoid cyclic search as much as possible, we use the "$<$" symbol in Eq. (8.9).

However, simply inserting G' before $O_{i,j}$ under the condition of Eq. (8.9) being satisfied does not guarantee that the resulting schedule (G') will be acyclic. Let Θ_k denote the set of operations processed by machine M_k in the original schedule (G^-) and ordered by increasing earliest start time, with the critical operation (co_x) not included in Θ_k. We then define Φ_k and Ψ_k as two subsequences of Θ_k as follows:

$$\Phi_k = \{v \in \Theta_k \mid ES^G(v) + p_{v,k} > ES^G(co_x)\}$$

(8.10)

$$\Psi_k = \{v \in \Theta_k \mid LS^G(v) < LS^G(co_x)\}$$

(8.11)

To do this, we define the set Y_k, which consists of all positions before the operations in $\Phi_k \backslash \Psi_k$ and after the operations in $\Phi_k \backslash \Psi_k$. Using this set, we establish the following theorem:

Using this set, we establish Theory 1, which states that the schedule obtained by inserting co_x into a position $\gamma \in Y_k$ is always feasible, and there exists an optimal position on the machine M_k in the set Y_k for co_x to insert into.

To prove this theory in detail, we refer to Mastrolilli and Gambardella [13]. As a direct corollary of Theory 1, ultimately leading to more effective and optimal scheduling solutions.

Corollary 1:

is a useful result in scheduling theory that states that if we can find a feasible and acceptable schedule by inserting a critical operation (co_x) into a certain position on the machine M_k, then we can always find another feasible and acceptable schedule We can add the element co_x to a specific position within the set Y_k.

To determine the optimal position to insert a critical operation (co_x) on machine M_k in a given schedule (G), If we find a position in Y_k that satisfies the conditions of Eq. (8.9), we can insert co_x into that position and obtain an acceptable schedule immediately. The process of finding a schedule that meets the required criteria and is obtained from the neighborhood structure N_1 is referred to as an acceptable schedule in detail in Algorithm 8.2.

Algorithm 8.2: GetAcceptableSchedule−I (**G**).

---

1. Get a critical path $S \rightarrow co_1 \rightarrow co_2 \dots \rightarrow co_w \rightarrow E$ in G
2. for $x = 1$ to w **do**
3.   Delete the operation co_x from G to get G^-
4.   **for** $k = 1$ to m **do**
5.   Get the set of position Y_k on the machine M_k
6.   **for** each position $\gamma \in Y_k$ **do**
7.   **if** γ satisfies Eq. (8.9) then
8.   Insert co_x into the position c to get the schedule G'
9.   **return** G'
10.   **end** if
11.   **end** for
12.   **end** for
13. end for
14. return a null schedule

To conduct a more thorough and intensive search for optimal scheduling solutions, we define a larger neighborhood structure called $N_2(G)$. This structure includes schedules that are obtained by moving not only one critical operation in a critical path of G but also two operations, at least one of which is critical. Compared to the previously defined neighborhood structure $N_1(G)$, $N_2(G)$ is much larger in size and complexity. However, it should be noted that $N_1(G)$ is a subset of $N_2(G)$, To obtain an acceptable schedule from the larger neighborhood structure N_2, we use Algorithm 8.3.

Algorithm 8.3: GetAcceptableSchedule—II (**G**).

---

1. $G' \leftarrow$ GetAcceptableSchedule-I (G)
2. **if** G' is not a null schedule **then**
3.   **return** G'
4. **end if**
5. **for** each critical operation ω_x on a critical path in G **then**
6.   Delete the operation ω_x from G to get G^-
7.   **for** each operation o in G^- **do**
8.   Delete the operation o from G^- to get $G^{-'}$
9.   **if** a suitable position γ in G^- is found for ω_x to insert into **then**
10.   Insert ω_x into γ to get $G^{-''}$
11.   **if** a suitable position γ' in $G^{-''}$ is found for o to insert into **then**
12.   Insert o into γ' to get G'
13.   **return** G'
14.   **end if**
15.   **end if**
16.   **end for**
17. **end for**
18. **return** a null schedule

Algorithm 8.3 shows that if moving one operation is successful, we do not move two operations, as it takes significantly more time. This means that we prioritize selecting an acceptable schedule from N_1, and only consider schedules in $N_2 \backslash N_1$ when no acceptable schedule is found in N_1. In steps 8−9 and 8−11, the "suitable position" refers to a position where inserting the operation does not cause a delay in $C_{\max}(G)$, as determined by Eq. (8.9), and results in a feasible schedule. The validity of Theorem 1 is not guaranteed when moving two operations, therefore it is crucial to verify whether the resulting graph is cyclic after inserting an operation. As the set $N_2 \backslash N_1$ contains a large number of potential insertions, not all of them are considered when moving two operations. Algorithm 8.3 demonstrates that once the operation ω_x and o has been successfully inserted into a suitable position for ω_x, the other possible suitable positions for ω_x are not explored, regardless of whether a suitable position is found for the other operation o to be inserted. This approach strikes a balance between optimizing the schedule and reducing computation costs.

8.3.5.3 Procedure of local search

Algorithm 8.4 outlines the steps involved in the local search procedure. In steps 8−3, instead of using Algorithm 8.2 to generate an acceptable schedule, we can utilize Algorithm 8.3 to achieve the same goal. If Algorithm 8.2 is used in the

Algorithm 8.4: LocalSearch (***G,iter_{max}***).

---

1. $i \leftarrow 0$
2. while G is not a null schedule and $i < iter_{max}$
3. $G \leftarrow$ GetAcceptableSchedule- I (G)
4. $i \leftarrow i + 1$
5. end while
6. return G

---

embedded local search, the resulting proposed HDE is referred to as HDE-N_1. If Algorithm 8.3 is utilized in the embedded local search, the proposed HDE is named HDE-N_2.

8.4 Experimental studies

8.4.1 Experimental setup

The HDE algorithms (HDE-N_1 and HDE-N_2) were coded in Java and executed on an Intel Xeon processor with a clock speed of 2.83 GHz and 15.9 Gb of RAM. To assess the effectiveness of the proposed HDE algorithms, we conducted experiments using four sets of widely-used benchmark instances from the FJSP literature.

(1) Kacem data: The dataset utilized in the study comprises five instances sourced from Kacem et al. [14]. These instances feature a diverse range of job, machine, and operation counts, with the number of jobs varying between 4 and 15, the number of machines ranging from 5 to 10, and each job containing 2—4 operations. The total number of operations involved across all jobs ranges from 12 to 56.

(2) BRdata: The dataset utilized in this study comprises 10 instances generated randomly using a uniform distribution within predefined limits. These instances were sourced from Brandimarte [15] and feature varying numbers of jobs, machines, and operations. The number of jobs ranges between 10 and 20, while the number of machines ranges from 4 to 15. Each job contains 5 to 15 operations, and the total number of operations across all jobs ranges from 55 to 240.

(3) BCdata: The dataset utilized in this study comprises 21 instances sourced from Barnes and Chambers [16]. These instances were obtained from three classical Job Shop Scheduling instances (mt10, la24, la40) that are known to pose significant challenges (Fisher and Thompson [17]; Lawrence [18]). The instances feature varying numbers of jobs, machines, and operations. The number of jobs ranges from 10 to 15, while the number of machines ranges from 11 to 18. Each job contains between 10 and 15 operations, and the total number of operations involved across all jobs ranges from 100 to 225.

(4) HUdata: The dataset used in this study comprises 129 instances sourced from Hurink et al. [19]. These instances were derived from three instances (mt06, mt10, mt20) created by Fisher and Thompson [17] and 40 instances (la01–la40) by Lawrence [18]. The dataset was divided into three subsets, namely Edata, Rdata, and Vdata, based on the average number of alternative machines available for each operation. The instances feature varying numbers of jobs, machines, and operations. The number of jobs ranges from 6 to 30, while the number of machines ranges from 5 to 15. Each job contains between 5 and 15 operations, and the total number of operations across all jobs ranges from 36 to 300.

To evaluate the performance of the proposed algorithms, multiple runs were conducted independently for each instance from different datasets. Specifically, 50 independent runs were executed for each instance sourced from Kacem data, BRdata, and BCdata. Due to the larger number of instances in HUdata, only 10 independent runs were performed for each instance in this dataset. The algorithms were evaluated based on four key metrics: the best makespan (Best), average makespan (AVG), standard deviation of makespan (SD), and the average computational time in seconds (CPU_{av}) required to execute the algorithms.

To demonstrate the effectiveness of our proposed HDE algorithms, we conducted a comparative analysis with some of the most competitive algorithms available in the literature for each dataset. We also introduced a new metric, mean relative error (MRE), to evaluate the quality of the solutions obtained. The MRE was used to analyze the relative error between the makespan obtained by the proposed algorithm and the best-known lower bound for a given instance. The relative error is defined as $RE = (MK - LB)/LB \times 100\%$, where MK is the makespan obtained by the algorithm and LB is the best known lower bound. For the analysis, the LB for instances from BRdata and BCdata datasets were sourced from Mastrolilli and Gambardella [13]. The LB for instances from HUdata datasets were computed by Jurisch [20]. However, the LB for Kacem instances was not available for this analysis.

When conducting a comprehensive evaluation of various algorithms for the FJSP is performed to determine their relative merits and demerits, one of the most significant issues is quantifying the computational effort. This is because different algorithms may use varying computing hardware, different software environments, programming tools, and levels of coding proficiency can significantly impact the development and implementation of algorithms for the FJSP, making direct comparisons challenging. It is also difficult to obtain a true amount of time taken by a program to execute, which is independent of the specific computer's processing power and is referred to as computer-independent CPU time. To address this issue in this chapter, we have provided additional information such as the CPU's initial designation and the programming language used to write the code are both significant aspects that influence the overall performance of a computer program, and an important metric used to

Table 8.2 Parameter settings of HDE algorithms

Parameter	Description	Kacem data	BRdata	BCdata	HUdata		
					Edata	Rdata	Vdata
NP	Population size	20	30	50	50	50	50
F	Mutation scale factor	0.1	0.1	0.5	0.5	0.1	0.1
Cr	Crossover probablity	0.3	0.3	0.1	0.1	0.3	0.3
$G_{\max}$	Maximum number of generations	100	200	700	700	700	700
P_l	Probability of carrying out local search	0.7	0.7	0.8	0.8	0.8	0.8
$iter_{\max}$	Maximum local iterations	80	80	90	90	120	150
δ	Bound factor	1.0	1.0	1.0	1.0	1.0	1.0

evaluate the efficiency and effectiveness of an algorithm in solving a particular task for each algorithm. This information allows us to obtain a basic understanding of the effectiveness of the algorithms being discussed, but a more detailed analysis is required to make conclusive assessments of their efficiency. This approach has been widely techniques currently employed in JSP research and is based on the existing literature and prior research studies, including studies conducted by Nasiri and Kianfar [21], Sha and Hsu [22], and Zhang et al. [23].

In our experiments, the proposed algorithms HDE-N_1 and HDE-N_2 were designed to use the same parameter settings. The details of the parameter settings for each dataset are presented in Table 8.2, allowing for easy reference and replicability of our experiments. By adopting these parameter settings, we were able to ensure that the proposed algorithms performed optimally and produced reliable results on the given datasets.

8.4.2 Results of Kacem instances

Our study focuses on the Kacem dataset as the first dataset under investigation. We conducted a comparative analysis of our proposed algorithms HDE-N_1 and HDE-N_2 with two recently proposed algorithms, TSPCB (a hybrid tabu search algorithm with a fast public critical block neighborhood structure) by Li et al. [24] and BEDA (a bi-population based estimation of distribution algorithm) by Wang et al. [5]. The results of this analysis are presented in Table 8.3, where the first column indicates the name of each instance, the second column shows the size of the instance, denoting the number of jobs and machines as n and m, respectively, and the third column lists the best-known solution (BKS) ever reported in

Table 8.3 Results of five Kacem instances.

Instances	$n \times m$	BKS	TSPCB[a]			BEDA[b]				HDE-N_1[c]				HDE-N_2[c]			
			Best	AVG	CPU$_{av}$	Best	AVG	SD	CPU$_{av}$	Best	AVG	SD	CPU$_{av}$	Best	AVG	SD	CPU$_{av}$
Case1	4×8	11	**11**	11.00	0.05	**11**	11.00	0.00	0.01	**11**	11.00	0.00	0.06	**11**	11.00	0.00	0.09
Case2	8×8	14	**14**	14.20	4.68	**14**	14.00	0.00	0.23	**14**	14.00	0.00	0.14	**14**	14.00	0.00	0.31
Case3	10×7	11	**11**	11.00	5.21	**11**	11.00	0.00	0.30	**11**	11.00	0.00	0.19	**11**	11.00	0.00	0.46
Case4	10×10	7	**7**	7.10	1.72	**7**	7.00	0.00	0.42	**7**	7.00	0.00	0.22	**7**	7.00	0.00	0.37
Case5	15×10	11	**11**	11.70	9.82	**11**	11.70	0.00	14.88	**11**	11.86	0.35	0.66	**11**	11.70	0.00	2.19

[a]The CPU time on a Pentium IV 1.6 GHz processor in C++.
[b]The CPU time on an Intel Core i5 3.2 GHz processor in C++.
[c]The CPU time on an Intel 2.83 GHz Xeon processor in Java.

the literature for each instance. The remaining columns present the computational results of TSPCB, BEDA, HDE-N_1, and HDE-N_2, respectively. Note that the SD values of TSPCB are not available. The best results are highlighted in bold in the table.

Table 8.3 presents a comprehensive comparison of the performance of four different algorithms on the Kacem dataset. The results demonstrate that BEDA and HDE-N_2 are the most effective algorithms, consistently obtaining the BKSs for all five instances. In terms of computational effort, HDE-N_2 is comparable to BEDA, although Java is generally less efficient than C++. Notably, HDE-N_2 outperforms both TSPCB and BEDA in solving the 15 × 10 instances, taking only about 2 s to complete the task. Our proposed algorithm, HDE-N_1, was unable to consistently obtain the best solution for the 15 × 10 instance. However, it appears to be the most efficient algorithm among them.

8.4.3 Results of BRdata instances

we also investigated the BRdata dataset as the second dataset in our study. We compared the performance of our proposed algorithms, TSPCB and BEDA. The results of this comparative analysis are presented in Table 8.4, which contains the same information as Table 8.3, including the name and size of each instance, the BKSs, and the computational results of the four algorithms.

The results presented in Table 8.4 indicate that HDE-N_1 is a highly effective, efficient, and robust algorithm for solving the BRdata instances, outperforming both TSPCB and BEDA. Specifically, HDE-N_1 achieves a better best makespan than TSPCB in 5 out of 10 instances and BEDA in 2 out of 10 instances. The SD values of HDE-N_1 are generally smaller than BEDA, indicating that HDE-N_1 is more robust. Additionally, HDE-N_1 exhibits better efficiency than TSPCB and BEDA, with an overall average computational time that is lower for most instances. The MRE analysis conducted in this study confirms the effectiveness of HDE-N_1 in solving the FJSP. HDE-N_1 achieves a MRE of 15.58% for the best makespan obtained, which is better than both TSPCB (18.66%) and BEDA (16.07%). Additionally, HDE-N_1 generates an MRE of 16.52% for the average makespan obtained, which is superior to TSPCB (18.95%) and BEDA (19.24%). While HDE-N_2 improves upon the best results for three instances (MK05, MK06, MK10) and matches eight BKSs, Although HDE-N_2 achieves better results than HDE-N_1 for certain instances, it requires more computational time, making it in terms of efficiency, the algorithm in question is inferior to both TSPCB and BEDA.

8.4.4 Results of BCdata instances

BCdata is a well-established benchmark dataset for evaluating the performance of algorithms designed to solve the FJSP. There have been several notable research works

Table 8.4 Results of 10 BRdata instances.

Instances	$n \times m$	BKS	TSPCB[a]			BEDA[b]				HDE-N_1[c]				HDE-N_2			
			Best	AVG	CPUav	Best	AVG	SD	CPUav	Best	AVG	SD	CPUav	Best	AVG	SD	CPUav
MK01	10 × 6	40	**40**	40.30	2.80	**40**	41.02	0.83	1.09	**40**	40.00	0.00	1.16	**40**	40.00	0.00	4.01
MK02	10 × 6	26	**26**	26.50	19.31	**26**	27.25	0.67	2.16	**26**	26.52	0.50	1.48	**26**	26.00	0.00	6.09
MK03	15 × 8	204	**204**	204.00	0.98	**204**	204.00	0.00	2.18	**204**	204.00	0.00	9.18	**204**	204.00	0.00	30.70
MK04	15 × 8	60	62	64.88	40.82	**60**	63.69	1.99	9.02	**60**	60.20	0.53	2.35	**60**	60.00	0.00	12.58
MK05	15 × 4	172	**172**	172.90	20.23	**172**	173.38	0.56	7.10	173	173.02	0.14	3.70	**172**	172.82	0.39	37.89
MK06	10 × 15	58	65	67.38	27.18	60	62.83	1.06	30.21	59	60.20	0.97	10.70	**57**	58.64	0.66	98.32
MK07	20 × 5	139	140	142.21	35.29	**139**	141.55	1.07	17.07	**139**	140.12	1.08	3.26	**139**	139.42	0.50	26.38
MK08	20 × 10	523	**523**	523.00	4.65	**523**	523.00	0.00	4.30	**523**	523.00	0.00	11.52	**523**	523.00	0.00	189.41
MK09	20 × 10	307	310	311.29	70.38	**307**	310.35	0.96	91.99	**307**	307.00	0.00	28.94	**307**	307.00	0.00	122.87
MK10	20 × 15	197	214	219.15	89.83	206	211.92	2.59	190.11	202	205.84	1.79	33.44	**198**	201.52	1.33	265.80
MRE (%)			18.66	18.95		16.07				15.58	16.52			14.67	154.46		

[a] The CPU time on a Pentium IV 1.6 GHz processor in C++.
[b] The CPU time on an Intel Core i5 3.2 GHz processor in C++.
[c] The CPU time on an Intel 2.83 GHz Xeon processor in Java.

on this dataset, including those by Bozejko et al. [25] and Oddi et al. [7]. Bozejko et al. [25] proposed a parallel TS algorithm that utilizes a high-performance GPU with 128 processors, resulting in the discovery of six new BKSs for the BCdata instances. Oddi et al. [7] proposed an IFS procedure that demonstrated exceptional performance on the BCdata instances, surpassing previous state-of-the-art results.

To evaluate the performance of our proposed HDE algorithms, we conducted experiments on the widely used BCdata set and present a detailed summary of the computational results in Table 8.5. Our results indicate that HDE-N_2 is a more effective algorithm than HDE-N_1, as it improves upon the best results for 10 instances and outperforms HDE-N_1 in terms of the average results for all 21 instances. Additionally, HDE-N_2 exhibits greater robustness than HDE-N_1, as evidenced by the SD values. However, it is worth noting that HDE-N_2 requires a significantly longer computational time than HDE-N_1.

To evaluate the effectiveness and efficiency of our proposed HDE algorithms, we conducted a comparative analysis with two state-of-the-art algorithms: TSBM^{2}h, proposed by Bozejko et al. [25], and IFS, proposed by Oddi et al. [7]. Specifically, we compared the best makespan and average computational time obtained by HDE-N_1 and HDE-N_2 with those obtained by TSBM^{2}h and IFS. The results of this comparison are presented in Table 8.6. It is worth noting that the performance of the IFS algorithm is dependent on the choice of the relaxing factor γ, and the table lists the results obtained by running IFS with γ values ranging from 0.2 to 0.7. Furthermore, to ensure a fair comparison, each run of the algorithm is subject to a strict maximum CPU time constraint of 3200 s. Table 8.6 provides a comprehensive comparison of the four algorithms based on their solution quality and computational efficiency. Our analysis indicates that HDE-N_2 is the most effective algorithm, outperforming all the other algorithms in terms of solution quality. Specifically, HDE-N_2 achieves 19 BKSs out of 21 instances, while even discovering a new BKS for the instance seti5c12 (improved from 1174 to 1171). Additionally, HDE-N_2 is only outperformed by TSBM^{2}h on one instance (seti5x) and outperforms TSBM^{2}h in 4 out of 21 instances. When considering all 21 instances, the MRE of HDE-N_2 is 22.39%, which is slightly better than TSBM^{2}h (22.45%), HDE-N_1 (22.55%), and IFS ($\gamma = 0.7$) (23.09%). In terms of computational efficiency, HDE-N_2 appears to be more efficient than IFS and is also comparable to TSBM^{2}h, considering the more advanced computing hardware used by TSBM^{2}h. On the other hand, HDE-N_1 requires significantly less computational time than the other algorithms, yet it still performs very effectively and matches 11 BKSs, demonstrating its effectiveness in solving the FJSP problem. Meanwhile, IFS achieves a total of nine BKSs, although this was achieved under different settings of γ.

8.4.5 Results of HUdata instances

The FJSP community widely recognizes the HUdata set as a benchmark for evaluating the performance of FJSP algorithms. In previous studies, two algorithms, namely TS

Table 8.5 Computational results of HDE algorithms on BCdata.

Instances	$n \times m$	HDE-N_1				HDE-N_2			
		Best	AVG	SD	CPUav	Best	AVG	SD	CPUav
mt10x	10 × 11	**918**	922.86	6.11	21.43	**918**	918.58	2.20	179.22
mt10xx	10 × 12	**918**	922.04	6.31	21.70	**918**	918.38	1.90	179.84
mt10xxx	10 × 13	**918**	919.94	3.96	23.05	**918**	918.00	0.00	179.39
mt10xy	10 × 12	**905**	906.52	1.09	22.51	**905**	905.56	0.79	169.77
mt10xyz	10 × 13	**847**	856.80	3.99	21.79	**847**	851.14	4.65	160.24
mt10c1	10 × 11	**927**	928.92	1.96	21.07	**927**	927.72	0.45	174.19
mt10cc	10 × 12	910	913.92	3.40	21.00	**908**	910.60	2.40	165.61
setb4x	15 × 11	**925**	931.50	2.48	33.04	**925**	925.82	2.11	338.30
setb4xx	15 × 12	**925**	930.38	3.29	29.76	**925**	925.64	1.98	336.24
setb4xxx	15 × 13	**925**	931.42	3.59	29.89	**925**	925.48	1.68	353.55
setb4xy	15 × 12	**910**	921.38	4.44	31.13	**910**	914.00	3.50	330.18
setb4xyz	15 × 13	905	913.40	4.21	30.39	**903**	905.28	1.16	314.64
setb4c9	15 × 11	**914**	919.32	2.87	32.19	**914**	917.12	2.52	313.02
setb4cc	15 × 12	909	912.58	3.81	32.00	**907**	909.58	1.89	316.89
seti5x	15 × 16	1204	1215.48	5.36	73.20	**1200**	1205.64	3.43	1112.77
seti5xx	15 × 17	1202	1205.66	2.56	72.52	**1197**	1202.68	2.02	1078.60
seti5xxx	15 × 18	1202	1206.10	3.18	72.07	**1197**	1202.26	2.37	1087.12
seti5xy	15 × 17	1138	1146.86	5.04	78.98	**1136**	1137.98	2.82	1250.62
seti5xyz	15 × 18	1130	1137.44	3.42	80.85	**1125**	1129.76	2.44	1244.22
sei5c12	15 × 16	1175	1182.54	7.62	69.06	**1171**	1175.42	1.63	1141.43
seti5cc	15 × 17	1137	1145.62		78.83	**1136**	1137.76	2.48	1222.53
MRE (%)		22.55	23.27			22.39	22.67		

Table 8.6 Comparison between the proposed HDE algorithms with TSBM^{2}h and IFS on BCdata.

Instances	$n \times m$	BKS	TSBM^{2}h[a]		IFS[b]						HDE-N_1[c]		HDE-N_2[c]	
			Best	CPUav	0.2	0.3	0.4	0.5	0.6	0.7	Best	CPUav	Best	CPUav
mt10x	10 × 11	918	922	55.11	980	936	936	934	**918**	**918**	**918**	21.43	**918**	179.22
mt10xx	10 × 12	918	**918**	50.18	936	929	936	933	**918**	926	**918**	21.70	**918**	179.84
mt10xxx	10 × 13	918	**918**	47.57	936	929	936	926	926	926	**918**	21.43	**918**	179.39
mt10xy	10 × 12	905	**905**	76.26	922	923	923	915	**905**	909	**905**	22.51	**905**	169.77
mt10xyz	10 × 13	847	849	110.13	878	858	851	862	**847**	851	**847**	21.79	**847**	160.24
mt10c1	10 × 11	927	**927**	44.50	943	937	986	934	934	**927**	**927**	21.07	**927**	174.19
mt10cc	10 × 12	908	**908**	65.74	926	923	919	919	910	911	910	21.00	**908**	165.61
setb4x	15 × 11	925	**925**	93.76	967	945	930	**925**	937	937	**925**	33.04	**925**	338.30
setb4xx	15 × 12	925	**925**	92.28	966	931	933	**925**	937	929	**925**	29.76	**925**	336.24
setb4xxx	15 × 13	925	**925**	89.405	941	930	950	950	942	935	**925**	29.89	**925**	353.55
setb4xy	15 × 12	910	**910**	150.83	**910**	941	936	936	916	914	**910**	31.13	**910**	330.18
setb4xyz	15 × 13	903	**903**	152.67	928	909	905	905	905	905	905	30.39	**903**	314.64
setb4c9	15 × 11	914	**914**	111.40	926	937	926	926	920	920	**914**	32.19	**914**	313.02
setb4cc	15 × 12	907	**907**	151.19	929	917	**907**	914	**907**	909	909	32.00	**907**	316.89
seti5x	15 × 16	1198	**1198**	257.75	1210	1199	1199	1205	1207	1209	1204	73.20	1200	1112.77
seti5xx	15 × 17	1197	**1197**	264.58	1216	1199	1205	1211	1207	1206	1202	72.52	**1197**	1078.60
seti5xxx	15 × 18	1197	**1197**	226.29	1205	1206	1206	1199	1206	1206	1202	72.07	**1197**	1087.12
seti5xy	15 × 17	1136	**1136**	675.40	1175	1171	1175	1166	1156	1148	1138	78.98	**1136**	1250.62
seti5xyz	15 × 18	1125	1128	717.60	1165	1149	1130	1134	1144	1131	1130	80.85	**1125**	1244.22
seti5c12	15 × 16	1174	1174	351.32	1196	1209	1200	1198	1198	1175	1175	69.06	**1171**	1141.43
seti5cc	15 × 17	1136	**1136**	670.35	1177	1155	1162	1166	1138	1150	1137	78.83	**1136**	1222.53
MRE (%)	–	–	22.45	–	25.48	24.25	24.44	23.96	23.28	23.09	22.55	–	22.39	–

[a]The CPU time of a Pentium IV 1.6 GHz processor in C++ environment.
[b]The CPU time of Intel Core i5 3.2 GHz processor in C++ environment.
[c]The CPU time of Intel 2.83 GHz Xeon processor in Java environment.

Table 8.7 Comparison of the proposed HDE algorithms with TS and hGA in the MRE on HUdata.

Instances	n × m	Edata				Rdata				Vdata			
		TS	hGA	HDE-N_1	HDE-N_2	TS	hGA	HDE-N_1	HDE-N_2	TS	hGA	HDE-N_1	HDE-N_2
mt06/ 10/20	6 × 6 / 10 × 10 / 20 × 5	**0.00** (0.10)	**0.00** (0.10)	0.05 (0.13)	**0.00** (0.07)	0.34 (0.36)	0.34 (0.34)	0.34 (0.45)	**0.34** (0.34)	**0.00** (0.00)	**0.00** (0.00)	**0.00** (0.01)	**0.00** (0.00)
la01–la05	10 × 5	**0.00** (0.00)	**0.00** (0.00)	**0.00** (0.00)	**0.00** (0.00)	0.11 (0.24)	0.07 (0.07)	0.11 (0.31)	**0.04** (0.10)	**0.00** (0.11)	**0.00** (0.00)	0.04 (0.19)	**0.00** (0.01)
la06–la10	15 × 5	**0.00** (0.00)	**0.00** (0.00)	**0.00** (0.00)	**0.00** (0.00)	0.03 (0.08)	**0.00** (0.00)	0.05 (0.10)	**0.00** (0.01)	**0.00** (0.03)	**0.00** (0.00)	0.03 (0.10)	**0.00** (0.00)
la11–la15	20 × 5	**0.29** (0.29)	**0.29** (0.29)	**0.29** (0.29)	**0.29** (0.29)	0.02 (0.02)	**0.00** (0.00)	**0.00** (0.02)	**0.00** (0.00)	**0.00** (0.01)	**0.00** (0.00)	**0.00** (0.01)	**0.00** (0.00)
la16–la20	10 × 10	**0.00** (0.00)	0.02 (0.02)	0.02 (0.48)	0.02 (0.02)	**1.64** (1.68)	**1.64** (1.64)	**1.64** (1.69)	**1.64** (1.69)	**0.00** (0.00)	**0.00** (0.00)	**0.00** (0.00)	**0.00** (0.00)
la21–la25	15 × 10	5.62 (5.93)	5.60 (5.66)	5.82 (6.41)	**5.46** (5.91)	3.82 (4.38)	3.57 (3.69)	3.73 (4.57)	**3.13** (3.66)	0.70 (0.85)	0.60 (0.68)	1.63 (2.15)	**0.57** (0.96)
la26–la30	20 × 10	3.47 (3.76)	3.28 (3.32)	3.89 (4.71)	**3.11** (3.64)	**0.59** (0.76)	0.64 (0.72)	1.04 (1.41)	0.60 (0.81)	0.11 (0.18)	0.11 (0.13)	0.42 (0.63)	**0.10** (0.19)
la31–la35	30 × 10	**0.30** (0.32)	0.32 (0.32)	0.50 (0.59)	0.32 (0.39)	0.09 (0.14)	0.09 (0.12)	0.22 (0.33)	**0.08** (0.13)	0.01 (0.03)	**0.00** (0.00)	0.12 (0.18)	0.03 (0.03)
la36–la40	15 × 15	8.99 (9.13)	**8.82** (8.95)	9.63 (10.43)	8.89 (9.36)	3.97 (4.47)	3.86 (3.92)	3.98 (4.92)	**3.38** (4.19)	**0.00** (0.00)	**0.00** (0.00)	**0.00** (0.01)	**0.00** (0.00)
MRE (%)		2.17 (2.27)	2.13 (2.17)	2.35 (2.68)	**2.11** (2.29)	1.24 (1.36)	1.19 (1.21)	1.28 (1.59)	**1.05** (1.26)	0.095 (0.13)	0.082 (0.09)	0.26 (0.38)	**0.080** (0.14)

proposed by Mastrolilli and Gambardella [13] and hGA proposed by Gao et al. [26], have demonstrated state-of-the-art performance on this data set. In Table 8.7, we present the MRE of the best makespan and average makespan obtained by HDE-N_1 and HDE-N_2 on HUdata and compare their results with those of TS and hGA. Our analysis shows that HDE-N_2 outperforms TS and hGA on all three subsets of HUdata in terms of the best makespan obtained. However, hGA exhibits the best performance among all four algorithms in terms of the average makespan obtained. It is also worth noting that TS, hGA, and HDE-N_2 all outperform HDE-N_1 solution quality.

Our proposed HDE-N_2 algorithm has achieved remarkable success in identifying new BKSs for the HUdata instances, including 22 new solutions (16 instances from Rdata and 6 instances from Vdata), out of which five are optimal solutions. This is an encouraging result that demonstrates the effectiveness of our proposed algorithm in solving the FJSP problem. In Table 8.8, we present a detailed comparison of the previously known best solutions with the new best solutions obtained by our algorithm.

Table 8.9 provides a comprehensive summary of the MRE of the best makespan obtained by various algorithms, including the proposed HDE algorithms, as well as other

Table 8.8 The makespan of new best known solutions identified by the proposed HDE-N_2 on HUdata

Instances	Dataset	LB	Prev. best known	New best known
la01	Rdata	570	571	570
la03	Rdata	477	478	477
la07	Rdata	749	750	749
la15	Rdata	1089	1090	1089
la21	Rdata	808	835	833
la22	Rdata	737	760	758
la23	Rdata	816	842	832
la24	Rdata	775	808	801
la25	Rdata	752	791	785
la27	Rdata	1085	1091	1090
la29	Rdata	993	998	997
la33	Rdata	1497	1499	1498
la36	Rdata	1016	1030	1028
la37	Rdata	989	1077	1066
la38	Rdata	943	962	960
la40	Rdata	955	970	956
la21	Vdata	800	806	805
la22	Vdata	733	739	735
la23	Vdata	809	815	813
la26	Vdata	1052	1054	1053
la27	Vdata	1084	1085	1084
la30	Vdata	1068	1070	1069

Table 8.9 Summary results of the MRE of the best makespan obtained by the proposed HDE algorithms and other known algorithms in the literature.

Algorithm	Edata		Rdata		Vdata	
	MRE (%)	Rank	MRE (%)	Rank	MRE (%)	Rank
HDE-N_1	2.35	5	1.28	4	0.26	5
HDE-N_2	2.11	1	1.05	1	0.080	1
TS [19]	4.50	7	2.30	7	0.40	6
GA [27]	5.59	8	4.41	9	2.59	10
TS [13]	2.17	3	1.24	3	0.095	3
GA [28]	9.01	11	8.34	11	3.24	11
hGA [26]	2.13	2	1.19	2	0.082	2
GA [29]	6.00	9	4.42	10	2.04	9
AIA [1]	6.83	10	3.98	8	1.29	8
PVNS [2]	3.86	6	1.88	6	0.42	7
CDDS [6]	2.32	4	1.34	5	0.12	4

algorithms reported in the literature. We have ranked all these algorithms based on their performance on each data set (Edata, Rdata, and Vdata). Our analysis reveals that both proposed HDE-N1 and HDE-N2 algorithms are highly effective on the HUdata set. Specifically, among all the 11 algorithms considered, HDE-N1 is ranked fifth on both Edata and Vdata, and fourth on Rdata. On the other hand, HDE-N2, has exhibited outstanding performance on the HUdata set, achieving the best results among all algorithms on all three subsets of the data, demonstrating its superior performance compared to the other algorithms.

8.4.6 Further performance analysis of hybrid differential evolution

8.4.6.1 Significance tests between hybrid differential evolution algorithms

To investigate whether the proposed HDE algorithms exhibit significant performance differences in different FJSP instances, we conducted a statistical analysis. Given that the makespan values obtained may not follow the makespan values obtained from the FJSP instances and do not exhibit normal distribution or homogeneity of variance, we adopted nonparametric tests, as recommended by Demšar [30]. Specifically, we employed the Wilcoxon signed-rank test, which is a pairwise nonparametric statistical test, to examine whether there are significant differences in the optimization performance of the two algorithms on each FJSP instance. Table 8.10 summarizes the results of our statistical analysis. The first column specifies the data set, while the second column displays the number of instances for each category. In the third column, we list the FJSP instances on which HDE-N_2 exhibits statistically significant improvement over HDE-N_1 at a significance level of 0.05. Our analysis suggests that HDE-N_1 is adequate for solving small-scale or relatively easy problems. For example, there are no

Table 8.10 Summary results of significance tests between HDE-N_1 and HDE-N_2 on each data set. The level of significance a is set to 0.05.

Data set	Num	Instances on which HDE-N_2 is significantly better than HDE-N_1
Kacem data	5	Case5
BRdata	10	MK02, MK05, MK06, MK07, MK10
BCdata	21	All the instances
Hurink Edata	43	mt20, la22, la24-la31, la34, la36-la40
Hurink Rdata	43	mt10, mt20, la01-la03, la06-la08, la10, la15, la21-la35, la37, la39, la40
Hurink Vdata	43	la01-la03, la06-la10, la15, la21-la35

significant differences in the makespan values obtained by HDE-N_1 and HDE-N_2 on instances mt06 and mt10 in Hurink Edata. On the other hand, HDE-N_2 appears to be more effective in handling large-scale or challenging problems. In particular, it is more likely for HDE-N_2 to obtain high-quality solutions for all problems in BCdata. However, as previously mentioned, he computational cost of HDE-N_2 is considerably higher compared to HDE-N_1, as it employs a larger neighborhood structure in the embedded local search. This results in a longer execution time for HDE-N_2.

8.4.6.2 Influence of parameters on hybrid differential evolution

Several experiments have been carried out to examine the impact of parameters to improve the performance of our HDE.

Initially, we focused on the influence of parameters NP and G_{max}. NP was varied from 10 to 40 in increments of 10, and G_{max} was varied from 100 to 250 in increments of 50. The remaining parameters were held constant in accordance with Table 8.2, and the algorithm was executed 50 times for each parameter configuration. The outcomes obtained for the MK06 instance are presented in Table 8.11. The findings in Table 8.11 reveal that augmenting either NP or G_{max} is advantageous for enhancing the solution quality at the outset. Nonetheless, there appears to be marginal impact in boosting NP or G_{max} beyond a certain threshold, and in some cases, the outcomes may even deteriorate. For instance, when NP is set to 30, the efficacy of HDE-N_2 remains unchanged with an increase in G_{max} from 200 to 250. Additionally, increasing either NP or G_{max} results in a higher computational burden.

Tables 8.12 and 8.13 present findings on the impact of parameters P_l and $iter_{max}$, as well as F and Cr, respectively, on the MK06 instance. According to Table 8.12, P_l and $iter_{max}$ exhibit a similar effect on HDE as NP and G_{max}. In terms of F and C_{max}, several parameter settings can maintain a high-performance level for HDE, while some configurations may yield subpar outcomes. For example, on the MK06 instance, a parameter combination of $F = 0.1$ and $Cr = 0.3$ appears to be an optimal choice for HDE, whereas $F = 0.7$ and $Cr = 0.7$ isn't a recommended option.

Table 8.11 Influence of parameters NP and G_{max} on HDE.

NP	$G_{max} = 100$						$G_{max} = 150$						$G_{max} = 200$						$G_{max} = 250$					
	HDE-N_1			HDE-N_2			HDE-N_1			HDE-N_2			HDE-N_1			HDE-N_2			HDE-N_1			HDE-N_2		
	AVG	SD	CPU$_{av}$	AVG	SD	CPU$_{av}$	AVG	SD	CPU$_{av}$	AVG	SD	CPU$_{av}$	AVG	SD	CPU$_{av}$	AVG	SD	CPU$_{av}$	AVG	SD	CPU$_{av}$	AVG	SD	CPU$_{av}$
10	61.68	1.11	1.87	60.02	1.10	16.53	61.38	1.01	2.68	59.62	0.88	24.35	61.14	1.07	3.38	59.30	0.79	31.66	60.68	0.87	4.14	59.58	0.81	38.64
20	61.02	0.87	3.90	59.36	0.72	32.93	60.70	0.81	5.48	59.20	0.76	50.16	60.76	0.96	7.18	59.14	0.78	65.53	60.32	1.00	8.64	58.78	0.74	80.55
30	60.98	0.98	5.91	59.04	0.67	49.33	60.38	0.83	8.36	58.78	0.71	75.61	60.20	0.95	10.56	58.64	0.66	98.32	60.20	1.01	12.80	58.70	0.65	123.35
40	60.64	0.88	7.67	59.08	0.80	66.82	60.22	0.79	11.40	58.80	0.61	97.78	60.02	0.65	13.95	58.58	0.57	130.62	59.62	0.85	17.44	58.54	0.61	164.79

Table 8.12 Influence of parameters P_l and $iter_{max}$ on HDE.

P_l	$iter_{max}=10$ HDE-N_1			HDE-N_2			$iter_{max}=40$ HDE-N_1			HDE-N_2			$iter_{max}=70$ HDE-N_1			HDE-N_2			$iter_{max}=100$ HDE-N_1			HDE-N_2		
	AVG	SD	CPU_{av}	AVG	SD	CPU_{av}	AVG	SD	CPU_{av}	AVG	SD	CPU_{av}	AVG	SD	CPU_{av}	AVG	SD	CPU_{av}	AVG	SD	CPU_{av}	AVG	SD	CPU_{av}
0.1	66.30	2.13	2.26	64.18	1.87	3.09	62.44	1.31	3.29	60.68	1.04	11.18	62.08	0.78	3.45	60.28	0.76	15.37	62.18	1.16	3.49	60.24	0.85	16.24
0.3	64.38	1.92	3.05	62.52	1.37	7.20	61.12	1.10	5.51	59.46	0.93	33.36	60.76	0.94	5.99	59.24	0.82	43.50	61.00	0.86	6.26	59.18	0.72	45.31
0.5	63.30	1.66	4.03	61.92	1.51	12.61	60.72	0.93	7.26	59.34	0.77	56.67	60.44	0.73	8.11	58.88	0.85	70.86	60.46	0.76	8.50	58.92	0.70	71.99
0.7	63.00	1.40	4.89	61.80	1.51	17.19	60.38	0.92	9.48	59.12	0.90	80.25	59.92	0.80	10.48	58.76	0.66	97.60	59.94	0.77	10.80	58.70	0.58	100.39
0.9	62.60	1.60	5.70	61.78	1.49	22.00	60.24	0.80	11.32	58.98	0.89	104.24	60.04	0.73	12.67	58.64	0.69	127.30	59.94	0.84	12.83	58.54	0.58	128.02

Table 8.13 Influence of parameters F and Cr on HDE.

F	Cr = 0.1						Cr = 0.3						Cr = 0.5						Cr = 0.7					
	HDE-N$_1$			HDE-N$_2$			HDE-N$_1$			HDE-N$_2$			HDE-N$_1$			HDE-N$_2$			HDE-N$_1$			HDE-N$_2$		
	AVG	SD	CPU$_{av}$	AVG	SD	CPU$_{av}$	AVG	SD	CPU$_{av}$	AVG	SD	CPU$_{av}$	AVG	SD	CPU$_{av}$	AVG	SD	CPU$_{av}$	AVG	SD	CPU$_{av}$	AVG	SD	CPU$_{av}$
0.1	61.04	0.57	9.53	59.34	0.48	92.60	60.20	0.97	10.70	58.64	0.66	98.32	60.48	1.09	7.73	59.38	0.88	82.04	62.74	1.32	5.30	60.76	1.27	70.96
0.3	60.68	0.62	12.24	59.26	0.69	99.96	60.68	0.77	17.79	58.72	0.73	110.41	60.58	0.88	19.98	59.42	0.84	105.02	60.88	1.12	19.64	59.50	1.02	100.77
0.5	60.94	0.65	12.66	59.16	0.55	101.86	61.18	0.77	19.67	59.38	0.60	108.57	61.74	0.72	22.82	59.56	0.73	96.37	62.08	1.19	24.21	60.12	0.87	84.88
0.7	60.97	0.62	13.92	59.06	0.51	104.67	61.90	0.68	21.91	59.94	0.47	102.15	63.04	0.83	25.22	60.90	0.79	75.54	64.18	1.24	25.87	62.20	0.99	49.57

We have also conducted experiments on several other problem instances to assess the impact of parameters. However, due to space constraints, we are unable to present the results here. In general, it is advisable to set NP and G_{max} (or P_l and $iter_{max}$) appropriately to strike a balance between optimization performance and computational effort. For larger problems, higher values of these parameters may be warranted, but this is not always the case for every problem instance. The performance of HDE is relatively insensitive to F and Cr parameters. Nevertheless, we have observed that $F = 0.5$ and $Cr = 0.1$ tend to be more effective for problems with lower flexibility (i.e., typically less than 1.5), while the parameter combination of $F = 0.1$ and $Cr = 0.3$ appears to be more suitable for other instances. Flexibility, in this context, refers to the mean number of feasible machines that can perform a given operation in the problem instance.

8.4.6.3 Effect of hybridizing differential evolution and local search algorithms

To assess the efficacy of combining global search algorithms based on DE with local search algorithms, we conducted experiments and comparisons between HDE algorithms with DE and multistart random local search (MRLS) algorithms.

Our study involved exploring the potential benefits of hybridizing global and local search algorithms. To this end, we developed two variants of the HDE algorithm: one that removes the local search procedure (DE), and another that replaces the DE operators with a random generation approach (MRLS). The MRLS algorithm generates a new solution randomly at each iteration and applies the local search to it with a probability threshold. This process is repeated until the maximum number of replications (R_{max}) is reached. Like the HDE algorithm, the MRLS algorithm also has two variants: MRLS-N_1 algorithm and MRLS-N_2 algorithm.

We present the performance evaluation of DE, MRLS, and HDE algorithms in terms of the MRE of the best makespan (MRE_b) and average makespan (MRE_{av}) obtained in Table 8.14. The parameters used for DE and MRLS are identical to those of the HDE algorithm. To ensure a fair comparison with the HDE, we set the unique parameter R_{max} of the MRLS algorithm as $NP \times G_{max}$. The results in Table 8.14 demonstrate that the HDE-N_1 (or HDE-N_2) algorithm outperforms the DE and MRLS-N_1 (or MRLS-N_2) algorithms on each dataset. To illustrate the advantage of hybridization, we plot the typical convergence rate curves for these algorithms based on the instance la40 in Hurink Edata in Fig. 8.8. The figure shows that the HDE algorithms converge faster to lower makespan values compared to the DE and MRLS algorithms. This finding is consistent across all other benchmark instances, indicating a reliable and consistent trend.

Having examined the results and comparisons, we can confidently assert that the HDE algorithm outperforms its constituent parts (DE and local search). This achievement can be attributed to the DE algorithm's ability to provide excellent starting points for the local search algorithm by performing global exploration. Additionally,

Table 8.14 Comparison of DE, MRLS and HDE algorithms.

Data set	Num	DE		MRLS-N_1		MRLS-N_2		HDE-N_1		HDE-N_1	
		MRE_b (%)	MRE_{av} (%)	MRE_b (%)	MRE_{av} (%)	MRE_b (%)	MRE_{av} (%)	MRE_b (%)	MRE_{av} (%)	MRE_b (%)	MRE_{av} (%)
BRdata	10	34.47	42.98	36.63	41.44	34.24	39.87	15.58	16.52	14.67	15.46
BCdata	21	24.76	28.53	25.52	27.78	23.78	25.37	22.55	23.27	22.39	22.67
Hurink Edata	43	5.26	6.79	4.70	5.42	3.70	4.28	2.35	2.68	2.11	2.29
Hurink Rdata	43	7.51	9.92	5.28	5.94	4.55	5.18	1.28	1.59	1.05	1.26
Hurink Vdata	43	5.50	7.86	4.18	5.08	3.77	4.79	0.26	0.38	0.080	0.14

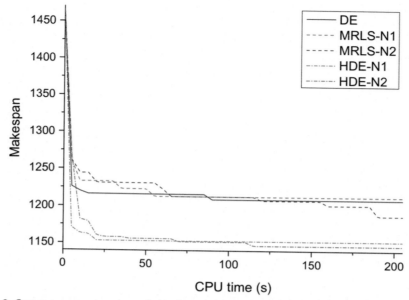

Figure 8.8 Convergence rate curve of the DE, MRLS, and HDE algorithms on the instance la40 in Hurink Edata.

Table 8.15 Results of P_{DE} and P_{LS} on each data set.

Data set	Num	HDE-N_1		HDE-N_2	
		P_{DE} (%)	P_{LS} (%)	P_{DE} (%)	P_{LS} (%)
Kacem data	5	24.01	75.99	2.39	97.61
BRdata	10	18.08	81.82	1.16	98.84
BCdata	21	15.11	84.89	1.27	98.73
Hurink Edata	43	11.44	88.56	1.25	98.75
Hurink Rdata	43	6.49	93.51	1.32	98.68

the local search algorithm enhances these solutions by conducting local exploitation and directing the DE algorithm toward more promising search spaces. In essence, the HDE algorithm combines the benefits of DE for diversification and local search for intensification to achieve a trade-off between exploring new search spaces and exploiting existing ones is essential for efficient optimization.

Table 8.15 provides insights into the computational efforts associated with DE and local search in the HDE algorithm, where P_{DE} and P_{LS} correspond to the percentage of DE and local search operations, respectively. The table reveals that the local search operation incurs the majority of computational cost, particularly in the case of

Table 8.16 Comparison of pure DE, GA of Chen, GA of Jia and GA of Pezzella on BRdata.

Instance	$n \times m$	DE	GA_Chen	GA_Jia	GA_Pezzella
MK01	10×6	40	40	40	40
MK02	10×6	27	29	28	26
MK03	15×8	204	204	204	204
MK04	15×8	60	63	61	60
MK05	15×4	173	181	176	173
MK06	10×15	63	60	62	63
MK07	20×5	144	148	145	139
MK08	20×10	523	523	523	523
MK09	20×10	311	308	310	311
MK10	20×15	223	212	216	212
MRE (%)		18.99	19.55	19.11	17.53

HDE-N_2. This finding is not unexpected since each iteration of the local search is significantly more computationally intensive than the vector evaluations.

8.4.6.4 Performance potential of pure differential evolution algorithm

While this chapter primarily focuses on hybrid algorithms, we would like to offer a brief demonstration of the performance potential of the pure DE algorithm. Although some results of DE were reported in Table 8.14, the parameters used were set according to HDE to showcase the effectiveness of hybridization. However, these parameters may not be optimal for pure DE. To explore the performance capabilities of pure DE, we set NP and G_{max} the population size and number of generations to 500 and 10,000, respectively. This resulted in a total of $NP \times G_{max} = 5 \times 10^6$ objective function evaluations, which is consistent with the approach used by Pezzella et al. [29]. In this context, the number of individuals in the population and the generation number are fixed at 5000 and 1000, respectively. Table 8.16 presents a comparison of the best makespan values obtained on BRdata by our DE algorithm with those obtained by three pure GA algorithms: GA of Chen et al. [27], GA of Jia et al. [28], and GA of Pezzella et al. [29]. The results in Table 8.16 show that DE performs only slightly worse than the GA of Pezzella et al. [29] overall. However, it is worth noting that the GA of Pezzella et al. [29] employs various strategies, such as problem-dependent initialization and intelligent mutation, which are tailored to specific problems. Our DE algorithm utilizes only fundamental DE operators to navigate the problem space.

8.5 Conclusion

This chapter introduced the HDE algorithms, which effectively address the FJSP with the makespan criterion, a vital problem in modern manufacturing environments.

To explore the problem space of the discrete FJSP, we devised a novel conversion mechanism that adapts the DE algorithm, originally designed for the continuous domain. It is worth highlighting that this conversion mechanism applies not only to DE but also to other continuous evolutionary algorithms, such as the harmony search [31] and ABC [32] algorithms, to tackle the FJSP. In this study, we aimed to improve the intensification search and balance the exploration and exploitation in the DE framework by incorporating a well-developed local search algorithm based on the critical path. To further enhance efficiency, we presented two neighborhood structures in the local search process, and a speed-up method was employed to quickly find acceptable schedules within the neighborhood. Our computational results and comparisons revealed that our proposed HDE-N_1 algorithm was highly effective and efficient for the FJSP, outperforming several recently proposed algorithms. Additionally, HDE-N_2 generated even higher-quality solutions than HDE-N_1 and was favorably compared with state-of-the-art approaches. Notably, HDE-N_2 even improved some of the BKSs for well-known benchmark instances. Moving forward, we plan to develop multiobjective HDE algorithms for the multiobjective FJSP and explore the application of the DE algorithm can be applied to a diverse range of combinational optimization problems beyond its current scope.

References

[1] Bagheri A, Zandieh M, Mahdavi I, et al. An artificial immune algorithm for the flexible job-shop scheduling problem. Future Generation Computer Systems 2010;26(4):533−41.
[2] Yazdani M, Amiri M, Zandieh M. Flexible job-shop scheduling with parallel variable neighborhood search algorithm. Expert Systems with Applications 2010;37(1):678−87.
[3] Xing LN, Chen YW, Wang P, et al. A knowledge-based ant colony optimization for flexible job shop scheduling problems. Applied Soft Computing 2010;10(3):888−96.
[4] Wang L, Zhou G, Xu Y, et al. An effective artificial bee colony algorithm for the flexible job-shop scheduling problem. International Journal of Advanced Manufacturing Technology 2012;60 (1−4):303−15.
[5] Wang L, Wang S, Xu Y, et al. A bi-population based estimation of distribution algorithm for the flexible job-shop scheduling problem. Computers & Industrial Engineering 2012;62(4):917−26.
[6] Hmida AB, Haouari M, Huguet MJ, et al. Discrepancy search for the flexible job shop scheduling problem. Computers & Operations Research 2010;37(12):2192−201.
[7] Oddi A, Rasconi R, Cesta A, et al. Iterative Flattening Search for the flexible job shop scheduling problem. Proceedings of the 22nd international joint conference; 2011.
[8] Pacino D, Van Hentenryck P. Large neighborhood search and adaptive randomized decompositions for flexible jobshop scheduling. Proceedings of the 22nd international joint conference; 2011. Vol. 11, p. 1997−2002.
[9] Storn R, Price K. Differential evolution-a simple and efficient heuristic for global optimization over continuous spaces. Journal of Global Optimization 1997;11(4):341.
[10] Panduro MA, Brizuela CA, Balderas LI, et al. A comparison of genetic algorithms, particle swarm optimization and the differential evolution method for the design of scannable circular antenna arrays. Progress in Electromagnetics Research B 2009;13:171−86.
[11] Michael LP. Scheduling: theory, algorithms, and systems. Springer International PU; 2022.

[12] Cheng R, Gen M, Tsujimura Y. A tutorial survey of job-shop scheduling problems using genetic algorithms—I. Representation. Computers & Industrial Engineering 1996;30(4):983—97.

[13] Mastrolilli M, Gambardella LM. Effective neighbourhood functions for the flexible job shop problem. Journal of Scheduling 2000;3(1):3—20.

[14] Kacem I, Hammadi S, Borne P. Pareto-optimality approach for flexible job-shop scheduling problems: hybridization of evolutionary algorithms and fuzzy logic. Mathematics and Computers in Simulation 2002;60(3—5):245—76.

[15] Brandimarte P. Routing and scheduling in a flexible job shop by tabu search. Annals of Operations Research 1993;41(3):157—83.

[16] Barnes JW, Chambers JB. Flexible job shop scheduling by tabu search. Graduate Program in Operations and Industrial Engineering, The University of Texas at Austin, Technical Report Series, ORP96-09, 1996.

[17] Fisher H. Probabilistic learning combinations of local job-shop scheduling rules. Industrial Scheduling 1963;225—51.

[18] Lawrence S. An experimental investigation of heuristic scheduling techniques. Supplement to resource constrained project scheduling, 1984.

[19] Hurink J, Jurisch B, Thole M. Tabu search for the job-shop scheduling problem with multi-purpose machines. Operations-Research-Spektrum 1994;15:205—15.

[20] Jurisch B. Scheduling jobs in shops with multi-purpose machines. University of Osnabrück, Germany, 1992.

[21] Nasiri MM, Kianfar F. A GES/TS algorithm for the job shop scheduling. Computers & Industrial Engineering 2012;62(4):946—52.

[22] Sha DY, Hsu CY. A hybrid particle swarm optimization for job shop scheduling problem. Computers & Industrial Engineering 2006;51(4):791—808.

[23] Zhang CY, Li PG, Rao YQ, et al. A very fast TS/SA algorithm for the job shop scheduling problem. Computers & Operations Research 2008;35(1):282—94.

[24] Li JQ, Pan QK, Suganthan PN, et al. A hybrid tabu search algorithm with an efficient neighborhood structure for the flexible job shop scheduling problem. The International Journal of Advanced Manufacturing Technology 2011;52:683—97.

[25] Bożejko W, Uchroński M, Wodecki M. Parallel hybrid metaheuristics for the flexible job shop problem. Computers & Industrial Engineering 2010;59(2):323—33.

[26] Gao J, Sun L, Gen M. A hybrid genetic and variable neighborhood descent algorithm for flexible job shop scheduling problems. Computers & Operations Research 2008;35(9):2892—907.

[27] Chen H., Ihlow J., Lehmann C. A genetic algorithm for flexible job-shop scheduling. Proceedings of the 15th IEEE international conference on robotics and automation; 1999. Vol. 2, p. 1120—5.

[28] Jia HZ, Nee AYC, Fuh JYH, et al. A modified genetic algorithm for distributed scheduling problems. Journal of Intelligent Manufacturing 2003;14:351—62.

[29] Pezzella F, Morganti G, Ciaschetti G. A genetic algorithm for the flexible job-shop scheduling problem. Computers & Operations Research 2008;35(10):3202—12.

[30] Demšar J. Statistical comparisons of classifiers over multiple data sets. The Journal of Machine Learning Research 2006;7:1—30.

[31] Geem ZW, Kim JH, Loganathan GV. A new heuristic optimization algorithm: harmony search. Simulation 2001;76(2):60—8.

[32] Karaboga D, Basturk B. A powerful and efficient algorithm for numerical function optimization: artificial bee colony (ABC) algorithm. Journal of Global Optimization 2007;39:459—71.

CHAPTER 9

An integrated search heuristic for large-scale flexible job shop scheduling problems

Contents

9.1 Introduction

Constraint-based approaches for addressing the flexible job shop scheduling problem (FJSP) primarily rely on constraint programming (CP) techniques. Given that the FJSP is fundamentally a constraint optimization problem, it is natural to apply CP to this problem. However, pure CP is only effective for solving small instances of the FJSP due to the exponentially growing search space. Fortunately, several significant advancements in CP, such as discrepancy search [1], large neighborhood search (LNS) [2], and iterative flattening search [3], have addressed this limitation. Recently, these

Intelligent Evolutionary Optimization
DOI: https://doi.org/10.1016/B978-0-443-27400-8.00009-5

techniques have undergone rigorous testing on the FJSP and have demonstrated outstanding performance in standard benchmark tests [4−6].

Given the successful application of both categories of techniques in solving the FJSP, their integration to create a more robust search mechanism is a promising avenue of research. This chapter presents the development of two algorithm modules for the FJSP with a makespan criterion: hybrid harmony search (HHS) and LNS, Corresponding to the evolutionary-based and constraint-based approaches, respectively, algorithm modules are developed in this chapter for the FJSP with a makespan criterion. The HHS algorithm employs the memetic paradigm to navigate the search space using harmony search (HS) [7]. In addition, a critical path-based local search procedure is incorporated into the HS to facilitate exploitation. The LNS algorithm is designed to continuously enhance the current solution by re-optimizing its subparts using CP-based search. Building on these two algorithms, an integrated search heuristic, referred to as HHS/LNS, a potential solution is being put forward to tackle FJSP challenges on a large scale.

Various factors are motivating the fusion of HHS and LNS in this chapter. The HHS algorithm can produce high-quality solutions rapidly. However, when the evolutionary procedure reaches a certain level, it becomes challenging to further improve the solution by tuning algorithm parameters. On the other hand, the LNS algorithm has a strong ability to intensify the search, but this ability diminishes with the increase of problem space. Another limitation of LNS is that it relies on the initial solution for addressing some large-scale instances, and a suboptimal initial solution may result in excessive computation time and low-quality results.

9.2 Hybrid harmony search

9.2.1 Outline of harmony search

The HS [7] is a recent evolutionary meta-heuristic that belongs to the population-based optimization methods. Originally designed for continuous optimization problems, it involves minimizing (or maximizing) the objective function $f(X)$ while satisfying the constraint that $x(j) \in \left[x_{\min}(j), x_{\max}(j) \right]$, where $X = \{x(1), x(2), \ldots, x(D)\}$ denotes a candidate solution consisting of D decision variables, and $x_{\min}(j)$ and $x_{\max}(j)$ represent the lower bound (LB) and upper bound (UB) for each decision variable, respectively. To tackle the problem, HS maintains a harmony memory (HM) which comprises harmony vectors and can be denoted as $HM = \{X_1, X_2, \ldots, X_{HMS}\}$, where HMS denotes the harmony memory size (HMS), and $X_i = \left\{ x_i(1), x_i(2), \ldots, x_i(D) \right\}$ represents the ith harmony vector in the HM. The best and worst harmony vectors in the HM are identified as X_{best} and X_{worst}, respectively. The workflow of HS can be summarized as follows: To begin, the initial HM is generated from a uniform distribution within the ranges $[x_{\min}(j), x_{\max}(j)]$, where $1 \leq j \leq D$. Next, a new candidate harmony is generated from the HM using three rules: memory consideration, pitch adjustment, and random selection. In this chapter, the modified pitch adjustment rule [8] is utilized, which effectively inherits a good solution structure from X_{best} and reduces the number of parameters in the algorithm. Algorithm 9.1 outlines the pseudocode for generating a new candidate harmony, also referred to as "improvisation" in the HS. Here, HMCR denotes the harmony memory considering rate, PAR represents the pitch adjusting rate, and $rand(0, 1)$ is a random function that returns a real number between 0 and 1 with uniform distribution. After improvisation, the HM is updated by replacing the worst harmony in the HM with the newly generated harmony, but only if its fitness (measured in terms of the objective function) is better than that of the worst harmony. The improvisation and updating procedures are repeated until the termination criterion is met. For additional information regarding HS, please refer to Refs. [7,9].

Algorithm 9.1: Pseudocode of the improvisation.

1: **for** each $j \in [1, D]$ **do**
2:     **if** $rand\,(0, 1) <$ HMCR **then**   ▷ *memory consideration*
3:         $x_{\text{new}}\,(j) \leftarrow x_i\,(j)$, where $i \in \{1, 2, \ldots, \text{HMS}\}$;
4:         **if** $rand\,(0, 1) <$ PAR **then**   ▷ *pitch adjustment*
5:             $x_{new}\,(j) \leftarrow x_{best}\,(j)$
6:         **end if**
7:     **else**   ▷ *random selection*
8:         $x_{new}\,(j) \leftarrow x_{new}\,(j) \in \left[x_{\min}\,(j), x_{\max}\,(j)\right]$
9:     **end if**
10: **end for**

9.2.2 Procedure of hybrid harmony search

The proposed HHS algorithm is based on HS, and its procedure is outlined in Algorithm 9.2. Unlike the basic HS, our algorithm involves a local search procedure to enhance the harmony vector generated in the improvisation phase, emphasizing exploitation. The improved harmony vector then enters the evolutionary process to replace the original one. Moreover, our HHS utilizes the total number of improvisations (NIs) as the stopping criterion. Specifically, the HHS terminates once the NI is reached.

Algorithm 9.2: Algorithmic flow of the proposed HHS algorithm.

1: Set the algorithm parameters and the stopping criterion.
2: Initialize the HM.
3: Evaluate each harmony vector in the HM and label the X_{best} and X_{worst}
4: while the stopping criterion is not met **do**
5:   Improvise a new harmony vector X_{new} from the HM.
6:   Perform the local search to X_{new} and yield X'_{new}
7:   Update the HM.
8: end while
9: return the best harmony vector found.

9.2.3 Adaptation of hybrid harmony search to the flexible job shop scheduling problem

Algorithm 9.2 indicates that there are four critical aspects to consider when adapting the proposed HHS to the FJSP: representation of a harmony vector, initialization of the HM, evaluation of a harmony vector, and the process of applying the procedure for the application of local search to a harmony vector.

Given that the HS algorithm operates in the continuous domain, the representation of a harmony vector in the HHS is characterized by continuous values to optimize the search mechanism of HS. In terms of initialization, the HM is randomly and uniformly initialized to preserve diversity.

To assess a harmony vector, it must be mapped to a schedule of the FJSP, and its fitness is determined by the makespan of the resulting schedule. However, this mapping is not straightforward due to the harmony vector's continuity and the schedule's discreteness. To address this, a discrete two-vector code is employed as a bridge. When evaluating a harmony vector, it is first converted to a two-vector code using forward conversion. Subsequently, the two-vector code is decoded into an active schedule, as illustrated in Fig. 9.1.

The computational flow for applying local search to a harmony vector is illustrated in Fig. 9.2. Notably, local search is not directly applied to the harmony vector, but rather to the corresponding schedule, which incorporates problem-specific knowledge. As depicted in Fig. 9.2, the evaluation operator is initially utilized to obtain the corresponding schedule for the harmony vector. Then, local search is applied to further improve the schedule. Subsequently, the improved schedule is transformed into a two-vector code, which is then converted back to an improved harmony vector employing reverse conversion.

The subsequent sections will provide a comprehensive overview of how the proposed HHS algorithm has been adapted to the FJSP.

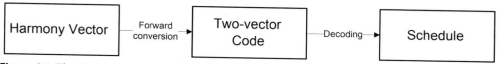

Figure 9.1 The computational flow of the evaluation.

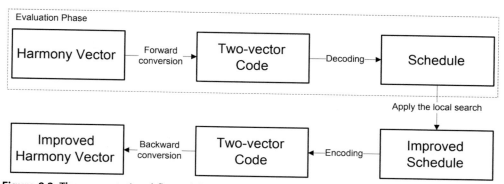

Figure 9.2 The computational flow of the local search to a harmony vector.

9.2.3.1 Representation and initialization

The proposed HHS algorithm uses a D-dimensional real vector to represent a harmony vector, $X_i = \{x_i(1), x_i(2), \ldots, x_i(D)\}$. The dimension D is constrained by $D = 2d$, where d denotes the total number of operations required to solve the FJSP. The first half of the harmony vector, $X_{i,1} = \{x_i(1), x_i(2), \ldots, x_i(d)\}$, describes the machine assignment information for each operation. The last half of the harmony vector, $X_{i,2} = \{x_i(d+1), x_i(d+2), \ldots, x_i(2d)\}$, typically performed through a combination of local search algorithms and other heuristic techniques. The proposed design is consistent with the two-vector code for the FJSP and facilitates convenient problem-solving. To simplify the problem, all intervals $[x_{min}(j), x_{max}(j)], j = 1, 2, \ldots, D$, are set as $[-\delta, \delta], \delta > 0$. The value δ is denoted as the bound factor in this chapter.

The population is initialized uniformly and randomly. To create a harmony vector, $X_i = \{x_i(1), x_i(2), \ldots, x_i(D)\}$, the following formula is used:

$$x_i(j) = -\delta + 2\delta \times rand\,(0, 1), \quad j = 1, 2, \ldots, D \tag{9.1}$$

9.2.3.2 Two-vector code

The two-vector code in the proposed algorithm comprises two vectors: the machine assignment vector and the operation sequence vector. These vectors are designed to address the two subproblems in the FJSP.

Table 9.1 Illustration of numbering scheme for operations.

Operation indicated	$O_{1,1}$	$O_{1,2}$	$O_{2,1}$	$O_{2,2}$	$O_{2,3}$	$O_{3,1}$	$O_{3,2}$
Fixed ID	1	2	3	4	5	6	7

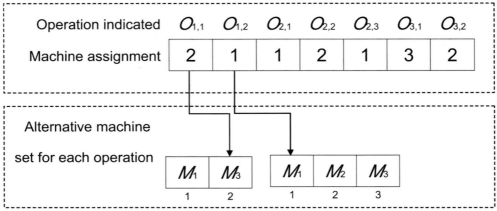

Figure 9.3 Illustration of the machine assignment vector.

To explain the two vectors, a unique ID is assigned to each operation based on its job number and order within the job. This numbering scheme is illustrated in Table 9.1. After numbering, each operation can be referred to by its unique ID. For instance, as shown in Table 9.1, operation 6 is equivalent to operation $O_{3,1}$ in terms of their respective positions within the production process.

The machine assignment vector, represented as $R_i = \{r_i(1), r_i(2), \ldots, r_i(d)\}$, is an array of d integer values. Each element $r_i(j)$ in this vector denotes the machine selected by operation j from its set of alternative machines. Fig. 9.3 illustrates a possible machine assignment vector and its corresponding interpretation. For instance, the value $r_i(1) = 2$ indicates that operation $O_{1,1}$ has chosen machine M_3, which is the second machine in its set of alternative machines.

The operation sequence vector in the proposed algorithm, denoted as $S_i = \{s_i(1), s_i(2), \ldots, s_i(d)\}$, represents an ID permutation of all the operations. The order of occurrence for each operation in S_i determines its scheduling priority. For instance, a possible operation sequence vector for this problem can be expressed as $S_i = \{3, 1, 4, 2, 6, 5, 7\}$. This sequence can be translated into a distinct list of operations arranged in a specific order.: $O_{2,1} \succ O_{1,1} \succ O_{2,2} \succ O_{1,2} \succ O_{3,1} \succ O_{2,3} \succ O_{3,2}$.

The operation with the highest priority, $O_{2,1}$, is scheduled first, followed by $O_{1,1}$, and so on. It is essential to recognize that not all ID permutations are viable for the operation sequence vector due to the designated priority order of operations within a job. Therefore, the relative priority order of operations within a job must be maintained in S_i.

The decoding process of the two-vector code is performed in two stages. The initial step involves assigning each operation to its selected machine based on R_i. The second stage deals with each operation in turn, following their order in S_i, to allocate them to the best available processing time for their respective machines. A schedule generated in this way is ensured to be an active schedule [10].

For a more straightforward encoding of a schedule solution to a two-vector code, R_i is obtained directly through the machine assignment in the schedule, while S_i is obtained by arranging all the operations in ascending chronological sequence based on the earliest possible starting time.

9.2.3.3 Conversion techniques

The proposed HHS algorithm involves two distinct types of conversions: forward conversion and backward conversion.

The forward conversion process aims to transform a harmony vector, denoted by the vector of real-valued parameters $X_i = \{x_i(1), x_i(2), \ldots, x_i(d), x_i(d+1), x_i(d+2), \ldots, x_i(2d)\}$, into a two-vector code composed of two integer-parameter vectors: $R_i = \{r_i(1), r_i(2), \ldots, r_i(d)\}$ and $S_i = \{s_i(1), s_i(2), \ldots, s_i(d)\}$. This conversion is split into two distinct parts. The first part involves converting $X_{i,1} = \{x_i(1), x_i(2), \ldots, x_i(d)\}$ into the vector representing machine assignments $R_i = \{r_i(1), r_i(2), \ldots, r_i(d)\}$.

Let $l(j)$ represent number of available machine options available for operation j, where $j = 1, 2, \ldots, d$. The conversion process involves mapping the real number $x_i(j) \in [-\delta, \delta]$; δ to the integer $r_i(j) \in [1, l(j)]$. The specific procedure is as follows: first, $x_i(j)$ is transformed into a real number within the range $[1, l(j)]$ using linear transformation. Then, $r_i(j)$ is assigned the integer value closest to it to the transformed real number, as shown in Eq. (9.2).

$$r_i(j) = round\left(\frac{1}{2\delta}(l(j)-1)(x_i(j)+\delta)+1\right), \ j = 1, 2, \ldots, d \qquad (9.2)$$

The purpose of the $round(x)$ function is to approximate a given number x to its closest whole number. In the second part of the conversion process, $X_{i,2} = \{x_i(d+1), x_i(d+2), \ldots, x_i(2d)\}$ is transformed into the operation sequence vector $S_i = \{s_i(1), s_i(2), \ldots, s_i(d)\}$. To achieve this transformation, the ID permutation of operations is constructed using the largest position value (LPV) rule [11], which involves arranging the operations in descending order of their position values.

Notwithstanding, as stated in Section 9.2, the arrangement obtained may not meet the requirements for S_i. Therefore, a repair procedure is performed to modify the relative order of operations within a job in the permutation. For instance, consider the vector $X_{i,2} = \{0.6, -0.4, 0.5, -0.2, 0.7, 0.3, -0.3\}$. Then, an instance of this conversion is demonstrated in Fig. 9.4.

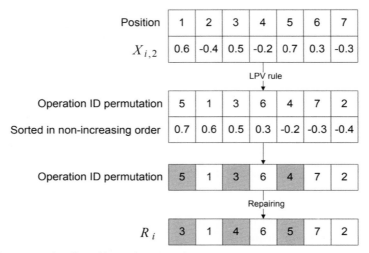

Figure 9.4 The conversion from $X_{i,2}$ to the operation sequence vector.

The process of backward conversion aims to convert a two-vector code back to a harmony vector, which is divided into two distinct parts. The first part is related to machine assignment, and it involves an inverse linear transformation of Eq. (9.2). However, when $l(j) = 1$, a unique case should be considered, and $x_i(j)$ should be randomly selected from the range $[-\delta, \delta]$ when $l(j) = 1$. The transformation can be carried out using the following steps:

$$x_i(j) = \begin{cases} \dfrac{2\delta}{l(j) - 1}(r_i(j) - 1) - \delta, & l(j) \neq 1 \\ x_i(j) \in [-\delta, \delta], & l(j) = 1 \end{cases} \tag{9.3}$$

In the second part, the vector $X_{i,2} = \{x_i(d+1), x_i(d+2), \ldots, x_i(2d)\}$ is obtained by rearranging the elements in the previous $X_{i,2}$ before being improved. This rearrangement ensures that the new $X_{i,2}$ matches the operation sequence vector of the optimized schedule, based on the LPV rule. where $j = 1, 2, \ldots, d$.

9.2.3.4 Local search strategy

Local search is implemented to improve the local exploitation capability of HS. It is applied to the schedule that corresponds to the harmony vector, as shown in Fig. 9.2.

A disjunctive graph $G = (V, C \cup D)$ [12,13] can be used to represent a schedule for the FJSP. The graph comprises a set V of nodes, where each node corresponds to an operation in the FJSP (including dummy starting and terminating operations). Additionally, C is the collection of all conjunctive arcs, which connect two successive operations within a job, and their directions indicate the order of processing among the pair of linked operations.

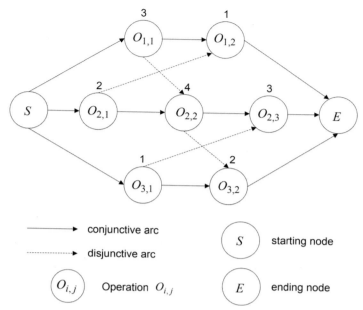

Figure 9.5 Illustration of disjunctive graph.

D represents a collection of disjunctive arcs, which link two neighboring operations carried out on the same machine, and their orientation indicates the sequence of processing. The processing duration for each operation is commonly denoted above the corresponding node and treated as the node's weight. A feasible timetable depicted by the disjunctive graph is shown in Fig. 9.5. In this timetable, operations $O_{3,1}$ and $O_{2,3}$ are executed consecutively on machine M_1, $O_{2,1}$ and $O_{1,2}$ are performed successively on machine M_2, and operations $O_{1,1}$, $O_{2,2}$, and $O_{3,2}$ are executed sequentially on machine M_3.

The critical path in a schedule is the longest sequence of operations from the starting node S to the ending node E, which determines the makespan for the schedule. Operations that fall on the critical path are referred to as critical operations. For example, in Fig. 9.5, the critical path is $S \rightarrow O_{1,1} \rightarrow O_{2,2} \rightarrow O_{2,3} \rightarrow E$, and the makespan for the schedule is 10. The critical operations in this case are $O_{1,1}$, $O_{2,2}$, and $O_{2,3}$.

The heterogeneous hyper-heuristic scheduler employs a local search inspired by the one employed in [13]. This local search generates a neighborhood of a schedule solution by relocating a single critical operation along a critical path in the disjunctive graph. This operation relocation is executed in two stages, involving deletion and insertion. Specifically, an operation is removed from the disjunctive graph and then reinserted at an appropriate position that ensures no scheduling deterioration. It's worth noting that the feasible position for an operation to be relocated can be on any other available machine. Therefore, the machine assignment for the operation will be reassigned when it's relocated to a different machine. For example, in the schedule depicted in Fig. 9.5, during the local search process, the critical path $S \rightarrow O_{1,1} \rightarrow O_{2,2} \rightarrow O_{2,3} \rightarrow E$ is first identified. Then, we attempt to relocate operation $O_{1,1}$ by finding a suitable position for it. If $O_{1,1}$ is successfully relocated (a feasible insertion point is located for $O_{1,1}$).

If a satisfactory insertion point is identified, the resulting schedule is deemed acceptable and becomes the current schedule to continue with the next iteration of local improvement. Otherwise, we attempt to relocate the operation $O_{2,2}$, and continue with subsequent operations along the critical path until one operation can be successfully moved. If it proves impossible to relocate any critical operation, it implies that the local search has reached a local optimum, that is, relocating a single operation on the critical path.

The key distinction in our local search approach is that, upon reaching the local optimum of relocating one critical operation, we refine the current solution by relocating two operations concurrently, with at least one operation being critical. However, since moving two operations requires more computational time, it is only attempted if relocating one critical operation is unsuccessful.

To summarize, Algorithm 9.3 delineates the process of obtaining an acceptable neighborhood in the local search. The keyword "return" within the loops indicates

---

Algorithm 9.3: Procedure of generating an acceptable neighborhood.

1: Get the critical path in the current solution represented by the disjunctive graph G.
2: for each operation cp in the critical path **do**
3:   Delete cp from G to yield G'
4:   **if** an available position is found for cp to insert into **then**
5:   Insert the operation cp to yield G''
6:   **return** the disjunctive graph G''
7:   **end if**
8: end for
9: for c each operation cp in the critical path **do**
10:   Delete cp from G to yield G'
11:   **for** each operation op in G' **do**
12:   Delete op from G' to yield G''
13:   **if** wo available positions are found for cp and op to insert into **then**
14:   Insert cop and op to yield G'''
15:   **return** the disjunctive graph G'''
16:   **end if**
17:   **end for**
18: end for
19: return an empty disjunctive graph.

---

that the algorithm terminates at that step, and the content returned is regarded as the final result of the algorithm. For additional information on operation relocation, please see [13]. Our local search algorithm terminates either when the maximum number of local iterations has been reached or when all designated relocations have failed.

9.3 Large neighborhood search

9.3.1 Outline of large neighborhood search

The LNS [2] is a robust optimization method that blends CP and local search. Unlike conventional local search algorithms that make minor adjustments to the current solution, such as relocating one or two operations in scheduling, LNS identifies a set of variables to temporarily remove from the problem's constraints. After identifying the variables, LNS temporarily removes them from the problem's constraints by unassigning them whilst maintaining constant values for the other variables. This process is referred to as "destruction." Subsequently, LNS searches for an improved solution by optimizing only the unassigned variables, which is called "construction." The LNS repeats these destruction and construction steps until the termination condition is satisfied. Algorithm 9.4 provides an overview of the fundamental structure of LNS.

Algorithm 9.4: LNS architecture.

1: Produce initial solution
2: **while** termination condition is not met **do**
3:     Choose a subset of variables to relax.
4:     Fix the remaining variables.
5: **if** search finds improvement **then**
6:     Update current solution.
7: **end if**
8: **end while**

In essence, the fundamental concept of LNS is straightforward. By utilizing the destruction operator, the original problem is simplified, and CP is then employed to solve the reduced problem. This approach overcomes the limitations of CP in exploring the vast search space. One significant advantage of LNS from a CP perspective is the ability to leverage powerful CP propagation techniques to more efficiently reduce the search space compared to pure tree search methods [14].

Our implementation of LNS utilizes COMET [15], a sophisticated optimization system that has gained increasing adoption in operations research. When employing LNS with COMET, the user must first model the problem by defining constraints, Further constraints are continually incorporated during Steps 4 and 5 of Algorithm 9.4. After a constraint has been established, the C_{OMET} system's built-in CP propagation is activated. This triggers the filtering of domains by all previously established constraints in a sequence until no more values can be removed from any domain. Additionally, each time a solution is discovered during the search, the system dynamically adds a constraint stating that the subsequent solution must be superior. For further information on the operational principles of C_{OMET} and its potential applications in solving diverse combinatorial optimization problems, please consult [16]. In the following sections, we will elucidate our implementation of LNS for the FJSP using C_{OMET}, encompassing the Limitation-oriented framework, deconstruction process, and assembly process.

9.3.2 Constraint-based model for the flexible job shop scheduling problem

In order to elucidate the limitation-oriented framework for the FJSP, two additional symbols are established according to Section 9.2. Let $\sigma_{i,j}, \mu_{i,j}$ denote the start time and the selected machine of operation $O_{i,j}$ in the schedule, respectively. Then, a solution to the FJSP is composed of pairs of values $(\sigma_{i,j}, \mu_{i,j})$ for all operations. A solution is deemed feasible if it meets the following three categories of constraints:

(1) Precedence constraint: Tasks contained in a work order must adhere to a specified priority order. The constraint is expressed as follows: $\forall i \in [1, n], \forall j \in [1, n_i - 1], \sigma_{i,j} + p_{i,j,\mu_{i,j}} \leq \sigma_{i,j+1}$.

(2) Resource constraint: a single task may exclusively be executed on its designated machines, such that $\forall O_{i,j}, \mu_{i,j} \in M_{i,j}$.

(3) Capacity constraint: A machine can only undertake a single operation at any given time. The constraint is expressed as follows: $\forall O_{x,y}, O_{\alpha,\beta}$, if $\mu_{x,y} = \mu_{\alpha,\beta}$, then $\sigma_{x,y} + p_{x,y,\mu_{x,y}} \leq \sigma_{\alpha,\beta}$ or $\sigma_{\alpha,\beta} + p_{\alpha,\beta,\mu_{\alpha,\beta}} \leq \sigma_{x,y}$.

The goal of the FJSP is to minimize the makespan, denoted as $C_{max} = \max_{1 \leq i \leq n, 1 \leq j \leq n_i} \{\sigma_{i,j} + p_{i,j,\mu_{i,j}}\}$, subject to the three constraints outlined above.

9.3.3 Destruction procedure

During the breakdown process, certain variables are selected for relaxation while others are fixed. The FJSP adopts the partial-order schedule (POS) relaxation [17], which initially selects a set Ω of operations. The remaining operations are then fixed to their current machines, while operations executed on the same machine maintain their relative precedence order in the current schedule. Let (σ, μ) denote the current schedule solution and (σ', μ') represent the schedule to be constructed. The POS relaxation can be expressed as follows: $\forall O_{x,y}, O_{\alpha,\beta} \notin R$ and $\mu_{x,y} = \mu_{\alpha,\beta}$, if $\sigma_{x,y} + p_{x,y,\mu_{x,y}} \leq \sigma_{\alpha,\beta}$, then $\sigma'_{x,y} + p_{x,y,\mu_{x,y}} \leq \sigma'_{\alpha,\beta}$ and $\mu'_{x,y} = \mu_{x,y}, \mu'_{\alpha,\beta} = \mu_{\alpha,\beta}$. It is advantageous for the POS relaxation to only fix the relative precedence order between the remaining operations, rather than their actual start times. This allows for more flexibility in re-optimization.

The selection of subset Υ, where each operation is fixed on its original machine, is referred to as the neighborhood heuristic in LNS, with Υ being a subset of Ω. In this study, the time-window neighborhood heuristic is utilized, which randomly generates the time-window $[t_{\min}, t_{\max}]$. The set Υ comprises all operations processed within the interval $[t_{\min}, t_{\max}]$. To enhance the search process, an extra neighborhood is established from the time-window neighborhood. This is achieved by selecting a subset $\Upsilon \subseteq \Omega$, where the machine assignment of operations in Υ is fixed. This is denoted as $\forall O_{i,j} \in r, \mu'_{i,j} = \mu_{i,j}$.

9.3.4 Construction procedure

The assembly process involves creating a new schedule solution from the current one using CP search. Our search approach is straightforward and relies on the fact that, once each operation is assigned to an available machine and operations, when operations are strictly sequenced within a single machine, subject to constraints, the smallest possible completion time is equal to the total duration of the tasks on the longest path in the precedence graph (disjunctive graph). In summary, the search is executed as follows: Assign operations to the selected machines, prioritizing those with the least number of machine selections.

Operations are then ranked separately on each machine, with priority given to machines with the least amount of slack. Following the ranking, the earliest and latest start times for each operation, as well as the makespan, are calculated based on the precedence graph. Finally, the earliest start time is set as the start time for all operations. To prevent excessively long search times, a failure limit is set for each LNS construction procedure. Additionally, our search controller employs a deep first search and, as the search is implemented on a constraint-based system, this approach can effectively leverage the advantages of constraint propagation in CP.

9.4 Integrated search heuristic: hybrid harmony search/large neighborhood search

Considering the intricacies of the two current algorithm modules, the integration method presented in this chapter is relatively straightforward. The HHS module is executed first. By replacing the worst harmony in the HM at each iteration, after running the HHS algorithm (NI is reached), the HM can be viewed as an elite solution pool. As the assignment of machines to operations is crucial in the FJSP, valuable machine assignment information can be extracted from the elite solutions in the HM before entering the LNS module. The extraction procedure functions as follows: For every task, the device with the optimal compatibility in the HM is appended to its list of usable devices. Additionally, if any remaining device is frequently selected by other top solutions and its selection frequency surpasses the adjustable parameter τ, it is also added to the list. Consequently, each task has a smaller pool of devices to consider during the extraction process. After the extraction, the HHS's top solution is employed as the initial solution for the LNS. The LNS is subsequently executed for a specified amount of CPU time to enhance the solution even further, ultimately returning the best solution discovered.

As previously mentioned, our integration approach has two main components. Firstly, the top solution obtained by the HHS serves as a favorable initial point for the LNS. Secondly, the extracted machine assignment data constrains the LNS search to a more advantageous problem space, thereby enhancing the intensification capabilities.

Undoubtedly, there are numerous additional avenues that we could explore. Nevertheless, this uncomplicated integration method straightforwardly and effectively accomplishes the objectives outlined in Section 9.1, as intended by our research.

9.5 Experimental study

9.5.1 Experimental setup

To evaluate the efficacy of our proposed algorithms, we have implemented the HHS module in Java and the LNS module in C_{OMET} [15] language. Both modules were executed on a Xeon processor with a clock speed of 2.83 GHz and 15.9 GB of RAM provided the hardware setup for our experiments.

Our experiment primarily focuses on utilizing two established FJSP benchmark sets. The first is the BRdata set of FJSP instances from Brandimarte [12], which we utilized to verify the efficiency of our proposed HHS algorithm. The second is a collection of more challenging and extensive instances provided by Dauzére-Pérés and Paulli [18], known as DPdata, which we employed to demonstrate the effectiveness of the HHS/LNS approach in resolving complex and large FJSP problems.

Furthermore, to provide a comprehensive assessment of the effectiveness of our proposed algorithms, we have included a summary of the results obtained from two additional benchmark data sets found in the literature. These data sets are the BCdata set from Barnes and Chambers [19], and the HUdataset from Hurink et al. [20], which is further divided into three distinct subsets: Edata, Rdata, and Vdata. To maintain consistency, the best LB and UB for each benchmark instance cited in this chapter are sourced from [21].

As a result of the inherent nondeterministic nature of our proposed algorithms, we conducted five separate runs on each problem instance to achieve reliable and significant outcomes, as recommended by prior studies [21–23]. We employed four distinct metrics to illustrate the computational results, namely the best makespan (BC_{max}), the average makespan ($AV(C_{max})$), the standard deviation (SD) of makespan, and the average computational time in seconds (AV(CPU)). The values for these metrics were obtained from the five runs.

To demonstrate the efficacy of our proposed algorithm, we compared the results obtained with those of existing algorithms found in the literature. The primary comparison metrics employed were BC_{max} and $AV(C_{max})$. We utilized the relative deviation criterion (dev) to compare the makespan, this is depicted as follows:

$$dev = \left(\left(MK_{comp} - MK_{proposed}\right)/MK_{comp}\right)] \times 100\% \qquad (9.4)$$

Here, $MK_{proposed}$ and MK_{comp} refer to the makespan values obtained by our proposed method and the comparative algorithm.

The HHS algorithm module comprises several parameters, including the HMS, HMCR, PAR, the bound factor (δ), the total NIs, and the maximum iterations of local search ($iter_{max}$). The LNS algorithm module, on the other hand, includes three distinct parameters: the failure limit for each construction procedure (maxFail), the probability of the operation in Ω belonging to $\Upsilon(Pl)$, and the maximum CPU time limit (T_{max}). The integrated approach of HHS/LNS involves an additional parameter τ, as discussed in Section 9.5, in addition to the parameters found in the HHS and LNS modules. The parameters utilized for each experiment will be explicitly outlined and fine-tuned to ensure a favorable balance in the trade-off between the quality of the solution and computational time.

9.5.2 Performance analysis of the hybrid harmony search module

This section focuses on analyzing the performance of the HHS algorithm. Initially, we scrutinize the BRdataset to verify the efficacy of our proposed HHS approach. The parameters utilized in the algorithmic approach of HHS for this specific group of cases are illustrated in Table 9.2.

Table 9.3 presents our computational outcomes for the HHS algorithm on the BRdata set. The first and second columns consist of the instance name and size, respectively. The third column details the total number of operations for each instance. The fourth column displays the mean count of available machinery options

Table 9.2 Parameters setting for the HHS on BRdata.

Parameter	Description	Value
HMS	Harmony memory size	5
HMCR	Harmony memory considering rate	0.95
PAR	Pitch adjusting rate	0.3
δ	Bound factor	1.0
NI	The total number of improvisations	3000
$iter_{max}$	The maximum iterations of local search	150

Table 9.3 Results of HHS on BRdata.

Instance	$n \times m$	d	Flex	(LB, UB)	HHS			
					BC_{max}	$AV(C_{max})$	SD	AV(CPU)
MK01	10×6	55	2.09	(36, 42)	40	40	0	3.87
MK02	10×6	58	4.10	(24, 32)	26	26.2	0.45	5.79
MK03	15×8	150	3.01	(204, 211)	204	204	0	36.60
MK04	15×8	90	1.91	(48, 81)	60	60	0	13.30
MK05	15×4	106	1.71	(168, 186)	172	172.8	0.45	35.78
MK06	10×15	150	3.27	(33, 86)	60	59.4	0.45	111.65
MK07	20×5	100	2.83	(133, 157)	139	139.8	0.45	36.16
MK08	20×10	225	1.43	523	523	523	0	171.10
MK09	20×10	240	2.53	(299, 369)	307	307	0	172.24
MK10	20×15	240	2.98	(165, 296)	202	203	1.00	437.69

per task, also known as "flexibility" in the FJSP. The fifth column indicates the optimal LB and UB for each instance denoted as (LB, UB), respectively. The subsequent columns delineate the quartet of measures referenced in Section 9.6.1.

Table 9.4 comprises a comparison between the HHS algorithm and several evolutionary-based algorithms recently proposed, such as GA by Pezzella et al. [22], KBACO by Xing et al. [24], AIA by Bagheri et al. [25], and ABC by Wang et al. [26]. The $AV(C_{max})$ metric for GA and AIA is unavailable. On the other hand, Table 9.5 provides a comparative analysis of our HHS algorithm against other categories of techniques, such as TS proposed by Mastrolilli and Gambardella [21], and CDDS developed by Hmida et al. [4].

Bold values in the tables indicate the algorithm with the best performance among the referenced approaches. For comparing the best makespan obtained between the HHS algorithm and the other methods, except for CDDS, we used dev. However, CDDS is different from the other aforementioned algorithms, as it is deterministic and comprises a group of four deterministic algorithms (CDDS-N_1, CDDS-N_2, CDDS-N_3, and CDDS-N_4). To ensure a more equitable comparison, the dev value for CDDS-N_1 (or CDDS-N_2, CDDS-N_3, CDDS-N_4) was computed by comparing the HHS algorithm against CDDS-N_1 (or CDDS-N_2, CDDS-N_3, CDDS-N_4) The dev value for CDDS-N_1 (or CDDS-N_2, CDDS-N_3, CDDS-N_4) was computed by comparing the HHS algorithm against CDDS-N_1 (or CDDS-N_2, CDDS-N_3, CDDS-N_4) by taking into account the average performance of HHS, rather than solely relying on the best performance.

Table 9.4 demonstrates that the proposed HHS algorithm performs favorably as compared to other evolutionary-based algorithms on the BRdataset. To be precise, when it comes to BC_{max}, the HHS algorithm outperforms the GA in 40% of the

Table 9.4 Comparison of the proposed HHS with four existing evolutionary-based algorithms on BRdata.

Instance	HHS		GA		KBACO			AIA		ABC		
	BC_{max}	AV (C_{max})	BC_{max}	dev (%)	BC_{max}	AV (C_{max})	dev (%)	BC_{max}	dev (%)	BC_{max}	AV (C_{max})	dev (%)
MK01	**40**	40	40	0	**39**	39.8	−2.56	40	0	40	40	0
MK02	**26**	26.2	**26**	0	29	29.1	+10.34	**26**	0	**26**	26.5	0
MK03	**204**	204	**204**	0	**204**	204	0	**204**	0	**204**	204	0
MK04	**60**	60	**60**	0	65	66.1	+7.69	**60**	0	**60**	61.22	0
MK05	**172**	172.8	173	+0.58	173	173.8	+0.58	173	+0.58	**172**	172.98	0
MK06	**59**	59.4	63	+6.35	67	69.1	+11.94	63	+6.35	60	64.48	+1.67
MK07	**139**	139.8	**139**	0	144	145.4	+3.47	140	+0.71	**139**	141.42	0
MK08	**523**	523	**523**	0	**523**	523	0	**523**	0	**523**	523	0
MK09	**307**	307	311	+1.29	311	312.2	+1.29	312	+1.60	**307**	308.76	0
MK10	**202**	203	212	+4.72	229	233.7	+11.79	214	+5.61	208	212.84	+2.88
Average improvement	—	—	—	+1.29	—	—	+4.45	—	+2.09	—	—	+0.46

Table 9.5 Comparison of the proposed HHS with other categories of techniques (TS, CDDS) on BRdata.

Instance	HHS		TS			CDDS							
	BC_{max}	$AV(C_{max})$	BC_{max}	$AV(C_{max})$	dev (%)	N_1	dev (%)	N_2	dev (%)	N_3	dev (%)	N_4	dev (%)
MK01	40	40	40	40	0	40	0	40	0	40	0	40	0
MK02	26	26.2	26	26	0	26	−0.77	26	−0.77	26	−0.77	26	−0.77
MK03	204	204	204	204	0	204	0	204	0	204	0	204	0
MK04	60	60	60	60	0	60	0	60	0	60	0	60	0
MK05	172	172.8	173	173	+0.58	175	+1.26	173	+0.12	173	+0.12	173	+0.12
MK06	59	59.4	58	58.4	−1.72	60	+1.00	59	−0.68	59	−0.68	58	−0.58
MK07	139	139.8	144	147	+3.47	139	−0.58	139	−0.58	139	−0.58	139	−0.58
MK08	523	523	523	523	0	523	0	523	0	523	0	523	0
MK09	307	307	307	307	0	307	0	307	0	307	0	307	0
MK10	202	203	198	199.2	−2.02	198	−2.53	197	−3.05	198	−2.53	198	−2.53
Average improvement					+0.03	–	−0.16	–	−0.50	–	−0.44	–	−0.62

instances, KBACO in 70% of the instances, AIA in 50% of the instances, and ABC in 20% of the instances. For the MK06 and MK10 instances, the HHS algorithm achieves better solutions than any of the other algorithms. Furthermore, the average relative deviation metrics indicate that the proposed HHS algorithm outperforms all four existing evolutionary-based algorithms. According to Table 9.5, the HHS algorithm is also comparable to TS and CDDS. Specifically, the HHS algorithm outperforms the other two algorithms in terms of BC_{max} in 8 out of 10 instances. In terms of the average relative deviation, the HHS algorithm performs slightly better than TS, but falls a bit short when compared to all four CDDS algorithms.

Table 9.3 indicates that the HHS algorithm exhibits not only robustness and efficiency but also a strong problem-solving capability. Half of the cases are resolved with an SD score of 0, whereas the other half show modest SD scores. Furthermore, all 10 instances can be computed in under 3 min, except instance MK10. Based on the results of the simulation tests and comparative study, it can be safely concluded that the HHS algorithm is highly effective, efficient, and robust enough to solve medium to large FJSP instances.

To further demonstrate the capabilities of the HHS algorithm, a large-scale FJSP instance (08a) from DPdata was selected. The HMS parameter was set to 8, while the other parameters were set according to Table 9.2. Fig. 9.6 displays the convergence curves that are typical of the HHS algorithm while solving instance 08a. As shown in the figure, the makespan decreases rapidly in the first ten generations of the process,

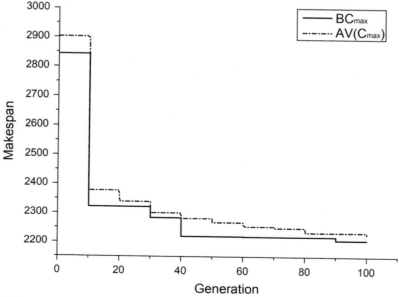

Figure 9.6 Convergence curves in solving the instance 08a by the proposed HHS.

Table 9.6 Performance of the HHS on the instance 08a under different parameter settings.

Experiment number	$iter_{max}$	NI = 1000			NI = 3000			NI = 5000		
		BC_{max}	AV (C_{max})	AV (CPU)	BC_{max}	AV (C_{max})	AV(CPU)	BC_{max}	AV (C_{max})	AV(CPU)
1	150	2136	2166	47.83	2124	2142.6	176.09	2124	2132.2	279.22
2	300	2086	2090.2	479.99	2082	2087	1455.79	2082	2085	2386.80
3	450	2086	2088.2	483.28	2080	2086.4	1460.77	2080	2083.2	2434.54

but the speed slows down notably in the subsequent iterations. This indicates that the HHS algorithm is capable of generating high-quality solutions in a relatively short amount of time, but further improvements to the solutions become more challenging as the evolutionary process advances.

Table 9.6 displays the results of the HHS algorithm on instance 08a with varying parameter settings. Specifically, we adjust the parameters $iter_{max}$ and NI, which are crucial for achieving high-quality solutions. The remaining parameters are kept fixed throughout the experiments. In Table 9.6, it is evident that the $iter_{max}$ parameter has a greater impact on the final solution quality. The completion times achieved in Experiment 2 are significantly better than those in Experiment 1, but at the cost of higher computation time.

The results obtained in Experiments 2 and 3 are almost identical. This is primarily because the local search is iterated 300 times, which is sufficient for finding the local optima in almost all cases. Thus, increasing the value of $iter_{max}$ beyond this point would not contribute significantly to the solution. Although increasing the value of the parameter NI can enhance the quality of the solution, its impact is comparatively limited in contrast to that of $iter_{max}$. It seems that increasing NI beyond a certain threshold has no discernible impact. Even when we increase NI from 3000 to 5000, the value of BC_{max} remains constant across all three experiments. The computational results presented in Table 9.6 indicate that it is quite challenging regardless of whether we increase the value of the parameter NI or $iter_{max}$, it appears to be quite challenging to further enhance the quality of the high-quality solution using the proposed HHS method.

9.5.3 Performance analysis of the large neighborhood search module

This section aims to evaluate the effectiveness of the LNS module using three different FJSP instances (07a, 08a, 09a) that exhibit a progressively expanding problem domain within the DPdata framework. Initially, we executed the LNS directly on all three instances, with the following parameter values: max$Fail = 200$; $P_l = 0:33$; $T_{max} = 2000$ s. The comprehensive outcomes are presented in Table 9.7. The first

Table 9.7 Performance of the LNS on instances 07a, 08a, 09a.

Instance	Initial	Time (s)				BKS
		500	1000	1500	2000	
07a	3094	2370	2357	2347	2327	2283
08a	4639	2893	2515	2409	2355	2069
09a	8447	7045	6561	6058	4888	2066

column of Table 9.7 displays the name of each instance, while the second column shows the initial solution obtained by the LNS for each instance. This refers to the initial feasible solution obtained using the CP-based search method. The subsequent four columns present the minimum makespan achieved by the LNS every 500 s. The final column of the table displays the most optimal solution currently documented in the literature. It is evident from Table 9.7 that the initial solution becomes increasingly inferior as the size of the problem space increases. Specifically, the preliminary solutions of the instances. 07a, 08a, and 09a are approximately 35.5%, 124.2%, and 308.8% worse than the respective optimal solutions on record. Regarding the solutions obtained at the end of the 2000-second time limit, the results are comparable. The solution for instance 07a is moderately acceptable, with a deviation of only 1.9% from the best-known solution. However, the solutions for instances 08a and 09a are relatively poor, with deviations of approximately 13.8% and 136.6%, respectively, from the best-known solutions. The suboptimal caliber of ultimate solutions for 08a and 09a instances can be attributed to their inadequate initial solutions. Therefore, it is crucial to provide the LNS with a better-quality initial solution. Additionally, for each instance, the makespan decreases as computation time increases, but the rate of decrease does not follow a precise pattern.

Next, we will examine the rate of decrease in makespan when applying the LNS algorithm to solve instances with varying problem spaces. Fig. 9.7 illustrates the makespan reduction for instances 07a, 08a, and 09a. To ensure a fair comparison, we initiate the reduction process from a starting solution equivalent to 10% of their respective best-known solutions. Based on the results depicted in Fig. 9.7, it is apparent that the makespan decreases at the fastest rate, for instance, 07a, while the rate is slowest for instance 09a. This suggests that the LNS algorithm generally exhibits a stronger intensification capability during the search process when dealing with instances that have a smaller problem space.

9.5.4 Effects of integration

Based on the preceding performance analysis, we can anticipate the effects of integration. Firstly, the experiments in Section 9.6.2 suggest that it becomes increasingly

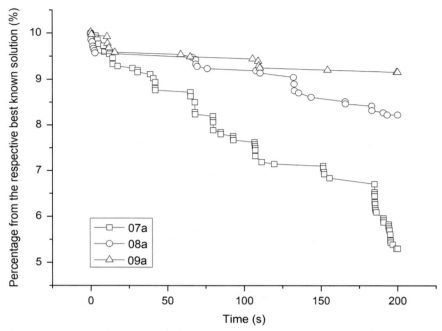

Figure 9.7 Decreasing of the makespan in solving instances 07a, 08a, and 09a by the LNS.

challenging to improve the solution further once the evolution procedure of the HHS attains a certain level. Secondly, the initial solution plays a crucial role in solving large-scale problems, and the LNS algorithm demonstrates greater search efficacy when dealing with problems that have smaller problem spaces. Furthermore, the outcomes presented in Table 9.7 demonstrate that the LNS algorithm alone is not an optimal instrument employed for the FJSP.

Fig. 9.8 illustrates the influence of extraction of information related to machine allocation using instance 08a. The curve with circle points represents the makespan reduction achieved by directly executing the LNS on the solution initially generated by the HHS algorithm, whereas the graph featuring triangular data markers depicts the performance after the extraction process. As shown in Fig. 9.8, the LNS algorithm can effectively enhance the high-quality solution generated by the HHS algorithm, and the benefits of the extraction process are evident.

9.5.5 Computational results on large-scale benchmark instances

The purpose of this section is to showcase the efficiency of the suggested combined exploration heuristic, HHS/LNS, in addressing large-scale FJSPs. To this end, we evaluate the HHS/LNS algorithm on instances from DPdata, which is one of the most challenging and extensive benchmark datasets. The common parameter values

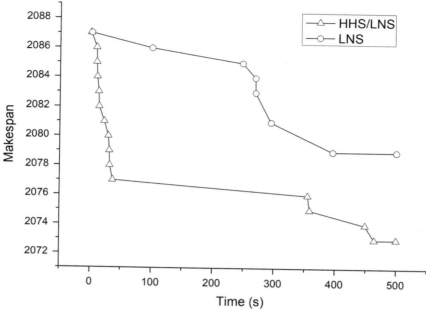

Figure 9.8 The impact of the machine assignment information extraction.

Table 9.8 Parameters setting for the HHS/LNS on DPdata.

Parameter	Description	Value
HMS	Harmony memory size	8
HMCR	Harmony memory considering rate	0.95
PAR	Pitch adjusting rate	0.3
NI	The total number of improvisations	3000
δ	Bound factor	1.0
$iter_{max}$	The maximum iterations of local search	200
maxFail	The failure limit for each construction procedure	200
P_l	The probability of the operation in Ω belonging to $\Upsilon(P_l)$	0.33
τ	The limit of selected frequency	3

utilized for the HHS/LNS algorithm on this set of instances are presented in Table 9.8. For the initial 12 instances (01a–12a), the maximum CPU time limit for the LNS in the HHS/LNS algorithm (T_{max}) is set to 500 s, while it is doubled for the other instances.

In Table 9.9, an exhaustive account of the computational outcomes for the instances evaluated in DPdata is presented. Columns 1–5 exhibit the same parameters as Table 9.3. In columns 6–8, the original outcomes attained by the HHS are

Table 9.9 Results on DPdata instances.

Instance	$n \times m$	d	Flex	(LB, UB)	HHS			LNS			HHS/LNS			
					BC_{max}	$AV(C_{max})$	SD	BC_{max}	$AV(C_{max})$	SD	BC_{max}	$AV(C_{max})$	SD	AV(CPU)
01a	10 × 5	196	1.13	(2505, 2530)	2525	2534	6.28	2554	2560	8.25	2505	2512.8	7.12	837.6
02a	10 × 5	196	1.69	(2228, 2244)	2242	2245.4	2.07	2233	2235.8	3.27	2230	2231.2	1.64	972.6
03a	10 × 5	196	2.56	(2228, 2235)	2229	2231.2	1.48	2230	2231.2	2.08	2228	2229	1.00	1164.6
04a	10 × 5	196	1.13	(2503, 2565)	2506	2517	8.34	2506	2522.4	25.81	2506	2506	0	849.6
05a	10 × 5	196	1.69	(2189, 2229)	2232	2234.6	2.41	2219	2222	3.94	2212	2215.2	2.39	931.2
06a	10 × 5	196	2.56	(2162, 2216)	2201	2206.8	3.77	2213	2215.6	1.82	2187	2191.8	2.77	1167.0
07a	15 × 8	293	1.24	(2187, 2408)	2323	2340.2	12.28	2327	2358.8	23.34	2288	2303	11.46	1547.4
08a	15 × 8	293	2.42	(2061, 2093)	2086	2087.6	1.52	2226	2278.6	73.08	2067	2073.8	5.16	1905.6
09a	15 × 8	293	4.03	(2061, 2074)	2074	2079	3.32	4004	4503	445.40	2069	2072.8	3.56	943.2
10a	15 × 8	293	1.24	(2178, 2362)	2341	2346.4	5.03	2357	2390.4	18.77	2297	2302.2	7.19	1590.0
11a	15 × 8	293	2.42	(2017, 2078)	2077	2079.8	2.77	2221	2289.2	55.92	2061	2066.6	3.28	1826.4
12a	15 × 8	293	4.03	(1969, 2047)	2045	2052.6	9.81	3765	4639	637.83	2027	2035.6	5.81	914.4
13a	20 × 10	387	1.34	(2161, 2302)	2280	2291.2	6.94	2365	2374.2	13.74	2263	2269.4	4.39	2900.3
14a	20 × 10	387	2.99	(2161, 2183)	2194	2195.2	1.10	3585	3743.2	162.67	2164	2167.6	2.07	3237.5
15a	20 × 10	387	5.02	(2161, 2171)	2220	2230.2	6.72	10081	10324.8	466.59	2163	2166.2	3.03	2112.3
16a	20 × 10	387	1.34	(2148, 2301)	2285	2289	5.10	2352	2372	15.76	2259	2266.4	5.46	2802.2
17a	20 × 10	387	2.99	(2088, 2169)	2160	2166.6	4.93	3568	3658	134.82	2137	2141.2	2.95	3096.4
18a	20 × 10	387	5.02	(2057, 2139)	2159	2170.2	6.53	10036	10683.8	594.23	2124	2128	3.87	2489.2

presented first. The results achieved by directly executing the LNS on DPdata instances are shown in columns 9—11 to provide a comparison with the HHS/LNS outcomes, where, concerning the 01a-12a and 13a-18a instances, the maximum CPU time limit of the LNS is increased to 2000 and 3000 s, respectively. The last four columns provide detailed information on the four measurements specified in Section 9.6.1 for the HHS/LNS algorithm. Table 9.9 compares the HHS/LNS algorithm with three state-of-the-art algorithms, namely TS by Mastrolilli and Gambardella [21], hGA by Gao et al. [23], and CDDS by Hmida et al. [4]. The variables BC_{max} and $AV(C_{max})$ represent the optimal and mean makespan attained across the five distinct executions, correspondingly, for the HHS/LNS, TS, and hGA algorithms. As CDDS are deterministic algorithms, we utilize the dev metric to make a fair comparison between the $AV(C_{max})$ of HHS/LNS and the results of CDDS.

Based on the data presented in Table 9.10, it is evident that our findings are highly competitive with the most advanced algorithms available. Compared to TS, hGA, and CDDS, the HHS/LNS approach exhibits a generally higher level of performance with regard to both BC_{max} and $AV(C_{max})$. Specifically, with regards to BC_{max}, the comparative performance of HHS/LNS against TS, hGA, CDDS-N_1, CDDS-N_2, CDDS-N_3, and CDDS-N_4, the former surpasses TS in 12 of 18 instances, outperforms hGA in 15 of 18 instances, and outperforms CDDS-N_1, CDDS-N_2, CDDS-N_3, and CDDS-N_4 in 15, 14, 16, and 14 of the 18 instances, respectively. The HHS/LNS approach falls short of producing the best results in only 6 instances, and even then, the difference is negligible, with an average deviation of only 0.2% from the top performers. On average, the HHS/LNS integrated search heuristic outperforms TS and hGA by 0.09% and 0.23%, respectively, across all 18 instances in relation to the mean deviation. In comparison to the CDDS algorithms, the HHS/LNS significantly outperforms all four variations, even while comparing the $AV(C_{max})$ of the HHS/LNS with the outcomes of CDDS, a notable difference is observed.

It is incredibly encouraging to note that the HHS/LNS approach was able to achieve 12 new best-known solutions for instances 01a, 02a, 03a, 05a, 06a, 08a, 11a, 12a, 14a, 15a, 17a, and 18a in DPdata. This remarkable feat demonstrates the effectiveness of the HHS/LNS in producing groundbreaking solutions with a reasonable amount of computing effort. Table 9.11 provides a comprehensive record of both our newly obtained best-known solutions and the previous ones for instances in DPdata.

Notably, for instances 01a and 03a, the best LB was previously reported to be 2505 and 2228, respectively [18], indicating that our integrated method has solved these instances optimally.

Upon examining Table 9.9, it is evident that the average computation time required for the HHS/LNS approach on DPdata is significantly longer than that of HHS on BRdata. This disparity is not surprising, given that instances in DPdata are generally more challenging and larger in scale, warranting a greater amount of search

Table 9.10 Comparison between the proposed HHS/LNS and state-of-the-art algorithms on DPdata.

Instace	HHS/LNS		TS			hGA			CDDS							
	BC_{max}	$AV(C_{max})$	BC_{max}	$AV(C_{max})$	dev (%)	BC_{max}	$AV(C_{max})$	dev (%)	N_1	dev (%)	N_2	dev (%)	N_3	dev (%)	N_4	dev (%)
01a	**2505**	2512.8	2518	2528	+0.52	2518	2518	+0.52	2518	+0.21	2530	+0.68	2530	+0.68	2520	+0.29
02a	**2230**	2231.2	2231	2234	+0.04	2231	2231	+0.04	2231	−0.01	2244	+0.57	2232	+0.04	2231	−0.01
03a	**2228**	2299	2229	2229.6	+0.04	2229	2229.3	+0.04	2229	0	2235	+0.27	2230	+0.04	2233	+0.18
04a	2506	2506	**2503**	2516.2	−0.12	2515	2518	+0.36	2510	+0.16	2520	+0.56	2507	+0.04	**2503**	−0.12
05a	**2212**	2215.2	2216	2220	+0.18	2217	2218	+0.23	2220	+0.22	2219	+0.17	2216	+0.04	2217	+0.08
06a	**2187**	2191.8	2203	2206.4	+0.73	2196	2198	+0.41	2199	+0.33	2214	+1.00	2201	+0.42	2196	+0.19
07a	2288	2303	**2283**	2297.6	−0.22	2307	2309.8	+0.82	2299	−0.17	**2283**	−0.88	2293	−0.44	2307	+0.17
08a	**2067**	2073.8	2069	2071.4	+0.10	2073	2076	+0.29	2069	−0.23	2069	−0.23	2069	−0.23	2069	−0.23
09a	2069	2072.8	**2066**	2067.4	−0.10	2067	2067	−0.10	2069	−0.18	**2066**	−0.33	**2066**	−0.33	**2066**	−0.33
10a	2297	2302.2	**2291**	2305.6	−0.74	2315	2315.2	+0.78	2301	−0.05	2291	−0.49	2307	+0.21	2311	+0.38
11a	**2061**	2066.6	2063	2065.6	+0.10	2071	2072	+0.48	2078	+0.55	2069	+0.12	2078	+0.55	2063	−0.17
12a	**2027**	2035.6	2034	2038	+0.34	2030	2030.6	+0.15	2034	−0.08	2031	−0.23	2040	+0.22	2031	−0.23
13a	2263	2269.4	2260	2266.2	−0.13	**2257**	2260	−0.27	**2257**	−0.55	2265	−0.19	2260	−0.42	2259	−0.46
14a	**2164**	2167.6	2167	2168	+0.14	2167	2167.6	+0.14	2167	−0.03	2189	+0.98	2183	+0.71	2176	+0.39
15a	**2163**	2166.2	2167	2167.2	+0.18	2165	2165.4	+0.09	2167	+0.04	2165	−0.06	2178	+0.54	2171	+0.22
16a	2259	2266.4	**2255**	2258.8	−0.18	2256	2258	−0.13	2259	−0.03	2265	−0.46	2260	−0.28	2256	−0.46
17a	**2137**	2141.2	2141	21.44	+0.19	2140	2142	+0.14	2143	+0.08	2140	−0.06	2156	+0.69	2143	+0.08
18a	**2124**	2128	2137	2140.2	+0.61	2127	2130.7	+0.14	2137	+0.42	2127	−0.05	2131	+0.14	2131	+0.14
Average improvement			–	–	+0.09	–	–	+0.23	–	+0.02	–	+0.08	–	+0.15	–	+0.01

Table 9.11 The makespan of new best-known solutions identified by the proposed HHS/LNS on DPdata.

Instance	(LB, UB)	Prev. best known	New best known
01a	(2505, 2530)	2518	2505
02a	(2228, 2244)	2231	2230
03a	(2228, 2235)	2229	2228
05a	(2189, 2229)	2216	2212
06a	(2162, 2216)	2196	2187
08a	(2061, 2093)	2069	2067
11a	(2017, 2078)	2063	2061
12a	(1969, 2047)	2030	2027
14a	(2161, 2183)	2167	2164
15a	(2161, 2171)	2165	2163
17a	(2088, 2169)	2140	2137
18a	(2057, 2139)	2127	2124

effort. It is worth noting from recent and related literature related to solving large FJSP instances that researchers have employed various strategies to manage computation time. For instance, Oddi et al. [6] established a maximum CPU runtime of 3200 s utilizing an AMD Phenom II X4 Quad 3.5 GHz processor to tackle a few large FJSP instances. Similarly, Beck and Feng [27] run their algorithm on a cluster containing nodes with 2 GHz Dual Core AMD Opteron 270 processors, each endowed with 2 GB of RAM, for 3600 s to handle some challenging JSPs. These approaches illustrate the importance of managing computation time in solving complex scheduling problems. to handle some difficult JSPs.

The effectiveness of our proposed HHS/LNS approach in solving large–scale FJSP instances is reasonably acceptable. The slightly larger SD values observed may be attributed to the fact that the HHS/LNS approach consists of two algorithm modules and may be influenced by more nondeterministic factors. Additionally, the large values of the duration of operation processing for the instances in DPdata. The results obtained by the pure LNS approach indicate that when considering instances with larger problem spaces, it becomes clear that the LNS approach cannot be compared to the HHS/LNS approach. The HHS/LNS approach exhibits a significantly higher level of performance and efficiency in solving complex problems, making it a more suitable choice for such instances. For instance, while the LNS approach achieves the same BC_{max} as the HHS/LNS approach for instance 04a, it produces suboptimal solutions for instance 12a.

Table 9.12 presents a comprehensive analysis of the computational effort necessary to execute HHS/LNS, TS, hGA, and CDDS algorithms. The CI-CPU row displays the total amount of average CPU time required, which is independent of the

Table 9.12 Comparison of total computational time (in seconds) required by HHS/LNS, TS, hGA, and CDDS on DPdata.

Algorithm	HHS/LNS	TS	hGA	CDDS
CI-CPU	6279	2467	6206	2890

computer used to perform the computations required by each algorithm on instances in DPdata. These values have been normalized using the coefficients provided by Dongarra [28], taking into account the varying performance levels of different CPUs. It is worth noting that our HHS and LNS algorithms are implemented in Java and C$_{OMET}$ language, respectively, in contrast, the remaining three algorithms have been implemented using C/C++ programming language. As is commonly known, Java programming language is generally less efficient than C/C++, and the C$_{OMET}$ language is approximately three to five times slower than equivalent C/C++ code [28]. To make a more accurate comparison between HHS/LNS and the other algorithms, we have divided the computational time required by HHS/LNS by a factor of 4. However, it is important to note that CPU time comparison is provided for indicative purposes only.

It is important to note that our CPU time comparison is based solely on available data, and other factors that may influence computation time, such as operating systems, software engineering decisions, and programming skills, are not taken into account. Based on the results presented in Table 9.12, it can be observed that the computational effort required by HHS/LNS is similar to that of hGA, but considerably higher than that of TS and CDDS. However, all four algorithms exhibit computational times within a factor of three while solving large-scale instances.

Tables 9.4 and 9.5 demonstrate that the HHS algorithm was unable to achieve the optimal solution for multiple instances in BRdata. Therefore, we conducted further experimentation by implementing the HHS/LNS algorithm on BRdata to enhance the solutions derived from the HHS algorithm. Although the instances in BRdata are generally less complex than those in DPdata, it was still of interest to investigate if the HHS/LNS algorithm could improve the results. Table 9.13 presents the best makespan values obtained by the HHS, LNS, and HHS/LNS algorithms on BRdata, wherein the UB of the CPU time for the pure LNS is established as 1000 s. Disappointingly, the results presented in Table 9.13 did not meet our expectations. The HHS/LNS algorithm was only able to improve the solutions for two instances (MK06 and MK10) when compared to the HHS algorithm alone and failed to obtain any novel optimal solution. The reason for this may be that the solutions generated by the HHS algorithm are already very close to the optimal solutions for the instances in BRdata. Importantly, it should be noted that the actual optimal solutions for the instances in BRdata are not available, apart from instances MK03 and MK09, for

Table 9.13 The comparison of best makespan obtained by the HHS, LNS, and HHS/LNS on BRdata.

Instance	HHS	LNS	HHS/LNS
MK01	40	40	40
MK02	26	26	26
MK03	204	204	204
MK04	60	60	60
MK05	172	173	172
MK06	59	60	58
MK07	139	140	139
MK08	523	523	523
MK09	307	307	307
MK10	202	206	198

Table 9.14 Mean relative error over best-known lower bound.

Data set	Num.	Alt.	HHS (%)	LNS (%)	HHS/LNS (%)	TS (%)	hGA (%)	CDDS (%)	M²h (%)
BRdata	10	2.59	15.52	16.20	14.98	15.14	14.92	14.98	N/A
DPdata	18	2.49	2.90	63.03	1.89	2.01	2.12	1.94	N/A
BCdata	21	1.18	22.86	22.73	22.43	22.53	22.61	22.54	22.53
Hurink Edata	43	1.15	2.34	2.32	2.11	2.17	2.13	2.32	N/A
Hurink Rdata	43	2.00	1.41	1.44	1.18	1.24	1.19	1.34	N/A
Hurink Vdata	43	1.31	0.19	30.27	0.11	0.095	0.082	0.12	N/A

which the LB values can be confirmed by the algorithms. Additionally, it is noteworthy that the pure LNS algorithm exhibits comparable performance to that of HHS and HHS/LNS algorithms when applied to BRdata. Considering the results obtained by the HHS/LNS algorithm on DPdata, it is more promising to use the HHS/LNS approach for solving relatively large and complex problems. This is because the true optimal solutions for these types of problems may be significantly far from the solutions generated by state-of-the-art algorithms. Additionally, it is noteworthy that the pure LNS algorithm exhibits comparable performance to that of HHS and HHS/LNS algorithms when applied to BRdata. Reflecting on the outcomes obtained by the HHS/LNS for DPdata, it is more promising to use the HHS/LNS approach for solving relatively large and complex problems. This is because the true optimal solutions for these types of problems may be significantly far from the solutions generated by state-of-the-art algorithms.

Table 9.14 presents an overview of the computational results for all the benchmark instances, measured in terms of the mean relative error (MRE). The first column specifies the name of the dataset, the second column indicates the number of instances included in each dataset, and the mean number of alternative machines for each operation is recorded in the third column. The remaining seven columns provide the MRE values for the best solutions obtained by various algorithms, including the HHS, pure LNS, HHS/LNS, Mastrolilli and Gambardella's TS algorithm [21], Gao et al.'s hGA algorithm [23], Hmida et al.'s CDDS algorithm [4], and Bozejko et al.'s M2h algorithm [29]. For BCdata and HUdata instances, the maximum CPU time limit for the pure LNS algorithm was set at 2000 s. The relative error (RE) for each instance was calculated using the formula $RE = [(MK-LB)/LB] \times 100\%$, where MK represents the best makespan generated by the algorithm and LB represents the best-known LB. Our experimentation revealed that the HHS algorithm alone could obtain optimal solutions for many instances in HUdata. Therefore, if an instance can be solved optimally using the HHS algorithm in the integrated HHS/LNS method, the LNS algorithm will not be run. Based on the results presented in Table 9.14, it is evident that the results presented in Table 9.14 demonstrate that our HHS/LNS algorithm outperforms all other algorithms on DPdata, BCdata, Hurink Edata, and Hurink Rdata instances. However, it is worth noting that the HHS/LNS algorithm is surpassed by the hGA and CDDS algorithms on BRdata, and by the TS and hGA algorithms on Hurink Vdata. Interestingly, the LNS algorithm alone exhibits favorable performance on BCdata and Hurink Edata, although it is still not as good as the HHS/LNS algorithm. This aligns with the findings of Pacino and Van Hentenryck [5], who reported that the expansive neighborhood search they put forward utilizes a random selection of relaxations and is highly effective on Hurink Edata. It appears that results suggest that the LNS algorithm is better suited for solving instances with reduced flexibility, such as those found in BCdata and Hurink Edata. However, it is worth noting that while the LNS algorithm performs well for instances with a lower degree of flexibility, its performance generally deteriorates while tackling larger-scale instances with a greater degree of flexibility. This is exemplified by the extremely poor results of the LNS algorithm on Hurink Vdata. Additionally, the results of the LNS algorithm affirm one of our primary motivations for conducting this study, namely, that the intensification ability of the LNS algorithm deteriorates significantly as the problem space increases.

9.6 Conclusion

This chapter outlines the development of two algorithm modules, referred to as HHS and LNS, for the FJSP to minimize the makespan. The HHS algorithm incorporates characteristics of evolutionary methods utilizing the memetic paradigm, whereas the LNS algorithm is a conventional constraint-based approach. Taking into account the advantages and limitations of these two algorithms, a combined exploration strategy, HHS/LNS, is established based on them. The HHS/LNS algorithm essentially comprises two stages. First, the HHS algorithm is executed, and then the LNS algorithm is employed to further enhance the solution derived from the HHS algorithm. To enhance the effectiveness of the LNS algorithm, a set of valuable elite solutions in the HM are employed to extract machine allocation information before entering the LNS module. This approach constrains the search space of the LNS algorithm to a more favorable region. The experimental findings indicate that the HHS/LNS algorithm proposed in this study performs comparably to cutting-edge algorithms for FJSPs of significant magnitude. Additionally, the study obtained new UBs for 12 out of 18 instances analyzed in DPdata. The remaining instances were within an average of 0.2% of the best-known solutions. Furthermore, the efficacy of the HHS/LNS is demonstrated by its performance on the remaining benchmarks.

We consider our integrated method to be more of a framework than a single algorithm. The solution procedures adopted in this study can be broadly classified into three steps: First, an evolutionary algorithm is executed on the problem until further improvements are difficult to achieve. Second, valuable information is extracted from the elite solutions derived from the evolutionary algorithm, and the problem space is reduced based on this information. Thirdly, a search technique with robust intensification capabilities is employed on the diminished problem to further refine the solution obtained via the evolutionary algorithm. We believe that the HHS/LNS algorithm is just one example of this framework, and other suitable alternatives can be used to replace HHS or LNS to develop new algorithms. The primary reason for utilizing the HHS in this chapter is its uncomplicated architecture and superior efficiency.

References

[1] Harvey WD. Nonsystematic backtracking search. Stanford University; 1995.
[2] Shaw P. Using constraint programming and local search methods to solve vehicle routing problems. Proceedings of the 4th principles and practice of constraint programming; 1998. p. 417–31.
[3] Cesta A, Oddi A, Smith SF. Iterative flattening: a scalable method for solving multi-capacity scheduling problems. Proceedings of the 17th association for the advancement of artificial intelligence/innovative applications of artificial intelligence; 2000. p. 742–7.
[4] Hmida AB, Haouari M, Huguet MJ, et al. Discrepancy search for the flexible job shop scheduling problem. Computers & Operations Research 2010;37(12):2192–201.
[5] Pacino D, Van Hentenryck P. Large neighborhood search and adaptive randomized decompositions for flexible jobshop scheduling. Proceedings of the 22nd international joint conference; 2011. Vol. 11, p. 1997–2002.
[6] Oddi A, Rasconi R, Cesta A, et al. Iterative flattening search for the flexible job shop scheduling problem. Proceedings of the 22nd international joint conference; 2011.
[7] Geem ZW, Kim JH, Loganathan GV. A new heuristic optimization algorithm: harmony search. Simulation 2001;76(2):60–8.
[8] Pan QK, Wang L, Gao L. A chaotic harmony search algorithm for the flow shop scheduling problem with limited buffers. Applied Soft Computing 2011;11(8):5270–80.
[9] Lee KS, Geem ZW. A new meta-heuristic algorithm for continuous engineering optimization: harmony search theory and practice. Computer Methods in Applied Mechanics and Engineering 2005;194(36–38):3902–33.

[10] Cheng R, Gen M, Tsujimura Y. A tutorial survey of job-shop scheduling problems using genetic algorithms—I. Representation. Computers & Industrial Engineering 1996;30(4):983—97.

[11] Wang L, Pan QK, Tasgetiren MF. Minimizing the total flow time in a flow shop with blocking by using hybrid harmony search algorithms. Expert Systems with Applications 2010;37(12):7929—36.

[12] Brandimarte P. Routing and scheduling in a flexible job shop by tabu search. Annals of Operations Research 1993;41(3):157—83.

[13] Tamaki H. A paralleled genetic algorithm based on a neighborthood model and its application to the jopshop scheduling. Parallel Problem Solving from Nature 1992;2:573—82.

[14] Carchrae T, Beck JC. Principles for the design of large neighborhood search. Journal of Mathematical Modelling and Algorithms 2009;8(3):245—70.

[15] Michel L, Hentenryck PV. A constraint-based architecture for local search. Proceedings of the 17th association for computing machinery special interest group on programming languages conference on object-oriented programming, systems, languages, and applications; 2002. p. 83—100.

[16] Comet Tutorial. ⟨https://public.tepper.cmu.edu/CPAIOR09/CPAIOR09_Tutorial.pdf⟩; 2010.

[17] Godard D, Laborie P, Nuijten W. Randomized large neighborhood search for cumulative scheduling. Proceedings of the 15th international conference on automated planning and scheduling; 2005. Vol. 5, p. 81—89.

[18] Dauzère-Pérès S, Paulli J. An integrated approach for modeling and solving the general multiprocessor job-shop scheduling problem using tabu search. Annals of Operations Research 1997;70(0):281—306.

[19] Barnes JW, Chambers JB. Flexible job shop scheduling by tabu search. Graduate program in operations and industrial engineering, The University of Texas at Austin, Technical Report Series, ORP96-09; 1996.

[20] Hurink J, Jurisch B, Thole M. Tabu search for the job-shop scheduling problem with multi-purpose machines. Operations-Research-Spektrum 1994;15:205—15.

[21] Mastrolilli M, Gambardella LM. Effective neighbourhood functions for the flexible job shop problem. Journal of Scheduling 2000;3(1):3—20.

[22] Pezzella F, Morganti G, Ciaschetti G. A genetic algorithm for the flexible job-shop scheduling problem. Computers & Operations Research 2008;35(10):3202—12.

[23] Gao J, Sun L, Gen M. A hybrid genetic and variable neighborhood descent algorithm for flexible job shop scheduling problems. Computers & Operations Research 2008;35(9):2892—907.

[24] Xing LN, Chen YW, Wang P, et al. A knowledge-based ant colony optimization for flexible job shop scheduling problems. Applied Soft Computing 2010;10(3):888—96.

[25] Bagheri A, Zandieh M, Mahdavi I, et al. An artificial immune algorithm for the flexible job-shop scheduling problem. Future Generation Computer Systems 2010;26(4):533—41.

[26] Wang L, Zhou G, Xu Y, et al. An effective artificial bee colony algorithm for the flexible job-shop scheduling problem. International Journal of Advanced Manufacturing Technology 2012;60(1—4):303—15.

[27] Beck JC, Feng TK, Watson JP. Combining constraint programming and local search for job-shop scheduling. INFORMS Journal on Computing 2011;23(1):1—14.

[28] Dongarra J. Performance of various computers using standard linear equations software. Association for Computing Machinery Special Interest Group on Computer Architecture Computer Architecture News 1992;20(3):22—44.

[29] Bozejko W, Uchronski M, Wodecki M. Parallel meta2heuristics for the flexible job shop problem. Proceedings of the 9th international conference on artificial intelligence and soft computing; 2010. No. 2, p. 395—402.

CHAPTER 10

Multiobjective flexible job shop scheduling using memetic algorithms

Contents

10.1 Introduction

Production scheduling is a critical area of focus, with the job shop scheduling problem (JSP) standing out as one of the most significant issues due to its complexity and practical relevance in real-world settings. The flexible job shop scheduling problem (FJSP) represents a generalization of the classical JSP. In the FJSP, a designated group of machines can handle each operation. as opposed to a single specified machine. In the FJSP, the challenge is not only to sequence the operations of each job but also to assign them to an appropriate machine. This added complexity makes the FJSP more

Intelligent Evolutionary Optimization
DOI: https://doi.org/10.1016/B978-0-443-27400-8.00010-1

challenging than the classical JSP. Research has shown that the FJSP is strongly NP-hard, even in cases where each job has a maximum of three operations and there are only two machines involved [1].

In the past few decades, there has been significant research on the single-objective FJSP (SO-FJSP), which typically involves minimizing the makespan, that is, the total time required to complete all jobs. This research has been documented extensively in the literature [2−9]. However, the research on the multiobjective flexible job shop scheduling problem (MO-FJSP) has been relatively limited. Nevertheless, multiple competing objectives often need to be concurrently optimized in many real-world scheduling problems. The MO-FJSP is a more realistic representation of production environments and deserves significant attention. In recent years, there has been a growing interest in the MO-FJSP, and numerous algorithms have been proposed to address it.

The priori approach in solving the MO-FJSP typically involves combining two or more objectives into a single measure using a linear weighting function. To illustrate, suppose there are n optimization criteria $f_1, f_2, \ldots, f_n$. A single-objective problem can be nsobtained by using $f = \sum_{i=1}^{n} w_i f_i$, subject to the constraints $0 \leq w_i \leq 1$ and $\sum_{i=1}^{n} w_i = 1$. However, this approach may not always accurately represent the trade-off relationship between objectives, and determining the weight coefficients w_i for each objective can be challenging. As a result, producers may need to run the priori approach multiple times to obtain a satisfactory solution. Earlier studies on the MO-FJSP focused primarily on the priori approach, as documented in the existing literature.

The posteriori approach is generally considered more desirable than the priori approach for addressing the MO-FJSP. In the posteriori approach, The Pareto dominance relation is employed to compare solutions. A solution x is dominant over a solution y if x is at least as good as y for all objectives and is strictly better than y for at least one objective. A solution is considered Pareto-optimal if no other solution dominates means that it is the best possible solution with respect to the given set of objectives. Unlike the priori approach. The former approach attempts to discover a singular optimal solution by aggregating objectives, whereas the posteriori approach seeks to identify the set of Pareto-optimal solutions. This approach does not require prior information and can demonstrate the distribution of solutions obtained from a single run enables the trade-off between objectives. This feature is particularly useful for producers who can evaluate these solutions and make informed decisions based on their preferences.

As previously mentioned, recent research on the MO-FJSP has shifted towards the posteriori approach, but there is still potential for further investigation. In this chapter, we propose novel memetic algorithms (MAs) that combine NSGA-II-based genetic search with local search, using the posteriori approach to address the MO-FJSP to minimize the makespan, total workload, and critical workload. Our contributions in this study are twofold: first, we introduce new state-of-the-art algorithms for solving the MO-FJSP, and second, we conduct comprehensive experimental analyses to demonstrate the effectiveness of our approach.

In algorithmic design, the novelty can be summarized as follows: A problem-specific local search operator that emphasizes the exploitation of the problem space and is based on critical operations is introduced for the MO-FJSP. A hierarchical strategy is employed in this local search to address the three objectives, with the highest priority given to minimizing makespan. the incorporation of the remaining two objectives is manifested in the sequence of attempting all feasible actions that can produce a satisfactory neighbor. Second, a genetic search centered on the exploration of the problem space is formulated for the MO-FJSP using a recently modified NSGA-II. This is accomplished through the development of expertly tailored chromosome encoding, decoding, and genetic operators. Thirdly, we incorporate a mechanism similar to the one proposed in [10] to pick members of the population chosen for proximal inquiry, which could promote maintaining a proportionate blend of immediate and evolutionary investigations in our MAs. As far as we are aware, this mechanism is introduced in the research on MO-FJSP.

Regarding the experimental analysis, the unique aspects are as follows. First, we conduct experiments to evaluate the impact of critical components in our MAs, including local search, on overall performance. This differs from previous works, where only the effectiveness of MAs is demonstrated without disclosing the contribution of each component to the overall performance. Second, the conventional technique of presenting algorithm performance in the literature on the MO-FJSP involves enumerating nondominated solutions obtained over a specific number of algorithms run. However, relying solely on this approach can make it difficult to assess the algorithm's precise performance, which is the evaluation process weighted towards qualitative measures rather than quantitative measures, making it crucial to include state-of-the-art quantitative indicators in multiobjective optimization to ensure a more impartial and robust evaluation. This practice is not uncommon in current research on various MO-COPs [10–13]. However, it is still relatively rare in the context of MO-FJSP.

10.2 Background

10.2.1 Formulation of the multiobjective flexible job shop scheduling problem

The formulation of MO-FJSP can be presented as follows: The problem involves a collection of n independent jobs $\mathcal{J} = \{J_1, J_2, \ldots, J_n\}$ and a set of m machines $\mathcal{M} = \{M_1, M_2, \ldots, M_m\}$. Each job J_i is composed of a sequence of n_i precedence-constrained operations $\{O_{i,1}, O_{i,2}, \ldots, O_{i,n_i}\}$ that must be executed consecutively, in a given order. Each operation $O_{i,j}$, representing the j th operation of job J_i, must be carried out on one machine chosen from a specified subset $\mathcal{M}_{i,j} \subseteq \mathcal{M}$. The duration of each operation is dependent on the selected machine, and $p_{i,j,k}$ represents the processing time of $O_{i,j}$ on machine M_k. The problem is divided into two subproblems: the machine assignment subproblem that assigns each operation to the appropriate machine and the operation sequencing subproblem that determines the sequence of operations on all machines. In this chapter, we aim to minimize three objectives: makespan, total workload, and critical workload. These objectives are defined as follows: Let C_i denote the completion time of job J_i, and let W_k be the sum of processing times of operations that are executed on machine M_k.

$$C_{\max} = \max\{C_i | i = 1, 2, \ldots, n\} \tag{10.1}$$

$$W_T = \sum_{k=1}^{m} W_k \tag{10.2}$$

$$W_{\max} = \max\{W_k | k = 1, 2, \ldots, m\} \tag{10.3}$$

This study is based on several assumptions, including the availability of all machines at time 0, the release of all jobs at time 0, the processing of only one operation at a time per machine, the completion of each operation without interruption once started, the predetermined order of operations for each job with no possibility of modification, and negligible machine setup and operation transfer times.

10.2.2 Disjunctive graph model

Originally designed to model JSP schedules, the disjunctive graph [14] can be readily adapted to describe FJSP schedules due to the FJSP's status as a JSP extension. We represent the disjunctive graph as $G = \{V, C \bigcup D\}$, Consider a set of nodes represented by V, where each node (excluding the start and end nodes) corresponds to an operation. C is a set of concatenated arcs that indicate precedence constraints within the same job, while D is a set of separate arcs that illustrate the precedence of operations executed on the same machine. In the disjunctive graph, each node representing an operation is assigned a label indicating the machine on which it is executed, and its corresponding processing time is labeled below and treated as the node's weight. The start and end nodes are assigned a weight of zero. In the event that the disjointed graph is without cycles, it represents a valid FJSP schedule. The critical path, which is the longest path from the start node to the end node, indicates the makespan, with the path length representing the makespan of the schedule. Any operation on the *critical path* is considered critical. We will use the terms operations and nodes, as well as schedules and disjunctive graphs interchangeably in the subsequent statements.

A feasible schedule, depicted in Fig. 10.1, can be represented using the disjunctive graph. In the disjunctive graph, two critical paths are present: $S \rightarrow O_{2,1} \rightarrow O_{2,2} \rightarrow O_{2,3} \rightarrow E$ and $S \rightarrow O_{3,1} \rightarrow O_{2,3} \rightarrow E$, both with a length of 5. Therefore the total time taken for executing this schedule is 5. Operations $O_{2,1}$, $O_{2,2}$, $O_{2,3}$, and $O_{3,1}$ are all important operations.

To facilitate algorithmic descriptions, we introduce certain Notations formulated from the disjointed graph G. Let $\mu(G, v)$ denote the ID of the selected machine for a generic node v in G. $ES(G, v)$ represents the earliest starting time of v, while $LS(G, v, T)$.

Indicates the latest viable initiation time that does not protract the required makespan T. Correspondingly, the earliest and latest completion times are labeled as $EC(G, v) = EC(G, v) + p_{v,u(G,v)}$ and $LC(G, v, T) = LS(G, v, T) + p_{v,u(G,v)}$, respectively, where $p_{v,u(G,v)}$ stands for the processing time of node v on machine $\mu(G, v)$. $PM(G, v)$ denotes the operation processed on the same machine immediately prior to v, while $SM(G, v)$ denotes the one immediately succeeding v. Let $PJ(v)$ be the operation immediately preceding v in the same job, and $SJ(v)$ be the one immediately succeeding $vnc(G)$ is the number of critical operations in G, and $\chi(G) = \{co_1, co_2, \ldots, co_{nc(G)}\}$ denote the collection of important operations.

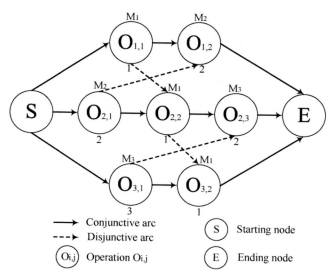

Figure 10.1 Illustration of the disjunctive graph.

An operation is classified as critical if and only if its earliest starting time $ES(G, v)$ is equal to its latest starting time $LS(G, v, C_{max}(G))$. Additionally, due to the fact that only active schedules [15] are taken into account in this study, the earliest starting time of an operation in G is considered to be its actual starting time. As an example, consider the disjunctive graph depicted in Fig. 10.1: operation $O_{2,2}$ is critical, with $ES(G, O_{2,2}) = LS(G, O_{2,2}, 5) = 2$. Operation $O_{1,2}$ is not critical, with $ES(G, O_{1,2}) = 2$ and $LS(G, O_{1,2}, 5) = 3$. Given a required makespan of $T = 6$, $LS(G, O_{1,2}, 6)$ is equivalent to 4.

10.2.3 Brief Introduction to nondominated sorting genetic algorithm II

The nondominated sorting genetic algorithm II (NSGA-II) [16] is a multiobjective evolutionary algorithm that operates at the population level. The fundamental steps of NSGA-II can be summarized as follows.

Assume that we are considering the t-th generation of NSGA-II, without any loss of generality. At this point, the parent population is denoted by P_t, while the child population is named Q_t, generated with the help of P_t and genetic operators. The size of both populations is N. Afterwards, P_t and Q_t are merged to form a new population $R_t = P_t \bigcup Q_t$, with a size of $2N$. To select the best N individuals from R_t for the next generation, a process known as nondominated sorting is first employed, which divides R_t into various nondomination tiers (F_1, F_2, etc.). After the nondominated sorting process divides the population R_t into various nondomination levels, the new population P_{t+1} is populated by selecting individuals from different nondomination levels, one level at a time. The population-filling process commences with the top nondomination level F_1 and progresses to the subsequent levels (F_2 and so on). Since R_t has a size of $2N$, it may not be possible to include all levels in P_{t+1}, and some may be disregarded. Additionally, in many cases, it may not be feasible to incorporate all solutions from the last accepted level. Instead of randomly discarding some members from the last level, none but the solutions that maximize the differentiation of selected solutions are chosen. NSGA-II accomplishes this by using a niche strategy, which calculates the distance between each member of the final level is calculated by adding the objective-based distances between its two nearest neighbors. Solutions with greater distance values are subsequently chosen. For a more indepth discussion of NSGA-II, please refer to [16].

10.2.4 Memetic algorithms for multiobjective combinatorial optimization

MAs are a class of algorithms that combine evolutionary algorithms with local search techniques. They have been demonstrated to possess excellent search capabilities for single-objective combinatorial optimization problems (SO-COPs). Several concerns regarding the design of these high-performing MAs for SO-COPs have also been investigated [17–19]. However, developing high-performing MAs for multiobjective combinatorial optimization problems (MO-COPs) presents an even greater challenge and has not been extensively explored.

When dealing with MAs for MO-COPs, a unique challenge arises when comparing solutions during local search. Typically, two approaches are employed to tackle this problem: one involves using a scalarizing function, while the other utilizes Pareto ranking. Research published in [20] has indicated that the scalarizing function approach yields better outcomes than the Pareto ranking approach. The weighted sum of objectives is the most commonly used scalarizing function, initially employed in the well-known multiobjective genetic local search (MOGLS) [21]. Recently, Sindhya et al. [22] conducted an extensive literature review on MAs for multiobjective optimization that utilized various scalarizing functions. In practical applications, numerous other factors can impact the efficacy of MAs for MO-COPs. Several such issues are outlined below:

1. How often should local search be applied?
2. To which solutions should local search be applied?
3. How long should local search be run?
4. Which local search procedure is to be used?

If the aforementioned issues are properly addressed, the designed MA will likely maintain a suitable balance between exploration (population-based) and exploitation (local improvement) throughout the search process, leading to superior performance. In the literature, several studies have addressed these issues. For instance, Ishibuchi et al. [10] investigated how to strike an optimal balance between genetic search and local search in MAs for the multiobjective permutation flow shop scheduling problem (MO-PFSP). Their experimental findings demonstrated the significance of this balance. In situations where the balance is not appropriately specified, the performance of multiobjective evolutionary algorithms is typically severely compromised when combined with local search. Additionally, Ishibuchi et al. [23] explored the influence of the local search probability specification The impact of local search probability specification on the efficacy of MAs for the MO-PFSP and multiobjective 0/1 knapsack problem was examined by Ishibuchi et al. [23].

In [24], the authors hypothesized a setting where every objective has its own highly effective heuristic local search algorithm. They proposed the notion of utilizing the heuristic local search methods for optimizing single objectives in MOGLS. The outcomes on the multiobjective 0/1 knapsack problem demonstrated that this approach improved the performance of MOGLS. Garrett and Dasgupta [25] undertook an empirical analysis of four MA methodologies for the multiobjective quadratic assignment problem. The four strategies can be roughly described as follows: "brief local search efforts on all individuals," "extended local search runs on all individuals," "short bursts of local search on randomly chosen individuals," and "extended local search runs on randomly chosen individuals."

10.3 Overview of the proposed memetic algorithms

The proposed MAs framework is based on the original NSGA-II [16], which is presented in Algorithm 10.1. To begin, an initial population of N chromosomes, where N represents the population size. Then, Steps 4–18 are repeated until the stopping criterion is met. At every iteration t, binary tournament selection, and genetic operators (crossover and mutation) are utilized to generate the offspring population Q_t. Next, the local search algorithm is employed on Q_t to generate the enhanced population Q'_t. In Step 6, the populations P_t, Q_t, and Q'_t are merged to form the population R_t. In Step 7, duplicates with the same objective values in R_t are eliminated through mutation. The superior N individuals are chosen from R_t using fast nondominated sorting and crowding distance to form the next population P_{t+1}.

Algorithm 10.1: Framework of the proposed MAs.

---

1. $P_0 \leftarrow$ Initialize Population ()
2. $t \leftarrow 0$
3. **while** the termination criterion is not met **do**
4. $\qquad Q_t \leftarrow$ Make Of springPopulation (P_t)
5. $\qquad Q'_t \leftarrow$ Local Search (Q_t)
6. $\qquad R_t \leftarrow P_t \cup Q_t \cup Q'_t$
7. $\qquad R_t \leftarrow$ Eliminate Duplicates (R_t)
8. $\qquad \{F_1, F_2, ...\} \leftarrow$ Fast NonDominatedSort (R_t)
9. $\qquad P_{t+1} \leftarrow \varnothing$
10. $i \leftarrow 1$
11. **while** $|P_{t+1}| + |F_i| < N$ **do**
12. $\qquad$ Crowding Distance Assignment (F_i)
13. $\qquad P_{t+1} \leftarrow P_{t+1} \cup F_i$
14. $\qquad i \leftarrow i + 1$
15. **end while**
16. Sort (F_i)
17. $P_{t+1} \leftarrow P_{t+1} \cup F_i[1:(N - |P_{t+1}|)]$
18. $t \leftarrow t + 1$
19. end while

Algorithm 10.1 indicates that the successful deployment of the proposed MAs revolves around two critical procedures. The first procedure deals with the creation of the offspring population through genetic search, which aligns with Step 4 outlined in Algorithm 10.1. The second procedure pertains to generating an improved population by applying local search to the offspring population, which corresponds to Step 5 in Algorithm 10.1.

10.4 Exploration using genetic search

This section will delve into the specifics of the genetic search implementation in the proposed MAs, covering critical aspects such as gene representation, gene interpretation, and genetic manipulation.

10.4.1 Chromosome encoding

The FJSP solution entails the allocation of operations to machines and the scheduling of these operations' performance on the machines. Consequently, the proposed MAs employ chromosomes that are composed of two vectors: the machine assignment vector and the operation sequence vector, which correspond precisely to the two subproblems inherent in the FJSP.

To begin, we assign a specific ID to each operation in sequence, in the form of j, where $j = 1, 2, ..., d$, with $d = \sum_{i=1}^{n} n_i$. This implies that operations 1 through n_1 belong to job J_1, $n_1 + 1$ through $n_1 + n_2$ belong to J_2, and so forth. Once numbered, it is possible to refer to a particular operation by its fixed ID.

The proposed MAs utilize two distinct vectors, with the first vector being the machine assignment vector, denoted as $\mathbf{u} = [u_1, u_2, ..., u_d]$. This vector is an array containing d integer values, where $1 \leq u_j \leq l_j$, and l_j represents the dimension of the backup machine set for operation j. We sort the available machines for operation j in the order of nondecreasing execution time. If equivalent processing times are necessary, priority is assigned to the machine with a smaller identification code. The integer value u_j indicates that operation j selects the u_j th machine in its sorted list of available machines.

The second vector used in the proposed MAs is the operation sequence vector, denoted as $\mathbf{v} = [v_1, v_2, ..., v_d]$. This vector represents a rearrangement of IDs for all the operations, in which the occurrence sequence of each operation in v denotes its prioritization in scheduling. A operation sequence vector is $\mathbf{v} = [6, 1, 7, 3, 4, 2, 5]$. This vector can be converted directly into a list of well-ordered operations that are distinct: $O_{3.1} \succ O_{1.1} \succ O_{3.2} \succ O_{2.1} \succ O_{2.2} \succ O_{1.2} \succ O_{2.3}$. In this case, the operation $O_{3.1}$ is granted the highest ranking and scheduled as the initial one, followed by the operation

$O_{1,1}$, and so on. It is important to note that not every ID permutation is feasible for the operation sequence vector, as the relative priority order of operations within a job must be maintained in $\mathbf{v}$.

10.4.2 Chromosome decoding

The process of decoding the chromosome involves assigning a specific period to each operation on its assigned machine, according to their order in the operation sequence vector (v). When processing an operation, its assigned machine is retrieved from $\mathbf{u}$. Next, the idle time intervals between previously scheduled operations on that machine are explored from left to right until an open time gap is identified. Let $s_{i,j}$ denote the starting time of a generic operation $O_{i,j}$ in the schedule, and $c_{i,j}$ represent its completion time. As an operation can only commence once its immediate predecessor operation within the same job has been completed, the idle time interval $[S_x, E_x]$ can be allocated to $O_{i,j}$ on machine M_k, provided that

$$\begin{cases} \max\{S_x, c_{i,j-1}\} + p_{i,j,k} \leq E_x, & \text{if } j \geq 2 \\ S_x + p_{i,j,k} \leq E_x, & \text{if } j = 1 \end{cases} \tag{10.4}$$

When allocating $O_{i,j}$ within the available interval $[S_x, E_x]$, the starting time is determined as $\max\{S_x, c_{i,j-1}\}$ for ($j \geq 2$) or S_x for ($j = 1$). If no available interval exists for $O_{i,j}$ on machine M_k, it is scheduled at the end of M_k. This decoding method guarantees that the generated schedule is active [26]. For example, after decoding the chromosome with the values $\mathbf{u} = [1, 1, 1, 1, 1, 2, 1]$ and $\mathbf{v} = [6, 1, 7, 3, 4, 2, 5]$, an active schedule can be generated. This schedule can be visualized using a Gantt chart, which is depicted in Fig. 10.2.

When using this decoding method, each operation is permitted to search for the earliest available idle time interval on its assigned machine during scheduling. Consequently, in cases where two operations, v_i and v_j, are assigned to the same machine, v_i may be scheduled earlier than v_j in the decoded schedule, even though v_j

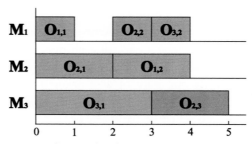

Figure 10.2 Gantt chart corresponding to the chromosome.

is listed before v_i in the operation sequence vector (**v**). To ensure proper inheritance of the operation sequence information, the operations in **v** are sorted according to their start times in the corresponding interpreted schedule before utilizing genetic operators to the chromosome.

10.4.3 Genetic operators

Our MAs employ genetic operators, which include both crossover and mutation, to generate offspring chromosomes. Crossover involves combining genetic information from a pair of chromosomes, while mutation involves altering the genetic information of a single chromosome.

The chromosome crossover process involves two distinct operators for the vectors **u** and **v**. For **u**, a random subset of positions is selected and the values at these positions are exchanged between the parents to generate the corresponding children. For **v**, a modified order crossover technique is used [27], which involves selecting two random points and copying the operations between them from the first parent to the first child. The remaining operations are then added to the child in the same order of priority as they appear in the second parent. However, these operations may not be feasible due to job constraints, so a repair procedure described in Algorithm 10.2 is applied to adjust the operation order within each job. The crossover process is illustrated for the problem in Table 10.1 in Fig. 10.3, and the same process is repeated for the second parent and its child.

Algorithm 10.2: RepairOperationSequence (**v**).

---

1. $[q_1, q_2, ..., q_n] \leftarrow [0, 0, ..., 0]$
2. **for** $i = 1$ to d **do**
3.   Get the job J_k that the operation v_i belongs to
4. $q_k \leftarrow q_k + 1$
5.   Get the fixed ID op for the operation O_{k,q_k}
6. $v_i \leftarrow$ op
7. **end for**

In addition to crossover, our genetic algorithm framework also incorporates mutation operators for both the u and v vectors. The mutation process has two parts. For the **u** vector, a single operation is randomly selected, and its machine assignment is changed to another available machine. For the **v** vector, a random operation and position are selected, and the operation is inserted into the chosen position **v** without violating the priority order among operations within the same job.

Table 10.1 Variants of the implemented algorithms.

Variant	Global search	Local search	
		Acceptance rule	Hierarchical strategy
MA-1	Genetic	Best	Yes
MA-2	Genetic	Pareto	Yes
MA-1-NH	Genetic	Best	No
MA-2-NH	Genetic	Pareto	No
MRLS-1	Random	Best	Yes
MRLS-2	Random	Pareto	Yes
NSGA-II	Genetic	—	—

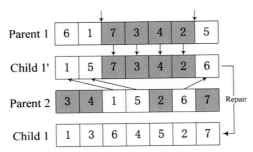

Figure 10.3 Illustration of the crossover for the v.

10.5 Exploitation using local search

In this part, we will provide a comprehensive explanation of our approach to performing a local search on the offspring population. The local search procedure can be divided into two main parts. The first part involves selecting individuals selected from the descendant population that will undergo local search. The second part involves refining the selected chromosomes using local search techniques to generate several improved solutions that will be integrated into the advanced population.

10.5.1 Selection of individuals for local search

Our genetic algorithm framework incorporates a selection mechanism that is similar to the approach presented in [10]. The selection process involves the use of an aggregation function, which is defined as follows:

$$f(\mathbf{x}, \boldsymbol{\lambda}) = \lambda_1 f_1(\mathbf{x}) + \lambda_2 f_2(\mathbf{x}) + \lambda_3 f_3(\mathbf{x}) \tag{10.5}$$

The aggregation function used in our genetic algorithm framework incorporates a weight vector, $\boldsymbol{\lambda} = [\lambda_1, \lambda_2, \lambda_3]$, and three objectives, $f_1(\mathbf{x})$, $f_2(\mathbf{x})$, and $f_3(\mathbf{x})$, which correspond to the triplet of objectives in MO-FJSP that are defined in Eqs. (10.1)–(10.3), respectively. The weight vector is used to balance the importance of each objective and to produce a single fitness value for each chromosome.

$$\lambda_1 + \lambda_2 + \lambda_3 = z, \lambda_i \in \{0, 1, ..., z\}, i = 1, 2, 3 \tag{10.6}$$

To ensure a thorough exploration of the Pareto front (PF), we generate a set of weight vectors using the formula C_{z+2}^2, where z is set to 23 in this chapter to produce 300 vectors for the three-objective problem. When opting for an individual for local refinement, a weight vector is randomly selected from an array of weight vectors. The existing population is evaluated using tournament selection with replacement based on Eq. (10.5) and the current weight vector. Finally, local search is employed on the selected individual to generate a set of improved solutions, E_i, which contains a certain number of solutions that have been refined through the local search process.

An additional inquiry pertains to the optimal frequency of implementing local search. To address this, we propose a probability parameter, P_{ls}, that governs the selection of individuals for local search. Specifically, $\lfloor N \times P_{ls} \rfloor$ individuals are chosen for local search, and this selection process is repeated $\lfloor N \times P_{ls} \rfloor$ times. The complete set of steps involved in this process is presented in Algorithm 10.3.

Algorithm 10.3: LocalSearch (Q_t).

---

1. $Q_t' \leftarrow \varnothing$
2. **for** $i = 1$ to $\lfloor N \times P_{ls} \rfloor$ **do**
3.   Randomly draw a weight vector λ from the weight vector set
4. $\{u, v\} \leftarrow$ Tournament Selection with Replacement (Q_t, λ)
5. $E_i \leftarrow$ LocalSearch For Individual ($\{u, v\}, \lambda$)
6. $Q_t' \leftarrow Q_t' \cup E_i$
7. **end for**
8. **return** Q_t'

10.5.2 Local search application to a chromosome

There is one more important issue that needs to be addressed in our genetic algorithm framework. Specifically, we need to determine the local search operator that will be applied to the selected chromosomes in Step 5 of Algorithm 10.3. In our approach, we do not apply local search directly to the chromosome itself. Instead, we apply local search to the decoded schedule of the chromosome, which allows us to incorporate problem-specific knowledge into the search process.

10.5.2.1 Neighbor generation in local search

Our local search approach involves generating neighboring solutions of a given schedule, G, by moving an operation. Given that the objective of minimizing makespan is relatively difficult, we only accept a neighbor, G', of G if its C_{max} value is less than or equal to that of G. To ensure that the move is beneficial, we propose the following theorem to ensure that the moves made during the local search process are beneficial and contribute to the overall optimization of the FJSP.

Theorem 1:

If we move an operation, $O_{i,j} \notin X(G)$, that is not already in the current schedule, G, to generate a new schedule, G', then we can state the following theorem: $C_{max}(G) \leq C_{max}(G')$.

Proof:

Suppose that there exists a critical path P in a graph G, which can be represented as a sequence of operations $S \to co_1 \to \ldots \to co_l \to E$. Since the operation $O_{i,j}$ is not included in the set of predecessors of the graph G, it is not part of the critical path P. There are three possible scenarios for moving the operation $O_{i,j}$:

1. relocated to a point between two operations on the same apparatus;
2. transferred to a place before all the operations on the machine in question; and
3. shifted to a spot after all the operations on the identical machine.

Assuming that $O_{i,j}$ is moved to a location between operations o_x and o_y on the same apparatus, if there exists no index $k \in \{1, 2, \ldots, l-1\}$ such that $co_k = o_x$ and $co_{k+1} = o_y$, then the critical path P would remain the same in the modified graph G'. Thus, $C_{max}(G) \leq C_{max}(G')$. However, if such an index k exists, then the modified graph G' would contain a new critical path $S \to co_1 \to \ldots co_k \to O_{i,j} \to co_{k+1} \ldots \to co_l \to E$, and the maximum completion time $C_{max}(G)$ would be less than that of $C_{max}(G')$.

According to Theorem 1, the makespan of a schedule can only be reduced by relocating critical operations. Therefore, our local search algorithm focuses exclusively on relocating critical operations to improve the schedule's performance.

To improve the schedule and obtain a feasible neighbor schedule G' with a shorter makespan than the original schedule G and $C_{max}(G') < C_{max}(G)$, we need to relocate a critical operation co_i in G. To do this, we first remove co_i from G and create a new graph G_i^- by deleting the disjunctive arcs connected to co_i. We then add a new disjunctive arc between the predecessor machine $PM(G, co_i)$ and the successor machine $SM(G, co_i)$ to maintain the graph's correctness. Additionally, we attribute a weight of 0 to node co_i. Next, co_i is inserted into another feasible position in G_i^-. If such a position is located before operation v on machine M_k, co_i should be started as early as $EC(G_i^-, PM(G_i^-, v))$, and can completed as late as $LS(G_i^-, v, C_{max}(G))$ without $C_{max}(G)$. Additionally, the fresh operation co_i must adhere to the precedence constraints within the same task. Therefore, for co_i to be inserted into a position before operation v, the following inequality must be satisfied to ensure that the position is available:

$$\max\{EC(G_i^-, PM(G_i^-, v)), EC(G_i^-, PJ(co_i))\} + p_{co_i,k} \leq \min\{LS(G_i^-, v, C_{max}(G)), LS(G_i^-, SJ(co_i), C_{max}(G))\} \quad (10.7)$$

The inequality used in our local search algorithm is actually "$<$" instead of "$\leq$" as stated in Eq. (10.7), and this is justified by the following theorem.

Theorem 2:
To obtain the neighbor schedule G', we insert the critical operation co_i into a feasible position before operation v on machine M_k in G_i^- using the inequality Eq. (10.7) with strict inequality (i.e., "$<$") rather than equality (i.e., "$\leq$"). If the makespan of G' is equal to the makespan of the original schedule G (i.e., $C_{max}(G') = C_{max}(G)$), then we can conclude that co_i is not the vital operation in G'.

Proof:
First, according to the definition, we have

$$ES\left(G', co_i\right) = \max\left\{EC\left(G', PM\left(G_i^-, v\right)\right), EC(G', PJ(co_i))\right\} \quad (10.8)$$

$$LS(G', co_i, C_{max}(G')) = \min\{LS(G', v, C_{max}(G')), LS(G', SJ(co_i), C_{max}(G'))\} - p_{co_i,k} \quad (10.9)$$

Inserting the critical operation co_i into a feasible position in G_i^- would not affect the earliest completion time of the predecessor machine $PM\left(G_i^-, v\right)$ and the earliest completion time of the other operations in the same job as co_i (i.e., $PJ(co_i)$). Similarly, it would not affect the latest start time of operation v and the latest start time of the other operations in the same job as co_i (i.e., $SJ(co_i)$). All of these constraints must be satisfied without delaying the maximum completion time $C_{max}(G)$ of the schedule, so we can write:

$$EC(G', PM(G_i^-, v)) = EC(G_i^-, PM(G_i^-, v)) \quad (10.10)$$

$$EC(G', PJ(co_i)) = EC(G_i^-, PJ(co_i)) \quad (10.11)$$

$$LS(G', v, C_{max}(G)) = LS(G_i^-, v, C_{max}(G)) \quad (10.12)$$

$$LS(G', SJ(co_i), C_{max}(G)) = LS(G_i^-, SJ(co_i), C_{max}(G)) \quad (10.13)$$

Since $C_{\max}(G') = C_{\max}(G)$, we have

$$ES(G', co_i) \neq LS(G', co_i, C_{\max}(G')) \tag{10.14}$$

based on Eqs. (10.8)–(10.13). Therefore, co_i is not the critical operation in G'.

Based on Theorem 2, if the makespan of the modified graph G' is the same as the original graph G, then the operation co_i cannot be the critical operation in G'. This ensures that co_i will not be selected for movement in the next local iteration from G' back to G. This approach can help minimize cyclic searches.

Although inserting the critical operation co_i before v using inequality Eq. (10.7) ensures that the resulting neighbor schedule G' does not increase the makespan of the original schedule G, it does not guarantee that G' will be acyclic. Therefore, we restrict the locations to be explored on machine M_k to only possible ones. in order to ensure the resulting schedule is acyclic. We denote the set of operations processed by machine M_k in G_i^- and ordered according to their earliest start times (excluding the critical operation co_i) as Θ_k. We define two subsequences of Θ_k, denoted as Φ_k and Ψ_k, as follows:

$$\Phi_k = \{r \in \Theta_k | ES(G, r) + p_{r,k} > ES(G_i^-, co_i)\} \tag{10.15}$$

$$\Psi_k = \{r \in \Theta_k | LS(G, r, C_{\max}(G)) < LS(G_i^-, co_i, C_{\max}(G))\} \tag{10.16}$$

Let Υ_k be the set of positions that are located before all the operations in $\Psi_k \backslash \Phi_k$ and after all the operations in $\Psi_k \backslash \Phi_k$ on machine M_k. Therefore, we can conclude the following theorem:

Theorem 3:

When inserting the critical operation co_i into a position $\gamma \in \Upsilon_k$ in G_i^-, the resulting neighbor schedule G' is always feasible. Moreover, there exists a specific position in the set Υ_k on machine M_k where inserting co_i yields the optimal makespan and no other position on the same machine would result in a better makespan.

The proof of this theorem can be found in reference [3]. Based on Theorem 3, we can derive the following corollary:

Corollary 1:

If a feasible neighbor schedule G' can be obtained by inserting the critical operation co_i into a position on machine M_k in G_i^- such that $C_{\max}(G') \leq C_{\max}(G)$, then there always exists a feasible schedule that can be obtained by embedding co_i into a place in the set Υ_k on machine M_k.

According to Corollary 1, when moving an assignment on machine M_k for the critical operation co_i in G_i^-, only the positions in Y_k need to be checked. Once a feasible position satisfying inequality Eq. (10.7) is found, co_i is inserted immediately into that position, and the resulting neighbor schedule G' is used to swap out the current program G. It is computationally expensive to check all positions for all critical operations, so we adopt a first-move strategy in our local search, where the first acceptable neighbor is accepted. We denote the action of finding a position on machine M_k for the critical operation co_i to be inserted into in G_i^- as $co_i \rightsquigarrow M_k$. Algorithm 10.4 summarizes the action $co_i \rightsquigarrow M_k$.

Algorithm 10.4: Insert operation on machine (G_i^-, co_i, k).

1. Get the set of positions Y_k on machine M_k
2. **for** each position γ in Y_k **do**
3.   **if** γ satisfies Eq. (10.7) **then**
4.   Insert co_i into γ in G_i^-
5.   **return true**
6.   **end if**
7. **end for**
8. **return false**

We define $\varphi(G)$ as the set of all possible actions $co_i \rightsquigarrow M_k$, where $i = 1, 2, ..., nc$ and $M_k \in \mathcal{M}_{co_i}$. This set consists of $\sum_{i=1}^{nc} l_{co_i}$ actions described in Algorithm 10.4 that can be used to construct an appropriate neighboring candidate G' of G. The order in which we try these actions reflects our concern for the entire operation load and significant operation load in our local refinement. For each action $co_i \rightsquigarrow M_k$ in $\varphi(G)$, we define two metrics as follows:

$$\Delta_t(co_i \rightsquigarrow M_k) = p_{co_i,k} - p_{co_i,\mu(co_i,G)} \tag{10.17}$$

$$\Delta_c(co_i \rightsquigarrow M_k) = W_k(G) + p_{co_i,k} \tag{10.18}$$

The metrics Δ_t and Δ_c take into account the total workload and critical workload objectives, respectively. These metrics are used to sort the actions in $\varphi(G)$ in Increasing order of Δ_t with no reduction. If two actions have the same Δ_t value, the one with a lower Δ_c value is given precedence. During one cycle of the local optimization, the actions are examined in sequence according to the sorted order until a desirable neighboring solution of G is discovered. Algorithm 10.5 illustrates this procedure.

Algorithm 10.5: Get neighbor schedule (**G**).

1. Get the set $\chi(G) = \{\omega_1, \omega_2, ..., \omega_{nc}\}$
2. $[G_1^-, G_2^-, ..., G_{nc}^-] \leftarrow [\varnothing, \varnothing, ..., \varnothing]$
3. Sort $\varphi(G)$ according to Δ_t and Δ_c
4.   **for** each action $\omega_i \rightsquigarrow M_k$ in the sorted $\varphi(G)$ **do**
5.   **if** $G_i^- = \varnothing$ **then**
6.   Clone a copy of G to G^{**}
7.   Delete ω_i from G^{**}
8. $G_i^- \leftarrow G^*$
9.   **end if**
10.   **if** Insert Operation on Machine (G_i^-, ω_i, k) **then**
11. $G' \leftarrow G_i^-$
12.   **return** G'
13.   **end if**
14. **end for**
15. **return** $\varnothing$

Our local search strategy employs a hierarchical approach to address the three objectives. This approach can be summarized as follows: to begin with, we create the neighborhood structure to maintain a nonincreasing makespan throughout a local search. Within this boundary, the neighbor with the lowest complete job burden is identified as the new schedule in every local iteration. If multiple neighbors have the same smallest total workload, the critical workload is considered to determine the optimal neighbor.

10.5.2.2 Acceptance rules in local search

We can transform the local search procedure into a chromosome, which is essentially an iterative application of Algorithm 10.5. The question now is which solutions generated during the local search should be accepted and added to the improved population. In our local search, we explore two different acceptance rules: "Best" and "Pareto." In this chapter, we refer to these rules as the "Best" and "Pareto" acceptance rules, respectively. In the process of local search, the acceptance criterion known as "Best" involves selecting the schedule with the minimum $f(G, \lambda)$ value as the optimized solution. Algorithm 10.6 summarizes the local search operator applied to a chromosome using the "Best" acceptance rule, where the parameter $iter_{max}$ denotes the maximum number of local search iterations. As previously mentioned, the recommended local refinement is not directly employed on a DNA strand. but rather to the decoded schedule generated from the chromosome. Therefore, the decoding technique has to be executed in Step 2 before the commencement of the local searches. Once the local iterations are completed, the accepted schedule must be encoded in Step 14 and returned as a genetic code configuration. Regarding the "Pareto"

Algorithm 10.6: Local search for individual ({**u**, **v**}, λ).

1. $i \leftarrow 0$
2. $G \leftarrow$ Chromo some Decoding (**u**, **v**)
3. $G_{best} \leftarrow G$
4. $flag \leftarrow 0$
5. **while** $G \neq \emptyset$ and $i < iter_{max}$ **do**
6. $G \leftarrow$ Get Neighbo rSchedule (G)
7.   **if** $G \neq \emptyset$ and $f(G, \lambda) < f(G_{best}, \lambda)$ **then**
8. $G_{best} \leftarrow G$
9. $flag \leftarrow 1$
10.   **end if**
11. $i \leftarrow i + 1$
12. **end while**
13. **if** $flag = 1$ **then**
14. $\{\mathbf{u}', \mathbf{v}'\} \leftarrow$ Chromo some Encoding (G_{best})
15.   **return** $\{\mathbf{u}', \mathbf{v}'\}$
16. **end if**
17.   **return** $\emptyset$

acceptance rule, it implies that, at each generation, the nonweak solutions among the schedules situated in all the local search directions for the local optimization individuals constitute the improved population.

10.6 Experimental studies

Behold, the proposed algorithms have been wrought in the Java tongue and are now set to blaze on an Intel Core i7–3520M processor, whose clock whirs to the tune of 2.9 GHz and is equipped with 8 gigs of RAM. To put these algorithms to the test, they have been thrust into the crucible of four venerable benchmarking sets. These sets comprise of 5 Kacem instances (ka4x5, ka08, ka10x7, ka10x10, ka15x10) [19], 10 BRdata instances (Mk01-Mk10) [2], 18 DPdata instances (01a–18a) [28], and 3 Hurink Vdata instances (la30, la35, la40) [29]. These sets encompass nearly all of the problem instances that have ever been adopted in the literary tomes on MO-FJSP. Verily, most of the research that has come before us has only dared to tackle a portion of these instances. But in our grand experimentations, we shall not shy away from any challenge. Nay, we shall make use of all 36 problem instances, so that we may render a comprehensive evaluation of every algorithm that we have wrought.

Owing to the sundry stratagems that are brought to bear during both the global and local search phases, a plethora of algorithmic variants shall be embroiled in our experiments, with all of them being duly chronicled in Table 10.1. It bears noting that

MA-2 diverges from MA-1 only insofar as it employs the "Pareto" acceptance rule during local search, rather than the "Best" rule. Furthermore, it is worth mentioning that MA-1-NH and MA-2-NH are but variations of MA-1 and MA-2, respectively, with the sole exception being that neither of them makes use of the hierarchical strategy during local search.

By the same token, when it comes to generating an acceptable neighbor during local search, MA-1-NH (MA-2-NH) scrutinizes the actions in the set $\varphi(G)$ in their original order until they chance upon an acceptable neighbor. Additionally, to put the genetic search through its paces, we have also devised the multistart random local search (MRLS) algorithms. To be more precise, MRLS-1 (MRLS-2) is concocted by dispensing with the genetic operators in MA-1 (MA-2) in favor of a random generation method, which is then used to derive fresh solutions. As for NSGA-II, it is a version that has been tailored to suit the MO-FJSP, with the chromosome representation and genetic operators that undergird the proposed MAs being directly brought to bear. It is a search algorithm that is wholly reliant on genetic-based methods, with no local search being employed.

The parameter configurations for the implemented algorithms have been faithfully recorded in Table 10.2. We have opted to apply identical parameter configurations for all algorithms. Moreover, each algorithm shall be deemed concluded once the predetermined quota of scrutinized solutions has been reached. For the Kacem instances, this limit has been set at 150,000, while for the BRdata instances, it is 500,000, and for all other instances, it is 1,000,000. This limit shall be the same for all implemented algorithms, thereby ensuring an equitable comparison. To comprehensively evaluate the algorithms, all the techniques mentioned in Table 10.1 shall be independently run 30 times for each problem instance.

10.6.1 Performance metrics

We shall measure the effectiveness of the proposed algorithms. To this end, we shall employ two metrics as harbingers of our experimental outcomes: the inverted generational distance (IGD) [30] and the set coverage [31]. These metrics may be formalized as such:

Table 10.2 Parameter settings of the implemented algorithms.

Parameter	Value
Population size (N)	300
Crossover probability (P_c)	1.0
Mutation probability (P_m)	0.1
Local search probability (P_{ls})	0.1
Maximal iterations of local search ($iter_{max}$)	50
Tournament size for local search solution selection (St)	20

10.6.1.1 Inverted generational distance

Let P^* denote a collection of points that are uniformly distributed across the PF. Assume A is an approximation of the PF. The IGD metric associated with the set A is formally defined as follows:

$$\text{IGD}(A, P^*) = \frac{1}{|P^*|} \sum_{x \in P^*} \min_{y \in A} d(x, y) \tag{10.19}$$

the Euclidean distance between each point x in A and its nearest neighbor y is computed using the function $d(x, y)$. If the set $|P^*|$ is of sufficient size to accurately represent the PF, then the $\text{IGD}(A, P^*)$ can be used to gauge both the convergence and diversity of the set A. For $\text{IGD}(A, P^*)$ to be small, A must be close to P^*, and must not omit any portion of P^*.

In this inquiry, the IGD metric shall be computed founded on the normalized objective vectors of the Pareto-optimal solutions. These vectors may be obtained through the following means:

$$\tilde{f}_i(\mathbf{x}) = \frac{f_i(\mathbf{x}) - f_i^{\min}}{f_i^{\max} - f_i^{\min}}, \quad i = 1, 2, 3 \tag{10.20}$$

the maximal and minimal values of $f_i(x)$ obtained from all results generated by the compared algorithms across all runs for the MO-FJSP shall be obtained, denoted as $f_i^{\max}$ and $f_i^{\min}$, respectively.

10.6.1.2 Set coverage

Let A and B be two approximations of the PF. The set coverage metric $C(A, B)$ is a measure of the proportion of solutions in B that are surpassed by at least one solution in A. In simple terms, it computes the fraction of solutions in B that are inferior to A and can be expressed mathematically as:

$$C(A, B) = \frac{|\{x \in B | \exists y \in A : y \text{ dominates } x\}|}{|B|} \tag{10.21}$$

Take heed, for it should be noted that $C(B, A)$ is not necessarily equivalent to $1 - C(B, A)$. If $C(B, A)$ is sizable and $C(B, A)$ is negligible, then A may be deemed superior to B in some respect.

As the true PFs for the test instances remain elusive, we have fashioned P^* by amassing all the nondominated solutions that have been unearthed by the implemented algorithms across all runs for each problem instance. Furthermore, we have augmented P^* by integrating nondominated solutions that have been obtained by algorithms that have been chronicled in the literature [32–35]. The sets of P^* that have been thusly compiled, along with granular computational results, have been made freely accessible on our website, and are intended for the benefit of future researchers.

10.6.2 Investigation of the acceptance rules in local search

To probe the ramifications of employing two disparate approval guidelines ("Top-notch" and "Pareto-optimal") in local search on the proposed multiagent systems (MAs), an appraisal of the performance of MA-1 and MA-2 shall be undertaken in this subsection.

Behold, Table 10.3 doth present the mean values of IGD and set coverage, computed over 30 autonomous runs of both MA-1 and MA-2, across all 36 instances of the problem. Furthermore, the table does furnish an overview of the salient features of each instance. The first column denotes the moniker of each instance, while the second column indicates the dimensions of said instance, with n being representative of the number of jobs and m serving as an emblem of the number of machines. The third column enumerates the pliability of each instance, this denotes the mean number of machines that may be utilized as a substitute for each assignment in the challenge. For each instance and performance metric (IGD and set coverage), we have performed a Wilcoxon signed-rank test [36] on the results obtained from 30 independent runs of the compared algorithms. Results that are significantly superior to the others (with a significance level of 0.05) shall be highlighted in bold. The tables that follow (Tables 10.4−10.6) shall contain the same bolded values, signifying significant differences in performance.

Table 10.3 reveals that MA-1 doth exhibit marked superiority over MA-2 on the ka10x10 instance, as well as on three DPdata instances. Conversely, MA-2 doth outshine MA-1 on a total of 15 instances, including three BRdata instances, nine DPdata instances, and all three Hurink Vdata instances. There remains 17 problem instances on which neither MA-1 nor MA-2 doth exhibit significant superiority over the other. Regarding the set coverage metric, MA-1 did evince notable superiority over MA-2 on the 08a and 13a instances. Conversely, MA-2 did surpass MA-1 on four BRdata instances, eight DPdata instances, and all three Hurink Vdata instances, with significant differences in performance. As for the 5 Kacem instances, 6 BRdata instances, and 8 DPdata instances, the results do not exhibit any statistically significant differences between MA-1 and MA-2.

In general, it does appear that MA-2 outperforms MA-1 with respect to the scrutinized problem examples. Nevertheless, MA-1 still demonstrates a slightly superior search ability than MA-2 in certain instances. Furthermore, almost half of all the instances do not exhibit significant superiority for either MA-1 or MA-2. In summation, the computational results suggest that the "Pareto" acceptance rule is the more favorable option for the proposed MAs. However, there may be certain instances in which the "Best" acceptance rule would be more appropriate.

Table 10.3 Comparison of two different acceptance rules in local search on average IGD and set coverage values over 30 independent runs for all 36 problem instances.

Instance	$n \times m$	Flex	IGD		MA-1 (A) vs MA-2 (B)	
			MA-1	MA-2	$C(A, B)$	$C(B, A)$
ka4x5	4 × 5	5	0.000000	0.000000	0.000000	0.000000
ka08	8 × 8	6.48	0.000000	0.000000	0.000000	0.000000
ka10x7	10 × 7	7	0.000000	0.000000	0.000000	0.000000
ka10x10	10 × 10	10	**0.033793**	0.092931	0.000000	0.000000
ka15x10	15 × 10	10	0.002778	0.000000	0.000000	0.044444
Mk01	10 × 6	2.09	0.001569	0.001774	0.035455	0.023333
Mk02	10 × 6	4.1	0.009685	**0.006263**	0.052315	**0.131944**
Mk03	15 × 8	3.01	0.000000	0.000000	0.000000	0.000000
Mk04	15 × 8	1.91	0.005937	0.006307	0.143948	0.122322
Mk05	15 × 4	1.71	0.003265	0.005062	0.003030	0.003030
Mk06	10 × 15	3.27	0.039592	0.040446	0.252925	**0.499238**
Mk07	20 × 5	2.83	0.000000	0.000181	0.006250	0.000000
Mk08	20 × 10	1.43	0.000000	0.000000	0.000000	0.000000
Mk09	20 × 10	2.52	0.002534	**0.001927**	0.110502	**0.220580**
Mk10	20 × 15	2.98	0.032299	**0.026703**	0.229056	**0.663331**
01a	10 × 5	1.13	0.142513	0.121680	0.366667	0.550000
02a	10 × 5	1.69	0.029790	0.034413	0.527354	0.364881
03a	10 × 5	2.56	**0.022955**	0.029485	0.582381	0.375278
04a	10 × 5	1.13	0.017067	0.020658	0.413626	0.282165
05a	10 × 5	1.69	0.029702	**0.027830**	0.373163	**0.525628**
06a	10 × 5	2.56	0.020006	0.020205	0.517712	0.410313
07a	15 × 8	1.24	0.138625	**0.104688**	0.376984	0.544444
08a	15 × 8	2.42	**0.025773**	0.038654	**0.602632**	0.282778
09a	15 × 8	4.03	0.035028	**0.026466**	0.266865	**0.613413**
10a	15 × 8	1.24	0.040129	0.036169	0.349751	0.606132
11a	15 × 8	2.42	0.024052	**0.020052**	0.285550	**0.603962**
12a	15 × 8	4.03	0.017390	**0.015395**	0.349964	**0.534587**
13a	20 × 10	1.34	0.058361	0.061297	**0.581839**	0.269497
14a	20 × 10	2.99	0.041484	**0.030463**	0.183185	**0.732829**
15a	20 × 10	5.02	0.036633	**0.021958**	0.161310	**0.809418**
16a	20 × 10	1.34	**0.043449**	0.047622	0.383714	0.498220
17a	20 × 10	2.99	0.022545	**0.015152**	0.142421	**0.742204**
18a	20 × 10	5.02	0.019398	**0.015005**	0.298604	**0.582840**
la30	20 × 10	4.65	0.040453	**0.035973**	0.196376	**0.700000**
la35	30 × 10	4.65	0.016722	**0.012918**	0.169444	**0.613889**
la40	15 × 15	6.48	0.028966	**0.016913**	0.181508	**0.717222**

Table 10.4 Performance evaluation of the effect of hybridizing genetic search and local search using average IGD values over 30 independent runs for all 36 problem instances.

Instance	IGD			IGD		
	MA-1	MRLS-1	NSGA-II	MA-2	MRLS-2	NSGA-II
ka4x5	0.000000	0.047126	0.000000	0.000000	0.004167	0.000000
ka08	0.000000	0.058269	0.000833	0.000000	0.009167	0.000833
ka10x7	0.000000	0.000000	0.007407	0.000000	0.000000	0.007407
ka10x10	0.033793	0.081590	0.134327	0.092931	0.052079	0.134327
ka15x10	**0.002778**	0.313175	0.280442	**0.000000**	0.294616	0.280442
Mk01	**0.001569**	0.101091	0.035556	**0.001774**	0.090541	0.035556
Mk02	**0.009685**	0.128757	0.050101	**0.006263**	0.119288	0.050101
Mk03	0.000000	1.007897	0.000202	0.000000	0.953574	0.000202
Mk04	**0.005937**	0.251465	0.023388	**0.006307**	0.233541	0.023388
Mk05	**0.003265**	0.243095	0.012698	**0.005062**	0.209437	0.012698
Mk06	**0.039592**	0.452603	0.073385	**0.040446**	0.453476	0.073385
Mk07	**0.000000**	0.292828	0.006943	**0.000181**	0.278908	0.006943
Mk08	0.000000	0.655307	0.000000	0.000000	0.603192	0.000000
Mk09	**0.002534**	0.462225	0.014184	**0.001927**	0.439581	0.014184
Mk10	**0.032299**	0.750063	0.071379	**0.026703**	0.723913	0.071379
01a	0.142513	0.648216	0.148463	**0.121680**	0.592304	0.148463
02a	**0.029790**	0.266288	0.059942	**0.034413**	0.248628	0.059942
03a	**0.022955**	0.260912	0.065892	**0.029485**	0.226697	0.065892
04a	**0.017067**	0.152115	0.029280	**0.020658**	0.130728	0.029280
05a	**0.029702**	0.351096	0.058806	**0.027830**	0.337028	0.058806
06a	**0.020006**	0.539079	0.086530	**0.020205**	0.510495	0.086530
07a	0.138625	0.419420	0.157773	**0.104688**	0.406506	0.157773
08a	**0.025773**	0.439693	0.112187	**0.038654**	0.425074	0.112187
09a	**0.035028**	0.408097	0.117332	**0.026466**	0.402469	0.117332
10a	**0.040129**	0.312350	0.092129	**0.036169**	0.300337	0.092129
11a	**0.024052**	0.535776	0.089533	**0.020052**	0.516628	0.089533
12a	**0.017390**	0.788284	0.113920	**0.015395**	0.767139	0.113920
13a	**0.058361**	0.528276	0.086919	**0.061297**	0.510652	0.086919
14a	**0.041484**	0.509893	0.140580	**0.030463**	0.491917	0.140580
15a	**0.036633**	0.509471	0.111058	**0.021958**	0.493920	0.111058
16a	**0.043449**	0.439592	0.102748	**0.047622**	0.422147	0.102748
17a	**0.022545**	0.707046	0.132775	**0.015152**	0.701669	0.132775
18a	**0.019398**	0.942038	0.187137	**0.015005**	0.919420	0.187137
la30	**0.040453**	0.332309	0.108040	**0.035973**	0.310914	0.108040
la35	**0.016722**	0.440808	0.089383	**0.012918**	0.432735	0.089383
la40	**0.028966**	0.417990	0.140409	**0.016913**	0.400358	0.140409

Table 10.5 Performance evaluation of the effect of Hybridizing genetic search and local search using average set coverage values over 30 independent runs for all 36 problem instances.

Instance	MA-1(A) vs MRLS-1(C)		MA-1(A) vs NSGA-II(E)		MA-2(B) vs MRLS-2(D)		MA-2(B) vs NSGA-II(E)	
	C (A, C)	C (C, A)	C (A, E)	C (E, A)	C (B, D)	C (D, B)	C (B, E)	C (E, B)
ka4x5	0.041667	0.000000	0.000000	0.000000	0.016667	0.000000	0.000000	0.000000
ka08	0.313333	0.000000	0.008333	0.000000	0.110000	0.000000	0.008333	0.000000
ka10x7	0.000000	0.000000	0.033333	0.000000	0.000000	0.000000	0.033333	0.000000
ka10x10	0.033333	0.000000	0.185000	0.000000	0.008333	0.000000	0.185000	0.000000
ka15x10	1.000000	0.000000	1.000000	0.000000	1.000000	0.000000	1.000000	0.000000
Mk01	0.943749	0.000000	0.747222	0.000000	0.945949	0.000000	0.752564	0.016061
Mk02	0.916005	0.000000	0.577838	0.003704	0.909114	0.000000	0.588899	0.000000
Mk03	1.000000	0.000000	0.025490	0.000000	1.000000	0.000000	0.025490	0.000000
Mk04	1.000000	0.000000	0.274072	0.004000	0.994444	0.000000	0.277258	0.004615
Mk05	0.896971	0.000000	0.070260	0.003030	0.780210	0.000000	0.076573	0.000000
Mk06	1.000000	0.000000	0.444094	0.259674	1.000000	0.000000	0.549810	0.162620
Mk07	1.000000	0.000000	0.176634	0.000000	1.000000	0.000000	0.176634	0.006250
Mk08	1.000000	0.000000	0.000000	0.000000	1.000000	0.000000	0.000000	0.000000
Mk09	1.000000	0.000000	0.808463	0.025715	1.000000	0.000000	0.824307	0.012114
Mk10	1.000000	0.000000	0.562177	0.235564	1.000000	0.000000	0.662532	0.167871
01a	1.000000	0.000000	0.600000	0.316667	1.000000	0.000000	0.600000	0.400000
02a	0.996296	0.000000	0.872778	0.110370	0.978782	0.000000	0.794444	0.137077
03a	0.994444	0.000000	0.937778	0.011111	0.974352	0.010833	0.891905	0.064127
04a	1.000000	0.000000	0.546229	0.143587	1.000000	0.000000	0.533477	0.166952
05a	1.000000	0.000000	0.754491	0.134465	1.000000	0.000000	0.790380	0.098991

(Continued)

Table 10.5 (Continued)

Instance	MA-1(A) vs MRLS-1(C)		MA-1(A) vs NSGA-II(E)		MA-2(B) vs MRLS-2(D)		MA-2(B) vs NSGA-II(E)	
	C (A, C)	C (C, A)	C (A, E)	C (E, A)	C (B, D)	C (D, B)	C (B, E)	C (E, B)
06a	1.000000	0.000000	0.985997	0.000641	1.000000	0.000000	0.982198	0.002925
07a	1.000000	0.000000	0.616667	0.311111	1.000000	0.000000	0.764444	0.173333
08a	1.000000	0.000000	0.906111	0.011111	0.997436	0.000000	0.886111	0.061706
09a	1.000000	0.000000	0.843980	0.018704	1.000000	0.000000	0.973016	0.000000
10a	1.000000	0.000000	0.877519	0.097341	0.999660	0.000000	0.871207	0.092518
11a	1.000000	0.000000	0.813326	0.066952	1.000000	0.000000	0.856821	0.041296
12a	1.000000	0.000000	0.994903	0.000290	1.000000	0.000000	0.994900	0.000233
13a	1.000000	0.000000	0.529982	0.170424	1.000000	0.000000	0.447590	0.215780
14a	1.000000	0.000000	0.849749	0.036574	1.000000	0.000000	0.987963	0.000000
15a	1.000000	0.000000	0.805833	0.047884	1.000000	0.000000	0.993333	0.000000
16a	1.000000	0.000000	0.656102	0.118672	1.000000	0.000000	0.661786	0.090860
17a	1.000000	0.000000	0.945089	0.005143	1.000000	0.000000	0.966387	0.000953
18a	1.000000	0.000000	0.999274	0.000000	1.000000	0.000000	1.000000	0.000000
la30	1.000000	0.000000	0.891534	0.010833	1.000000	0.000000	0.947222	0.014286
la35	1.000000	0.000000	0.985000	0.000000	1.000000	0.000000	1.000000	0.000000
la40	1.000000	0.000000	0.823611	0.008466	1.000000	0.000000	0.936667	0.000000

Table 10.6 Performance evaluation of the effect of the hierarchical strategy in local search using average IGD and set coverage values over 30 independent runs for all 36 problem instances.

Instance	IGD		MA-1 (A) vs MA-1-NH (C)		IGD		MA-2 (B) vs MA-2-NH (D)	
	MA-1	MA-1-NH	C (A, C)	C (C, A)	MA-2	MA-2-NH	C (B, D)	C (D, B)
ka4x5	0.000000	0.000000	0.000000	0.000000	0.000000	0.000000	0.000000	0.000000
ka08	0.000000	0.000000	0.000000	0.000000	0.000000	0.000000	0.000000	0.000000
ka10x7	0.000000	0.000000	0.000000	0.000000	0.000000	0.000000	0.000000	0.000000
ka10x10	**0.033793**	0.070134	**0.116667**	0.000000	0.092931	0.071523	**0.127778**	0.000000
ka15x10	**0.002778**	0.156178	**0.900000**	0.000000	**0.000000**	0.136906	**0.838889**	0.000000
Mk01	**0.001569**	0.022960	**0.489172**	0.000000	**0.001774**	0.015994	**0.348780**	0.016061
Mk02	**0.009685**	0.034411	**0.483089**	0.020370	**0.006263**	0.027675	**0.424478**	0.012500
Mk03	**0.000000**	0.000202	**0.025490**	0.000000	**0.000000**	0.000136	**0.019390**	0.000000
Mk04	**0.005937**	0.009063	**0.379759**	0.020682	**0.006307**	0.008421	**0.321268**	0.040832
Mk05	0.003265	0.000000	0.000000	0.003030	0.005062	0.000000	0.000000	0.003030
Mk06	**0.039592**	0.057145	**0.732628**	0.121220	**0.040446**	0.054947	**0.829041**	0.061756
Mk07	0.000000	0.001130	0.042361	0.000000	**0.000181**	0.002145	**0.065833**	0.000000
Mk08	0.000000	0.000000	0.000000	0.000000	0.000000	0.000000	0.000000	0.000000
Mk09	**0.002534**	0.017960	**0.908416**	0.006954	**0.001927**	0.019248	**0.921462**	0.005524
Mk10	**0.032299**	0.096543	**0.924833**	0.014070	**0.026703**	0.082840	**0.923299**	0.011510
01a	0.142513	0.130129	0.433333	0.533333	0.121680	0.114516	0.455556	0.500000
02a	0.029790	0.034487	0.509114	0.429167	0.034413	0.043247	0.559841	0.377315
03a	0.022955	0.027293	**0.606349**	0.263175	0.029485	0.031024	0.436905	0.471164
04a	**0.017067**	0.021816	0.389245	0.249457	0.020658	0.018123	0.275728	0.366822

(*Continued*)

Table 10.6 (Continued)

Instance	IGD		MA-1 (A) vs MA-1-NH (C)		IGD		MA-2 (B) vs MA-2-NH (D)	
	MA-1	MA-1-NH	C (A, C)	C (C, A)	MA-2	MA-2-NH	C (B, D)	C (D, B)
05a	**0.029702**	0.044304	**0.811556**	0.118395	**0.027830**	0.042991	**0.877537**	0.077069
06a	**0.020006**	0.073221	**0.996160**	0.000000	**0.020205**	0.068212	**0.985961**	0.002807
07a	0.138625	0.137809	0.525000	0.392222	0.104688	0.116383	0.516667	0.405556
08a	**0.025773**	0.034817	0.538175	0.336746	0.038654	0.039831	0.495794	0.365913
09a	0.035028	0.036091	0.496890	0.425767	**0.026466**	0.038417	**0.613968**	0.272315
10a	**0.040129**	0.054284	**0.716120**	0.236064	**0.036169**	0.045667	**0.711205**	0.242898
11a	**0.024052**	0.109806	**0.998012**	0.000000	**0.020052**	0.111832	**0.997280**	0.000000
12a	**0.017390**	0.221964	**1.000000**	0.000000	**0.015395**	0.248510	**1.000000**	0.000000
13a	**0.058361**	0.073867	**0.621165**	0.148909	**0.061297**	0.091838	**0.707024**	0.213000
14a	0.041484	0.035127	0.352652	0.526402	**0.030463**	0.050004	**0.732103**	0.189431
15a	0.036633	**0.028674**	0.333018	**0.580291**	**0.021958**	0.028285	**0.606548**	0.295503
16a	**0.043449**	0.071278	**0.816502**	0.057209	**0.047622**	0.063839	**0.758392**	0.099110
17a	**0.022545**	0.184460	**1.000000**	0.000000	**0.015152**	0.214329	**1.000000**	0.000000
18a	**0.019398**	0.343793	**1.000000**	0.000000	**0.015005**	0.439499	**1.000000**	0.000000
la30	0.040453	0.042556	0.362513	0.494643	**0.035973**	0.046167	**0.717460**	0.203624
la35	0.016722	**0.012202**	0.266667	**0.627778**	0.012918	0.012686	0.405556	0.410000
la40	**0.028966**	0.042734	**0.684101**	0.250544	**0.016913**	0.059628	**0.953889**	0.020357

10.6.3 Effect of hybridizing genetic search and local search

In this particular subsection, we have embarked on a series of experiments and comparisons between MA-1 (MA-2) and NSGA-II, as well as MRLS-1 (MRLS-2) algorithms, to demonstrate the efficacy of combining hereditary-oriented planetary search with task-specific nearby exploration. We aim to obtain a more comprehensive understanding of the underlying mechanisms that account for the success of the proposed MAs, as elucidated by these experiments.

Table 10.4 provides the mean values of IGD, computed over 30 independent runs for all 36 instances of the problem. The four variants of the algorithm have been segregated into two distinct groups: {MA-1, MRLS-1, NSGA-II} and {MA-2, MRLS-2, NSGA-II}, to facilitate comparisons. Within the first group, it is evident that MA-1 reigns supreme, as the IGD results generated by MA-1 doth significantly surpass those produced by MRLS-1 and NSGA-II in the vast majority of all instances. Moreover, the remaining problem instances did not show any statistically significant dissimilarities among the three algorithms. Regarding the second group, the scenario bears a resemblance to the first. It is readily discernible that MA-2 doth exhibit a significantly superior performance in terms of the IGD metric, MRLS-2 and NSGA-II achieved better results than the other algorithms on 31 out of the 36 instances. Neither MRLS-2 nor NSGA-II manifests any significant superiority over the other two algorithms in any of the instances. Table 10.5 reveals the consequences of set containment examination, acquired by comparing MA-1 (MA-2) with MRLS-1 (MRLS-2) and NSGA-II. The outcomes illustrated in Table 10.5 doth make it abundantly clear that the results generated by A-1 (MA-2) doth far surpass those produced by MRLS-1 (MRLS-2) and NSGA-II.

Drawing upon the aforementioned results and comparisons, we may safely assert that MA-1 (MA-2) doth exhibit a substantially greater efficacy than MRLS-1 (MRLS-2) and NSGA-II, providing ample evidence of the effectiveness of genetic search, local search, and their combination. The triumph of our MAs stems from the seamless integration of the respective strengths of the hereditary-oriented search for heterogeneity and domain-specific exploration for enhancement. This harmonious blend enables the algorithm to strike a perfect equilibrium between exploration and exploitation, thereby achieving an optimal outcome.

10.6.4 Effect of the hierarchical strategy in local search

In this particular subsection, we aim to provide a demonstration of the effectiveness of the hierarchical strategy that has been incorporated into the local search process. To this end, we have conducted a comparison between MA-1 (MA-2) and MA-1-NH (MA-2-NH). The results presented in Table 10.6 doth serve to illustrate that the application of the hierarchical approach in local search leads to more progress in the effectiveness of the proposed MAS.

With regard to the IGD metric, it is noteworthy that MA-1 exhibits a significant improvement over MA-1-NH on 2 instances of Kacem, 7 instances of BRdata, and 11 instances of DPdata, while being outperformed by MA-1-NH on only 2 instances, namely 15a and la35. With respect to the set coverage metric, MA-1 doth manifest a significant superiority over MA-1-NH on 20 out of the total 36 instances, while MA-1-NH doth exhibit a significant improvement over MA-1 solely on situations 15a and la35. The hierarchical strategy implemented in MA-2 demonstrates a similar level of efficacy. It is worth highlighting that MA-2 exhibits a marked superiority over MA-2-NH, in as many as 24 out of the 36 instances, in relation to both the IGD criterion and the set inclusion criterion. It is worth noting that MA-2-NH demonstrates a significant improvement over MA-2 in only one instance, namely Mk05, in terms of the IGD metric. However, it does not exhibit any significant superiority over MA-2 in any instance, according to the set encompassment indicator. It is also worth highlighting that the proposed hierarchical strategy does appear to be particularly advantageous in tackling instances that feature an increased number of nonweak solutions, such as Mk09, Mk10, 11a, and the like.

10.6.5 Comparison with state-of-the-art algorithms

In this particular subsection, we have sought to compare the performance of the proposed MAs (MA-1 and MA-2), which have exhibited an exceptional level of efficacy, with that of the existing state-of-the-art methods. It is worth noting that, from our present knowledge, there does not exist any algorithm in the literature on the MO-FJSP which has been examined on all 36 problem instances scrutinized in this chapter. Therefore, we have selected the most representative benchmark algorithms from each data set. Additionally, it is worth reiterating that, as noted in Section 10.1, the standard practice in the literature on MO-FJSP is to present the performance of an algorithm by enumerating all the nondominated solutions that have been obtained over a specified number of runs. Nevertheless, there are only a limited number of algorithms that provide a detailed account of the results for each individual run. As a result, it appears highly unlikely that a statistical comparison, similar to the ones that have been conducted in the preceding three subsections, can be carried out contrasting the proposed MAs with the established algorithms in the literature. We do, however, believe that such a comparison would be more reasonable than the comparison of nondominated solutions that have been obtained over several runs. In the present comparison, we have computed the metrics of IGD and set coverage for the set of nondominated solutions that have been obtained over a series of runs, for each individual problem and all algorithms. Moreover, the minimum number of trials used by the compared algorithms has been set as the number of trials for MA-1 (MA-2) on each dataset. to ensure that no undue advantage is taken of the compared algorithms.

We have compared the performance of MA-1 (MA-2) with that of four algorithms that have been recently proposed for the MO-FJSP, and which have been referred to as HSFLA [32], PLS [33], SEA [34], and CMA [35], distinctively, in the present chapter.

HSFLA has not been evaluated on the ka4x5 and ka10x7 instances, while PLS has only been considered for four of the ten BRdata instances. Both HSFLA and PLS have been executed 20 times for each instance, while SEA has only been run 10 times. On the other hand, four different variants of parameters have been used for CMA, and each variant has been executed 10 times. It is of note that CMA is run a total of 40 times for each instance, owing to the utilization of four different parameter variants, each of which is executed 10 times. In contrast, the proposed MA-1 (MA-2) has been executed only 10 times for each instance.

Upon close inspection of Tables 10.7–10.9, one can observe that all six algorithms, including the proposed MAs, have succeeded in identifying all of the nonweak solutions in the baseline set for each Kacem problem. within the specified number of runs. Turning our attention to the BRdata instances, it becomes apparent that MA-1 attains the best results, in terms of the IGD metric, on 7 out of the 10 instances, while MA-2 performs best on 8 out of the 10 instances, except for Mk04 and Mk06. It appears that both HSFLA and PLS do not perform as well as the other four algorithms, this can be

Table 10.7 Comparison between the proposed memetic algorithms and the existing algorithms in the literature using IGD values of the solutions found over a certain number of independent runs for Kacem instances and BRdata instances.

Instance	IGD					
	MA-1	**MA-2**	**HSFLA**	**PLS**	**SEA**	**CMA**
ka4x5	**0.000000**	**0.000000**	—	**0.000000**	**0.000000**	**0.000000**
ka08	**0.000000**	**0.000000**	**0.000000**	**0.000000**	**0.000000**	**0.000000**
ka10x7	**0.000000**	**0.000000**	—	**0.000000**	**0.000000**	**0.000000**
ka10x10	**0.000000**	**0.000000**	**0.000000**	**0.000000**	**0.000000**	**0.000000**
ka15x10	**0.000000**	**0.000000**	**0.000000**	**0.000000**	**0.000000**	**0.000000**
Mk01	**0.000000**	**0.000000**	0.202123	0.111817	0.010644	**0.000000**
Mk02	**0.000000**	**0.000000**	0.141176	0.060069	0.038961	0.009524
Mk03	**0.000000**	**0.000000**	0.222437	0.222437	**0.000000**	**0.000000**
Mk04	**0.002610**	0.002705	0.189767	—	0.012537	0.003653
Mk05	**0.000000**	**0.000000**	0.018541	—	0.024490	**0.000000**
Mk06	0.028061	0.025240	0.114675	—	0.053591	**0.022556**
Mk07	**0.000000**	**0.000000**	0.049865	—	0.015284	0.007078
Mk08	**0.000000**	**0.000000**	0.111717	0.111717	0.006982	**0.000000**
Mk09	0.000908	**0.000663**	0.118504	—	0.009631	0.001470
Mk10	0.019261	**0.015448**	0.086488	—	0.079933	0.044289

For each instance, the minimal IGD values obtained by the compared algorithms are marked in bold.

Table 10.8 Comparison between MA-1 and the existing algorithms in the literature using set coverage values of the solutions found over a certain number of independent runs for Kacem instances and BRdata instances.

Instance	MA-1 (A) vs HSFLA (B)		MA-1 (A) vs PLS (C)		MA-1 (A) vs SEA (D)		MA-1 (A) vs CMA (E)	
	C (A, B)	C (B, A)	C (A, C)	C (C, A)	C (A, D)	C (D, A)	C (A, E)	C (E, A)
ka4x5	—	—	0.000000	0.000000	0.000000	0.000000	0.000000	0.000000
ka08	0.000000	0.000000	0.000000	0.000000	0.000000	0.000000	0.000000	0.000000
ka10x7	—	—	0.000000	0.000000	0.000000	0.000000	0.000000	0.000000
ka10x10	0.000000	0.000000	0.000000	0.000000	0.000000	0.000000	0.000000	0.000000
ka15x10	0.000000	0.000000	0.000000	0.000000	0.000000	0.000000	0.000000	0.000000
Mk01	0.909091	0.000000	1.000000	0.000000	0.272727	0.000000	0.250000	0.000000
Mk02	1.000000	0.000000	0.750000	0.000000	0.142857	0.000000	0.250000	0.000000
Mk03	0.857143	0.000000	0.857143	0.000000	0.000000	0.000000	0.000000	0.000000
Mk04	1.000000	0.000000	—	—	0.100000	0.000000	0.043478	0.074074
Mk05	0.428571	0.000000	—	—	0.000000	0.000000	0.000000	0.000000
Mk06	1.000000	0.000000	—	—	0.669903	0.009434	0.598425	0.179245
Mk07	0.666667	0.000000	—	—	0.000000	0.000000	0.250000	0.000000
Mk08	0.625000	0.000000	0.625000	0.000000	0.000000	0.000000	0.000000	0.000000
Mk09	1.000000	0.000000	—	—	0.687500	0.000000	0.052632	0.050000
Mk10	0.733333	0.035176	—	—	0.934783	0.010050	0.762590	0.120603

For each instance, the greater set coverage values obtained by the compared algorithms are marked in bold.

Table 10.9 Comparison between MA-2 and the existing algorithms in the literature using set coverage values of the solutions found over a certain number of independent runs for Kacem instances and BRdata instances.

Instance	MA-2 (A) vs HSFLA (B)		MA-2 (A) vs PLS (C)		MA-2 (A) vs SEA (D)		MA-2 (A) vs CMA (E)	
	C (A, B)	C (B, A)	C (A, C)	C (C, A)	C (A, D)	C (D, A)	C (A, E)	C (E, A)
ka4x5	—	—	0.000000	0.000000	0.000000	0.000000	0.000000	0.000000
ka08	0.000000	0.000000	0.000000	0.000000	0.000000	0.000000	0.000000	0.000000
ka10x7	—	—	0.000000	0.000000	0.000000	0.000000	0.000000	0.000000
ka10x10	0.000000	0.000000	0.000000	0.000000	0.000000	0.000000	0.000000	0.000000
ka15x10	0.000000	0.000000	0.000000	0.000000	0.000000	0.000000	0.000000	0.000000
Mk01	0.909091	0.000000	1.000000	0.000000	0.272727	0.000000	0.000000	0.000000
Mk02	1.000000	0.000000	0.750000	0.000000	0.142857	0.000000	0.250000	0.000000
Mk03	0.857143	0.000000	0.857143	0.000000	0.000000	0.000000	0.000000	0.000000
Mk04	1.000000	0.000000	—	—	0.200000	0.000000	0.043478	0.000000
Mk05	0.428571	0.000000	—	—	0.000000	0.000000	0.000000	0.000000
Mk06	1.000000	0.000000	—	—	0.689320	0.000000	0.677165	0.064220
Mk07	0.666667	0.000000	—	—	0.000000	0.000000	0.250000	0.000000
Mk08	0.625000	0.000000	0.625000	0.000000	0.000000	0.000000	0.000000	0.000000
Mk09	1.000000	0.000000	—	—	0.703125	0.000000	0.052632	0.016667
Mk10	0.866667	0.005181	—	—	0.920290	0.010363	0.830935	0.051813

For each instance, the greater set coverage values obtained by the compared algorithms are marked in bold. For each instance, the greater set coverage values obtained by the compared algorithms are marked in bold.

attributed to the fact that both HSFLA and PLS have failed to achieve results that are as impressive as those of the other algorithms, in terms of the IGD metric, across all of the BRdata instances.

It is noteworthy that CMA has achieved the best IGD value on the Mk06 instance. However, it should be noted that this superiority is based on a considerably larger number of runs than the proposed MAs. Additionally, we have discovered that if the number of runs for MA-1 (MA-2) is increased to 30, the apparent dominance of CMA on the Mk06 instance would no longer be evident. Furthermore, in Tables 10.8 and 10.9, the other algorithms are compared separately with MA-1 and MA-2, respectively., using set coverage values. These tables unequivocally demonstrate that MA-1 (MA-2) is superior to all of the compared algorithms in terms of exploring undominated solutions. Table 10.10 presents a comparison of the average running times for MA-1, MA-2, and HSFLA. However, due to the differences in computing machinery, coding frameworks, and programming knowledge employed in each algorithm, conducting such a comparison can be quite challenging [37]. Therefore, we have included the original CPU name, programming language, and running time for each algorithm, which should provide us with a general idea of the efficiency of the respective algorithms. This approach has been commonly utilized in prior investigations of the JSP [38,39]. Based on the results presented in Table 10.10, it appears that HSFLA is generally associated with higher computational costs than the proposed MAs.

Table 10.10 The average CPU time (in seconds) consumed by MA-1, MA-2, and HSFLA on Kacem instances and BRdata instances.

Instance	MA-1[a]	MA-2[a]	HSFLA[b]
ka4x5	5.77	5.03	1.26
ka08	5.39	6.15	—
ka10x7	5.37	5.08	10.14
ka10x10	5.80	6.53	—
ka15x10	8.91	7.46	21.13
Mk01	20.30	20.16	172.18
Mk02	26.99	28.21	229.56
Mk03	56.60	53.76	139.87
Mk04	30.71	30.53	426.12
Mk05	37.50	36.36	153.12
Mk06	81.41	80.61	577.80
Mk07	38.54	37.74	185.23
Mk08	79.40	77.71	165.48
Mk09	74.74	75.23	565.70
Mk10	85.39	90.75	1072.20

[a]The CPU time on an Intel Core i7−3520M 2.9 GHz processor in Java.
[b]The CPU time on a Pentium IV 1.8 GHz processor in C++.

Table 10.11 presents a comparison between MA-1 (MA-2) and MOGA [40] on DPdata instances, with each algorithm being independently executed 10 times. The IGD results reveal that MA-1 (MA-2) achieves significantly superior performance over MOGA on the DPdata instances. Additionally, MA-1 (MA-2) also demonstrates superiority in terms of computational time for the majority of the considered instances. Furthermore, the complete superiority of MA-1 (MA-2) over MOGA can be more effectively displayed through the use of set coverage values. These values demonstrate that, for each instance, MA-1 (MA-2) outperforms every solution obtained by MOGA, with each MOGA solution being inferior to at least one solution found by MA-1 (MA-2), whereas none of the solutions achieved by MA-1 (MA-2) is outperformed by any MOGA solution.

Table 10.12 presents a comparison of the proposed MA-1 (MA-2) with MOEA-GLS [41] on three Hurink Vdata instances, with each algorithm being executed 30 times. Since the three instances under consideration have only a limited number of nondominated solutions, the solutions obtained by each algorithm over the 30 independent runs are explicitly listed in Table 10.12. In the case of the la30 and

Table 10.11 Comparison between the proposed memetic algorithms and MOGA using IGD values and average CPU time (in seconds) for DPdata instances.

Instance	MA-1[a]		MA-2[a]		MOGA[b]	
	IGD	CPU	IGD	CPU	IGD	CPU
01a	0.040359	198.33	**0.035874**	185.72	0.224215	122.50
02a	**0.004321**	155.34	0.016988	166.01	0.101119	153.40
03a	**0.007921**	150.80	0.013462	157.96	0.207378	174.00
04a	**0.006372**	121.34	0.011408	87.25	0.308259	124.20
05a	**0.014391**	121.04	0.014910	117.03	0.536145	142.40
06a	**0.012423**	138.70	0.013342	135.07	0.808465	185.60
07a	**0.022060**	200.52	0.039878	215.18	0.259504	457.80
08a	**0.003637**	122.56	0.010671	164.33	0.186362	496.00
09a	0.013067	106.50	**0.002006**	153.70	0.197739	609.60
10a	0.023802	188.23	**0.017439**	180.87	0.226811	452.80
11a	0.014375	176.87	**0.010544**	163.37	0.697549	608.20
12a	0.009872	192.45	**0.007111**	165.14	0.895897	715.40
13a	0.026774	195.87	**0.026426**	196.45	0.304963	1439.40
14a	0.024124	122.11	**0.009541**	153.67	0.352456	1743.20
15a	0.016359	123.93	**0.004840**	148.75	0.173609	1997.10
16a	0.026806	185.04	**0.023212**	194.71	0.394364	1291.40
17a	0.011310	184.15	**0.005050**	203.10	0.735482	1708.00
18a	0.008480	175.72	**0.006298**	191.23	0.922706	1980.40

[a]The CPU time on an Intel Core i7–3520M 2.9 GHz processor in Java.
[b]The CPU time on a 2 GHz processor in C++ For each instance, the minimal IGD values obtained by the compared algorithms are marked in bold.

Table 10.12 Solutions found over 30 independent runs by MA-1, MA-2, and MOEA-GLS for 3 Hurink Vdata instances.

Instance	MA-1			MA-2			MOEA-GLS		
	C_{max}	W_T	W_{max}	C_{max}	W_T	W_{max}	C_{max}	W_T	W_{max}
	1076	10,680	1075	**1072**	**10680**	**1072**	1075	10,680	1075
	1078	10,680	1074	**1073**	**10680**	**1071**	1077	10,680	1073
la30	1079	10680	1073	**1082**	**10680**	**1070**	1079	10,680	1072
	1080	10,680	1072	**1135**	**10680**	**1069**	—	—	—
	1086	10,680	1071	—	—	—	—	—	—
	1097	10,680	1070	—	—	—	—	—	—
la35	**1550**	**15,485**	**1550**	**1550**	**15485**	**1550**	**1550**	**15,485**	**1550**
la40	955	11,472	772	**955**	**11472**	**769**	955	11,472	783
	956	11,472	771	**956**	**11472**	**768**	957	11,472	780
	959	11,472	770	—	—	—	963	11,472	779
	967	11,472	769	—	—	—	964	11,472	777
	—	—	—	—	—	—	966	11,472	775

For each instance, the solution that is not dominated by any other solution is marked in bold.

Table 10.13 The average CPU time (in seconds) consumed by MA-1, MA-2, and MOEA-GLS on 3 Hurink Vdata instances.

Instance	MA-1[a]	MA-2[a]	MOEA-GLS[b]
la30	47.95	53.43	2110.83
la35	67.29	83.03	355.20
la40	62.13	55.81	928.80

[a]The CPU time on an Intel Core i7−3520M 2.9 GHz processor in Java.
[b]The CPU time on a 2 GHz processor in C++.

la40 instances, MA-2 outperforms all solutions obtained by MOEA-GLS and MA-1, with each MOEA-GLS and MA-1 solution being inferior to at least one solution found by MA-2, whereas none of the solutions obtained by MA-2 is outperformed by any solution from the other two algorithms. As for the la35 instance, all three algorithms converge to the same nondominated solution. Based on Table 10.13, it appears that MA-1 (MA-2) requires significantly less computational time than MOEA-GLS.

Although our MA-1 (MA-2) is tailored for the MO-FJSP, where the minimization of makespan is the primary focus, in addition, we have evaluated their performance in relation to the top makespan attained with two advanced algorithms for the SO-FJSP. namely Mastrolilli and Gambardella's TS algorithm [3], and Hmida et al.'s CDDS method [7], as presented in Table 10.14. The fourth column of Table 10.14 lists the best-known solution (BKS) noted in earlier works for each scenario. Table 10.14 shows that MA-1 (MA-2) performs comparably well to TS and CDDS when solving the SO-FJSP. An intriguing observation is that MA-1 (MA-2) was able to achieve novel optimal solutions for multiple examples. Specifically, MA-1 discovered a new

Table 10.14 Comparison of the best makespan obtained on all 36 problem instances.

Instance	BKS	MA-1	MA-2	TS	CDDS
ka4x5	11	11	11	—	—
ka08	14	14	14	—	—
ka10x7	11	11	11	—	—
ka10x10	7	7	—	—	—
ka15x10	11	11	11	—	—
Mk01	40	40	40	40	40
Mk02	26	26	26	26	26
Mk03	204	204	204	204	204
Mk04	60	60	60	60	60
Mk05	172	172	172	173	173
Mk06	58	60	59	58	58
Mk07	139	139	139	144	139
Mk08	523	523	523	523	523
Mk09	307	307	307	307	307
Mk10	197	205	202	198	197
01a	2505	2520	2521	2518	2518
02a	2230	2236	2244	2231	2231
03a	2228	2231	2234	2229	2229
04a	2503	2510	2513	2503	2503
05a	2212	2208	2211	2216	2216
06a	2187	2173	2172	2203	2196
07a	2283	2371	2365	2283	2283
08a	2067	2083	2087	2069	2069
09a	2066	2081	2075	2066	2066
10a	2291	2340	2327	2291	2291
11a	2061	2067	2057	2063	2063
12a	2027	1998	1992	2034	2031
13a	2257	2306	2311	2260	2257
14a	2167	2192	2187	2167	2167
15a	2165	2186	2180	2167	2165
16a	2255	2292	2293	2255	2256
17a	2140	2129	2119	2141	2140
18a	2127	2086	2077	2137	2127
la30	1069	1076	1072	1069	—
la35	1549	1550	1550	1549	—
la40	955	955	955	955	—

For each instance, the minimal makespan values obtained by the compared algorithms are marked in bold.

best-known solution for instance 05a, while MA-2 achieved 5 new best-known solutions for instances 06a, 11a, 12a, 17a, and 18a. Notably, the best-known solutions for instances 06a, 12a, 17a, and 18a were significantly improved by MA-2, although the underlying reasons for this improvement remain unclear. It appears that the optimization of multiple objectives in parallel has an indirect effect of encouraging the improvement of job scheduling efficiency for these scenarios.

Based on the aforementioned computational results and comparisons, it can be inferred that the proposed MA-1 and MA-2 algorithms generally exhibit superior performance compared to the existing state-of-the-art methods for addressing the MO-FJSP. Additionally, they demonstrate a remarkable ability to minimize the makespan, and as a result, they were able to further improve the best documented total job duration values for several examples.

10.7 Conclusion

This chapter focuses on addressing the MO-FJSP, which is highly relevant to real-world manufacturing scenarios and involves optimizing multiple criteria, comprising completion duration, total task load, and pivotal workload. To develop effective MAs, we begin by adapting the classical NSGA-II approach to the MO-FJSP using a carefully designed chromosome encoding/decoding scheme and genetic operators. Additionally, we introduce a novel local search mechanism tailored specifically to the MO-FJSP, which is based on critical operations. Of particular significance is our adoption of a hierarchical approach in the local search mechanism, which serves to improve its capability to handle the optimization of multiple objectives.

Our hierarchical approach assigns the highest priority to minimizing the makespan, followed by considering the total workload and critical workload in a subsequent order based on the possible actions that could lead to acceptable neighbors. This approach is integrated into the adapted NSGA-II framework to reinforce the search process, ultimately resulting in the development of our proposed MAs. While both acceptance rules employed in the local search mechanism have a minor impact on the performance of the MAs, the "Pareto" acceptance rule is generally preferred. We conducted a thorough evaluation of the key components of our MAs, including the genetic search, local search, and hierarchical strategy employed in the local search mechanism. Additionally, we compared the performance of our proposed MAs with existing state-of-the-art algorithms across various datasets. Our computational results demonstrate that the proposed MAs significantly outperform all other algorithms by a substantial margin. These outcomes underscore the effectiveness of leveraging traditional multiobjective evolutionary techniques in combination with problem-specific search algorithms to achieve optimal solutions.

10.8 Summary of this part

In the first part, we delve into innovative approaches for solving the FJSP and the MO-FJSP. In Chapter 1, we propose the hybrid harmony search (HHS) algorithm, which transforms continuous harmony vectors into discrete codes to adapt the harmony search algorithm for the FJSP. The algorithm combines heuristic and random strategies for effective initialization and incorporates a local search procedure to enhance exploitation. Empirical results demonstrate its competitiveness and efficiency in solving the FJSP. Chapter 2 introduces the hybrid differential evolution (HDE) approach, which employs a novel conversion mechanism to explore the discrete problem space of the FJSP. It integrates a local search algorithm based on the critical path to balance exploration and exploitation. Extensive experiments show that the proposed algorithms achieve state-of-the-art performance and even discover new best-known solutions. In Chapter 3, we present two algorithm modules, hybrid harmony search (HHS) and large neighborhood search (LNS), for optimizing the FJSP. The combined search heuristic HHS/LNS exhibits improved performance on large-scale FJSP problems and reveals new upper bounds through computational simulations. Finally, chapter 4 addresses the MO-FJSP using MAs that optimize multiple objectives. The MAs, based on the NSGA-II, incorporate a unique local search algorithm and hierarchical strategy. Extensive experiments and comparisons demonstrate the superiority of the proposed MAs over other algorithms. These contributions provide valuable insights and effective solutions for scheduling optimization, advancing the research and application of multiobjective optimization in job shop scheduling.

References

[1] Garey MR, Johnson DS, Sethi R. The complexity of flowshop and jobshop scheduling. Mathematics of Operations Research 1976;1(2):117−29.
[2] Brandimarte P. Routing and scheduling in a flexible job shop by tabu search. Annals of Operations Research 1993;41(3):157−83.
[3] Mastrolilli M, Gambardella LM. Effective neighbourhood functions for the flexible job shop problem. Journal of Scheduling 2000;3(1):3−20.
[4] Ho NB, Tay JC, Lai EMK. An effective architecture for learning and evolving flexible job-shop schedules. European Journal of Operational Research 2007;179(2):316−33.
[5] Pezzella F, Morganti G, Ciaschetti G. A genetic algorithm for the flexible job-shop scheduling problem. Computers & Operations Research 2008;35(10):3202−12.
[6] Bożejko W, Uchroński M, Wodecki M. Parallel hybrid metaheuristics for the flexible job shop problem. Computers & Industrial Engineering 2010;59(2):323−33.
[7] Hmida AB, Haouari M, Huguet MJ, et al. Discrepancy search for the flexible job shop scheduling problem. Computers & Operations Research 2010;37(12):2192−201.
[8] Yuan Y, Xu H, Yang J. A hybrid harmony search algorithm for the flexible job shop scheduling problem. Applied Soft Computing 2013;13(7):3259−72.
[9] Yuan Y, Xu H. An integrated search heuristic for large-scale flexible job shop scheduling problems. Computers & Operations Research 2013;40(12):2864−77.
[10] Ishibuchi H, Yoshida T, Murata T. Balance between genetic search and local search in memetic algorithms for multiobjective permutation flowshop scheduling. IEEE Transactions on Evolutionary Computation 2003;7(2):204−23.
[11] Minella G, Ruiz R, Ciavotta M. A review and evaluation of multiobjective algorithms for the flowshop scheduling problem. INFORMS Journal on Computing 2008;20(3):451−71.

[12] Mei Y, Tang K, Yao X. Decomposition-based memetic algorithm for multiobjective capacitated arc routing problem. IEEE Transactions on Evolutionary Computation 2011;15(2):151−65.

[13] Ke L, Zhang Q, Battiti R. MOEA/D-ACO: a multiobjective evolutionary algorithm using decomposition and antcolony. IEEE Transactions on Cybernetics 2013;43(6):1845−59.

[14] Roy B, Sussmann B. Les problemesd'ordonnancement avec contraintes disjonctives. Note DS 1964;9.

[15] Michael LP. Scheduling: theory, algorithms, and systems. Springer International Pu; 2022.

[16] Deb K, Pratap A, Agarwal S, et al. A fast and elitist multiobjective genetic algorithm: NSGA-II. IEEE Transactions on Evolutionary Computation 2002;6(2):182−97.

[17] Krasnogor N, Smith J. A tutorial for competent memetic algorithms: model, taxonomy, and design issues. IEEE Transactions on Evolutionary Computation 2005;9(5):474−88.

[18] Ong YS, Keane AJ. Meta-Lamarckian learning in memetic algorithms. IEEE Transactions on Evolutionary Computation 2004;8(2):99−110.

[19] Ong YS, Lim MH, Zhu N, et al. Classification of adaptive memetic algorithms: a comparative study. IEEE Transactions on Systems, Man, and Cybernetics, Part B (Cybernetics) 2006;36 (1):141−52.

[20] Ishibuchi H., Narukawa K. Some issues on the implementation of local search in evolutionary multiobjective optimization. Proceedings of the 6th annual conference on genetic and evolutionary computation; 2004. p. 1246−58.

[21] Ishibuchi H, Murata T. A multi-objective genetic local search algorithm and its application to flow-shop scheduling. IEEE Transactions on Systems, Man, and Cybernetics, Part C (Applications and Reviews) 1998;28(3):392−403.

[22] Sindhya K, Deb K, Miettinen K. Improving convergence of evolutionary multi-objective optimization with local search: a concurrent-hybrid algorithm. Natural Computing 2011;10:1407−30.

[23] Ishibuchi H., Hitotsuyanagi Y., Nojima Y. An empirical study on the specification of the local search application probability in multiobjective memetic algorithms. Proceedings of the 15th IEEE congress on evolutionary computation; 2007. p. 2788−95.

[24] Ishibuchi H., Hitotsuyanagi Y., Tsukamoto N., et al. Use of heuristic local search for single-objective optimization in multiobjective memetic algorithms. Proceedings of the 7th internadtional conference on parallel problem solving from nature; 2008. p. 743−52.

[25] Garrett D., Dasgupta D. An empirical comparison of memetic algorithm strategies on the multiobjective quadratic assignment problem[C]. Proceedings of the 6th IEEE symposium on computational intelligence in multi-criteria decision-making (MCDM). IEEE; 2009. p. 80−87.

[26] Cheng R, Gen M, Tsujimura Y. A tutorial survey of job-shop scheduling problems using genetic algorithms—I. Representation. Computers & Industrial Engineering 1996;30(4):983−97.

[27] Oliver I.M., Smith D.J., Holland J.R.C. A study of permutation crossover operators on the traveling salesman problem. Proceedings of the 3rd genetic algorithms and their applications; 2013. p. 224−30.

[28] Dauzère-Pérès S, Paulli J. An integrated approach for modeling and solving the general multiprocessor job-shop scheduling problem using tabu search. Annals of Operations Research 1997;70 (0):281−306.

[29] Hurink J, Jurisch B, Thole M. Tabu search for the job-shop scheduling problem with multi-purpose machines. Operations-Research-Spektrum 1994;15:205−15.

[30] Coello CAC, Cortés NC. Solving multiobjective optimization problems using an artificial immune system. Genetic Programming and Evolvable Machines 2005;6:163−90.

[31] Zitzler E, Deb K, Thiele L. Comparison of multiobjective evolutionary algorithms: Empirical results. Evolutionary Computation 2000;8(2):173−95.

[32] Li J, Pan Q, Xie S. An effective shuffled frog-leaping algorithm for multi-objective flexible job shop scheduling problems. Applied Mathematics and Computation 2012;218(18):9353−71.

[33] Li JQ, Pan QK, Chen J. A hybrid Pareto-based local search algorithm for multi-objective flexible job shop scheduling problems. International Journal of Production Research 2012;50(4):1063−78.

[34] Chiang TC, Lin HJ. A simple and effective evolutionary algorithm for multiobjective flexible job shop scheduling. International Journal of Production Economics 2013;141(1):87−98.

[35] Chiang T.C., Lin H.J. Flexible job shop scheduling using a multiobjective memetic algorithm. Proceedings of the 7th advanced intelligent computing theories and applications; 2012. p. 49–56.

[36] Demšar J. Statistical comparisons of classifiers over multiple data sets. The Journal of Machine Learning Research 2006;7:1–30.

[37] Beck JC, Feng TK, Watson JP. Combining constraint programming and local search for job-shop scheduling. INFORMS Journal on Computing 2011;23(1):1–14.

[38] Sha DY, Hsu CY. A hybrid particle swarm optimization for job shop scheduling problem. Computers & Industrial Engineering 2006;51(4):791–808.

[39] Zhang CY, Li PG, Rao YQ, et al. A very fast TS/SA algorithm for the job shop scheduling problem. Computers & Operations Research 2008;35(1):282–94.

[40] Wang X, Gao L, Zhang C, et al. A multi-objective genetic algorithm based on immune and entropy principle for flexible job-shop scheduling problem. The International Journal of Advanced Manufacturing Technology 2010;51(5–8):757–67.

[41] Ho NB, Tay JC. Solving multiple-objective flexible job shop problems by evolution and local search. IEEE Transactions on Systems, Man, and Cybernetics, Part C (Applications and Reviews) 2008;38(5):674–85.

Summary of part II

Since Brandimarte proposed the tabu search method in 1993, research on the flexible job shop scheduling (FJS) problem has experienced rigorous development. The team to which the authors belong proposed the hybrid harmony search (HHS) method incorporating problem knowledge in 2013, the integrated search method combining HHS and large neighborhood search, and the memetic evolutionary method based on target importance decomposition in 2015 (discussed in the relevant content of the second part of this book). These contributions are considered significant milestones in the field and have received high praise from the academic community and widespread application in the industry. The Deputy Editor-in-Chief of *IEEE Transactions on Automation Science and Engineering* (*IEEE TASE*) stated that the research addressed a class of challenging practical scheduling problems, proposing a refined and effective algorithm. Papers presenting these results were among the top 20 most popular papers in IEEE TASE. The International Transactions on Operation Research recognized the algorithms in this book as seven of the best-performing classical algorithms among all flexible job shop scheduling problem (FJSP) algorithms. *The European Journal of Operational Research* regarded the methods in this book as a representative class of evolutionary computation in solving FJSPs. The internationally renowned citation system, local citation references, ranked our algorithms among the top 10 classical FJSP algorithms, with a ranking of 4.

In terms of industrial applications and evaluations, Professor Duc Truong Pham, a Fellow of the Royal Academy of Engineering in the UK, applied the algorithms in this book to optimize scheduling in multiindustrial collaborative robotic systems. Professor Panos M. Pardalos, a pioneer in global optimization and combinatorial optimization and a Fellow of AAAS, utilized the variable neighborhood search algorithm in this book to solve complex instances of FJS. Professor Enrique Alba, the chair of ACM GECCO 2013, considered the achievements in this book as a representative class of search optimization scheduling methods in the past decade. Professor Jiao Licheng, a Fellow of the European/Russian Academies of Sciences, IEEE Fellow, and IET Fellow, regarded the achievements in this book as one of the four classical algorithms successfully applied for practical and efficient FJSP-solving in real production scenarios.

Despite achieving certain research results in the field of FJSP-solving methods, ongoing and in-depth research is needed to address the challenges posed by real-world scenarios and diverse industry applications. Especially with the rise of deep learning and large model technologies in the field of artificial intelligence in recent years, the team of authors will continue to conduct research in this area and promptly present relevant results to the readers.

Appendix A: Symbol cross-reference table

ABC	artificial bee colony
ACO	ant colony optimization
AIA	artificial immune algorithm
AR	average ranking
BBO	biogeography-based optimization
BKS	best-known solution
CCG	controlling the maximum number of crossed genes
CEC	congress on evolutionary computation
CNB	Complement Naive Bayes
CP	constraint programming
DCI	diversity comparison indicator
DE	differential evolution
DEV	deviation criterion
DIV	division
DMOPSO	decomposition-based multiobjective particle swarm optimizer
DS	discrepancy search
EA	evolutionary algorithm
EC	evolutionary computation
EDA	estimation of distribution algorithm
EDN	expected dominance number
EFR	ensemble fitness ranking
EGO	efficient global optimization
EI	expected improvement
EMO	evolutionary multiobjective optimization
FJSP	flexible job shop scheduling problem
FNNs	feedforward neural networks
FNN	feedforward neural network
GA	genetic algorithm
GD	generational distance
GECCO	genetic and evolutionary computation conference
GrEA	grid-based evolutionary algorithm
HDE	hybrid differential evolution
HHS	hybrid harmony search
HHS/LNS	hybrid harmony search and large neighborhood search
HM	harmony memory
HMCR	harmony memory considering rate
HMS	harmony memory size
HS	harmony search
HV	hypervolume
IBEA	indicator-based evolutionary algorithm
ID	identification
IFS	iterative flattening search
IGD	inverted generational distance

JSP	job shop scheduling problem
KBACO	knowledge-based ant colony optimization
LB	lower bound
LNS	large neighborhood search
LPV	largest position value
MaxGen	maximum number of generations
MaxEval	maximum number of evaluations
MaOP	many-objective optimization problem
MAs	multiagent systems
MO-CMA-ES	multiobjective covariance matrix adaptation evolution strategy
MO-COPs	multiobjective combinatorial optimization problems
MOEA	multiobjective evolutionary algorithm
MO-FJSP	ultiobjective flexible job shop scheduling problem
MOGA	multiobjective genetic algorithm
MOGLS	multiobjective genetic local search
MOMBI	many-objective metaheuristic based on the R2 indicator
MO-PFSP	multiobjective permutation flowshop scheduling problem
MOP	multiobjective optimization problem
MR	maximum ranking
MRE	mean relative error
MRLS	multistart random local search
MSOPS	multiple single-objective Pareto sampling
MVU	maximum variance unfolding
MWR	most work remaining
NI	number of improvisations
NSGA-II	nondominated sorting genetic algorithm II
PAR	pitch adjusting rate
PBI	penalty boundary intersection
PCA	principal component analysis
PCSEA	Pareto corner search evolutionary algorithm
PESA-II	Pareto envelope-based selection algorithm II
PF	Pareto front
POGA	preference ordering genetic algorithm
POS	partial-order schedule
PSO	particle swarm optimization
PS	Pareto set
PVNS	parallel variable neighborhood search
RE	relative error
ReLU	rectified linear unit
RF	random forest
Rmax	maximum number of replications
SA	simulated annealing
SBX	simulated binary crossover
SD	standard deviation of makespan
SDE	shift-based density estimation
SMS-EMOA	S metric selection evolutionary algorithm
SO-COPs	single-objective combinatorial optimization problems
SO-FJSP	single-objective FJSP

SOP	single-objective optimization problem
SPEA2	strength Pareto evolutionary algorithm 2
SVM	support vector machine
TS	tabu search
UB	upper bound
VND	variable neighborhood descent
VNS	variable neighborhood search

Index

Note: Page numbers followed by "*f*" and "*t*" refer to figures and tables, respectively.

Printed in the United States
by Baker & Taylor Publisher Services